Adrian C. Ritchie, MA (*Manc.*), Doct de l'Univ. (Strasbourg), is Lecturer in French at the School of Modern Languages, University College of North Wales, Bangor.

FRENCH FOR ADMINISTRATION, BUSINESS AND COMMERCE

AN ENGLISH–FRENCH GLOSSARY

Adrian C. Ritchie

CARDIFF
UNIVERSITY OF WALES PRESS
1993

© Adrian C. Ritchie, 1993

British Library Cataloguing-in-Publication Data.
A catalogue record for this book is available from the British
Library.

ISBN 0-7083-1178-4 paperback   1746412
ISBN 0-7083-1199-7 hardback

Cover design by Michael Reader.
Typeset by Megaron, Cardiff.
Printed in Great Britain by Bath Press, Bath.

INTRODUCTION

Scope and purpose

This glossary, which complements my *Newspaper French* (1990), is written for the student, businessman, journalist, politician and general reader alike. It is intended to help the layman read, understand, write and converse in the language and idiom of contemporary French. It focuses principally on the vocabulary of **administration, business** and **commerce**, but I have also included some of the more common lexis associated with **politics, legal reporting**, and **social affairs**.

Many specialist dictionaries, however comprehensive in their coverage, are far from user-friendly. They may offer multiple variants on a given headword, but few if any offer much informative illustration of the different uses and meanings of words and expressions.

Building on the success of the earlier volume, I have tried in this vocabulary to provide actual examples of usage to illustrate the different contexts and fields in which a given English word might be used in contemporary French.

In most cases, the headword is followed by a comprehensive range of illustrations drawn from the vocabulary which is to be found in the 'quality' French dailies, news periodicals and specialized texts.

The coming into being of the European Community and the implementation of the single European Market only increases the need for a working knowledge of administrative, political, commercial and other lexis. I have deliberately restricted myself to the most frequently met and useful terms and expressions, my aim being to compile a guide to the French language and idiom of today which is both handy and up-to-date.

I have every hope that this book will prove an invaluable companion for student and general reader alike – in fact for all those called upon to have more than a passing contact with France and who wish to master the language and idiom of our closest continental neighbour.

How to use the glossary

It should be noted that a strict alphabetical sequence has been adopted for all entries: thus **police**, **policeman**, **police record**, **police station** and **policing** occur as separate entries and in that order.

For reasons of clarity, those French words and phrases within the illustrations which correspond directly and precisely to the headword are printed in **bold**: [e.g. **banned** (*adj*): le divorce, qui reste **interdit** dans ce pays (*banned, illegal*)].

Translations [italicized] of emboldened material are supplied in such a way as to distinguish clearly the different meanings of the examples given: [e.g. **barrier** (*n*): ⟨Econ⟩ la cherté du crédit est une **entrave** au commerce (*barrier*); la City fait le pari du **décloisonnement** (*m*) et de l'ouverture (*bringing down barriers*)]. Where no translation is given for any of the examples, the translation of the emboldened material is the same as the headword. Where no translation is given for one or more examples, the immediately succeeding translation is applicable.

Within translations, a comma separates near synonyms; a semicolon indicates a distinct shift in meaning.

In the many cases [often legal or financial and commercial terms] where either (*a*) the headword or (*b*) the French word or concept included in the illustration has no precise equivalent in the other language [e.g. (*a*) **direct debit**, **managing director**, **magistrate**, **mortgage**, **policeman**, or **solicitor**; or (*b*) 'aménagement du territoire', or 'commission des sages'], the nearest cultural equivalent is given in the other language.

For ease of reference, compounds which consist of attributive uses of English nouns or other words (e.g. 'consumer spending') or word groups and collocations which function in a similar way (e.g. 'conspiracy to defraud') are generally to be found under the first word of the expression. Some compounds or other collocations, [e.g. 'community policing', 'job creation', 'share ownership', 'wage restraint'], however, are given a separate entry, by virtue of their importance and frequency. So, 'black market' does not appear under **market** but under **black**. There is inevitably an element of subjectivity in such decisions.

Headwords on which a large number of compounds are formed [e.g. **job**, **wage**, **put**, **give**], are broken down into separate entries by meaning, for ease of reference. Thus, **give in**, **give up**, **give way**, and **giving up** occur as separate headwords. Within entries, particularly the longer ones [as in: 'business, 'executive', 'fall', 'growth', 'return', 'tax' etc.], examples are grouped as far as possible by semantic field.

Cross-references are extensive but not absolutely systematic or comprehensive. Under **overmanning**, for example, a cross-reference alerts the user to the synonym **overstaffing**, so that French equivalents can be found under both words. In a few cases where such duplication seemed unjustified, examples are given under one word only, there being a cross-reference under the other word. Thus, **invitation** has a cross-reference to **bid** and to **tender**, and **bailing out** to **refloating**. For words like **rise**, **fall**, **increase**, **order**, **fund**, such cross-references are unavoidably numerous: under **increase**, for example, the user is referred to **raise**, **rise**, and **grow**.

Headwords which can have both substantival and adjectival meanings [e.g. **majority**] are marked (*n/adj*). However, in the case of long and unwieldy entries [e.g. **public**], separate entries are provided for noun and adjective. Verbal and noun uses are of course kept separate [e.g. **package**, **parole**, **grant**, **aid**, etc.].

Where it seems necessary, some syntactical information [prepositions etc.] is included in both example and translation. Under the verb **infringe**, both verb and relevant preposition in the French renderings ['enfreindre à', 'contrevenir à', and 'tomber sous le coup de'] are emboldened to help the non-native speaker to use the word or expression correctly.

Symbols and abbreviations

In the interest of clarity and ease of reference, much lexicographical data normally provided in dictionaries [phonetic transcription of headwords, and style labels etc.] has been omitted.

I have however incorporated a minimum of information, indicating the main parts of speech, the number [where necessary], and the gender of French nouns. Also included are semantic categories, and field labels where these help to make important distinctions of meaning and context.

The following are the most commonly used symbols:

(*n*): noun
(*npl*): plural noun
(*m*): masculine noun
(*f*): feminine noun
(*mpl*): masculine plural noun
(*fpl*): feminine plural noun
(*adj*): adjective
(*n/adj*): noun and adjective
(*adv*): adverb
(*pref*): prefix
(*prep*): preposition
⟨ ⟩ field labels are shown within oblique brackets
[ ] extra information is given in square brackets

The field names for the range of vocabulary used are as follows:

⟨Admin⟩ Administrative		⟨Ins⟩ Insurance
⟨Agric⟩ Agricultural		⟨Jur⟩ Juridical
⟨Comm⟩ Commercial		⟨Med⟩ Medical
⟨Econ⟩ Economic		⟨Mil⟩ Military
⟨Educ⟩ Educational		⟨Pol⟩ Political
⟨Fin⟩ Financial		⟨Rel⟩ Religious
⟨Fisc⟩ Fiscal		⟨Soc⟩ Social
⟨Ind⟩ Industrial		

A list of acronyms [generally French] occurring within illustrative material is appended at the end of the volume.

Adrian C. Ritchie   Bangor, February 1993

A

abandon (*v*): **renoncer** à la lutte armée; les Blancs décident d'**enterrer** l'apartheid (*abandon, give up, renounce*); si le gouvernement de Bonn devait **lâcher** la France (*abandon, leave, walk out on*)

abandonment (*n*): l'**abandon** (*m*) des armes nucléaires tactiques (*abandonment, giving up*); l'**enterrement** (*m*) de la réforme tant de fois annoncée (*abandonment, laying aside*); le nouveau texte **enterre** le projet de texte fiscal (*signal the abandonment/abandoning of*); SEE ALSO **giving up, surrender**

abduct (*v*): en mal d'enfant, elle **enleva** celui de sa voisine; **kidnapper** un enfant de huit ans

abduction (*n*): il y a crime si le **détournement de mineur** s'accompagne de violences (*abduction of a minor*); plusieurs **enlèvements** (*m*) **d'enfant** défrayent la chronique (*child abduction/kidnapping*)

ability (*n*): la **capacité** de l'opposition à remporter seule les élections; conserver sa **capacité** (*f*) d'intervention en Europe (*ability, capability*)

abode (*n*): ⟨Jur/Soc⟩ les SDF, ou personnes **n'ayant pas de domicile** (*m*) **fixe** (*without fixed abode*)

abolish (*v*): **abolir** une taxe jugée inéquitable; le poste de vice-président est **supprimé**

abolition (*n*): l'**abolition** (*f*) de la peine de mort en 1981 (*abolition*); ces accords prévoient la **suppression** des frontières (*abolition, elimination*)

abortion (*n*): ⟨Med⟩ légaliser l'**interruption** (*f*) **volontaire de la grossesse [IVG]** (*abortion, termination of pregnancy*); les **avortements** (*m*) spontanés, ou fausses couches (*[spontaneous] abortion*); la Cour suprême autorise l'adolescente violée à **avorter**; aller **se faire avorter** à l'étranger (*have an abortion*)

abortive (*adj*): ⟨Pol⟩ coup d'État **avorté** en Guinée (*abortive, failed*); le **putsch avorté** en Union soviétique (*abortive/failed coup*); SEE ALSO **failed**

about-turn (*n*): la **volte-face** fiscale de l'administration américaine (*about-turn, volte-face*)

abroad (*adv*): ⟨Econ/Comm⟩ des acquisitions importantes **à l'étranger** (*m*) notamment; des firmes japonaises installées **hors frontières** (*f*); les entreprises ont énormément investi **hors de nos frontières**

absorb (*v*): 〈Econ〉 **absorber** une entreprise concurrente (*absorb, take over*); 〈Fin〉 **éponger** de lourdes dettes outre-Atlantique; **éponger les pertes** (*f*) d'une filiale (*absorb [esp. debt/loss]*)

abstain (*v*): 〈Pol〉 de plus en plus d'électeurs **s'abstiennent** (*abstain, not to vote*); les électeurs hier ont **boudé les urnes** (*abstain from voting, not go to the polling-booth*)

abstention (*n*): 〈Pol〉 on craint un **taux d'abstention** (*f*) supérieur à 50% (*abstention rate*)

abuse (*n*): un **abus** inacceptable du droit de grève; les **dérapages** (*m*) que pourrait entraîner l'application de ce décret (*abuse, excess*); accusé de **forfaiture** (*f*) dans une affaire de ventes d'armes (*abuse of influence*)

abuse (*v*): **abuser** des droits que lui accorde la Constitution (*abuse, misuse*); 〈Soc〉 les enfants **victimes d'abus** (*mpl*) **sexuels** (*sexually abused*)

accede (*v*): 〈Pol〉 **accéder à** la plupart des revendications (*accede to, grant; comply with*); son ambition: **monter sur le trône** (*accede to the throne*)

accept (*v*): un engagement à **endosser** la responsabilité des dommages causés (*accept; take on, bear*); SEE ALSO **accommodate**, **admit**

acceptance (*n*): l'**acceptation** (*f*) par Bagdad du plan soviétique; leur **acceptation** des conditions à un cessez-le-feu formel

access (*n*): l'inégalité de l'**accès** (*m*) à la justice; les femmes peuvent **accéder à** des postes de responsabilité (*have access to, attain to*)

accession (*n*): 〈Pol〉 l'**avènement** (*m*) du roi (*accession to throne*); son **accession** (*f*) **au** pouvoir (*accession to*); l'**adhésion** (*f*) d'autres pays à cette organisation (*accession; joining*)

accessory (*n/adj*): 〈Jur〉 **complice** (*m/f*) d'une série d'escroqueries; **se faire complice** d'un assassinat (*be an accessory to a crime*)

accident (*n*): 〈Ins〉 un formulaire de déclaration de **sinistre** (*m*); dans la branche **assurance-dommages** (*accident insurance*)

accommodate (*v*): 12% des enfants en bas âge sont **accueillis** dans une crèche collective (*accommodate, admit*); comment **héberger** tous les sans-abris (*accommodate, give shelter to*)

accommodation (*n*): 〈Soc〉 l'**accueil** (*m*) des personnes âgées; logé dans des conditions normales d'**accueil**; les frais d'**hébergement** (*m*) et de nourriture (*accommodation*); des avantages en nature, comme un **logement de fonction** (*f*) (*accommodation going with a post*)

accompanied (*adj*): un ultimatum **assorti** d'un embargo sur les livraisons de · pétrole; 〈Jur〉 des peines de 15 mois, **assorties** d'amendes de 50.000F (*accompanied by, with the addition of*)

accompanying (*adj*): 〈Pol/Soc〉 l'**accompagnement** (*m*) **social** aux grandes opérations de réhabilitation (*accompanying social measures*)

accomplice (*n*): les gardiens de paix ripoux et leur **complice** (*m/f*)

accordance (*n*): ceci serait **conforme à** la constitution (*in accordance with*); ⟨Jur⟩ décider, **conformément à la loi** (*in accordance/conformity with the law*)

account (*n*): ⟨Admin⟩ le **compte-rendu** interne du comité (*account, report*); ces dispositions **prennent acte** (*m*) **de** la nouvelle configuration de la frontière (*take account of*); trois éléments doivent être **pris en compte** (*m*); **tenir compte** ni des grèves ni du chômage technique (*take into account*); ⟨Fin⟩ les enquêteurs ont épluché la **comptabilité** de la firme; approuver les **comptes** de l'exercice en cours (*[financial] accounts*); l'examen détaillé du **livre de comptes** (*accounts book*); **verser un acompte** lie les parties irrévocablement (*pay a sum on account*); SEE ALSO **accounting, down payment**

accountability (*n*): SEE **responsibility**

accountable (*adj*): le maire doit **répondre de** sa gestion (*be accountable for*); ⟨Pol⟩ les ministres sont **responsables** de leurs décisions devant le Parlement (*be accountable, be answerable*)

accountancy (*n*): ⟨Fin⟩ un grand **cabinet comptable** (*accountancy firm*); la loi sur la **profession comptable** (*accountancy profession*); la formation complète à l'**expertise** (*f*) **comptable** (*chartered accountancy*); SEE ALSO **accountant**

accountant (*n*): ⟨Fin⟩ une célèbre **société d'audit** (*m*) britannique (*firm of accountants, accountancy firm*)

account holder (*n*): ⟨Fin⟩ les noms des **titulaires** (*m*) **de comptes** en Suisse

accounting (*n*): ⟨Fin⟩ la **comptabilité** est en règle (*accounting*); tenir une **comptabilité** précise (*accounting, accounts*); une simplification des obligations **comptables** (*accounting*); clôture de l'**exercice** (*m*) **comptable** (*accounting year*)

accredit (*v*): ⟨Educ⟩ des établissements dont les diplômes sont **visés** par l'État (*accredit, give accreditation*)

accreditation (*n*): ⟨Educ⟩ le **visa** du diplôme; SEE ALSO **accredit**

accredited (*adj*): le représentant **attitré** de la France dans ce pays (*accredited, authorized*)

accuracy (*n*): contester l'**exactitude** (*f*) des chiffres avancés; la **précision** des statistiques établies par le FAO (*accuracy*); être sûr de la **justesse** de ses prévisions (*accuracy, correctness*)

accurate (*adj*): des chiffres **exacts** (*accurate, precise*); une traduction **fidèle**; faire des **prévisions** (*f*) **exactes** des ventes (*accurate forecast*)

accusation (*n*): SEE **charge**

accuse (*v*): **reprocher à** son associé 14 MF de détournements (*accuse*); un article de journal le **met en cause** (*accuse, incriminate*); ⟨Jur⟩ **être inculpé** et écroué (*be accused/charged*); **accusé** de viol, et conduit au commissariat; les deux agents **incriminés** (*accused; charged*)

3

accused (*n*/*adj*): ⟨Jur⟩ tout **prévenu** (*m*) est présumé innocent; une formule qui offre des garanties aux **justiciables** (*m*) (*accused person, person accused of a crime*)

achieve (*v*): le premier des objectifs de la France est **atteint** (*achieved*); comment va **se réaliser** l'union monétaire souhaitée? (*be achieved*)

achievement (*n*): les **acquis** (*m*) de la politique agricole commune; il souligna les **réalisations** (*f*) du gouvernement; la décentralisation, l'œuvre (*f*) majeure de ce gouvernement (*achievement, attainment*)

acknowledge (*v*): **accuser réception** (*f*) d'une lettre (*acknowledge receipt*)

acknowledgement (*n*): vous recevrez un **avis** de dépôt de demande; sa lettre n'a pas reçu d'**accusé** (*m*) **de réception** (*acknowledgement [of receipt]*)

acquire (*v*): **se doter** d'un ordinateur pour le traitement des commandes (*acquire, equip o.s. with*); ⟨Econ⟩ des sociétés ont été cédées et d'autres **acquises**; le magnat britannique **s'est rendu acquéreur** (*m*) du *Daily News* de New York (*acquire, purchase*)

acquisition (*n*): ⟨Econ⟩ l'échec du projet de **reprise** (*f*) de la société; le **rachat**, par OPA, des actions détenues par le public; SEE ALSO **take-over**

acquit (*v*): ⟨Jur⟩ jugé et **acquitté**, il est maintenu en détention

acquittal (*n*): ⟨Jur⟩ malgré son **acquittement** (*m*), il reste inculpé d'autres délits criminels; SEE ALSO **discharge, release**

act (*n*): ⟨Pol⟩ une **loi** sera votée dans la nouvelle session (*Act of Parliament*); ⟨Jur⟩ **prendre en flagrant délit** (*m*) de vol; **pris sur le fait**, il ne pouvait nier sa participation (*catch in the act, in flagrante delicto*)

act (*v*): le gouvernement doit **prendre des mesures** (*f*), et de toute urgence (*act, take action*)

action (*n*): ⟨Jur⟩ le plaignant pourrait **se constituer partie** (*f*) **civile** (*bring an independent action for damages*); aucune **action en dommages** (*mpl*) **et intérêts** ne peut être engagée contre un syndicat (*action for damages*); le ministère public **apprécie les suites** (*f*) **à donner** à l'affaire (*consider what action to take*)

active (*adj*): un **militant** de l'association Frères des hommes (*active member*); ceux et celles qui **militent** dans les diocèses (*be active [esp. in organization or political party]*)

activism (*n*): ⟨Pol⟩ la participation à un parti va de l'adhésion au **militantisme**

activist (*n*): ⟨Pol⟩ où sont les **militants** (*m*) d'autrefois, dévoués au syndicat? (*[political] activist, militant*); **militer** dans un parti ou un syndicat (*be a [political] activist*); SEE ALSO **militant**

activity (*n*): une enquête officielle sur leurs **agissements** (*m*) a été ouverte (*[criminal/nefarious] activities*)

adapt (*v*): ils ont su **s'adapter** à des conditions très particulières (*adapt*); l'**inadaptation** (*f*) des institutions (*failure/inability to adapt*); SEE ALSO **adjust**

adaptability (*n*): on peut douter des **capacités** (*f*) **d'adaptation** du personnel

addition (*n*): grâce au **cumul** de leurs salaires, ils touchent 28.000F par mois (*addition, adding together*)

additional (*adj*): cet organisme bénéficiera d'un **surcroît de crédits** (*mpl*) (*additional funds*)

adequate (*adj*): faute de crédits **suffisants**; en l'absence de volontaires **en nombre** (*m*) **suffisant** (*adequate, sufficient*)

adjacent (*adj*): dans les rues **adjacentes** (*adjacent*); la campagne **jouxtant** la ville nouvelle (*be adjacent to*)

adjourn (*v*): le sommet a été **ajourné** (*adjourn, defer, put off*); **suspendre** une séance (*adjourn, suspend*); SEE ALSO **postpone**

adjournment (*n*): l'**ajournement** (*m*) des modalités d'application de la réforme (*adjournment*); ⟨Pol⟩ la **suspension** des débats; il demande la **clôture** (*adjournment [esp. of parliamentary debate]*); SEE ALSO **postponement**

adjust (*v*): la bureaucratie et l'**inadaptation** (*f*) de l'éducation nationale (*failure to adjust/adapt*)

adjustment (*n*): ⟨Econ⟩ difficultés d'**ajustement** (*m*) de l'offre et de la demande (*adjustment*); quelques **aménagements** (*m*) ont été faits, mais la rigueur est maintenue; une **modulation** des prestations familiales en fonction des revenus (*adjustment, modification*)

administer (*v*): ⟨Admin⟩ les citoyens estiment que la municipalité est bien **gérée**; première femme à **diriger** une grande métropole (*administer, run*)

administration (*n*): ⟨Admin⟩ confier l'**administration** (*f*) de la société au directeur-adjoint (*administration*); la Chine veut se mêler de la **gestion** de Hong-Kong (*administration, government*)

administrative (*adj*): le poste à pourvoir exige de réelles qualités **administratives** (*administrative, pertaining to administration*)

administrator (*n*): les **gestionnaires** (*m*) du parc HLM; les associations, principales **gestionnaires** du tourisme social; ⟨Comm⟩ la SARL est administrée par un **gérant** (*administrator [of limited-liability company]*)

admissible (*adj*): ⟨Jur⟩ les référés ont été déclarés **recevables** par les juges (*admissible, allowable*)

admission (*n*): ⟨Educ⟩ l'**admissibilité** (*f*) à l'École Polytechnique (*admission, entrance to*); avec l'**intégration** (*f*) de l'ex-RDA dans la nouvelle Allemagne (*admission, entry*)

admit (*v*): ⟨Pol⟩ **laisser entrer** les réfugiés; l'État ne peut pas **accueillir** tous les demandeurs d'asile (*admit, let in*); SEE ALSO **accommodate, confess**

adopt (*v*): ⟨Pol⟩ les députés **adoptent** le projet de loi (*adopt, pass*); **retenir** une série de mesures concrètes (*adopt, decide on*); **investir** un candidat

5

(*adopt [esp. as election candidate]*); ⟨Soc⟩ l'enfant qu'on souhaite **adopter** (*adopt, foster*)

adoption (*n*): ⟨Pol⟩ l'**adoption** (*f*) d'un plan d'action (*adoption*); ⟨Soc⟩ vérifier si l'**adoption** est conforme à l'intérêt de l'enfant (*adoption; fostering*)

advance (*n*): ⟨Comm⟩ une **avance** sur la prime d'intéressement sera distribuée aux salariés (*advance*); ⟨Fin⟩ une limite d'**encours** (*m*) mensuel est indiquée aux bénéficiaires de cartes de crédit (*cash advance*)

advance (*v*): aider à **faire progresser** les pourparlers de paix

advanced (*adj*): des formations spécifiques, très **pointues** (*advanced; specialized*); une **technologie de pointe** (*f*) (*advanced technology*)

advancement (*n*): le diplôme pour tous ne veut pas dire l'**avancement** (*m*) pour tous; SEE ALSO **promotion**

advent (*n*): le prix à payer pour l'**avènement** (*m*) d'une société plus égalitaire; un acte d'importance majeure pour l'**avènement** de l'Europe (*advent, coming into being*)

advertise (*v*): **faire de la réclame** pour vanter les qualités du produit; **faire de la publicité** dans les journaux

advertisement (*n*): mettre une **annonce** dans un journal (*advertisement*); les **spots** (*m*) **publicitaires**, le dernier cri en matière de publicité médiatique (*advert[isement], commercial [esp. TV]*)

advertiser (*n*): les **annonceurs** (*m*) reçoivent un exemplaire gratuit

advertising (*n*): sans la **publicité**, le journal ne paraîtrait pas; abuser de la **réclame** (*advertising, publicity*); la récession a réduit les **recettes** (*f*) **de publicité** (*advertising revenue*); ⟨Journ⟩ un **encart publicitaire** pleine page (*advertising/publicity insert*); SEE ALSO **insert**

advice (*n*): après **avis** (*m*) des syndicats (*advice, opinion*); un **conseil** qu'il suit à la lettre (*advice, piece of advice*); ⟨Jur⟩ on lui conseille de **consulter un avocat** (*take legal advice*)

advise (*v*): le rapport **préconise** un retour aux vieilles méthodes (*advise, recommend*); on les en avait **avisés** trop tard (*advise, notify, inform*)

adviser (*n*): le président consulta ses **conseillers** (*m*)

advisory (*adj*): assister à une réunion **à titre** (*m*) **consultatif** (*in an advisory capacity*)

advocate (*n*): les **adeptes** (*m*) de l'interventionnisme; **partisan** (*m*) de la peine de mort; un **tenant** de la ligne dure; les **zélateurs** (*m*) du protectionnisme (*advocate, champion*); SEE ALSO **supporter**

advocate (*v*): ceux qui **préconisent** la poursuite de la Révolution; **prôner** l'octroi d'une aide occidentale à Moscou; **se faire l'avocat** (*m*) de la fabrication de l'arme nucléaire (*advocate, be in favour of*); SEE ALSO **support**

affect (*v*): ceci **influera sur** notre décision (*affect, influence*); la crise qui **frappe** le transport aérien (*affect, hit*); cette décision **touche** 77 des 339 salariés (*affect, concern*); SEE ALSO **impair**

affiliate (*v*): 2.000 membres supplémentaires **se sont affiliés** cette année (*be affiliated; join*)

affiliated (*adj*): ⟨Ind⟩ les **centrales** (*f*) **syndicales** restent divisées (*[group of] affiliated trade unions*)

affiliation (*n*): on ignore leur **appartenance** (*f*) précise (*affiliation*); aucune distinction de religion ou d'**appartenance politique** (*political affiliation*)

affluent (*adj*): les couches **aisées** de la population (*affluent, prosperous*); par rapport aux autres salariés, ils sont des **nantis** (*affluent/prosperous person*)

against (*prep*): des sanctions **à l'encontre de** l'Afrique du Sud; ⟨Jur⟩ le tribunal a prononcé **à son encontre** la peine maximale

age-group (*n*): l'accès de 80% d'une **classe d'âge** au baccalauréat; dans la **tranche d'âge** 15-44 ans; le chômage décroît dans ces **catégories** (*f*) **d'âge** (*age group, age band/bracket*)

ageing (*n*): ⟨Soc⟩ la crainte d'un **vieillissement** de la population

agency (*n*): ⟨Admin⟩ la Croix-Rouge établit une **antenne** permanente à Phnom Penh; ⟨Comm⟩ les industriels français ont rouvert des **représentations** (*f*) à Pékin (*agency; branch*)

agenda (*n*): **à l'ordre** (*m*) **du jour** de la réunion (*on the agenda*); **insérer à l'ordre du jour** un débat sur les droits des minorités (*put on the agenda*)

aggravate (*v*): la crise du Golfe ne fait qu'**aggraver** la situation; SEE ALSO **worsen**

aggravating (*adj*): ⟨Jur⟩ ce qui constitue une **circonstance aggravante** (*aggravating circumstance*)

agitate (*v*): ⟨Pol⟩ **militer** pour les droits des immigrés; SEE ALSO **campaign**

agitation (*n*): cette annonce a provoqué un certain **émoi** chez les experts-comptables (*agitation, emotion*)

agitator (*n*): la police a arrêté les **fauteurs** (*m*) **de troubles**; des **meneurs** (*m*) qui entretenaient la violence dans la rue

agree (*v*): les deux pays ont **convenu** de se consulter à intervalles réguliers; l'OPEP **s'accorde** à limiter sa production; les pays du Golfe **se mettent d'accord** sur un nouveau plafond de production; la Chine et la Grande-Bretagne **s'entendent** sur la construction d'un nouvel aéroport (*agree, come to an agreement*); SEE ALSO **commitment**

agreed (*adj*): des négociations qui débouchent sur un **règlement à l'amiable** (*agreed settlement*); SEE ALSO **out-of-court**

agreement (*n*): ⟨Pol⟩ arriver enfin à un **accord** (*agreement*); il dénonce la **convention** qui liait les deux pays (*agreement, convention*); ⟨Jur⟩ lire tous les termes d'un **engagement** (*agreement, commitment*); un **terrain d'entente** (*f*) a été trouvé (*area/basis of agreement*); ⟨Comm⟩ OPEP: **entente** Koweït-Arabie Saoudite (*commercial agreement [esp. illicit]*)

agricultural (*adj*): ⟨Agric⟩ un désaccord sur les **prix** (*m*) **agricoles** divise l'Europe (*agricultural prices*); l'**Europe** (*f*) **verte**, ou le secteur agricole de la CEE (*European agricultural policy*); confronté à la colère des **paysans** (*m*); toute la **paysannerie** d'Europe devait manifester ce jour-là (*agricultural/farming community*)

agriculture (*n*): ⟨Agric⟩ les aides à l'**agriculture** (*f*) toujours à l'ordre du jour des sommets européens (*agriculture, farming*)

aid (*n*): ⟨Pol⟩ l'octroi d'une **aide** occidentale à Moscou (*aid*); l'**assistance** (*f*) **militaire** fournie par la France (*military aid*); ⟨Soc⟩ une population d'**assistés** (*m*) où tous les risques sont pris en charge par l'État (*person receiving state aid*); comment sortir d'une condition d'**assistanat** (*m*)?; du chômage massif et une économie d'**assistance** (*dependence on State aid*)

aid (*v*): il faudrait **venir en aide** aux plus démunis (*aid, help*); les personnes officiellement **secourues** (*aided; in receipt of [State] aid*)

aim (*n*): les **visées** (*f*) annexionnistes de ses voisins (*aim, design*); cette loi **vise un double objectif** (*have a dual aim/purpose*); l'ONU **s'est fixé un objectif** ambitieux (*set o.s. an aim/objective*); SEE ALSO **ambition**

aim (*v*): des mesures **visant** à améliorer la protection sociale; un projet de loi **visant** l'abrogation de la loi (*aim at, have as its aim*)

alarm (*n*): **alerte** (*f*) à l'attentat sur un avion d'Air France (*alert, warning, scare*)

alert (*n*): l'**état** (*m*) **d'alerte** décrété le 5 décembre (*state of alert*); les unités de l'armée sont **placées en état d'alerte** (*f*) (*place/put on alert/stand-by*)

alienate (*v*): le gouvernement ne veut pas **s'aliéner** le soutien de ses alliés conservateurs; il risque de **se mettre à dos** les libéraux (*alienate, antagonize*)

align (*v*): la France doit tôt ou tard **s'aligner** sur la pratique communautaire (*align o.s.; fall into line with*)

alignment (*n*): on devrait **aligner** la politique française sur les dispositions en vigueur dans d'autres pays (*bring into alignment*)

alimony (*n*): ⟨Soc⟩ une réduction d'impôt pour **aide** (*f*) **alimentaire**; indexer une **pension alimentaire** sur le coût de la vie (*alimony, maintenance payment*)

allegation (*n*): les **allégations** (*f*) portées contre eux étaient infondées; la vérité de ses **assertions** (*f*) n'est pas prouvée; faire la preuve de la vérité des **faits** (*m*) **allégués**; il a appris officiellement les **faits qui lui sont reprochés** (*allegation, assertion*)

alleged (*adj*): la signature de l'auteur **supposé** du document; pallier le **prétendu** déficit de l'assurance-maladie (*alleged, supposed*)

allegiance (*n*): ⟨Rel⟩ les sectes d'**obédience** (*f*) musulmane (*allegiance, [religious] persuasion*); ⟨Pol⟩ le gouvernement **d'obédience** marxiste-léniniste (*allegiance [esp. political]*); son parti se **réclame des** mêmes valeurs que la droite (*claim allegiance to; profess*)

alleviate (*v*): on a pu **atténuer** les souffrances de la population

alleviation (*n*): une priorité: l'**allégement** (*m*) de la pauvreté la plus criante

alliance (*n*): ⟨Pol⟩ pas d'**alliance** (*f*) RPR-UDC pour le second tour des élections; un **rapprochement** inattendu entre les écologistes et la Droite (*alliance [esp. electoral]*); ⟨Econ⟩ un **regroupement** entre Thomson, Siemens et Philips (*alliance, link-up*)

allocate (*v*): ⟨Fin⟩ les 4,5 milliards **alloués** aux lycées; les sommes **affectées** à la réfection des bâtiments scolaires; SEE ALSO **allot, earmark**

allocation (*n*): l'opposition s'inquiète de l'**affectation** (*f*) de ces sommes (*allocation, use*); l'**attribution** (*f*) des logements à loyer modéré (*allocation, distribution*)

allot (*v*): un local **affecté** à la Perception (*allot, assign, allocate*); deux heures sont **allouées** aux activités d'éveil (*allot, devote*); ⟨Pol⟩ plusieurs sièges sont encore à **pourvoir** (*allot, distribute*); SEE ALSO **earmark**

allow (*v*): le travail de nuit des femmes va être **autorisé** (*allow, permit*); SEE ALSO **permit**

allowance (*n*): ⟨Fin⟩ on va annuler l'**allocation** (*f*) de parent unique; une hausse des **indemnités** (*f*) de chauffage et de logement (*allowance*); ⟨Pol⟩ un parlementaire touche une **indemnité** mensuelle de 36.000F (*allowance, pay*); SEE ALSO **cost of living, tax allowance**

ally (*n*): ⟨Pol⟩ le groupe socialiste, y compris ses quinze **apparentés** (*m*), a voté l'amnistie; sans compter les modérés et **assimilés** (*m*)

alternate (*v*): la droite et la gauche **alternent** au pouvoir

alternative (*n/adj*): chercher une solution **de rechange** (*m*); à leur avis, il n'existe pas de **politique** (*f*) **de rechange** (*alternative policy*)

amalgamate (*v*): ⟨Econ⟩ leur décision de **fusionner** au sein d'une nouvelle entité; SEE ALSO **merge**

amalgamation (*n*): ⟨Econ⟩ comment réussir la **fusion** de deux sociétés elles-mêmes en difficultés?; SEE ALSO **merger**

ambition (*n*): ⟨Pol⟩ les **velléités** (*f*) sécessionnistes de la Slovénie; le nationalisme kurde face à la **volonté** assimilatrice de la Turquie (*ambition, aim*)

amend (*v*): ⟨Pol⟩ il peut voter le budget et **amender** les textes; la législation a été **remaniée** à plusieurs reprises (*amend, modify*)

amendment (*n*): ⟨Pol⟩ sur 246 **amendements** (*m*) enregistrés, 79 furent adoptés (*amendment [esp. to parliamentary bill]*); ⟨Jur⟩ le seul syndicat à avoir signé l'**avenant** (*m*) à la convention

amenity (*n*): une maison avec piscine et une foule d'autres **avantages** (*m*) (*amenities*); préserver un équilibre entre emplois, logements et **équipements** (*m*) **collectifs** (*amenities, community facilities*); SEE ALSO **facilities**

amicable (*adj*): ⟨Jur⟩ les parties sont arrivées à un **règlement à l'amiable** (*amicable settlement*); une volonté d'**arrangement** (*m*) **à l'amiable** (*amicable/friendly arrangement*); SEE ALSO **out-of-court**

amnesty (*n*): ⟨Pol⟩ **amnistie** (*f*) des délits politico-financiers (*amnesty, general pardon*)

amnesty (*v*): ⟨Pol⟩ le général chrétien, **amnistié** par le gouvernement libanais; **amnistier** ceux qui ont financé des partis politiques (*amnesty, give a general pardon*)

amount (*n*): le **montant** de ses gains (*amount, sum*); le **total** n'a pas été fixé (*total amount*); une allocation est versée **jusqu'à concurrence** (*f*) **de** 300F par enfant à charge (*up to the amount/limit of*)

amount (*v*): le coût total **se chiffre à** quelque 10.000F; les économies **se montent à** un total de 37 MF (*amount to*)

analyse (*v*): SEE **break down**

analysis (*n*): SEE **breakdown**

ancestry (*n*): l'association des Français d'**ascendance** (*f*) polonaise (*ancestry, stock*)

annex (*v*): ⟨Pol/Mil⟩ un pays qui avale en l'**annexant** un pays voisin

annexation (*n*): ⟨Pol/Mil⟩ depuis l'**annexion** (*f*) de l'Ukraine par l'Union soviétique

announce (*v*): il a **fait état** de sa décision de se rendre à Moscou; **faire part** de son intention de démissionner (*announce*); ⟨Ins⟩ le Lloyds **affiche** un bilan catastrophique (*announce, report*)

announcement (*n*): le jour de l'**annonce** (*f*) de sa décision

annual (*adj*): ⟨Fin⟩ une économie de 62.000F sur les **annuités** (*f*) **des prêts**; il doit rembourser 59.000F d'**annuités d'emprunt** (*annual instalment on a loan*)

annul (*v*): ⟨Jur⟩ faire **annuler** son mariage (*annul*); la chambre d'accusation **infirme** les ordonnances prises par le juge d'instruction (*annul, quash*); SEE ALSO **repeal**

annulment (*n*): l'**abrogation** (*f*) de la loi; il réclame l'**abolition** (*f*) de la loi de 1904 (*annulment, repeal*)

answer (*v*): ⟨Jur⟩ contraint de **répondre en justice** (*f*) des accusations portés contre lui (*answer [esp. a charge]*)

anticipate (*v*): on aurait pu **prévoir** un pourrissement de la situation (*anticipate, foresee*)

anticipation (*n*): **en prévision** (*f*) **de** l'ouverture des frontières (*in anticipation of*)

anxiety (*n*): l'OCDE manifeste sur ce point de réelles **inquiétudes** (*f*) (*anxiety, concern*)

anxious (*adj*): les Douze, **soucieux** de se démarquer des États-Unis; Washington, de plus en plus **inquiet** du sort de la Yougoslavie (*anxious, concerned*)

apartment (*n*): 2.000F de prime par **logement** (*m*) **collectif**; les **habitats** (*m*) **collectifs**, notamment les logements sociaux (*apartment block*)

apolitical (*adj*): ⟨Pol⟩ on disait la jeunesse **apolitique** et individualiste

apparatus (*n*): ⟨Pol⟩ 30% des fonds collectés vont à l'**appareil** (*m*) **du parti** (*party apparatus/machinery*); la mainmise d'un **appareil étatique** sur la vie publique (*State apparatus/machine*)

appeal (*n*): ⟨Jur⟩ il avait été relaxé **en appel** (*m*); si la condamnation était confirmée **en appel** (*on appeal*); le défenseur a déposé un **pourvoi en cassation** (*f*) devant les tribunaux; le **recours en grâce** fut rejeté (*appeal for clemency*); une **saisie** de la commission des monopoles s'impose (*appeal, lodging of an appeal*)

appeal (*v*): l'opposition **appelle au** boycottage des élections; l'ex-URSS **plaide pour** un espace économique commun (*appeal/call for*); la direction a **lancé un appel** à la reprise du travail; ⟨Jur⟩ les parties disposent d'un délai d'un mois pour **interjeter appel**; les condamnés peuvent **se pourvoir en cassation** (*f*) (*lodge an appeal*); **déposer un recours** devant le Conseil constitutionnel; il a décidé de **faire appel de la décision** du tribunal (*appeal against a decision*)

appear (*v*): ⟨Jur⟩ les détenus ont **comparu** devant la chambre correctionnelle; **comparaître à audience** (*f*) devant un tribunal à Rabat (*appear [before a court]*)

appearance (*n*): ⟨Jur⟩ en attendant une **comparution** devant le conseil de discipline (*appearance [before a court/tribunal]*); le RPR demande l'**audition** (*f*) du journaliste devant une commission d'enquête (*appearance [esp. before committee of inquiry]*); SEE ALSO **publication**

appellant (*n*): ⟨Jur⟩ l'appel étant injustifié, l'**appelant** (*m*) est condamné aux dépens

applicant (*n*): dix **postulants** (*m*) pour une place; les **candidats** (*m*) à l'immigration; les qualifications des deux **prétendants** (*m*) au poste; le **demandeur** doit pouvoir justifier d'une résidence de trois ans (*applicant, candidate*)

application (*n*): sa **candidature** (*f*) a des chances d'être retenue; leur **demande** (*f*) sera soumise à un jury (*application*); remplir un **formulaire de demande** (*application form*); faire parvenir une **lettre de sollicitation** (*f*) (*letter of application*); ⟨Pol⟩ l'**application** (*f*) de la charte des Nations unies; la **mise en œuvre** intégrale de la résolution de l'ONU (*application, putting into effect*); SEE ALSO **implementation**

apply (*v*): on **affecta** ces sommes à l'aide au tiers monde (*apply, make use of*); la Suède se prépare à **poser sa candidature**; **postuler** la place vacante (*apply/make application for*)

appoint (*v*): avant d'être **affecté** au bureau de Tokyo (*appoint, post*); il vient d'être **nommé** au poste de directeur-général (*appoint [esp. to a post]*); SEE ALSO **nominate**

appointee (*n*): le **candidat retenu** devra être titulaire d'une licence; le **titulaire** alliera à un esprit d'initiative une bonne faculté d'adaptation

appointment (*n*): la **désignation** d'un successeur ne saurait tarder; depuis la **nomination** du nouveau garde des Sceaux (*appointment; selection*); recevoir une **lettre d'embauche** (*f*) (*letter of appointment [to a job]*)

appreciate (*v*): ⟨Fin⟩ le DMark **apprécie** sur tous les marchés financiers; la valeur de leurs actifs ne pouvait que **s'apprécier** (*appreciate, increase in value*)

appreciation (*n*): ⟨Econ/Fin⟩ l'**appréciation** (*f*) du franc facilitera les importations

apprehend (*v*): l'agresseur, un mineur, est **interpellé** (*apprehend; stop for questioning*)

apprentice (*n*) ⟨Ind⟩ des **apprentis** (*m*) formés en deux ans; des centres de formation d'**apprentis**

apprenticeship (*m*) ⟨Ind⟩ un **apprentissage** permet d'obtenir une qualification; le but: mettre en **apprentissage** 400.000 jeunes dans les cinq ans

approach (*n*): une **démarche** conjointe pourrait réussir (*approach*); Paris **fait des ouvertures** (*f*) à Bonn (*make approaches/overtures*)

approach (*v*): ⟨Comm⟩ **démarcher** systématiquement toutes les sociétés implantées aux États-Unis (*approach, canvass*)

appropriate (*adj*): trouver des solutions **adéquates** à ces problèmes; une solution **adaptée** à leurs besoins (*appropriate, suitable*); SEE ALSO **suitable**

appropriateness (*n*): il mettait en question l'**opportunité** (*f*) de ces mesures (*appropriateness; timing*)

approval (*n*): avec l'**approbation** (*f*) tacite du reste du monde arabe; l'**agrément** (*m*) préalable des pouvoirs publics est requis; après **avis** (*m*) **favorable** de l'Inspection du travail (*approval, consent*); SEE ALSO **consent**

approve (*v*): une réduction dont le principe a été **agréé** lors du sommet; ⟨Pol⟩ le vote a **sanctionné** la politique française au Proche-Orient; le refus de Bruxelles d'**avaliser** le rachat de la firme canadienne (*approve, endorse*); il refuse de **cautionner** une manifestation qu'il juge anti-patriotique (*approve, support*)

approved (*adj*): ⟨Admin⟩ les associations **reconnues d'utilité** (*f*) **publique** (*officially approved*)

arbitrate (*v*): c'est au chef de l'État d'**arbitrer** les disputes entre ministres; un magistrat chargé de **trancher** les désaccords entre l'administration et les élus (*arbitrate, decide*)

arbitration (*n*): les députés demandent l'**arbitrage** (*m*) du Premier ministre (*arbitration, decision*); ⟨Ind⟩ l'**arbitrage** intervient après l'échec de la médiation (*arbitration procedure*); une **commission d'arbitrage** composée de cinq juristes européens (*arbitration committee/board*)

arbitrator (*n*): servir de médiateur, sinon d'**arbitre** (*m*) entre les deux pays

area (*n*): ⟨Comm⟩ dans le **quartier commercial** de la ville (*business area*); son **secteur de vente** (*f*) comprend toute la région parisienne (*sales area*); ⟨Econ⟩ une vaste **zone de libre-échange** (*free trade area*); les pays de la **zone sterling** (*sterling area*); SEE ALSO **sector**

argue (*v*): en **arguant** que cela ne constitue pas une garantie suffisante; **soutenir** le contraire (*argue, maintain*); les adversaires du projet **font valoir** qu'il sera très coûteux (*argue; point out*)

argument (*n*): l'**argumentation** (*f*) du ministre en dit long sur l'évolution de sa pensée; le **raisonnement** selon lequel il fallait continuer la guerre (*argument, reasoning*); la **thèse** libérale a prévalu (*argument, thesis*)

arm (*n*): ⟨Mil⟩ avec 100.000 hommes **sous les drapeaux** (*mpl*) (*under arms*); ⟨Mil/Econ⟩ les **dépenses** (*f*) **d'armements** de la Belgique (*arms expenditure*); l'**armement** (*m*) espagnol multiplie les alliances (*arms industry*); un important **trafic d'armes** (*f*) avec les pays bordant sa frontière sud (*arms trade*); entre **marchands** (*m*) **de canons** la bataille sera rude (*arms dealer/supplier*); ⟨Pol⟩ négociation sur le **contrôle des armes**: l'impasse (*arms control*)

arm (*v*): ⟨Mil⟩ **armer** des volontaires; quelle folie de **fournir en armes** (*f*) les rebelles! (*arm, equip with arms*)

armed (*adj*): ⟨Mil⟩ une diminution des effectifs des **forces** (*f*) **armées** (*armed forces*); renoncer à la **lutte armée** (*armed struggle*)

arouse (*v*): l'affaire **soulève** une certaine émotion à Paris; l'enthousiasme que **suscite** la révolution islamique (*arouse, give rise to*)

arrange (*v*): la réunion **fixée** au 15 mai a été annulée

arrangement (*n*): Paris est arrivée à un **arrangement** avec Alger; des **dispositions** (*f*) ont été prises pour leur rapatriement; une fois les ultimes **dispositions sécuritaires** prises (*safety arrangement/ precautions*)

arrears (*npl*): ⟨Fin⟩ les **arrérages** (*mpl*) de loyer et les factures impayées; à cause de ses 10.000F d'**impayés** (*mpl*) **de loyer** (*arrears of rent*); les **arriérés** (*m*) **de paiement** dûs aux fournisseurs français (*arrears of payment*); ⟨Fisc⟩ un **redressement fiscal** pour 200.000F lui a été adressé (*notification to pay arrears of tax*)

arrest (*n*): ⟨Jur⟩ trois **arrestations** (*f*) à la suite d'émeutes (*arrest*); lancer un **mandat d'amener** contre les deux fuyards; un **mandat d'arrêt** (*m*) international a été délivré à son encontre (*arrest warrant*)

arrest (*v*): **arrêté**, puis transféré à la centrale de Colmar; **appréhender** un suspect (*arrest, put under arrest*)

arrival (*n*): ⟨Comm⟩ un **arrivage** de vivres en provenance d'Europe (*arrival; consignment, delivery*)

arrive (*v*): le seul moyen d'**aboutir à** une paix durable; les Douze **parviennent à** un accord (*arrive at, reach*)

arson (*n*): ⟨Jur⟩ une série d'**incendies** (*m*) **d'origine criminelle**; trois **incendies volontaires** dans le Var hier (*case of arson*)

ask (*v*): ⟨Pol⟩ la Grande-Bretagne, **sollicitée** d'y participer, réserve sa réponse (*ask, request*); ⟨Jur⟩ l'avocat général avait **requis** une peine de cinq ans (*ask for, demand [esp. sentence]*)

assailant (*n*): ⟨Jur⟩ il n'a pas reconnu son **agresseur** (*m*)

assault (*n*): ⟨Jur⟩ inculpés pour **coups** (*mpl*) **et blessures**; une procédure judiciaire pour outrage et **voies** (*fpl*) **de fait** (*assault and battery*)

assemble (*v*): une foule **rassemblée** sur la place Rouge (*assemble, gather*)

assembly (*n*): ⟨Pol⟩ il a fait toute sa carrière à l'**Assemblée** (*f*) **nationale** (*[Fr] National Assembly*); ⟨Ind⟩ le travail répétitif d'une **chaîne de montage** (*m*) (*assembly line*)

assent (*n*): la France a donné son **acquiescement** (*m*); obtenir l'**assentiment** (*m*) de la population (*assent, agreement*)

assent (*v*): l'Allemagne est prête à **acquiescer** à cette demande (*assent, acquiesce*)

assert (*v*): il tenait à **faire valoir ses droits** (*m*) (*assert one's rights*); ⟨Jur⟩ tout au long de l'audience, il **protesta de son innocence** (*f*) (*assert one's innocence*)

assertion (*n*): le tribunal doit trancher de la vérité de ses **assertions** (*f*) (*assertion, affirmation*); SEE ALSO **allegation**

assess (*v*): **estimer** le montant des dégâts (*assess, calculate*); on **chiffre** la perte à près de 3.000F (*assess, put a figure on/to*)

assessment (*n*): l'**évaluation** (*f*) des dommages-intérêts

asset (*n*): l'horlogerie, un des principaux **atouts** économiques de la Franche-Comté (*asset*); ⟨Fin⟩ après le gel des **avoirs** (*m*) panaméens aux États-Unis (*assets, holdings*); l'**actif** (*m*) **immobilisé** comprend les bâtiments et les machines (*fixed assets*); la **réalisation des actifs** était dès lors indispensable (*realizing of assets*); SEE ALSO **liquid assets**

assign (*v*): le poste à responsabilité qui lui était **imparti**; SEE ALSO **allot**

assignment (*n*): il espérait une **affectation** en Extrême-Orient (*assignment, posting*); **envoyé en mission** (*f*) en Yougoslavie (*send on an assignment/ mission*)

assist (*v*): ⟨Mil⟩ la France a envoyé des troupes pour **prêter main-forte** (*f*); **venir en aide** (*f*) aux forces tchadiennes (*assist, help, come to the help of*)

assistance (*n*): ⟨Econ⟩ l'Auvergne, beaucoup plus **aidée** que la moyenne des autres provinces (*in receipt of assistance, assisted*); SEE ALSO **aid**

assistant (*n*): employé en tant qu'**adjoint** (*m*) au directeur; le jeune directeur **adjoint**; SEE ALSO **deputy**

assize court (*n*): ⟨Jur⟩ la **Cour d'assises** (*fpl*) seule peut juger les crimes

associate (*n*): la firme recrute de nouveaux **collaborateurs** (*m*) à l'étranger

associate (*v*): la France **s'associe** aux autres pays occidentaux (*associate with, join*)

association (*n*): ⟨Jur⟩ la loi de 1901 régit toutes les **associations** (*f*) (*association, society*); ⟨Jur⟩ les **statuts** (*mpl*) peuvent limiter les pouvoirs du gérant; la société a déposé ses **statuts** au Registre du Commerce (*articles of association*)

asylum (*n*): ⟨Pol⟩ 2.000 demandes d'**asile** (*m*) politique enregistrées en novembre (*[political] asylum*); le **droit d'asile** ne peut être demandé que dans ce cas précis (*right of asylum*); dans le cas d'un étranger **demandeur** (*m*) **d'asile politique** (*asylum seeker*)

attach (*v*): ⟨Pol/Admin⟩ le ministre l'a **attaché** à son cabinet (*attach, add*); il est **attaché** au ministère des Affaires étrangères; il sera **affecté** au service contrôle de gestion (*attach, post*)

attached (*adj*): le document **ci-joint** (*attached, enclosed*)

attack (*n*): **attentats** (*m*) contre des installations militaires (*[terrorist] attack*); il **monte au créneau** et exige des éclaircissements (*go onto the attack*); les médecins sont **dans le collimateur** (*under attack, in the line of fire*); la France, particulièrement **épinglée** (*under attack*)

attack (*v*): il raconte avoir été **agressé** par deux faux policiers (*attack, assault*); le gouvernement, toujours prêt à **s'en prendre à** la presse (*attack, criticize*)

attempt (*n*): la première **tentative** a été un échec

attempt (*v*): les Douze **tentent** en vain de persuader Washington

attempted (*adj*): échec d'une **tentative de coup** (*m*) **d'État** (*attempted coup*); une **tentative de vol** (*m*) a échoué (*attempted theft*)

attend (*v*): il refusa d'**assister** à la conférence; le ministre n'a pas pu **être présent** (*attend, be present*)

attendance (*n*): la **présence** des parents serait souhaitable (*attendance, presence*); devant une nombreuse **assistance** (*attendance, audience*); ⟨Educ⟩ l'**assiduité** (*f*) aux cours est obligatoire (*regular attendance*); ⟨Jur⟩ un système de semi-détention comme la **prison de weekend** (*attendance centre for young offenders*)

attention (*n*): la grève a **mis en avant** les justes revendications des salariés (*draw attention to*)

attest (*v*): il **affirma sous serment** (*m*) la véracité de leurs dires (*attest*); cet accueil **témoigne de** l'importance que la France accorde à ses rapports avec le Maroc (*attest to, show*)

15

attestation (*n*): joindre au dossier l'**attestation** (*f*) de prise en charge Sécurité sociale (*attestation, certificate, statement*)

attorney (*n*): ⟨Jur⟩ **signer une procuration** pour qu'un autre puisse toucher un mandat à sa place (*give power of attorney*); SEE ALSO **proxy**

attract (*v*): une idée qui **séduit** les conservateurs; ⟨Econ⟩ la Chine cherche à **séduire** les investisseurs occidentaux

attraction (*n*): les marchés étrangers exercent un fort **pouvoir attractif**

attractive (*adj*): des perspectives **alléchantes** pour les entreprises exportatrices; la banque propose des conditions très **intéressantes** (*attractive*); une idée qui paraît **séduisante** sur le papier (*attractive, interesting*)

attractiveness (*n*): la faible **attractivité** de ce pays pour les quartiers-généraux de sociétés étrangères

auction (*n*): ⟨Comm⟩ la **vente aux enchères** (*fpl*) de la compagnie sidérurgique; ces concessions feront l'objet de **mises** (*f*) **aux enchères**

auction (*v*): ⟨Comm⟩ les articles de valeur furent **mis aux enchères** (*f*) (*auction, put up for auction*)

audience (*n*): il ne cacha pas à son **auditoire** (*m*) la gravité de la situation; exposer ses idées devant une **audience** très attentive; un **public** clairsemé assista aux débats

audit (*n*): ⟨Fin⟩ procéder au **contrôle des comptes** (*m*); un **audit** a mis en lumière de graves irrégularités de gestion (*financial audit*)

audit (*v*): ⟨Fin⟩ **apurer** un compte (*audit*); nous avons **procédé au contrôle des comptes** (*audit accounts*)

auditor (*n*): ⟨Fin⟩ les **commissaires** (*m*) **aux comptes** ont été réélus (*[financial] auditor*); un **expert-comptable** est le conseil naturel des petites entreprises (*[independent] auditor*); SEE ALSO **accountant**

austerity (*n*): ⟨Pol⟩ le **budget d'austérité** (*f*) est vivement contesté (*austerity budget*); ⟨Econ⟩ Chine: maintien de l'**austérité** en 1991 (*austerity measures*); les effets du **plan de rigueur** (*f*) se sont vite fait sentir (*austerity plan*)

authenticate (*v*): ⟨Jur⟩ les greffiers **authentifient** les actes de procédure; **certifier conforme** la traduction d'une pièce d'identité

author (*n*): ⟨Journ⟩ les **rédacteurs** (*m*) du document

authoritarian (*adj*): ⟨Pol⟩ partout des régimes **autoritaires** sont tombés

authority (*n*): l'**autorité** (*f*) du ministre a été bafouée; placé sous la **tutelle** du ministre du Travail (*authority*); agissant **par délégation** (*f*) directe du gouvernement (*on/with the authority of*); conformément à l'**autorisation** (*f*) donnée par les actionnaires (*authority, authorization*); ⟨Pol/Admin⟩ les **autorités** empêchent les journalistes de faire leur métier; les **pouvoirs** (*m*) **publics** ont décrété le couvre-feu; l'afflux de réfugiés inquiète les **responsables** (*m*) algériens; une réunion des plus hautes **instances** (*f*) iraniennes (*authorities*)

16

authorization (*n*): obtenir l'**autorisation** (*f*) de licencier du personnel; la radio émet **sans autorisation** (*without authorization*)

authorize (*v*): ⟨Comm⟩ en son absence, son adjoint **a qualité** (*f*) **pour signer** (*be authorized/empowered to sign*)

authorized (*adj*): ⟨Comm⟩ le distributeur **agréé** de la marque dans l'Est; une société importante ayant un correspondant **attitré** en Grande-Bretagne

autonomous (*adj*): ⟨Pol⟩ un territoire **autonome**, s'administrant librement (*autonomous, independent*)

autonomy (*n*): ⟨Pol⟩ l'aspiration à l'**autonomie** (*f*) sinon à l'indépendance (*autonomy, independence*); SEE ALSO **independence**

avail (*v*): le conseil municipal **usa** de son droit de préemption pour se réserver le terrain (*avail o.s. of, use*)

availability (*n*): les qualités du conciliateur: la **disponibilité** et l'impartialité (*availability*); de bonnes **disponibilités** en logements pour les employés (*availability, supply*); la **mise à disponibilité** de prêts bancaires (*availability; making available*); SEE ALSO **supply**

available (*adj*): on propose des cadres expérimentés immédiatement **disponibles**

average (*n/adj*): le prix **moyen** des logements dans la capitale a doublé (*average*); pour le nombre de jours fériés, la France se situe dans la **moyenne** (*average [position]*); la **moyenne d'âge** (*m*) est de 45 ans (*average age*)

avert (*v*): la crise de Wall Street n'est pas **conjurée**; des précautions furent prises pour **prévenir** ce type d'accident; **éviter** des heurts entre les deux communautés (*avert, avoid*)

avoid (*v*): on peut en **éviter** les inconvénients en prenant des précautions

avoidable (*adj*): une guerre commerciale paraît difficilement **évitable**

award (*n*): le **prix** était la juste récompense de ses travaux (*award, prize*); l'**attribution** (*f*) d'un contrat de recherche par le Pentagone; ces études aboutissent à la **délivrance** d'un diplôme (*award, awarding*); l'**octroi** (*m*) d'un jour de congé par mois (*awarding, granting*); SEE ALSO **contract**

award (*v*): il vient de se voir **décerner** le prix Nobel d'économie; une prime de fin d'année **octroyée** au personnel; ⟨Educ⟩ le collège ne **délivre** aucun diplôme (*award, grant*)

aware (*adj*): les Français **ont-ils conscience** (*f*) **de** l'importance du phénomène? (*be aware of*); il faudrait **sensibiliser** le grand public (*make aware*); un problème de **sensibilisation** (*f*) de l'opinion (*making aware*)

awareness (*n*): la **conscience** qu'on avait de l'enjeu de la guerre (*awareness*); un **programme de sensibilisation** (*f*) est le meilleur moyen de faire passer le message (*awareness programme*)

axe (*v*): ⟨Econ⟩ on **supprime les emplois** (*m*) par milliers dans tous les secteurs (*axe jobs*)

17

axis (*n*): l'**axe** (*m*) autour duquel est constitué l'équilibre européen; l'**axe** germano-nippon domine actuellement

B

back (*v*): faire grève pour **appuyer** leurs revendications (*back, support, give approval*); il ne veut pas **cautionner** une manifestation à ses yeux anti-républicaine (*back, give support to*); SEE ALSO **endorse, guarantee, secure, support**

backer (*n*): ⟨Fin⟩ ses **bailleurs** (*m*) **de fonds** étrangers lui apportent une aide considérable (*[financial] backer*)

backhander (*n*): ⟨Comm⟩ toucher un **dessous de table** de 700 MF; les **dessous de table** y sont devenus monnaie courante (*backhander, under-the-counter payment*)

backing (*n*): avec l'**appui** (*m*) des Centristes, le texte fut voté (*backing, support*); le protocole attend l'**aval** (*m*) des pouvoirs publics (*backing, approval*); le seul à ne pas **apporter sa caution** au président (*give one's backing*)

backlash (*n*): l'industrie subit le **contrecoup** d'un doublement de la TVA

back pay (*n*): toucher un **rappel** [de salaire] de 2.000F; la compagnie doit lui verser un **arriéré** de $200.000 (*back pay, arrears of salary*)

backward (*adj*): un pays dont l'économie est l'une des plus **arriérées**; une société très **en retard** en ce qui concerne l'évolution des mœurs (*backward, underdeveloped*)

backwardness (*n*): un **déficit** technologique rend l'Espagne très dépendante de l'étranger; comment combler notre **retard** (*m*) industriel?

bad (*adj*): ⟨Fin⟩ la banque a accumulé une série de **créances** (*f*) **douteuses**; le coût des **créances irrécouvrables** (*bad debt, write-off*); pousser les **mauvais payeurs** (*m*) à rembourser leurs dettes (*bad debtor*); SEE ALSO **debtor**

bail (*n*): ⟨Jur⟩ une mise en liberté avec versement d'une **caution** (*bail [bond]*); l'inculpé a été **mis en liberté** (*f*) **provisoire sous caution** (*release on bail*); bénéficier d'une **libération sous caution** (*[release on] bail*); comment **se porter caution pour** un repris de justice notoire? (*go/stand bail for*); SEE ALSO **release**

bail (*v*): ⟨Jur⟩ il a été **mis en liberté sous caution** (*f*) de 100.000 DM (*bail, release on bail*); SEE ALSO **release**

bailiff (*n*): l'**huissier** (*m*) est venu expulser les locataires; recevoir une **citation d'huissier** (*bailiff's summons*)

bailing out (*n*) ⟨Fin⟩: SEE **refloating**

bail out (*v*): ⟨Fin⟩ une filiale constamment **renflouée** par la maison mère; SEE ALSO **refloat**

balance (*n*): un plus juste **équilibre** entre hôpitaux publics et cliniques privées (*balance*); ⟨Comm⟩ les échanges agro-alimentaires presque **équilibrés** (*in balance*); Renault prévoyait l'**équilibre financier** pour l'année (*a budget in balance*); dès réception du **reste** de la commande (*balance, remainder*); ⟨Fin⟩ virer la **somme restant due**; le **solde** sera réglé à la livraison (*balance [owing]*); ⟨Econ⟩ la **balance des paiements** (*m*) **courants** est déficitaire (*balance of current account*); la **balance commerciale** de l'industrie cotonnière est déficitaire de 2,7 milliards en 1986 (*balance of trade*); SEE ALSO **remainder**

balance (*v*): industrie et agriculture **s'équilibrent** (*balance one another; be in balance*); ⟨Fin⟩ la Poste est tenue d'**équilibrer** ses recettes et ses dépenses; la Poste **équilibre son budget** en 1992; un quart des familles seulement parvient à **boucler son budget** (*balance the budget*)

balance sheet (*n*): ⟨Fin⟩ le **bilan** de l'exercice révèle un important déficit d'exploitation

balanced (*adj*): un accord juste et **équilibré**

ballot (*n*): ⟨Pol⟩ le premier **tour de scrutin** (*m*) (*ballot*); adopter le **scrutin uninominal à un tour** pour les prochaines législatives (*single-ballot voting system*); les Français **se rendent aux urnes** (*f*) (*go to the ballot-box, vote*); après dépouillement des **bulletins** (*m*) **de vote** (*ballot-paper, voting slip*); SEE ALSO **vote**

ban (*n*): la **défense** de fumer dans les lieux à usage collectif; l'**interdiction** (*f*) faite aux séropositifs étrangers d'entrer sur le territoire américain; SEE ALSO **banning, embargo**

ban (*v*): le pouvoir **frappe d'interdiction** (*f*) la seule agence de presse non officielle; il est question d'**interdire** de tels spectacles; **mettre hors la loi** la publicité pour le tabac (*ban, outlaw*)

band (*n*): la **tranche supérieure** des classes moyennes (*upper band/bracket*)

banishment (*n*): ⟨Pol⟩ le **bannissement** de douze Palestiniens des territoires occupés (*banishment, expulsion*)

bank (*n*): ⟨Fin⟩ les titulaires de **comptes** (*m*) **bancaires** (*bank account*); les nouveaux **crédits** (*m*) **bancaires** accordés en octobre (*bank loans*); la Banque de Japon relaxe son **taux d'escompte** (*m*) (*bank/discount rate*)

bank (*v*): les régions viticoles **parient sur** leur notoriété; **miser sur** son agriculture (*bank/count on; rely completely on*)

banker (*n*): ⟨Fin⟩ régler un abonnement par **virement** (*m*) **bancaire** (*banker's order*); la banque nous avisa de l'acceptation de la **traite** (*banker's draft*)

banking (*n/adj*): ⟨Fin⟩ une carrière dans la **banque** (*banking, banking profession*); le coût prohibitif des **opérations** (*f*) **bancaires** courantes (*banking services*)

19

banknote (*n*): plusieurs **coupures** (*f*) de 1.000F ont disparu

bankrupt (*adj*): ⟨Fin/Econ⟩ une économie **en pleine banqueroute** (*f*) (*bankrupt, failed*); les commerçants **faillis**; selon le maire, la ville est **en cessation** (*f*) **de paiements**; le nombre des sociétés **mises en faillite** (*f*) (*[declared] bankrupt*); SEE ALSO **insolvent**

bankruptcy (*n*): ⟨Fin⟩ le fabricant belge est au bord de la **faillite**; divers délits financiers, dont une **banqueroute** frauduleuse (*[fraudulent] bankruptcy*); l'ouverture d'une **procédure de faillite** (*bankruptcy proceedings*); les créanciers demandent une **mise en faillite** de la société (*declaration of bankruptcy*); **déposer son bilan** auprès du Tribunal de commerce (*file for bankruptcy*); l'annonce du **dépôt de bilan** a surpris les milieux d'affaires (*filing of bankruptcy proceedings*)

banned (*adj*): le divorce, qui reste **interdit** dans ce pays (*banned, illegal*)

banning (*n*): l'**interdiction** (*f*) des partis d'extrême-droite (*banning, outlawing*); SEE ALSO **ban**

bar (*n*): ⟨Jur⟩ les avocats font partie d'un **barreau**, une organisation autonome; un citoyen syrien **mis sous les verrous** (*m*) en France (*put behind prison bars; imprison*)

bar (*v*): les statuts de l'association **excluent** les étrangers (*bar, debar, exclude*)

bargain (*n*): ⟨Comm⟩ une **[bonne] affaire** pour celui qui aurait des sommes à investir; il y a des **affaires à saisir** (*bargain*); **prix** (*mpl*) **sacrifiés** sur tout le stock (*bargain prices*); en vente **à un prix exceptionnel** (*at a bargain price*); profiter des **soldes** (*fpl*) de janvier (*[bargain] sales*)

bargaining (*n*): SEE **collective**, **haggling**

barrier (*n*): ⟨Econ⟩ la cherté du crédit est une **entrave** au commerce (*barrier, obstacle*); la City fait le pari du **décloisonnement** et de l'ouverture (*bringing down barriers [esp. trading]*)

barrister (*n*): ⟨Jur⟩ l'inculpé n'avait pas pris d'**avocat** (*m*) pour sa défense; depuis 1971 les **avoués** (*m*) n'exerçaient plus que devant les Cours d'appel (*barrister*); se destiner au **barreau** (*profession of barrister; the bar*)

barter (*n*): ⟨Comm⟩ la généralisation du **troc** (*barter, bartering*); dans le cadre d'un **accord de troc** (*m*) conclu récemment (*barter agreement/ deal*); SEE ALSO **exchange**

barter (*v*): ⟨Comm⟩ **troquant** sa place contre quelques promesses pour l'avenir (*barter, exchange, swap*)

base (*n*): l'**ancrage** (*m*) du parti socialiste dans le Midi reste solide; le parti a besoin d'élargir son **assise** (*f*) dans le Nord

base (*v*): l'agriculture y demeure **axée** sur l'élevage (*base, centre*); employeur et salarié versent une cotisation **assise** sur le salaire brut (*based, calculated*)

baseless (*adj*): les accusations sont **sans fondement** (*m*) (*baseless, unjustified*)

basic (*adj*): ⟨Comm⟩ l'accès à des services bancaires **de base**; la charte des droits sociaux **fondamentaux** (*basic*); outre les commissions, il touche un **fixe** mensuel (*basic wage*)

basis (*n*): les **bases** (*f*) d'un accord existent, il suffit de régler les détails

bearish (*adj*): ⟨Fin⟩ les cambistes sont devenus **baissiers** sur le franc

beat (*v*): il **bat** le candidat socialiste de 1.565 voix; la liste communiste **coiffée** par la liste socialiste (*beat/defeat narrowly*)

begin (*v*): on ne voit pas **s'amorcer** cette amélioration tant souhaitée; une triple bataille qui **s'engage** à Washington (*begin, start*); les négociations **s'ouvrent** demain à Genève (*begin, open*)

beginning (*n*): une **amorce** de solution (*beginning, beginnings of sth*); les **balbutiements** (*m*) du multipartisme en Afrique (*[earliest] beginnings; infancy*)

behind (*prep*): la France arrive cinquième, **talonnant** l'Italie (*be just behind*); la France **distancée** dans la course aux contrats (*leave behind, outstrip*)

bench (*n*): SEE **government, judge**

beneficial (*adj*): cela aura un effet **bénéfique** sur les négociations à venir

beneficiary (*n*): les principaux **bénéficiaires** (*m*) de l'aide communautaire; ⟨Fisc⟩ la transmission à un **bénéficiaire** unique (*beneficiary [esp. of will/testament]*); ⟨Soc⟩ l'abaissement de l'âge de la retraite augmentera le nombre des **ayants droit** (*m*) (*beneficiary [esp. of aid/benefit]*); SEE ALSO **recipient**

benefit (*n*): les **bienfaits** (*m*) issus de la crise (*benefit*); sans perdre le **bénéfice** du parapluie militaire de l'OTAN (*benefit, advantage*); ⟨Soc⟩ les **prestations** (*f*) **sociales** y sont parmi les plus élevées du monde (*State social security benefit*); SEE ALSO **fringe, unemployment**

benefit (*v*): chercher à **tirer profit** (*m*) de la crise (*benefit*); les pays occidentaux **profitent du** désarroi à l'Est (*benefit from, profit by*)

bequeath (*v*): il a **légué** la totalité de sa succession à un étranger à sa famille

bequest (*n*): un **legs** au profit d'une personne sans lien de famille avec le défunt; l'association peut recevoir des dons et **legs** en exonération de tout droit de mutation; SEE ALSO **legacy, inheritance**

bid (*n*): ⟨Fin⟩ il prépare une **surenchère** à l'offre de l'industriel australien (*higher/counter bid*); SEE ALSO **tender**

bid (*v*): ⟨Pol⟩ avoir l'intention de **briguer** l'Élysée aux élections présidentielles (*bid for; canvass for*); ⟨Fin⟩ **renchérir** sur toute OPA lancée sur le fabricant de whisky (*raise the bid; outbid*); ⟨Comm⟩ procéder à un **appel d'offres** (*invitation to bid*); SEE ALSO **tender**

bidder (*n*): ⟨Comm⟩ le droit de vendre au **plus offrant** (*highest bidder*); SEE ALSO **lowest**

bidding (*n*): l'arrivée des Japonais a **fait monter les enchères** (*f*) (*raise the bidding*)

bilateral (*adj*): ⟨Pol⟩ des discussions **bilatérales** entre Paris et Bonn

bill (*n*): ⟨Pol⟩ le **projet de loi** (*f*) réformant le statut des dockers (*[parliamentary] bill*); une **proposition de loi** émanant d'un groupe de conservateurs (*private bill*); ⟨Comm⟩ la **facture** pétrolière est payée en dollars (*bill, invoice*); l'**affichage** (*m*), le média le plus connu du public; une campagne d'**affichage** à l'échelon national (*billsticking, billposting*); SEE ALSO **debt**

bill (*v*): ⟨Comm⟩ des achats **facturés** en dollars (*bill, invoice*); SEE ALSO **invoice**

billing (*n*): ⟨Comm⟩ une **facturation** en francs suisses (*billing, invoicing*)

bind (*v*): contrairement aux arrhes, l'acompte **engage** totalement l'acheteur (*bind, be binding upon*)

binding (*adj*): ⟨Jur⟩ une clause **qui engage** (*binding*); un document qui est **légalement contraignant** (*legally binding*)

bind over (*v*): ⟨Jur⟩ il a été **mis en liberté** (*f*) **conditionnelle**; il a été **relaxé sous peine de comparaître en cas de récidive** dans les neuf mois (*be bound over*); SEE ALSO **conditional**

birth rate (*n*): ⟨Soc⟩ le déclin de la **natalité**; le **taux de natalité** est partout en baisse (*birth rate*); il déplora la **chute du taux des naissances** (*n*) (*declining/falling birth rate*)

bitter (*adj*): son adversaire le plus **acharné** (*bitter, fierce*); à l'issue d'une **âpre** campagne électorale (*bitter, hard-fought*); si la situation venait à **s'envenimer** encore (*become more bitter/acrimonious*)

bitterly (*adv*): l'Italie critique **avec âpreté** (*f*) le compromis de Bruxelles

black (*adj*): ⟨Fin⟩ la Gauche laissait la Sécurité sociale **en excédent** (*m*) (*in the black; in surplus*); la **politique du pire** jouée par la direction explique la défaite du parti (*policy of painting things as black as possible*)

black (*v*): ⟨Ind⟩ SEE **boycott**

black economy (*n*): ⟨Econ⟩ URSS: l'**économie** (*f*) **parallèle** réalise un chiffre d'affaires record

blackleg (*n*): ⟨Ind⟩ traités de **briseurs** (*m*) **de grève** pour avoir travaillé

blackmail (*n*): par un **chantage** ignoble, on les empêchait de parler

blackmail (*v*): il a **fait du chantage**, pour les forcer à céder

black market (*n*): ⟨Comm⟩ à Moscou, le **marché noir** peut tout fournir; les **marchés noirs** ont connu une véritable explosion

blame (*n*): il encourt les **reproches** (*m*) de ses collègues; **rejetter la responsabilité** de l'échec sur Washington (*lay the blame for*); c'est lui qui **fera les frais** (*m*) d'un nouvel échec (*take the blame*)

blame (*v*): il est difficile de leur **donner tort**; la Turquie semble ne pas **tenir rigueur** à Alger; le rapport israélien **met en cause** le chef de la police (*blame; implicate*)

blatant (*adj*): les déséquilibres **criants** entre les forts et les faibles

bloc (*n*): ⟨Pol⟩ les pays de l'ancien **bloc** (*m*) soviétique (*bloc*); l'écroulement du **bloc de l'Est** (*Eastern bloc*)

block (*n*): dans certains **îlots** (*m*) frappés par la délinquance (*[housing] block*); SEE ALSO **office**

block (*v*): accuser la CEE d'**entraver** la libéralisation des échanges

blockade (*n*): ⟨Mil/Pol⟩ imposer un **blocus** aux exportations irakiennes; le **blocus** des casernes fédérales par les rebelles

blockage (*n*): le syndicat a constaté un **blocage** total des négociations (*blockage, deadlock*)

blood (*n*): un nouvel attentat **ensanglante** le pays (*bathe in blood*)

bloody (*adj*): malgré une **sanglante** répression; une **meutrière** répression des manifestants (*bloody; murderous*)

blow (*n*): nouveau **coup dur** (*m*) pour les agriculteurs français! (*blow, setback*)

blue-chip (*n/adj*): ⟨Fin⟩ acquérir des **valeurs** (*f*) **de premier ordre** (*blue-chip/gild-edged stock*); l'indice CAC 40 des **valeurs vedettes** (*blue-chip securities [Fr]*); SEE ALSO **gilt-edged**

board (*n*): ⟨Admin⟩ le **conseil d'administration** élit le président (*board of directors*); le président du **directoire** de la firme automobile (*executive board, directorate*); lors de la dernière **réunion du conseil d'administration** (*board meeting*); SEE ALSO **directorate**

body (*n*): ⟨Admin/Pol⟩ l'**instance** (*f*) la plus élevée en matière judiciaire (*[official] body*)

bond (*n*): ⟨Fin⟩ le fonds est composé d'**obligations** (*f*) **d'État** françaises (*[government] bond*); les **obligations** représentent près de 80% des transactions des bourses françaises (*bond; debenture*); SEE ALSO **debenture**

bonus (*n*): ⟨Econ⟩ l'octroi d'une **prime de fin** (*f*) **d'année** (*end-of-year bonus*); une **bonification d'ancienneté** (*f*) d'un mois par année d'exercice (*length of service bonus*); mettre en place un **programme de stimulants** (*mpl*) **salariaux** (*bonus incentive scheme*)

booklet (*n*): réaliser une **plaquette** à des fins de publicité; diffuser une **brochure** à l'intention des électeurs (*booklet, pamphlet*)

boom (*n*): ⟨Econ⟩ les ventes de caméscopes connaissent un véritable **essor**

boost (*n*): ⟨Econ⟩ un **gonflement** de la demande (*boost, expansion*); **donner une vigoureuse impulsion** aux exportations (*give a boost to*); SEE ALSO **fillip**

boost (*v*): ⟨Comm/Econ⟩ une dévaluation aura pour effet de **relancer** les exportations; les ventes à l'étranger, **dopées** par la baisse du Mark (*boost*); **donner un coup de fouet** aux réformes économiques (*boost, stimulate*)

border (*n*): les pays qui n'ont pas de **frontière** (*f*) commune avec le Kurdistan; les Vosges et la Lorraine, provinces **limitrophes** de l'Alsace (*on the borders of; bordering on*)

borough (*n*): 84 communes, dont six **bourgs** (*m*) et 49 districts (*borough, market town*)

borrow (*v*): ⟨Fin⟩ en **empruntant** à 15%, on court à la ruine; **emprunter** pour financer de grosses réparations (*borrow, borrow money*)

borrower (*n*): ⟨Fin⟩ les **emprunteurs** (*m*) paient 10% à la banque (*borrower*); si le **débiteur** n'exécute pas ses obligations, le créancier peut l'y contraindre (*borrower, debtor*)

borrowing (*n*): ⟨Fin/Econ⟩ recourir à l'**emprunt** (*m*) ou à l'autofinancement (*borrowing*); cette diminution du **coût du crédit** (*cost of borrowing/ credit*); les PME, victimes de la **cherté du crédit** (*high cost of borrowing/ credit*); SEE ALSO **loan**

boss (*n*): le **patron** d'usine accueillait les invités (*boss; manager*); le ministre débattra de l'affaire avec tous les **partenaires** (*m*) **sociaux** (*boss/ employer and unions*)

bottle-neck (*n*): ⟨Comm⟩ on perd des ventes en raison de **goulets** (*m*) **d'étranglement** dans la production

bottom (*n*): ⟨Fin⟩ le Franc tombe près de son **cours plancher** (*bottom price; lower limit*)

bottom out (*v*): ⟨Fin⟩ le dollar **atteint son niveau plancher**

boundary (*n*): ⟨Pol⟩ le **redécoupage électoral** permet la création de nouveaux cantons urbains (*boundary changes*); SEE ALSO **redrawing**

boycott (*n*): son parti appelle au **boycottage** des élections; Liban: appel au **boycott** des élections (*boycott, boycotting*)

boycott (*v*): la ménagère française **boycotte** la viande importée

brainwashing (*n*): ⟨Pol/Comm⟩ il dénonce la campagne d'**intox[ication]** (*f*) de la droite (*brainwashing; indoctrination*)

branch (*n*): l'**antenne** (*f*) régionale du parti (*branch; outpost*); ⟨Comm⟩ les banques vont fermer des **succursales** (*f*) dans les petites communes (*branch; branch office*)

breach (*n*): toute **infraction** (*f*) à la loi sera punie; une **violation** de la Constitution; un **manquement** au devoir de réserve d'un chef de l'État (*breach, infringement*); ⟨Jur⟩ être **en rupture** (*f*) **de contrat** (*in breach of contract*); comportement qui constitue un **attentat à l'ordre** (*m*) **public** (*breach of the peace*); SEE ALSO **breaking, infringement**

breach (*v*): un monopole qui sera **battu en brèche** (*f*) par les chaînes satellites (*breach, break*)

break (*n*): une **rupture** totale avec la politique suivie jusqu'alors; la **cassure** entre les syndicats et la base

break (*v*): le parti a **rompu** ses accords avec l'extrême droite; **faire éclater** le monopole de l'État (*break, split*); ⟨Jur⟩ **violer la loi** sur l'avortement; **être en infraction** (*f*) par rapport à la loi (*break the law*); SEE ALSO **infringe**

breakaway (*n/adj*): l'Église polonaise est au bord de la **dissidence**; ⟨Pol⟩ les leaders **séparatistes** boudent la réunion de conciliation; le **groupe dissident** défie le parti (*breakaway group*)

breakdown (*n*): l'**échec** (*m*) des négociations salariales; ⟨Soc⟩ le constat de **rupture** (*f*) du mariage (*breakdown, failure*); ⟨Pol⟩ en attendant l'ultime **décompte** (*m*) des voix; ⟨Fin/Econ⟩ l'**analyse** (*f*) des résultats révèle les points faibles du groupe; la **ventilation** du commerce extérieur par pays et par produits (*breakdown; analysis*); **donner le détail** des frais encourus (*give a breakdown*)

break down (*v*): **faire le détail** d'une liste; **ventiler** les dépenses entre frais fixes et frais variables (*break down, analyse*)

break-even (*adj*): ⟨Fin/Comm⟩ atteindre le **seuil de rentabilité** (*f*) (*break-even point*)

break even (*v*): ⟨Fin/Econ⟩ après une année désastreuse, on devrait **atteindre l'équilibre** (*m*) **financier** cette année; **rentrer dans ses frais** (*m*) après deux années déficitaires

break-in (*n*): une seconde **effraction** par les mêmes cambrioleurs; SEE ALSO **breaking**

break in (*v*): **entrer par effraction** (*f*) après la fermeture des locaux

breaking (*n*): ⟨Pol/Jur⟩ une **violation** flagrante du traité (*breaking, violating*); ⟨Jur⟩ inculpé de **vol** (*m*) **avec effraction**; la **pénétration par effraction** (*f*) est sévèrement sanctionnée (*breaking and entering*)

breaking-even (*n*): ⟨Fin⟩ seul un **équilibre d'exploitation** (*f*) est espéré fin 1993

breaking-off (*n*): la menace d'une **rupture** entre la France et le monde arabe (*breaking-off/severing of relations*); la **rupture des relations** (*f*) **diplomatiques** avec la Syrie (*breaking-off/severing diplomatic relations*)

breaking-up (*n*): le mouvement est menacé d'**éclatement** (*m*)

break off (*v*): les deux partis **rompent** leurs accords régionaux

break out (*v*): un important incendie **s'est déclaré** hier en fin d'après-midi; quand **éclate** une crise comme celle du Golfe (*break out [of fire, disease]*); deux détenus **s'évadent** de la prison de Strasbourg (*break out, escape*)

break-out (*n*): nouvelle **évasion** (*f*) de la prison des Baumettes (*break-out, escape*)

breakthrough (*n*): ⟨Comm⟩ réussir une première **percée** en Europe centrale; ⟨Pol⟩ **percée** de l'extrême droite en Allemagne

break up (*v*): ⟨Econ⟩ **casser** les monopoles existants ou en cours de constitution (*break up, dismantle*); ⟨Admin⟩ le conseil **s'est séparé** sans être arrivé à voter aucun des projets (*break up, disperse*)

breakup (*n*): éviter la **cassure** de la société urbaine; ⟨Soc⟩ l'**éclatement** (*m*) de la famille, puis le placement des enfants dans des foyers de l'enfance; ⟨Pol⟩ la **dislocation** de l'empire soviétique; la **désagrégation** de l'empire se poursuit (*breakup, disintegration*)

break with (*v*): quitte à **rompre avec** les vieux mythes socialistes (*break with, abandon*); **déroger à** l'usage établi en la matière (*break with, depart from*)

bribe (*n*): décrocher des marchés grâce à des **pots-de-vin** (*m*) (*bribe, backhander*); obligé de démissionner pour **corruption** (*f*) (*offering/accepting bribes; bribery*)

bribe (*v*): ⟨Jur/Comm⟩ poursuivi pour avoir **versé des pots-de-vin** (*m*); ⟨Jur⟩ **acheter** un témoin; essayer de **suborner** le témoin principal

bribery (*n*): ⟨Jur⟩ un cas de **corruption** (*f*) de fonctionnaire (*bribery [and corruption]*)

bribing (*n*): ⟨Jur⟩ inculpé pour **subornation** (*f*) **de témoin** (*bribing a witness*)

bridgehead (*n*): ⟨Mil/Comm⟩ les industriels étrangers trouvent ainsi une **tête de pont** en France

bring about (*v*): le redressement économique **opéré** dès 1982; les conditions ont **entraîné** une vague de fusions-acquisitions (*bring about, cause*)

bring back (*v*): **rétablir** le scrutin proportionnel; **rétablir** la peine de mort (*bring back, restore*); SEE ALSO **restore**

bring before (*v*): treize personnes ont été **traduites en justice** (*f*) (*bring before the courts*)

bring down (*v*): envisager de **ramener** à 60 ans l'âge limite du travail; son objectif, **faire reculer** le chômage et les exclusions (*bring down, reduce*); le chômage en France au fil des mois **se résorbe** (*be reduced/brought down*); SEE ALSO **reduce**

bring forward (*v*): prendre la décision d'**avancer** la date du congrès

bring in (*v*): ⟨Fin⟩ cet impôt devra **rapporter** 33 milliards de francs; le lancement de l'emprunt a déjà **drainé** 90 MF (*bring in, yield [esp. revenue]*)

bring together (*v*): la manifestation a **rassemblé** quelque 100.000 jeunes dans toute la France; la réunion **associe** le Pakistan et les autres pays de la région; les Progressistes **regroupent** tous les mécontents du pays (*bring together*); on s'efforce de **rapprocher** les législations nationales (*bring [closer] together*)

broad (*adj*): il y a en Europe un **large consensus** à ce sujet (*broad consensus*)

broadcast (*n*): un contrat pour la **diffusion** de quatre programmes (*broadcast, broadcasting*)

broadcast (*v*): un communiqué **diffusé** dimanche soir; la radio **émet** depuis un endroit indéterminé de la région

broadcasting (*n*): les grandes agences de **diffusion** (*f*) des informations (*broadcasting*); les sociétés privées partageront le **temps d'antenne** (*f*) (*broadcasting time*); SEE ALSO **schedule**

broaden (*v*): l'extrême-droite peut encore **élargir son assise** (*f*) (*broaden one's base*)

brochure (*n*): ⟨Comm⟩ le **prospectus** présente brièvement le produit (*brochure; leaflet*)

broken (*adj*): ⟨Soc⟩ on sait l'influence des **foyers** (*m*) **brisés** dans la formation des attitudes délinquantes (*broken home*); SEE ALSO **promise**

broker (*n*): ⟨Fin⟩ les **agents** (*m*) **de change** à la Bourse de Paris (*[stock]broker*); ⟨Ins⟩ une réunion de **courtiers** (*m*) **en assurances** britanniques (*insurance broker*); SEE ALSO **stockbroker**

brokerage (*n*): une société de **courtage** (*m*) immobilier, située près de Bruxelles

budget (*n*): ⟨Fin⟩ le **budget** enregistre les dépenses et les recettes de l'État (*budget*); le Chancelier **présente le projet de loi de Finance** (*deliver the Budget speech [GB]*); le quatrième **poste budgétaire** de l'État (*budget heading*); il y a **excédent** (*m*) **budgétaire** quand les ressources sont supérieures aux charges (*budget surplus*); il laisse une **impasse budgétaire** de 10 milliards de francs (*budget deficit*); ⟨Fin/Econ⟩ le groupe prévoit une **enveloppe d'investissements** (*mpl*) de 45 MF pour 1995 (*investment budget*)

buffer (*n/adj*): une **zone tampon** (*m*) servant de cordon sanitaire aux localités frontalières (*buffer zone*)

build (*v*): on a su **bâtir** une Europe forte et unie; la nécessité d'**édifier** des logements sociaux (*build, construct*); l'Europe **se construit** lentement (*be built*)

building (*n*): un retard dans la **construction** de l'échangeur; poursuivre l'**édification** (*f*) de la CEE; la **mise en place** d'un carrefour autoroutier (*building, construction*); la bonne activité du **bâtiment** et des travaux publics (*building industry*); les **mises en chantier** (*m*) de logements en progression de 16% (*building start*); le manque de **terrains** (*m*) **à bâtir** s'aggrave (*building land*); les **grands travaux** (*mpl*) créent des milliers d'emplois (*major building works*); un important **programme immobilier** autour du port de plaisance (*building programme/scheme*); la **taxe sur le foncier bâti** est payée par les propriétaires (*local tax on buildings*)

building society (*n*): ⟨Fin⟩ toutes les **sociétés** (*f*) **de crédits hypothécaires**; la deuxième **société de crédit** (*m*) **immobilier** de la Grande-Bretagne

buildup (*n*): lutte contre l'**accumulation** (*f*) des déchets ménagers (*buildup, accumulation*); ⟨Ind⟩ la CGT, vite dépassée par la **surenchère** de la base (*increasing buildup of demands*)

build up (*v*): un moyen sûr de **se constituer** un capital (*build up, amass*)

bullish (*adj*): ⟨Fin⟩ la tendance **haussière** de l'indice FT

27

buoyant (*adj*): ⟨Econ/Fin⟩ la conjoncture **euphorique** de cette fin d'année (*buoyant*); **euphorie** (*f*) sur le billet vert (*buoyant mood; confidence*); la demande reste **soutenue** (*buoyant, sustained*); l'électronique de loisirs, un autre **marché porteur**; dans un **marché soutenu**, le cuivre fait preuve de fermeté (*buoyant market*)

burden (*n*): le **fardeau** de la dette extérieure (*burden*); l'État en a transféré la **charge** sur les collectivités locales (*burden, charge*); ces hausses vont **grever** le budget des ménages (*put a burden/strain upon*); le maintien à domicile des personnes âgées a permis d'**alléger les charges** (*lighten the [financial] burden*)

bureaucracy (*n*): ⟨Admin⟩ l'ensemble des fonctionnaires, ou la **bureaucratie** (*bureaucracy*); se plaindre du **pouvoir excessif de l'administration** (*f*) (*excessive [administrative] bureaucracy*)

bureaucrat (*n*): ⟨Admin⟩ parmi les **bureaucrates** (*m*) de la Commission

bureaucratic (*adj*): ⟨Admin⟩ tous se plaignent des lenteurs **bureaucratiques**

burglar (*n*): un **cambrioleur** connu des services de la police

burglary (*n*): un policier avait commis une douzaine de **cambriolages** (*m*)

bursary (*n*): ⟨Fin/Scol⟩ la Région finance les **bourses** (*f*) et le matériel pédagogique (*bursary, grant*)

business (*n*): ⟨Econ⟩ les **affaires** (*fpl*) sont florissantes dans le secteur du bâtiment (*business*); vendre le **fonds de commerce** (*business, concern*); la perte de confiance des **milieux** (*m*) **d'affaires** (*business community*); l'**activité** (*f*) **industrielle** reprend peu à peu (*industrial activity*); **commercer** avec les pays de l'Est; l'espoir de **réaliser des affaires** avec la Chine (*do business*); pour **lancer une affaire** il faut des capitaux (*start up a/in business*); il entend **se mettre à son compte** (*set up in business*); la société alsacienne en difficultés a **cessé ses activités** (*go out of business*); SEE ALSO **firm**, **company**

businessman (*n*): ⟨Comm⟩ **homme** (*m*) **d'affaires** dynamique et entreprenant; fille d'un **gros industriel** du Nord (*businessman, manufacturer; industrialist*)

business tax (*n*): ⟨Fisc⟩ le remplacement de la **patente** par la taxe professionnelle; la commune va quintupler ses recettes grâce à la **taxe professionnelle** (*local business tax*)

busy (*adj*): les aéroports parisiens moins **encombrés** que d'ordinaire

buy (*v*): ⟨Comm⟩ Péchiney **rachète** une société du Texas; une tonne d'aluminium **se traite** aujourd'hui à 23.000 dollars (*be bought/traded; sell at*)

buyer (*n*): ⟨Comm⟩ l'appareil devrait donc trouver **acquéreur** (*m*) (*buyer*); à Drouot, la moitié des œuvres n'ont pas **trouvé preneur** (*m*) (*find a buyer*); les administrateurs chargés de trouver un **repreneur** (*buyer, purchaser [esp. of ailing business]*)

buy-out (*n*): ⟨Comm⟩ l'entreprise alsacienne est un autre candidat potentiel au **rachat** (*buy-out, take-over*)

28

buy out (*v*): ⟨Comm⟩ mal en point, la société fut **rachetée** par son concurrent allemand

by-election (*n*): ⟨Pol⟩ des **élections** (*f*) **partielles** auront lieu dans deux circonscriptions; le second tour de la [municipale] **partielle**

by-law (*n*): ⟨Pol/Admin⟩ par **arrêté** (*m*) **municipal**; sauf **réglementation** (*f*) **municipale** contraire

bypass (*n*): une **rocade** bloquée par des routiers en colère; une seconde **bretelle de contournement** (*m*) de l'agglomération rennaise; création d'une **voie de contournement** près de Guingamp (*bypass, ring-road*); SEE ALSO **ring-road**

bypass (*v*): SEE **circumvent**

C

cabinet (*n*): ⟨Pol⟩ le **cabinet** a été renversé (*cabinet, government*); au cours d'une **réunion du cabinet** (*cabinet meeting*); présenter un plan **en conseil** (*m*) **des ministres** (*in cabinet*); **crise** (*f*) **ministérielle** en Pologne (*cabinet crisis*); SEE ALSO **reshuffle**

calculate (*v*): ⟨Fin⟩ **calculer** le coût de l'opération; **comptabiliser** les heures de travail effectuées par chaque salarié

calculation (*n*): leur **calcul** (*m*) s'est avéré juste; ⟨Fin⟩ l'assiette de **calcul** des pensions (*calculation, computation*)

calendar (*n*): pendant trente **jours** (*m*) **calendaires** après réception de cette notification (*calendar day*)

call (*n*): ⟨Admin⟩ plus de 39 heures de travail et d'**astreinte** (*f*) par semaine (*being on call/standby*); ⟨Fin⟩ procéder à un **appel de fonds** (*mpl*) (*call for capital*)

call (*v*): ⟨Pol⟩ **convoquer** une conférence sur le désarmement; les élections **convoquées** par le chef de l'État (*call, convoke*)

call for (*v*): **réclamer** l'arrêt des opérations militaires; l'opposition **appelle à** la grève générale (*call/appeal for*); ⟨Jur⟩ l'avocat a **requis** une peine de prison de dix ans (*call for, request, demand*)

call on (*v*): ⟨Pol⟩ **interpeller** le Président pour qu'il se saisisse du problème

call-up (*n*): ⟨Mil⟩ les étudiants peuvent repousser leur **incorporation** (*f*); on peut devancer le **rappel** sous certaines conditions (*call-up for military service*)

call up (*v*): ⟨Mil⟩ les jeunes sont **appelés** à l'âge de 19 ans; il fut **incorporé** au régiment d'infanterie de Metz (*call up*); Washington **bat le rappel** des réservistes (*call up for national service; call to arms*)

calm (*n*): lancer un appel au **calme**; il appelle à la **sérénité** dans le débat sur le port du foulard islamique (*calm; dispassionateness, objectivity*)

calm (*v*): le ministre s'efforce de **dépassionner** le débat; **calmer** le jeu politique

campaign (*n*): ⟨Pol⟩ la **campagne** électorale bat son plein

campaign (*v*): ⟨Pol⟩ **faire campagne** (*f*) pour l'ordre et la sécurité; **militer** pour la création d'une grande métropole Orléans-Blois-Tours; SEE ALSO **agitate**

cancel (*v*): on a **décommandé** la visite du ministre (*cancel, call off*); ⟨Comm⟩ des contrats **annulés** par des pays d'Europe de l'Est (*cancel*); ⟨Jur/ Comm⟩ chacune des parties prenantes au contrat est libre de le **résilier** (*cancel, rescind [esp. agreement]*); ⟨Fin⟩ **tirer un trait** sur les 21 milliards de dollars qui leur étaient dûs (*cancel [esp. a debt]*)

cancellation (*n*): les Japonais déçus par l'**annulation** (*f*) de sa visite à Tokyo (*cancellation*); on peut demander la **résiliation** de son contrat de location (*cancellation, termination*); ⟨Fin⟩ des **remises** (*f*) **de dettes** pour les pays les plus pauvres (*cancellation of debt*)

candidacy (*n*): le principe des **candidatures** (*f*) communes a été affirmé (*candidacy; candidate*)

candidate (*n*): le député sortant, **candidat** (*m*) à sa propre succession

capability (*n*): SEE **ability**

capacity (*n*): ⟨Soc⟩ la **capacité d'accueil** (*m*) du centre passera à 250 (*capacity*); ⟨Écon⟩ augmenter ses **moyens** (*m*) **de production** (*productive capacity*); ⟨Admin⟩ **en sa qualité de** diplomate (*in one's capacity as*); SEE ALSO **output, yield**

capital (*n*): ⟨Fin⟩ toute entreprise a besoin de **capitaux** (*mpl*) (*capital*); l'entreprise souffre d'une trop faible **capitalisation** (*capital base*); la société s'apprête à **lever** plus de cinq milliards de francs (*issue, raise [esp. capital]*)

capital expenditure (*n*): ⟨Écon⟩ le transfert aux communes de certaines **dépenses** (*f*) **d'équipement**

capital gain (*n*): ⟨Fin⟩ une **plus-value** dégagée d'une vente; l'impôt sur l'éventuelle **plus-value** financière; ⟨Fisc⟩ l'imposition des **gains** (*m*) **en capital** est un impôt sur le revenu et non pas sur le patrimoine

care (*n*): ⟨Soc⟩ un centre spécialisé dans la **prise en charge** (*f*) des toxicomanes (*care, treatment*)

career (*n*): remotiver les hommes en leur proposant de nouvelles **perspectives** (*f*) **de carrière** (*career prospects*); la réforme leur assure un meilleur **déroulement de carrière** (*f*); les grévistes exigent un **plan de carrière** adapté aux gains de productivité réalisés (*career structure*); **faire carrière** dans le privé (*make a career*); ⟨Mil⟩ le déficit en **personnel** (*m*) **de carrière** dans l'armée de terre (*career personnel [esp. military]*)

careless (*adj*): une gestion **imprévoyante**; SEE ALSO **foresight**

carriage (*n*): ⟨Comm⟩ les frais de **port** (*m*) et d'emballage demeurent à la charge de l'acheteur

carrying out (*n*): ⟨Admin⟩ son objet: retarder l'**exécution** (*f*) des résolutions des Nations unies (*carrying out, implementation*); deux journalistes tués dans l'**exercice** (*m*) de leur mission (*carrying out, discharge*); SEE ALSO **exercise, implementation**

carry on (*v*): SEE **continue**

carry out (*v*): une mission secrète **effectuée** au Moyen-Orient; **assurer** des missions de police civile et militaire; **réaliser** un sondage (*carry out*); des arrestations **opérées** hier soir par la police; l'armée **se livre** à une répression sanglante (*carry out, conduct*); le transfert des fonds **s'est opéré** à l'insu des autorités (*be carried out; take place*)

cartel (*n*): ⟨Econ⟩ l'entente, dont la forme la plus connue est le **cartel**

case (*n*): ⟨Jur⟩ l'**affaire** (*f*) a été portée devant les tribunaux; le **dossier** a été classé sans suite (*case, affair*); un **cas de divorce** qui fit grand bruit (*divorce case*); un célèbre avocat **plaida sa cause** (*plead a case/cause*); il a fini par **perdre son procès** (*lose a court case*); plusieurs jugements qui sont venus amender profondément la **jurisprudence** (*case law; jurisprudence*); SEE ALSO **precedent**

cash (*n/adj*): ⟨Fin⟩ effectuer des retraits **en espèces** (*fpl*); des versements officieux payés **en liquide** (*m*); modes de paiement: **en numéraire** (*m*) ou par chèque bancaire (*in cash*); de nouvelles formes de services bancaires comme les **cartes** (*f*) **de retrait d'espèces** (*cash card*); ⟨Comm⟩ une remise sur tout **achat** (*m*) **comptant** (*cash purchase*)

cash flow (*n*): ⟨Fin/Comm⟩ un problème de **liquidité** (*f*) de fin de mois; une baisse de sa **trésorerie** (*cash flow*); la Sécurité sociale **en crise** (*f*) **de trésorerie** (*with a cash-flow problem*)

castigate (*v*): il a **fustigé** les dépenses excessives en matière de défense (*castigate, criticize strongly*)

casual (*adj*): on préfère licencier un **employé temporaire** (*casual/temporary employee*); des **travailleurs** (*m*) **intermittents**, payés à la journée (*casual/intermittent worker*); un **journalier**, rémunéré à la journée (*casual labourer [esp. on farm]*)

catching up (*n*): le **rattrapage** du pouvoir d'achat

catch up (*v*): les entreprises françaises ont **rattrapé leur retard** (*m*) en matière d'internationalisation (*catch up*); les prix dans les magasins **rattrapent** le pouvoir d'achat (*catch up with*)

cause (*n*): les **causes** (*f*) du déclin de la Lorraine sont multiples

cause (*v*): l'attentat a **provoqué** d'importants dégâts matériels; son discours **suscita** bien des controverses; une perte de marché qui **engendre** le chômage; l'évolution technologique **entraîne** un besoin croissant de personnel qualifié (*cause, bring about*); la révolte **issue** du mécontentement populaire; des problèmes sociaux **issus** de l'urbanisme des années 60 (*caused by, born of, stemming from*)

caution

caution (*n*): faire preuve de **prudence** (*f*); **circonspection** (*f*) à Washington (*caution; cautious reaction/response/attitude*)

cautious (*adj*): observer une attitude **attentiste** (*cautious; wait-and-see*)

cease-fire (*n*): ⟨Mil⟩ le **cessez-le-feu** a peu de chances de durer; l'**accord** (*m*) **de cessez-le-feu** intervenu hier (*cease-fire agreement*)

ceiling (*n*): ⟨Fin⟩ le **plafond** pour le calcul des cotisations (*ceiling*); le **plafonnement** à 80.000F de la prime (*setting of a ceiling/upper limit*); le projet de **déplafonnement** (*m*) des allocations familiales (*removal of ceiling/upper limit*); le D-Mark est à 2 centimes de son **cours-plafond**, à 3,41F (*ceiling price*); la loi qui réglemente et **plafonne** ces dépenses (*impose a ceiling/upper limit*); on est remboursé **dans la limite de** 2.000F par an et par famille (*up to a ceiling of*); SEE ALSO **limit**

censure (*n*): ⟨Pol⟩ les communistes prêts à voter la **censure** (*censure motion*)

censure (*v*): ⟨Pol⟩ l'opposition s'unit pour **censurer** le gouvernement (*pass a vote of censure/no confidence*)

census (*n*): les chiffres sont ceux du **recensement** de 1990 (*census*); impossible de **recenser** les sans-abri (*take a census of; count*)

centralism (*n*): ⟨Pol/Admin⟩ pratiquer un **centralisme** administratif et stratégique excessif

centralization (*n*): ⟨Pol/Admin⟩ la **centralisation**, battue en brèche par la loi de 1982

centralizer (*n*): ⟨Pol/Admin⟩ pour ce **jacobin** de toujours, l'État doit donner l'exemple (*centralizer, Jacobin*)

centralizing (*adj*): ⟨Pol/Admin⟩ imposer une politique **centralisatrice**; on a trop longtemps supporté la loi de l'État **jacobin** (*centralizing, Jacobin*)

centre (*n*): un **foyer** traditionnel de l'industrie manufacturière; Besançon, le **pôle** national des industries de haute précision (*centre, home*); ⟨Pol⟩ une opération de **recentrage** (*m*) opérée par la gauche (*moving to the centre*)

cessation (*n*): les autorités proclament l'**arrêt** (*m*) des hostilités (*cessation of hostilities; cease-fire*)

chain (*n*): ⟨Comm⟩ la deuxième **chaîne** britannique de magasins de confection (*chain [of stores]*); toutes les formes de distribution, dont les **magasins** (*m*) **à succursales multiples** (*chain store*)

chair (*n*): ⟨Admin⟩ prendre la **présidence** de l'assemblée générale; occuper le **fauteuil présidentiel** (*take the chair*); ⟨Educ⟩ **être titulaire** (*m*) **d'une chaire** à la faculté (*hold a chair*)

chair (*v*): ⟨Admin⟩ l'adjoint au maire **présida**; en l'absence du président, elle accepta d'**assurer la présidence** (*chair, chair a meeting/committee*)

chairman (*n*): qui sera **nommé à la présidence**? (*appoint [as] chairman/person*); le **président du conseil d'administration** y siège d'office (*chairman/person of a board of directors*); devant le **président-directeur général [PDG]** de la société (*chairman/person and managing director*)

chairmanship (*n*): ⟨Admin⟩ la **présidence** portugaise de la CEE; SEE ALSO **presidency**

challenge (*n*): malgré la **contestation** interne, il a recueilli la confiance de 95% des responsables (*challenge, opposition*); un **défi** politique et économique (*challenge, difficult task*); il faut **relever le défi** (*take up a challenge*); **gagner le pari** du développement et de la démocratie (*meet a challenge successfully*)

challenge (*v*): **contester** une décision (*challenge, contest*); susceptible de **mettre en cause** (*f*) la suprématie mondiale des États-Unis; ⟨Econ⟩ fortement **concurrencé** sur son marché traditionnel (*challenge, threaten*); SEE ALSO **competition**

chance (*n*): une **occasion** dont il faut profiter; les **opportunités** (*f*) qu'offre le marché unique de 1993 (*chance, opportunity*)

chancellor (*n*): ⟨Pol⟩ le **chancelier** de l'Allemagne (*Chancellor, Prime Minister*); le candidat à la **Chancellerie** du parti social-démocrate (*office of Chancellor*); le poste de **Chancelier de l'Échiquier** (*m*) (*Chancellor of the Exchequer*)

change (*n*): ⟨Pol⟩ PCF: le **changement** n'est pas à l'ordre du jour (*change*); une période de **mutation** (*f*) profonde de l'économie (*change, transformation*); un **revirement** de la politique européenne; le **virage** de 1983 explique la défaite électorale de 1986 (*change/reversal of policy*)

change (*v*): les choses **évoluent** très vite; les pouvoirs publics devront **s'adapter** (*change, evolve*); on ne saurait **faire table** (*f*) **rase** de la législation actuelle (*change completely*)

channel (*n*): de nouvelles **filières** (*f*) pour passer de la drogue (*channel; network*); ⟨Admin/Scol⟩ il avait suivi la **filière** classique: ENA, Polytechnique (*channel, path [esp. educational]*); être obligé de **passer par la voie hiérarchique** (*go through official channels*)

channel (*v*): une élection permettra de **canaliser** le mécontentement populaire

charge (*n*): ⟨Econ/Fin⟩ la **tarification** de l'ensemble des services bancaires (*making a charge; charging*); la **grille du barème** a été supprimée en 1986; une banque aux **tarifs** (*m*) et prestations compétitifs (*scale of charges*); ⟨Jur⟩ aucune **charge** (*f*) n'a été retenue contre lui (*charge*); détention, sans **inculpation** (*f*) ni jugement (*charge, being charged*); trois **chefs** (*m*) **d'inculpation** furent retenus contre lui (*charge, count*); SEE ALSO **indictment**

charge (*v*): ⟨Comm/Fin⟩ les banques voudraient **facturer** les comptes et les chèques (*charge/make a charge for*); bien que **pratiquant des tarifs** (*m*) **très élevés** (*charge high rates*); les frais sont **à la charge de** l'assuré (*charged to/payable by*); les cartes bancaires sont **tarifées** deux fois plus cher à l'étranger (*charge, bill, invoice*); ⟨Jur⟩ un policier **inculpé** après la mort d'un jeune voleur (*charge with a crime*); le nombre de **prévenus** (*m*) qui encombrent les prisons (*person charged with a crime*)

charitable

charitable (*adj*): le régime fiscal appliqué aux **organisations** (*f*) **caritatives** (*charitable organization*); SEE ALSO **charity**

charity (*n*): donner de l'argent à une **œuvre de bienfaisance** (*f*) (*charity; charitable organization*)

charter (*n*): ⟨Pol/Soc⟩ adhérer à la **charte sociale** (*social charter*); ⟨Comm⟩ recentrer son activité sur les **vols** (*m*) **à la demande**; le transport des passagers en **vol charter** (*m*) (*charter flight*)

charter (*v*): un avion gros porteur, **affrété** par la Croix-Rouge

cheap (*adj*): une main-d'œuvre abondante et **bon marché**; la protection des approvisionnements **à bas prix** (*m*) (*cheap/low cost*)

cheaply (*adv*): ⟨Comm⟩ vendre des produits **à un moindre coût** (*more cheaply*); on cherche le pays où les fabriquer **au moindre coût** (*most cheaply*

cheat (*v*): les contribuables salariés ne pourront plus **frauder**; SEE ALSO **defraud**

check (*n*): les **contrôles** (*m*) aux douanes; les services de police ont procédé à des **vérifications** (*f*) pour port d'arme prohibée (*check, control, verification*)

check (*v*): contrôler les voitures et **vérifier** les identités (*check, verify*); l'objectif est d'**enrayer** toute spirale inflationniste (*check, curb*)

chicanery (*n*): ⟨Pol⟩ l'Opposition parle de **magouille** (*f*) à propos du redécoupage électoral

chief (*n/adj*): ⟨Mil⟩ l'armée obéit à ses **chefs** (*m*) (*chief*); **chef d'état-major** (*m*) de l'armée de l'air (*Chief of Staff*); ⟨Pol⟩ au **préfet [de police]** est confiée la direction de la police à Paris (*chief of police*); ⟨Admin⟩ le **directeur-général** de la BBC (*chief executive [officer]*)

child (*n*): ⟨Soc⟩ les conditions d'accès pour l'**allocation** (*f*) **pour jeune enfant** (*child benefit*); aider les salariés pour la **garde des enfants** après l'école; les emplois familiaux tels que la **garde d'enfants à domicile** (*child-minding*)

choice (*n/adj*): un grand **choix** de marchandises (*choice, selection*); ⟨Pol⟩ la politique économique va imposer des **arbitrages** (*m*) douloureux (*choice, decision*); des marchandises **de choix** (*choice, select*)

choose (*v*): on l'a **choisi** parmi 35 candidats au poste (*choose, select*); les Français **élisent** leur Président (*choose, elect*)

circular (*n*): ⟨Pol/Admin⟩ une **circulaire** portant sur les conditions de l'emploi obligatoire de la langue arabe

circulate (*v*): le document, **diffusé** à 50 exemplaires (*circulate, distribute*); la rumeur s'**est propagée** vite (*circulate, spread*)

circulation (*n*): ⟨Journ⟩ une baisse sensible des **tirages** (*m*) (*circulation*); avec une **diffusion** de 44.000 exemplaires (*circulation, sales*); SEE ALSO **copy**

circumstance (*n*): la **conjoncture** n'y est guère favorable (*circumstances, situation [esp. economic]*); SEE ALSO **mitigating**

circumvent (*v*): la Lituanie tente de **contourner** le blocus économique; les firmes d'armements **tournent** l'embargo vers le golfe Persique (*circumvent, get round/past, bypass*)

citation (*n*): ⟨Jur⟩ une **citation** ou sommation de comparaître en justice (*citation, summons*); SEE ALSO **summons**

cite (*v*): ⟨Jur⟩ **cité à comparaître** le 29 juin (*cite, summons to appear in court*)

citizen (*n*): ⟨Pol⟩ le maire est soutenu par la majorité de ses **administrés** (*m*) (*citizen*); tout **ressortissant** (*m*) de la Communauté pourra voter (*citizen; national*)

citizenship (*n*): ⟨Pol⟩ pour faciliter l'accession à la **citoyenneté**; il est possible d'imaginer une **citoyenneté** européenne

city (*n*): les deux **municipalités** (*f*) vont discuter de la question (*city/town council*); il travaillait dans la **Cité** [de Londres] (*City of London*)

civil (*adj*): le **mariage civil** précédait la cérémonie religieuse (*civil wedding*); ⟨Pol⟩ une campagne de **désobéissance** (*f*) **civique** (*civil disobedience*); la **guerre civile** reprend en 1988 (*civil war*)

civilian (*n/adj*): la nomination d'un **civil** à la tête du ministère de la Défense (*civilian*); sur les quelque 19.000 guérilleros revenus à la **vie civile** (*civilian life*)

civil rights (*npl*): ⟨Pol⟩ la campagne pour les **droits** (*m*) **civils** aux États-Unis; œuvrer pour les **droits civiques** des Noirs (*civil rights*)

civil servant (*n*): ⟨Admin⟩ les employés de l'administration sont appelés **fonctionnaires** (*m*); les fonctionnaires *stricto sensu*, c'est-à-dire les **agents** (*m*) **de l'État** (*civil servant; State employee*); l'ENA, pépinière des **grands commis** (*m*) **de l'État** (*high-ranking/top civil servant*)

civil service (*n*): ⟨Admin⟩ une longue carrière dans la **fonction publique**; l'**Administration** (*f*) ou l'ensemble des services de l'État

claim (*n*): des **revendications** (*f*) salariales légitimes (*claim, demand*); ⟨Ins⟩ toute **réclamation** (*f*) doit être faite dans les huit jours (*claim*); complètement sinistrés, ils ont **fait une demande d'indemnité** (*f*) (*put in a claim [esp. insurance]*); ⟨Fin⟩ les deux tiers des **créances** (*f*) sur la Pologne (*financial claim, debt*); SEE ALSO **debt**

claim (*v*): les insurgés **affirment** progresser au nord (*claim*); il **se veut** un champion de l'ouverture (*claim to be*); **se prévaloir** d'avoir mené cette stratégie à bien (*claim with justification*); **se prévaloir** de la qualité de français (*claim, lay claim to*); **prétendre à** des allocations d'assurance-chômage (*claim; submit a claim for*); ⟨Pol⟩ l'IRA **s'attribuait** le nouvel attentat; l'organisation terroriste **revendique** l'attentat (*claim responsibility [esp. for terrorist act]*)

claimant (*n*): le **demandeur** doit pouvoir justifier d'une résidence de trois ans

clash (*n*): des **heurts** (*m*) violents pendant une manifestation d'agriculteurs; des **accrochages** (*m*) opposant manifestants et police; les **affrontements** (*m*) ont fait dix morts (*clash, confrontation*); le **choc des cultures** (*f*) entre Italiens et Polonais (*clash of cultures*); SEE ALSO **skirmish**

clash (*v*): la foule **se heurte** à l'armée; des troupes gouvernementales **s'étaient affrontées** avec les émeutiers

clause (*n*): ⟨Pol/Jur⟩ une **disposition** qui ne figure pas dans l'accord; les **dispositions** modifiant le traité (*clause, provision*)

clean up (*v*): des mesures pour **assainir** la vie politique; ces textes vont **moraliser** le financement de la vie politique (*clean up; cleanse [esp. of corruption]*); la profession **s'est moralisée** depuis (*clean oneself up; put one's house in order*)

cleaning up (*n*): l'**assainissement** (*m*) de la route forestière (*cleaning up*); la nécessité d'une **moralisation** des mœurs politiques en France (*cleaning up, cleansing [esp. of corruption]*)

clear (*v*): la police a mis deux heures pour **dégager** la rue des manifestants (*clear*); ⟨Jur⟩ accusé de vol mais **innocenté** par la Cour d'appel; **mis hors de cause** (*f*) après une longue audition (*clear, exonerate, pronounce innocent*); il en est sorti **blanchi** (*with one's name cleared*); SEE ALSO **exonerate**

clearing (*n*): ⟨Jur⟩ l'**innocentement** (*m*) d'un suspect; la **disculpation** d'un prévenu (*clearing, acquittal*)

cliché (*n*): un discours plein de **poncifs** (*m*) et de lieux-communs

client (*n*): ⟨Comm⟩ le **client** a toujours raison; SEE ALSO **customer**

climate (*n*): des signes manifestes du mécontentement **ambiant** (*climate of*); SEE ALSO **current**

close (*adj*): une **étroite** coopération entre les deux pays (*close, intimate*); un **proche** du ministre de l'Économie (*close [esp. friend/ally/colleague]*); chez un **proche parent** (*close relation*)

close (*n*): ⟨Fin⟩ la **clôture** de la Bourse (*close*); les cours de la Bourse **en clôture** (*at close of trading*)

close (*v*): ⟨Comm⟩ la Bourse **chôme** en raison de la fête de la Toussaint; la conférence **s'est clôturée** en laissant un sentiment d'inachevé (*close, end*); ⟨Jur⟩ **clore** un dossier, faute d'éléments; les tribunaux espagnols **classent** provisoirement le dossier (*close [esp. a file/case]*)

closed (*adj*): ⟨Pol/Jur⟩ au cours d'une **séance à huis clos** (*closed session*); ⟨Écon/Ind⟩ un accord permettant au syndicat l'**exclusivité** (*f*) **d'embauche** dans l'entreprise; la fin du **monopole syndical d'embauche** (*f*) (*closed shop*)

close down (*v*): ⟨Comm⟩ l'usine a **cessé toute activité** (*f*); l'entreprise va devoir **fermer ses portes** (*f*); l'affaire ayant périclité, le patron **met la clef sous la porte** (*close down, cease operating/trading*)

36

close-fought (*adj*): la lutte s'annonce **serrée** (*close-fought, tight*)

closeness (*n*): il réaffirma l'**étroitesse** (*f*) de la coopération entre les deux pays

closure (*n*): ⟨Econ⟩ la **fermeture** de cinquante puits de mines (*closure, closing down*); ⟨Comm⟩ de nouveaux licenciements et des **fermetures d'entreprises** (*closure/closing down [esp. of business/firm]*)

club (*n*): ⟨Pol⟩ fondateur de l'Union des **clubs** (*m*) pour le renouveau de la Gauche (*political club/association*)

coalition (*n*): ⟨Pol⟩ passation de pouvoirs à un **gouvernement de coalition** (*f*) (*coalition government*); ⟨Mil⟩ optimisme du côté des **coalisés** (*mpl*) (*coalition powers*); le retrait des **forces** (*f*) **coalisées** de l'Irak (*coalition forces*)

code (*n*): un **code de déontologie** (*f*) fixé par la profession (*code of conduct/ethics*)

coeducation (*n*): ⟨Scol⟩ l'**éducation** (*f*) **mixte** est la norme; partisan de la **mixité à l'école** (*coeducation; mixed schools*)

coffer (*n*): apporter d'abondantes recettes dans les **caisses** (*f*) de l'État; ce sont 33 milliards de francs qui sont entrés dans l'**escarcelle** (*f*) **de l'État** (*coffers/purse of the State*)

cohabit (*v*): ⟨Soc⟩ les époux ne sont plus tenus de **cohabiter**; choisir de **vivre en couple** (*m*), sans se marier; les couples qui **vivent maritalement**; des personnes **vivant en union** (*f*) **libre** (*cohabit, live together*)

cohabitation (*n*): ⟨Soc⟩ après sept ans de **vie** (*f*) **commune**; la **vie en couple** (*m*) est le choix de la grande majorité; favoriser le **concubinage** au détriment du mariage (*cohabitation; living together*)

collaborate (*v*): ⟨Comm⟩ deux géants de l'édition vont **se rapprocher** (*collaborate; combine*)

collaboration (*n*): ⟨Comm⟩ la tendance à la **coopération** entre les industriels (*collaboration*); l'accord vise à favoriser des **rapprochements** (*m*) **d'entreprise** (*collaboration/link-up of firm*)

collapse (*n*): ⟨Econ⟩ les **défaillances** (*f*) du tissu industriel de la Lorraine; l'**écroulement** (*m*) de l'économie est-allemande; l'**effondrement** (*m*) des exportations (*collapse*); la **déconfiture** des compagnies les plus menacées; la **ruine** de l'économie (*collapse, bankruptcy*)

collapse (*v*): ⟨Fin⟩ des sociétés bien cotées ont vu leurs cours **s'effondrer**; ⟨Comm⟩ les ventes **se sont effondrées** (*collapse; fall dramatically*)

collect (*v*): les informations **rassemblées** au cours de l'enquête (*collect, assemble*); les dossiers sont à **retirer** et à déposer avant le 31 mai (*collect; pick up*); ⟨Fin⟩ l'argent **recueilli** sera alloué à un fonds spécial; ⟨Fisc⟩ une baisse des revenus **perçus** par l'État (*collect*); le fonctionnaire qui **perçoit les impôts** (*m*) (*collect taxes*)

collection (*n*): des **collectes** (*f*) organisées pour aider les réfugiés (*collection*); ⟨Fisc⟩ assurer le **recouvrement des impôts**; une meilleure **perception des**

impôts; le rôle du fisc, c'est la **collecte de l'impôt** (*collection of taxes/dues*)

collective (*adj*): ⟨Econ⟩ patronat et syndicats ont signé une **convention collective** (*collective agreement*); au Portugal, la **négociation collective** est peu développée (*collective bargaining*); ⟨Mil⟩ qui pourrait organiser la **sécurité collective** dans la région? (*collective security*)

college (*n*): ⟨Pol⟩ désigné par un **collège** de notables

collegial (*adj*): ⟨Pol⟩ la présidence **collégiale**, dirigée à tour de rôle par chaque République; les décisions se prennent **collégialement** (*in a collegial manner*)

column (*n*): ⟨Journ⟩ la **rubrique** financière du *Monde*; la **chronique** musicale du *Figaro* (*newspaper column/page/section*)

combine (*n*): ⟨Econ⟩ les **ententes** (*f*) faussent le jeu de la concurrence; l'énorme **combinat** (*m*) **d'État** de l'ex-RDA (*State combine*); SEE ALSO **cartel**

combine (*v*): l'État et la Ville **conjuguent** leurs efforts; ⟨Comm⟩ les deux sociétés vont **allier leurs activités** (*combine*); deux géants de l'agro-alimentaire **s'associent** (*combine, link up*); la société **regroupe** ses activités micro-électroniques; ⟨Pol⟩ on parle de **panacher** les listes RPR et FN au second tour (*combine [esp. electoral lists]*)

command (*n*): ⟨Admin⟩ respecter la **hiérarchie** (*chain of command; hierarchy*); ⟨Mil⟩ **prendre le commandement de** la force d'interposition de l'ONU (*take command of*)

command (*v*): **commander** les forces alliées (*command*); le Président leur **commande** de poursuivre l'effort militaire (*command, give orders*)

commerce (*n*): le **commerce** international (*commerce, trade*); une carrière dans les **affaires** (*fpl*) (*commerce, business*); la bonne tenue des **échanges** (*mpl*) avec le Japon (*commerce, trade*)

commercial (*adj*): ⟨Comm⟩ premier partenaire **commercial** de la Chine (*commercial, trading*); ⟨Jur/Comm⟩ les principales questions du **droit commercial** (*commercial law*)

commission (*n*): ⟨Fin/Comm⟩ toucher une **commission** de 10%; moyennant de substantielles **commissions** (*commission*); l'architecte se rémunère **à la commission** (*on a commission basis*); ⟨Jur⟩ chacun des inculpés aurait pu empêcher la **commission** du délit (*commission, committing*)

commit (*v*): ⟨Jur⟩ **commettre** un crime (*commit*); accusé d'avoir **perpétré** cet ignoble assassinat (*commit, carry out, perpetrate*); après les avoir inculpés, le juge d'instruction les **fit incarcérer** (*commit to prison*); la chambre d'accusation le **renvoya devant la cour d'assises** (*commit for trial*); SEE ALSO **offence**

commitment (*n*): son **engagement** (*m*) en faveur de la réunification allemande; être lié par des **engagements** à trop long terme (*commitment, promise*); la **vocation exportatrice** de l'entreprise (*commitment to exporting*); SEE ALSO **agreement**

committal (*n*): ⟨Jur⟩ placer sous **mandat** (*m*) **de dépôt** (*committal order*); sa **mise en accusation** lui a été signifiée (*committal for trial*)

committee (*n*): ⟨Admin⟩ le **bureau** syndical, élu à l'unanimité; nommé rapporteur de la **Commission** des finances (*committee*); seuls les **commissaires** (*m*) socialistes ont voté contre (*committee/commission member*); une **commission d'enquête** (*f*) a été chargée d'en étudier les causes (*committee/commission of inquiry*); ⟨Pol⟩ la proposition est au stade de l'**étude** (*f*) **en commissions** (*[parliamentary] committee stage*); SEE ALSO **joint, select**

commodity (*n*): ⟨Comm⟩ une **denrée** très rare en Union soviétique; des **marchandises** (*f*) offertes sur le marché noir; SEE ALSO **produce**

common law (*n*): ⟨Jur⟩ une simple affaire de **droit** (*m*) **commun**; cent **prisonniers** (*m*) **de droit commun** ont été graciés au Maroc (*common law prisoner*); ⟨Soc⟩ un couple qui **vit en concubinage** (*m*) **notoire** (*have a common-law marriage*); SEE ALSO **cohabitation**

commonplace (*adj*): la télématique **se banalise**; plus inquiétant, l'emploi des armes à feu **se banalise** (*become commonplace*); la **banalisation** des assassinats mafieux (*becoming commonplace/more frequent*); SEE ALSO **spread**

commons (*npl*): ⟨Pol⟩ les **Communes** (*fpl*), la Chambre basse du parlement

community (*n/adj*): ⟨Soc⟩ son dévouement au service de la **communauté** (*community, society in general*); le manque de **vie** (*f*) **associative** dans les cités nouvelles (*community life*); dans un **local associatif** en banlieue (*community room/hall*); il faut des **animateurs** (*m*) **socio-culturels** pour encadrer la jeunesse désœuvrée (*community worker*); ⟨Pol⟩ la réglementation **communautaire** est très stricte (*community [esp. relating to EEC]*)

community policing (*n*): ⟨Jur⟩ la mise en place de l'**îlotage** (*m*) dans les cités ouvrières; les efforts en matière de **police** (*f*) **de proximité** commencent à porter leurs fruits

community service (*n*): ⟨Soc/Jur⟩ les **travaux** (*m*) **d'intérêt général** accomplis au profit d'une collectivité publique; imposer aux délinquants des **prestations** (*f*) **non rémunérées** prélevées sur le temps de loisirs (*community service order for young offender*)

commute (*v*): ⟨Jur⟩ **commuer** une condamnation à mort en une peine de prison

company (*n*): ⟨Econ⟩ la **firme** a décroché d'importants contrats en Corée; des **sociétés** (*f*) menacées par la crise économique (*company*); une **grosse société** avec plus de 100.000 actionnaires (*large company*); un salaire mensuel généreux et une **maison de fonction** (*f*) (*company house*); le nombre des **défaillances** (*f*) **d'entreprises** a progressé de 18% (*company failure*); ⟨Jur/Scol⟩ des épreuves de **droit** (*m*) **de l'entreprise** (*company law*)

compensate (*v*): comment **pallier** la perte de 50.000 emplois? (*compensate/make up for*); ⟨Ins⟩ **dédommager** les sinistrés de la perte de leurs biens (*compensate, pay compensation*); SEE ALSO **indemnify**

compensation (*n*): verser un gros **dédommagement**; le versement de leurs **indemnisations** (*f*); les **indemnités** (*f*) auxquelles le salarié licencié a droit; SEE ALSO **indemnification, indemnity**

compete (*v*): Belfort **dispute** à Besançon le monopole universitaire; ils **se disputent** un marché potentiel énorme (*compete for*); un pôle financier capable de **concurrencer** le Japon (*compete with*)

competence (*n*): faire appel aux **compétences** (*f*) d'un spécialiste (*competence, skill*); ⟨Jur⟩ on n'a aucune **compétence** pour intervenir (*competence, right*); un service de police **ayant compétence** sur l'ensemble du territoire (*have competence [esp. legal/administrative]*)

competent (*adj*): les régions sont **compétentes** en matière d'urbanisme; ⟨Jur⟩ le **tribunal compétent** est le tribunal de police (*court of competent jurisdiction*)

competing (*adj*): des commerces **concurrents** (*competing, rival*)

competition (*n*): ⟨Comm⟩ un renforcement de la **concurrence** américaine; au sein d'une sévère **compétition** internationale (*competition*); ce secteur **concurrencé** par l'électronique japonaise (*faced with competition*)

competitive (*adj*): ⟨Comm⟩ une agriculture **compétitive**; les entreprises les plus **performantes**; l'entreprise la plus **concurrentielle** sur le marché américain (*competitive, successful*); avoir une **avance sur ses concurrents** (*have a competitive edge*); SEE ALSO **education**

competitiveness (*n*): ⟨Comm⟩ l'aptitude à supporter la concurrence, ou la **compétitivité**

competitor (*n*): ⟨Comm⟩ Anvers, le **concurrent** direct du port normand (*competitor; rival*)

complain (*v*): la France va **porter plainte** (*f*) (*complain, lodge a complaint*); il **s'est ému** auprès du ministre (*complain, express displeasure*)

complaint (*n*): face aux **doléances** (*f*) africaines, la France a fait quelques concessions; un projet qui provoque quelques **grognes** (*f*) chez les agriculteurs (*complaint*); ⟨Jur⟩ ces agressions ont suscité plus de 50 **plaintes** (*f*) [en justice] (*official complaint*)

complement (*n*): le PDG prit la parole devant l'**effectif** (*m*) **complet**; le cabinet était présent **au grand complet** (*full complement; in full*)

complete (*adj*): le texte **intégral** de son discours (*complete, integral*)

complete (*v*): aller à Téhéran pour **achever** la réconciliation franco-iranienne (*complete*); cette année verra **s'achever** la construction de l'autoroute (*be completed*); **boucler** le dossier avant mars (*complete, finish, tie up*); **parfaire** sa formation (*complete, perfect*)

completion (*n*): l'**achèvement** (*m*) des travaux, prévu pour 1994; vous serez assuré de voir les **travaux** (*m*) **achevés** (*completion of the work*); ⟨Admin⟩ lors de l'**exécution** (*f*) du transfert de la propriété (*completion of house purchase*)

compliance (*n*): vérifier que les travaux sont **en conformité** (*f*) **avec** les plans; ⟨Jur⟩ **conformément au** règlement (*in compliance with*); SEE ALSO **accordance**

complicity (*n*): bénéficier de la **complicité** de Jérusalem (*complicity*); la **connivence** sinon la responsabilité du gouvernement d'alors (*complicity; connivance*)

comply (*v*): devant leur refus d'**obtempérer**, le policier fit usage de son arme (*comply, obey*); **se conformer au** règlement; **respecter** les dispositions légales (*comply with, respect*)

comprise (*v*): l'activité lainière **compte** 150 entreprises (*comprise*); un comité consultatif qui **regroupe** patronat et syndicats; un groupe qui **rassemble** tous les secteurs de la machine-outil (*comprise, include, bring together*)

compromise (*n*): son refus de tout **compromis** (*m*); un accord sur le **texte de compromis** (*compromise text*); ses **compromissions** (*f*) avec la dictature (*[dishonest] compromise, deal*)

compromise (*v*): les États-Unis refusent de **transiger** avec les principes (*compromise [esp. principle]*); **se compromettre** dans une affaire d'espionnage (*compromise o.s.; be compromised*); SEE ALSO **jeopardize**

compulsory (*adj*): la procédure d'**expropriation** (*f*) ne signifie pas l'expulsion; les dispositions du Code de l'**expropriation pour cause d'utilité publique** (*compulsory purchase by the state*)

computer (*n*): l'ère de l'**ordinateur** (*m*) (*computer*); une connaissance de l'**informatique** (*f*) s'impose (*computer science, computing*)

computerize (*v*): **informatiser** le système de contrôle des stocks (*computerize*); **mettre sur ordinateur** (*m*) les données les plus importantes; les avantages de la **gestion informatisée** (*computerized management*)

concede (*v*): il n'a rien **cédé** sur sa vision politique (*concede; make a concession*); SEE ALSO **concession**

concentrate (*v*): ⟨Econ⟩ la firme de Sochaux entend **se recentrer** sur la pharmacie; notre action **s'est focalisée** sur l'équilibre régional (*concentrate on; focus on*)

concentration (*n*): ⟨Econ⟩ le groupe achève son **recentrage** en vendant sa filiale suisse (*concentration on core activities*)

concern (*n*): son **souci** principal: aider les plus démunis (*concern, preoccupation*); **s'inquiéter** des conséquences probables (*express concern, disquiet*); SEE ALSO **business**, **firm**

concern (*v*): ⟨Admin⟩ cela **relève** du Premier ministre; les zones non urbaines **relèvent** de la gendarmerie (*concern; be a matter for*)

concerned (*adj*): la France, **soucieuse** de promouvoir la stabilité des taux de change (*concerned, anxious*); les élus, **inquiets** des répercussions économiques sur leur région; la volonté de l'**intéressé** (*m*) d'obtenir sa naturalisation (*person concerned*)

41

concerning (*adj*): deux rapports **ayant trait** (*m*) aux droits des détenus; deux dispositions **intéressant** les étrangers vivant en France (*concerning, pertaining to*)

concerted (*adj*): une politique **concertée** au niveau de la CEE (*concerted*); une **concertation** pour l'emploi; une **mobilisation** accrue pour la protection de l'environnement (*concerted action*); SEE ALSO **combine**

concession (*n*): une **concession** de taille (*concession*); **ne pas céder** sur ce chapitre crucial (*make no concessions*); SEE ALSO **concede**

conciliation (*n*): ⟨Jur/Ind⟩ la **conciliation** permet d'éviter un procès; la **conciliation** se limite aux petits litiges individuels (*conciliation procedure*)

conciliator (*n*): ⟨Ind⟩ le conflit se prolongeant, le ministre nomma un **conciliateur** (*conciliator [esp. in industrial dispute]*)

conclude (*v*): un traité **conclu** entre les États riverains

conclusion (*n*): la France souhaite l'**aboutissement** (*m*) des négociations (*successful conclusion/outcome*); le **constat** des enquêteurs est sévère (*conclusion, finding[s]*); dresser un **premier bilan** (*preliminary conclusion*)

concurrent (*adj*): ⟨Jur⟩ le système de la **confusion des peines** (*f*) réduira la durée de sa détention (*serving concurrent sentences*)

concurrently (*adv*): on peut **cumuler** deux mandats électifs (*hold concurrently*)

condemn (*v*): ⟨Jur⟩ la loi **condamne** l'usage de stupéfiants (*condemn, forbid*); **condamner à mort** un criminel (*condemn/sentence to death*)

condemnation (*n*): ⟨Jur⟩ la **condamnation** par le Conseil de sécurité de la répression en Irak

condition (*n*): la CEE **conditionne** une aide financière à une amélioration de la situation dans ce pays (*pose as a prior condition; make conditional*); ⟨Econ/Jur⟩ la stricte contrainte des **cahiers** (*m*) **des charges** (*schedule of conditions; conditions of a contract*)

conditional (*adj*): ⟨Jur⟩ bénéficier d'une mesure de **libération** (*f*) **conditionnelle** (*conditional discharge*)

conference (*n*): ⟨Pol⟩ établir l'ordre du jour du **congrès** (*conference*); le parti a **tenu ses assises** (*fpl*) **annuelles** à Pau (*hold its annual conference*)

confess (*v*): ⟨Jur⟩ il **reconnaît** avoir dérobé la somme; les auteurs de l'attentat ont **avoué** (*confess, admit*)

confession (*n*): un **aveu** d'impuissance devant la montée de l'insécurité (*confession, admission*); ⟨Jur⟩ des **aveux** (*mpl*) extorqués par la violence (*confession [esp. to a crime]*); **passer des aveux complets** après trois heures de garde à vue (*make a full confession*)

confide (*v*): il a **confié** aux journalistes ses espoirs

confidence

confidence (*n*): malgré la crise, les banques gardent leur **sérénité** (*f*) (*confidence, optimism*); ⟨Comm⟩ avec la fin des hostilités, le retour à la **confiance**; surmonter les conservatismes, les **frilosités** (*f*) (*lack of confidence*); ⟨Pol⟩ ils sont 37% seulement à lui **faire confiance** (*pass a vote of confidence*); le parti conservateur lui **retira sa confiance** (*pass a vote of no confidence*)

confident (*adj*): il est **confiant** dans la capacité de l'industrie française; le parti, **serein** à l'approche des élections (*confident, optimistic*)

confirm (*v*): ⟨Comm⟩ avoir bon espoir que les commandes d'avions **se concrétiseront** (*be confirmed*)

confirmation (*n*): ⟨Comm⟩ sur **confirmation** (*f*) de la commande; la **concrétisation** des commandes en cours de négociation

conflict (*n*): faire cesser les **affrontements** (*m*) inter-ethniques; les grévistes obtiennent satisfaction sur deux **sujets** (*m*) **conflictuels** (*area of conflict; subject of disagreement*)

conflict (*v*): leurs idées **se heurtent aux** conceptions françaises (*conflict with*)

confront (*v*): décider de **confronter** l'accusé avec le témoin (*confront*); les islamistes **affrontent** le pouvoir tunisien (*confront, clash with*); SEE ALSO **face**

confrontation (*n*): dans une atmosphère d'**affrontement** (*m*) entre républiques; le **face à face** de ces deux adversaires de toujours; **épreuve** (*f*) **de force** entre les rebelles et l'armée fédérale (*confrontation; showdown*); SEE ALSO **trial of strength**

conjuncture (*n*): ⟨Econ⟩ la **conjoncture**, c'est-à-dire la situation économique présente et son évolution possible dans un futur proche (*[economic] conjuncture*)

connect (*v*): payer pour **se faire raccorder** au tout-à-l'égout (*be connected [esp. to telephone/drainage/sewerage etc. system]*)

connection (*n*): le **raccord** de l'aéroport au TGV; le droit de participation pour **raccordement** (*m*) à l'égout public (*connection, connecting*); SEE ALSO **connect**

conscript (*n*): ⟨Mil⟩ un **appelé** effectuant son service national; envoyer les **soldats** (*m*) **du contingent** pour rétablir la paix; l'armée comptait 2,5 millions de **conscrits** (*m*) (*conscript, conscripted soldier*)

conscript (*v*): SEE **call up**

conscription (*n*): ⟨Mil⟩ ou une armée de métier, ou la **conscription** traditionnelle

consensus (*n*): le modèle allemand repose sur un **consensus** social fort; le **consensus** était difficile à dégager

consent (*n*): ⟨Admin⟩ l'**agrément** (*m*) du maire est nécessaire; l'ouverture de nouvelles grandes surfaces est soumis à l'**agrément** des pouvoirs publics (*consent, approval*); SEE ALSO **mutual**

conservatism (*n*): ⟨Pol⟩ l'**immobilisme** (*m*) de la politique européenne du gouvernement (*conservatism; resistance to change*)

conservative (*n/adj*): ⟨Pol⟩ les réformistes contre les **partisans** (*m*) **de l'immobilisme**; se heurter à l'opposition des forces **conservatrices**; quatrième victoire consécutive pour les **Conservateurs** (*m*) (*Conservative Party [esp. British]*)

considerable (*adj*): subir des dégâts **importants**; Bruxelles préconise des baisses **sensibles** des prix agricoles; ces systèmes offrent des avantages **non négligeables**; l'obstacle est **de taille** (*f*) (*considerable, sizeable*)

considerably (*adv*): un réseau routier **sensiblement** amélioré

consideration (*n*): la mise en service d'un tramway **est à l'étude** (*f*) (*be under consideration, be studied*)

consistency (*n*): préserver la **cohérence** de notre politique à long terme

consistent (*adj*): une politique sociale **suivie** (*consistent; coherent*)

consolidate (*v*): il ne reste plus qu'à **bétonner** la nouvelle formation; les entreprises soucieuses de **conforter** ou d'accroître leurs parts de marché (*consolidate, strengthen*)

consolidation (*n*): ⟨Agric⟩ le **remembrement** ou le regroupement des propriétés rurales morcelées (*[land] consolidation*)

consortium (*n*): ⟨Econ/Fin⟩ détenir 37% du **consortium** européen; un **consortium** prend souvent la forme du groupement d'intérêt économique [GIE]

conspiracy (*n*): ⟨Jur⟩ accusés de meurtre et d'**association** (*f*) **de malfaiteurs** (*[criminal] conspiracy*); inculpés de **complicité** (*f*) **d'escroquerie** (*conspiracy to defraud*)

constituency (*n*): ⟨Pol⟩ le député en visite dans sa **circonscription**; SEE ALSO **electoral**

constraint (*n*): des **contraintes** (*f*) liées à l'insularité corse

construct (*v*): peu à peu, on **bâtit** l'Europe (*construct, build*)

construction (*n*): la **construction** de l'Europe est loin d'être réalisée; au fil des sommets, l'**édification** (*f*) de l'Europe continue; SEE ALSO **building**

consult (*v*): il faut écouter, dialoguer, **se concerter** (*consult together/each other*); ⟨Ind⟩ les dirigeants refusent de **consulter la base** (*consult the membership*)

consultancy (*n*): assurer une **mission de conseil** (*m*) pour le compte d'une société

consultant (*n*): ⟨Econ/Comm⟩ **consultant** (*m*) dans un cabinet parisien réputé (*consultant*); **expert-conseil** (*m*) auprès d'une grande société (*[acting as] consultant*); faire appel à un **conseiller en gestion** (*f*) **d'entreprise** (*management consultant*); consulter un **conseiller fiscal** (*tax consultant*)

consultation (*n*): ⟨Pol⟩ les **délibérations** (*f*) se poursuivent; cette mesure n'a fait l'objet d'aucune **consultation** (*consultation, exchange of views*); décider sans **concertation** (*f*) avec les principaux intéressés; le patient n'a pas à payer les frais de la **consultation** (*consultation [esp. medical]*)

consume (*v*): ⟨Econ⟩ les pays de l'Occident **consomment** de trop; on découvre chaque année plus de gaz qu'on n'en **consomme** (*consume, use up*)

consumer (*n*): ⟨Econ⟩ le **consommateur** boude les soldes de juillet (*consumer*); des milliers d'**abonnés** (*m*) privés d'eau courante (*consumer; customer [esp. of a public service]*); habillement, meubles et autres **biens** (*m*) **de consommation courante** (*consumer goods*); les prêts aux ménages, ce qu'on appelle le **crédit à la consommation** (*consumer credit/lending*); les **dépenses** (*f*) **de consommation** n'ont augmenté que de 0,9% (*consumer spending*)

consumption (*n*): la **consommation** a augmenté de 50% (*consumption; spending*)

contain (*v*): la région ne **compte** pas de très grandes villes (*contain, possess*); **contenir** le pouvoir d'achat (*contain, keep under control*)

contempt (*n*): ⟨Jur⟩ condamné pour **outrage** (*m*) **à la Cour** pour avoir tu ce qu'il savait; inculpé d'**outrage à magistrat** (*contempt of court*)

contention (*n*): ⟨Pol⟩ dix candidats étaient **en lice** (*f*) pour le premier tour des élections (*in contention*)

contest (*v*): la Maison Blanche et le Congrès **se disputent** la maîtrise de la politique extérieure; SEE ALSO **compete**

continuation (*n*): ⟨Pol⟩ la **poursuite** de l'action diplomatique par d'autres moyens (*continuation, pursuit*)

continue (*v*): on **poursuit** les discussions (*continue, pursue*); l'évacuation des otages **se poursuit** (*continue, carry on*); un boom de la consommation qui **ne se dément pas** (*continue unabated/unchecked*)

continued (*adj*): SEE **sustained**

continuing (*adj*): ⟨Scol⟩ des actions en **formation** (*f*) **continue** financées par les entreprises (*continuing education*)

contract (*n*): deux **affaires** (*f*) importantes sont en négociations au Nigéria; le **marché** qu'il a proposé à la Pologne; revoir des **contrats** (*m*) passés avec la France (*contract, deal*); la **passation de marchés** pour la réhabilitation d'habitats anciens (*awarding/signing of contracts*)

contract (*v*): la demande des pays occidentaux **se contracte** (*contract, diminish*); ⟨Jur⟩ **s'engager par contrat** (*m*) à compléter le travail (*contract, sign a contract*); ⟨Comm⟩ la société **a un contrat pour** la construction de l'hôpital (*have contracted for*)

contraction (*n*): le **tassement** de la consommation de l'énergie primaire continue

45

contractor (*n*): ⟨Econ⟩ la vitalité des **entrepreneurs** (*m*) locaux (*contractor; businessman*); la mairie est le **maître d'œuvre** du projet (*main contractor*); trois firmes se disputent la **maîtrise d'œuvre** de cet énorme projet (*role of main contractor*)

contravene (*v*): les pays riches n'hésitent pas à **contrevenir aux règles** (*f*) (*contravene, breach [esp. legislation]*)

contravention (*n*): SEE **breach**

contribute (*v*): ⟨Journ⟩ il avait **collaboré** à plusieurs journaux; ⟨Fin⟩ la Ville **s'est engagée** à hauteur de 100.000F

contribution (*n*): ⟨Econ⟩ l'**apport** (*m*) du tourisme étranger; le total de sa **participation** s'élève à 39.000F (*contribution*); la **quote-part** que devrait acquitter la Grande-Bretagne (*contribution, share*); ⟨Fin⟩ **cotiser** pour le montant qui vous convient (*pay a contribution/due*); ⟨Fisc⟩ la réduction du nombre de **cotisants** (*m*) est due au chômage (*person paying contributions [esp. National Insurance]*); allégement des **charges** (*f*) **sociales** (*social security contributions*)

contributor (*n*): ⟨Journ⟩ **collaborer** à une revue (*be a [regular] contributor*)

contributory pension scheme (*n*): ⟨Fin⟩ les employés cotisent tous à une **caisse de retraite** (*f*)

control (*n*): la **maîtrise** des dépenses de santé (*keeping under control*); le danger d'un **dérapage** (*m*) de l'inflation (*getting out of control*); l'économie donne déjà des signes d'**emballement** (*m*) (*getting out of control*); éviter que le crédit à la consommation ne **s'emballe** (*get out of control*); une économie **à la dérive** (*out of control*); SEE ALSO **hold**

control (*v*): une urgence: **contrôler** les dépenses de santé; l'inflation est difficile à **maîtriser** (*control, keep under control*); une loi visant à **réglementer** la publicité pour le tabac (*control, regulate*)

controversial (*adj*): une question des plus **controversées**; le conflit sera un des **sujets brûlants** évoqués (*controversial subject; hotly debated/burning issue*)

controversy (*n*): la décision suscita de vives **controverses** (*f*) en Grande-Bretagne

convalescent home (*n*): ⟨Soc⟩ une hospitalisation suivie d'un séjour en **maison** (*f*) **de repos**

convene (*v*): ⟨Pol/Admin⟩ les députés **convoqués** en session extraordinaire; il avait été prévu de **réunir** le parlement russe (*convene, convoke*)

convening (*n*): faire obstacle à la **convocation** d'une réunion (*convening, convoking*)

convention (*n*): mandaté par les **assises** (*fpl*) du parti (*convention, conference*)

conversation (*n*): leurs **entretiens** (*m*) sont à la une de tous les journaux (*conversations, discussions*)

converse (*v*): il a pu **s'entretenir** brièvement avec son homologue allemand (*converse, have a conversation*)

conversion (*n*): ⟨Pol⟩ son récent **ralliement** à la cause socialiste; ⟨Econ⟩ la **reconversion** de l'industrie militaire

convert (*v*): ⟨Econ⟩ **reconvertir** l'industrie militaire au civil; **se reconvertir** dans le petit appareillage domestique; **se déployer** dans la chimie (*convert into; convert [esp. production into new activity]*)

converting (*n*): l'**aménagement** (*m*) d'anciens entrepôts en résidences de grand standing

convict (*n*): ⟨Jur⟩ un **repris de justice** notoire activement recherché par la police; trois **détenus** (*m*) **en cavale** (*escaped convict, convict on the run*)

convict (*v*): ⟨Jur⟩ faire **condamner** un innocent; il a été **condamné** pour détournement de fonds (*convict*); les deux hommes **convaincus** de participation à l'attentat (*convicted*)

conviction (*n*): ⟨Jur⟩ il a trois **condamnations** (*f*) à son actif; une **condamnation** assortie du sursis avec mise à l'épreuve

convocation (*n*): SEE **convening**

convoke (*v*): SEE **convene**

cool (*adj*): l'accueil de son hôte fut plutôt **frais** (*cool, chilly*)

coolly (*adv*): la France **accueille fraîchement** cette proposition (*greet coolly*)

coolness (*n*): sa visite mettra fin à une période de **froid** (*m*) diplomatique; le long **gel** des relations sino-soviétiques (*coolness, frost*)

co-operate (*v*): les firmes d'armement sont condamnées à **coopérer**; la Ville et l'État **conjuguent leurs efforts** (*m*) (*co-operate, combine one's efforts*)

co-operation (*n*): l'importance de la **concertation** (*f*) et du dialogue

co-operative (*n*): ⟨Comm⟩ une **coopérative** cherche avant tout à satisfaire les intérêts de ses membres; les grandes enseignes de la **coopération** (*co-operative movement*)

co-owner (*n*): lors de l'assemblée générale des **copropriétaires** (*m*) (*co-owner, joint owner*)

co-ownership (*n*): posséder un bien immobilier en **copropriété** (*f*) (*co-ownership*); acheter un appartement dans un **immeuble en copropriété** (*block of flats in co-ownership*)

copy (*n*): conserver un **double** de vos déclarations (*copy, duplicate*); se vendre à plus de 30.000 **exemplaires** (*m*) (*copy [esp. of book/newspaper]*); SEE ALSO **circulation**

corner-stone (*n*): **pierre** (*f*) **angulaire** depuis longtemps de l'Alliance atlantique; SEE ALSO **keystone**

corporate (*adj*): ⟨Admin/Comm⟩ les **raisons** (*f*) **sociales** successives du groupe (*corporate name*); ⟨Fisc⟩ l'abattement est plafonné à 30.000F pour une **personne morale** (*corporate/legal entity*); ⟨Econ⟩ un nouveau **plan social** pour 1994 portant sur des centaines de salariés (*corporate/company plan [esp. involving redundancies]*)

47

corporation

corporation (*n*): ⟨Econ⟩ la Poste, France-Télécom et d'autres **établissements** (*m*) **publics** (*public corporation*); ⟨Fisc⟩ l'**impôt** (*m*) **sur les sociétés** diminue de 1% (*corporation tax [GB]*)

correct (*v*): ⟨Pol/Admin⟩ la circulaire du ministre vise à y **remédier** (*correct [esp. an abuse]*); SEE ALSO **solve**

correction (*n*): ⟨Journ⟩ *Le Figaro* a publié un **rectificatif** dans ses éditions d'hier

corrupt (*adj*): une société **pourrie** (*corrupt, rotten*); le scandale des policiers **ripoux** (*corrupt, 'bent' [esp. police officer]*)

corruption (*n*): une sombre histoire de **trafic** (*m*) **d'influence** (*corruption, bribery*); son nom a été lié à des **malversations** (*f*) financières (*corruption; corrupt practices*); SEE ALSO **bribery**

cost (*n*): ⟨Fin/Econ⟩ l'énorme **coût** (*m*) de l'unification; la **charge** sociale des jeunes sans qualification; **faire les frais** (*m*) de l'opération (*pay/bear the cost of*); manifestation contre la **vie chère** (*high cost of living; high prices*); de sévères **réductions** (*f*) **de coûts** (*cost-cutting*); ⟨Jur⟩ acquitté, il a été **condamné aux dépens** (*mpl*) (*order to pay costs of a trial*); il fallait payer les **frais de procédure** (*legal/court costs*); SEE ALSO **expense**

cost (*v*): erreurs qui leur ont **fait perdre** des parts de marché (*cost; make to lose*); ⟨Fin/Comm⟩ **chiffrer** les propositions qui ont été déjà présentées (*cost; calculate the cost of*); ⟨Comm⟩ il s'agit d'**établir le prix**, avant de procéder (*cost an operation*)

cost-cutting (*n*): ⟨Econ⟩ dans le cadre d'un programme de **réduction** (*f*) **des coûts**

costly (*adv*): une opération très **coûteuse** pour une petite entreprise; SEE ALSO **dear**, **expensive**

cost of living (*n*): ⟨Econ⟩ toucher une **indemnité de vie chère** pour travailler à Paris (*cost-of-living allowance*)

cottage industry (*n*): ⟨Econ⟩ les structures d'accueil relèvent encore de l'**artisanat** (*m*); SEE ALSO **craft industry**

council (*n*): ⟨Pol⟩ les communes s'administrent librement par des **conseils** (*m*) élus

councillor (*n*): ⟨Pol⟩ les **conseillers** (*m*) **municipaux** ont procédé à l'élection du maire (*town/city councillor*); **conseiller général** et maire de la ville (*county/departmental councillor*); **conseiller régional** d'Alsace et porte-parole des Verts (*regional councillor*)

count (*n*): au dernier **recensement** de la population (*count, census*); SEE ALSO **census**, **charge**, **counting**

count (*v*): on **dénombrait** 26,7 millions de femmes en France; ⟨Admin⟩ **recenser** les habitants d'une région (*count, do a census*); ⟨Pol⟩ **dépouiller** les bulletins de vote (*count, check*); les personnes dont il **escomptait** la coopération; **tabler sur** une croissance de 1,9% de la production (*count/rely on, expect*)

counter (*n*): Banques: **guichets** (*mpl*) fermés demain mardi (*counter [esp. in bank/post-office]*); des paiements **en sous-main** (*under-the-counter, secret*)

counter (*v*): pour **contrer** la propagande du parti travailliste (*counter; combat*)

counterbalance (*v*): la seule région susceptible de **faire contrepoids** (*m*) à la région parisienne

counterfoil (*n*): ⟨Fin⟩ la **souche** d'un chéquier; inscrire le montant d'un chèque sur le **talon** (*counterfoil*); ⟨Comm⟩ le **bordereau** annuel de renouvellement d'adhésion au club (*counterfoil, slip; form*)

countermeasure (*n*): ⟨Mil/Econ⟩ si des **contre-mesures** (*f*) de rétorsion devaient être adoptées

counterpart (*n*): la banque vénézuélienne et son **homologue** colombien (*counterpart, equivalent, opposite number*)

counterweight (*n*): Metz est un utile **contrepoids** à Nancy à cet égard

counting (*n*): la **prise en compte** du temps de service dans le calcul de la retraite (*counting, calculating*); ⟨Pol⟩ le **comptage** des voix; procéder au **dépouillement** du vote (*counting of votes*)

country (*n*): le **pays** a soutenu son Président; on a constaté un recul de la criminalité en **zone** (*f*) **rurale** (*country area*)

countryside (*n*): **espace** (*m*) **rural**: cri d'alarme des écologistes; la défense du **monde rural** (*countryside; agricultural/rural community*)

coup (*n*): ⟨Pol⟩ le **coup d'État** d'hier a échoué (*coup*); destitution du président dans un **coup d'État sans effusion** (*f*) **de sang** (*bloodless coup*)

course (*n*): d'autres **voies** (*f*) pourraient alors être adoptées (*course, path*); ⟨Educ⟩ l'université a mis en place une **formation** nouvelle et originale; proposer des **cursus** (*m*) de trois ou quatre ans

court (*n*): ⟨Jur⟩ la **juridiction** compétente en matière pénale (*court, court of law*); une **action** (*f*) **judiciaire** paraît improbable (*court action*); la ville **assigne en justice** (*f*) ses créanciers; il va les **attaquer en justice**; treize personnes ont été **traduites en justice** (*take s.o. to court*); avant **d'agir en justice**, pensez au conciliateur; le gouvernement va **porter l'affaire devant les tribunaux**; il y a lieu d'**engager une action en justice** (*bring a court action, take a case to court*)

court of appeal (*n*): ⟨Jur⟩ un recours possible devant la **Cour de cassation** (*court of final appeal*)

courtroom (*n*): ⟨Jur⟩ l'accès à la **salle d'audience** (*f*) sera strictement limité

cover (*n*): ⟨Ins⟩ la **couverture** de tous les risques (*cover*); ⟨Soc⟩ votre rémunération et **couverture sociale** [retraite, assurance chômage] (*social security cover*); ⟨Pol⟩ la livraison de matériel de guerre avec la **couverture** des autorités (*cover, protection*)

cover (*v*): ⟨Ins⟩ la Sécurité sociale **couvre** les risques sociaux (*cover*); **se prémunir** contre l'éventualité d'un sinistre (*cover/protect o.s.*)

coverage (*n*): ⟨Journ⟩ la **couverture** tendancieuse de certains journaux (*coverage, reporting*); la **couverture médiatique** des événements laisse à désirer (*media coverage/reporting*)

cover up (*v*): ⟨Pol⟩ la vérité sur cette affaire a été **étouffée**; des tentatives pour **étouffer** l'affaire (*cover up, conceal*); SEE ALSO **hush up**, **suppress**

crackdown (*n*): la **répression** de la fraude fiscale; SEE ALSO **repression**

crack down (*v*): défaut de port de casque: la police va **sévir**; SEE ALSO **repress**

craft industry (*n*): ⟨Comm⟩ des **activités** (*f*) **artisanales** lucratives; SEE ALSO **cottage industry**

craftsman (*n*): ⟨Comm⟩ les petits commerçants et les **artisans** (*m*) sont les plus nombreux (*[self-employed] craftsman, artisan*)

crash (*n*): ⟨Econ⟩ des **faillites** (*f*) retentissantes (*crash, [company] collapse*); le **krach boursier** de 1989 fait toujours des vagues (*stock market crash*)

credentials (*n*): ⟨Pol⟩ l'ambassadeur présente ses **lettres** (*f*) **de créance** au roi

credibility (*n*): porter un nouveau coup à la **crédibilité** de la Communauté (*credibility, reputation*)

credible (*adj*): aucune dissuasion purement conventionnelle n'est **crédible**

credit (*n*): ⟨Fin⟩ le contrôle de l'État sur le fonctionnement du **crédit** (*credit, lending*); un **solde créditeur** de 5.000F (*credit balance*); ⟨Econ⟩ le **resserrement du crédit** commence à se faire sentir (*credit squeeze*); avec la levée de l'**encadrement** (*m*) **du crédit** (*credit controls*); à l'époque, le **crédit était encadré** (*credit controls be in force*); ⟨Fin/Comm⟩ accorder un **crédit à 3 mois** (*ninety-day credit*); **faire crédit** à un client à concurrence de 100.000F (*give credit*)

credit (*v*): ⟨Fin⟩ **approvisionner** un compte en banque (*credit [esp. an account]*); **alimenter un compte** régulièrement par des versements de fonds (*credit/pay into an account; fund, supply with funds*); **être crédité** du montant de la somme due (*be credited*)

creditor (*n*): les **créanciers** (*m*) commencent à serrer la vis; la France est le second **créancier** de l'Égypte (*creditor, lender*)

crime (*n*): ⟨Jur⟩ la Cour d'assises juge les auteurs d'**infractions** (*f*) **criminelles** (*crime, criminal offence, felony*); la **délinquance** quotidienne a doublé en vingt ans; la **grande délinquance** a beaucoup décru (*serious crime*); la lutte continue contre la **petite criminalité** (*petty crime*); lutter contre le **grand banditisme** (*organized crime*); une semaine internationale de la **prévention de la délinquance** (*crime prevention*)

criminal (*adj*): ⟨Jur⟩ soupçonné fortement d'autres **activités** (*f*) **délictueuses** (*criminal activity*); les inculpés sont connus pour leurs **antécédents** (*mpl*) **judiciaires** (*criminal history/record*); les honoraires des avocats **en matière** (*f*) **pénale** (*in criminal cases*); un **avocat d'assise** (*f*) jouissant d'une certaine notoriété (*criminal lawyer*); SEE ALSO **police record**

criminal (*n*): un truand et **malfaiteur** (*m*), au casier judiciaire chargé

criminal court (*n*): ⟨Jur⟩ le **tribunal correctionnel** statue sur les petits délits (*criminal court, magistrate's court*); deux fois récidiviste, il fut **traduit en correctionnelle** (*f*) (*bring before a criminal court*)

criminality (*n*): SEE **crime**

crisis (*n*): la **crise** qui secoue les partis de la droite (*crisis*); ⟨Econ⟩ depuis le premier **choc pétrolier** en 1973 (*oil crisis*)

critical (*adj*): très **critique** à l'égard des accords; **trouver à redire à** la politique de la Gauche (*be critical of, criticize*); ⟨Econ⟩ prendre la tête d'une société **en perdition** (*f*) (*in a critical state*)

cross (*v*): **traverser** le continent d'est en ouest (*cross, traverse*); en **franchissant** la ligne de cessez-le-feu (*cross, step over*)

crossing (*n*): la **traversée** la plus rapide de la Manche; le **franchissement** symbolique de la ligne de partage (*crossing, crossing over*)

crossroads (*n*): le rôle de **carrefour** (*m*) européen joué par l'Alsace

cruelty (*n*): SEE **ill-treatment**

crush (*v*): une rébellion **écrasée** par les troupes fidèles au régime

crushing (*n*): l'**écrasement** (*m*) de la révolte kurde en 1991

curb (*v*): on a à peu près **maîtrisé** l'inflation; **juguler** l'inflation (*curb, halt*); comment **endiguer** la croissance des inégalités?; **enrayer** la détérioration des transports publics (*curb, halt, arrest*)

cure (*v*): SEE **remedy**

curfew (*n*): ⟨Pol/Mil⟩ le camp a été placé sous **couvre-feu** (*m*); lever le **couvre-feu** imposé il y a quinze jours

currency (*n*): ⟨Fin⟩ la **devise** américaine est très demandée; une **monnaie** reflète notamment l'état de santé du pays; la logique de la **monnaie unique** (*single currency*); les réserves de **change** (*m*) britanniques (*foreign currency*)

current (*adj*): la xénophobie **ambiante**, exacerbée par la présence de réfugiés (*current; fashionable*); les négociations **en cours** (*m*) sur l'union politique européenne; le président **en exercice** (*m*) (*current, present*); SEE ALSO **liquid assets**

current account (*n*): ⟨Fin⟩ ouvrir un **compte courant**; ⟨Econ⟩ détérioration de la **balance des paiements** (*m*) **courants** (*current account balance*); le **déficit courant** a été de 608 millions de dollars en avril (*current account deficit*)

custody (*n*): ⟨Jur⟩ après six mois de **détention** (*f*) **préventive** (*preventive custody*); le seul inculpé à être maintenu **sous dépôt** (*m*) (*in custody/jail*); 140 des personnes arrêtées sont toujours **en garde** (*f*) **à vue** (*in police custody*); ⟨Soc⟩ recevoir la **garde** de l'enfant; donner à la mère le **droit de garde** (*f*) de l'enfant (*custody/care [esp. of child]*); SEE ALSO **detention**

custom (*n*): ⟨Comm⟩ retirer sa **clientèle** (*custom, business*); on risque de **perdre des clients** (*m*) (*lose custom/business*); ⟨Soc⟩ une règle fixée par les **usages** (*m*) **locaux** (*local custom*)

customer (*n*): ⟨Comm⟩ SNCF: grogne des **usagers** (*m*) (*customer, user [esp. of a public service]*); la **clientèle** se fait rare sur les vols sur long-courrier (*customers*); conserver des services peu rentables pour **fidéliser la clientèle** (*develop customer loyalty*)

customs (*npl*): ⟨Econ/Fisc⟩ tous les **droits** (*m*) **de douane** ont été supprimés entre les États membres (*customs duties*); la coopération **douanière** (*of/ by the customs*); l'office britannique des **douanes** (*f*) **et accises** (*customs and excise*)

cut (*n*): ⟨Econ⟩ subir une nouvelle **ponction** sur les revenus; pratiquer de réelles **coupes** (*f*) dans les dépenses

cut (*v*): **tailler dans** les programmes sociaux; **trancher dans** les effectifs et dans les équipements (*cut drastically*); ⟨Comm⟩ pour gagner les clients, les compagnies **bradent les prix** (*cut/slash prices*)

cut-back (*n*): ⟨Econ⟩ s'opposer à toute tentative de **compression** (*f*) **des effectifs** (*cut-back of staff*); **coupe** (*f*) **claire** dans la fonction publique: 37.000 suppressions d'emplois (*severe cutback*)

cut back (*v*): ⟨Econ⟩ le groupe **réduit** ses effectifs et ses investissements; SEE ALSO **reduce**

cut off (*v*): le blocus qui **isole** toujours la moitié du pays; ne pas faire l'autoroute, ce serait **enclaver** cette région (*cut off, isolate*)

cut-price (*adj*): ⟨Comm⟩ dans un **magasin de vente** (*f*) **au rabais** (*cut-price/ discount store*); **solder** les excédents céréaliers; **vendre à prix** (*mpl*) **réduits** pour écouler le stock (*sell at cut-price*)

cut short (*v*): les négociations ont **tourné court** (*be cut short; come to a sudden end*)

cycle (*n*): ⟨Econ⟩ le **cycle** d'inflation actuel ne saurait continuer

cyclical (*adj*): ⟨Econ⟩ des conditions d'ordre **conjoncturel**; du chômage **dû à la conjoncture** (*cyclical; according to circumstances*); la situation s'explique par des **facteurs** (*m*) **conjoncturels** (*cyclical factors*)

D

daily (*n/adj*): ⟨Journ⟩ les principaux **quotidiens** (*m*) de la presse écrite (*daily newspaper*); assurer le ménage **quotidien** des bureaux; une indemnité **journalière** (*daily, per day*)

damage (*n*): les **dégâts** (*m*) sont évalués à 80.000F; ⟨Ins⟩ certains **dommages** (*m*) sont pris en charge par l'assureur (*damage, losses*); ⟨Jur⟩ il demande 10.000F de **dommages et intérêts** (*damages*); l'ouverture d'une information pour **'dégradation de biens'** (*damage to property*); lors de la perte ou de la **détérioration** d'un article (*damage to/damaging* *of*); récupérer la somme de 2 milliards à titre de **préjudice** (*m*) (*damage, loss*)

damage (*v*): **dégrader** les ressources naturelles (*damage, cause damage to*); **porter atteinte** (*f*) à la crédibilité du gouvernement (*damage, harm*)

damaged (*adj*): ⟨Comm⟩ des produits **avariés** (*damaged*); le vendeur doit rembourser ou échanger les **articles** (*m*) **détériorés** (*damaged goods*)

damning (*adj*): le témoignage de son ancien collaborateur était **accablant**

data (*npl*): SEE **datum**

date (*n*): cette **échéance** va servir à concentrer les esprits (*expiry date*); ⟨Pol⟩ à la veille de l'**échéance électorale** de 1988 (*electoral date, election*)

date (*v*): le chèque est **daté** et signé (*dated*); la décentralisation **date de** 1982; la dernière augmentation **remonte à** janvier 1991 (*date from, go back to*)

datum (*n*): la pauvreté n'est pas une **donnée** objective et mesurable; disposer de **données** (*fpl*) scientifiques suffisamment fiables (*data*)

day (*n*): ⟨Ind⟩ une nouvelle **journée d'action** (*f*) nationale; les syndicats s'associent à la **journée revendicative** (*day of action/protest*); ⟨Soc⟩ un **centre spécialisé de jour** pour le troisième âge; un **accueil de jour** pour personnes âgées (*day centre*)

deadline (*n*): une **échéance** qui va obliger les deux antagonistes à s'entendre (*deadline*); la nouvelle **date butoir** est le 15 décembre (*deadline; final date*)

deadlock (*n*): menaces de grève: toujours l'**impasse** (*f*) (*deadlock*); tenter de **débloquer** les négociations (*end/break a deadlock*); SEE ALSO **stalemate**

deadlocked (*adj*): Haïti: les négociations **dans l'impasse** (*f*) (*deadlocked, in deadlock*)

deal (*n*): ⟨Comm⟩ le **marché** qu'il a proposé à la Pologne; les **affaires** (*f*) **conclues** l'an passé par Rhône-Poulenc (*deal; contract*)

deal (*v*): ⟨Comm⟩ **traiter** avec une entreprise étrangère (*deal/do business with*); **être dans le commerce** du bois (*deal/trade in*); SEE ALSO **traffic**

dealer (*n*): ⟨Comm⟩ chez les **négociants** (*m*) français de céréales (*dealer, trader*); un **trafiquant** en voitures volées (*dealer, trafficker*); SEE ALSO **arm**

dealing (*n*): ⟨Comm⟩ impliqué dans un **trafic d'armes** (*dealing in arms, arms dealing*); ⟨Fin⟩ des **opérations** (*f*) **de Bourse** illégales (*Stock Exchange dealings*); SEE ALSO **transaction**

dear (*adj*): la vie est **chère**; SEE ALSO **expensive**, **costly**

dearer (*adj*): ⟨Comm⟩ on a vu le brut **renchérir** constamment (*get dearer, increase in price*); **renchérir** de 1.000F le prix du mètre carré (*make dearer, increase the price of*)

death (*n*): le Sida: première cause de **décès** (*m*) de la population masculine africaine (*death*); ⟨Fisc⟩ le paiement des **droits** (*m*) **de succession** (*death* *duty*); ⟨Jur⟩ un juge qui prononce un **arrêt de mort**; encourir la **peine de mort** (*death penalty/sentence*)

debate (*n*): ⟨Pol⟩ les **débats** (*m*) **parlementaires** (*parliamentary debate*); une contribution à la **réflexion** sur l'avenir de la défense nationale (*debate, discussion*); la décision suscite de vives **polémiques** (*f*) (*[lively] debate, discussion*)

debate (*v*): la réforme proposée sera **débattue** en janvier

debenture (*n*): ⟨Fin⟩ l'émission d'une **obligation** correspond à un emprunt remboursable (*debenture*); l'argent des souscripteurs est placé sur le **marché obligataire** (*debenture market*); SEE ALSO **bond**

debit (*n*): ⟨Fin⟩ le compte de la société est **débiteur** de 50.000F; les États les plus fortement **débiteurs** (*in debit*); le **solde débiteur** était de 13.000F (*debit balance*); effectuer des versements par **virement** (*m*) **automatique**; régler par **prélèvement** (*m*) **automatique** (*direct debit*)

debit (*v*): ⟨Fin⟩ on **débitera** le compte de son créancier

debt (*n*): ⟨Econ⟩ l'**endettement** (*m*) du Tiers-Monde (*debt; being in debt*); le **surendettement** des ménages (*running up huge debts*); ils ont peur de se **surendetter** (*run up huge debts; overextend o.s.*); **s'endetter** pour un logement trop coûteux (*get/go into debt*); les pays **endettés** de l'hémisphère sud (*in debt*); soucieux de **désendetter** l'État (*get out of debt*); ⟨Fin⟩ le renoncement d'une **créance** (*debt, money owed*); des pratiques peu scrupuleuses de **recouvrement** (*m*) **de créances** (*debt recovery/collection*); SEE ALSO **bad debt, cancellation, indebtedness, write off**

debtor (*n*): ⟨Fin⟩ la condamnation du **mauvais payeur** étant des plus dissuasives (*bad debtor*)

decade (*n*): 4.500 emplois industriels auront disparu en une **décennie** (*decade, ten-year period*)

decay (*n*): URSS: **décomposition** (*f*) du pouvoir central; le **délabrement** des économies des pays de l'Est (*state of decay*)

deceit (*n*): une expertise a permis de conclure à une **supercherie** (*deceit, swindle, hoax*); SEE ALSO **deception**

deceive (*v*): SEE **delude**

decency (*n*): ⟨Jur⟩ coupable d'**outrage** (*m*) **aux bonnes mœurs** (*affront to public decency*)

decentralization (*n*): ⟨Pol⟩ la **décentralisation** opérée par la loi socialiste de 1982; ⟨Admin⟩ accélérer la **déconcentration** de la gestion; SEE ALSO **devolution**

decentralize (*v*): ⟨Econ⟩ moderniser et **décentraliser** le contrôle de gestion; on va **déménager en province** (*f*) l'atelier de Paris (*decentralize, move from the centre*); ceci a permis une certaine **déconcentration des décisions** (*f*) (*decentralizing of decision-taking*)

deception (*n*): ⟨Jur⟩ trois mois de prison ferme pour **tromperie** (*f*) sur la marchandise; SEE ALSO **fraud**

deceptive (*adj*): cette image **mensongère** de la situation

decide (*v*): ⟨Pol⟩ le conseil municipal vote et **arrête** le budget (*decide, finalize*); le gouvernement a **retenu** une série de neuf mesures concrètes (*decide on; adopt*); les élections **trancheront** (*decide/settle an issue*); ⟨Jur⟩ le ministère public **appréciera les suites à donner** (*decide what action to take*)

deciding (*adj*): le délai de livraison était **déterminant**; le rôle de l'État est **déterminant** (*a deciding/determining factor*)

decision (*n*): aucune **décision** n'a été arrêtée (*decision*); le gouvernement **se prononcera** rapidement (*reach/come to a decision*); ⟨Jur⟩ un **arrêt** de la cour d'appel; le pourvoi formé contre le **décret** de la cour (*decision, ruling*); casser un **jugement** (*decision/verdict [of a court]*); ⟨Pol/ Admin⟩ participer au processus de **prise** (*f*) **de décision** (*decision-taking*); l'accès des femmes aux **instances** (*f*) **de décision** (*decision-taking body*); disposer de **pouvoirs** (*mpl*) **décisionnels** (*decision-taking powers*); un journal lu par tous les **décideurs** (*m*) (*decision-maker*)

decisive (*adj*): le rôle de l'État est **déterminant** (*decisive; a decisive factor*); ⟨Pol⟩ une nouvelle diplomatie plus **volontariste** et plus affirmée (*decisive, firm, resolute*); SEE ALSO **determined**

declaration (*n*): ⟨Admin⟩ une **déclaration** de changement de domicile (*declaration*); ⟨Pol⟩ malgré l'**instauration** (*f*) de l'état d'urgence (*declaration, establishment*); ⟨Fisc⟩ remplir une **déclaration de revenu** et l'envoyer au fisc (*declaration of income*); il faut **déclarer** les indemnités reçues (*make a declaration [to the tax authorities]*)

declare (*v*): ⟨Admin⟩ **déclarer** une naissance à la mairie (*declare, register*); ⟨Fisc⟩ **déclarer** des objets de valeur à la douane (*declare [esp. to customs]*); ⟨Mil⟩ **déclarer la guerre** à un pays (*declare war*); SEE ALSO **independence**

declared (*adj*): son approbation **affichée** de cette politique; les partisans **avoués** de l'Europe dominent (*declared, open*); la destitution du roi était le **but avoué** (*declared/avowed aim*)

decline (*n*): la faillite économique s'accompagne d'un **déclin** moral; malgré la **dégradation** de l'économie britannique (*decline, deterioration*); le **fléchissement** de la demande de logements s'accentue; la consommation des biens manufacturés a connu un **repli** sensible (*decline, fall*); les libéraux sont **en recul** (*m*) (*on the decline*); SEE ALSO **decrease, fall**

decline (*v*): le marché **décroît** au rythme de 5% par an; la proportion d'actifs **diminue** régulièrement; le commerce mondial du pétrole a fortement **reculé** (*decline, reduce*); on est libre de **décliner** la nationalité (*decline, refuse*); le porte-parole du gouvernement **se refuse à tout commentaire** (*decline/refuse to comment*)

declining (*adj*): ⟨Econ⟩ des secteurs à la valeur ajoutée **déclinante** (*declining*); une production industrielle **en déclin** (*m*) (*declining, on the decline*)

decontrol (*v*): ⟨Econ⟩ la loi a **libéré** les loyers des logements vacants; laisser jouer la concurrence en **revenant à la liberté des prix** (*decontrol prices, end price controls*)

decontrolling (*n*): ⟨Econ⟩ le projet de **déréglementation** (*f*) des Télécoms; la **libéralisation** du ciel français se poursuit; la loi sur la **libération des loyers** (*rent decontrolling*); SEE ALSO **deregulation**

decrease (*n*): **baisse** (*f*) des commandes aux industries américaines; un net **fléchissement** de la criminalité en 1992; la **décrue** du chômage se confirme (*decrease, reduction*); **diminution** (*f*) des accidents de la route (*decrease, fall/drop in number*)

decrease (*v*): ⟨Econ/Comm⟩ les taux de natalité ont tendance à **décroître**; l'activité devrait **diminuer** d'autant l'an prochain (*decrease, fall*); l'écart **s'amenuisa** encore en 1992 (*decrease, diminish, dwindle*)

decree (*n*): ⟨Pol⟩ le SMIC sera augmenté par **arrêté** (*m*) du ministre; le parlement albanais a approuvé un **décret** présidentiel; avoir recours à des **ordonnances** (*f*) pour accélérer les choses (*decree*); l'État a **édicté une réglementation** dans ce sens (*issue a decree*)

decree (*v*): ⟨Pol⟩ la décision de **décréter** un embargo sur les livraisons d'armes; renvoyer les clandestins: plus facile à **décréter** qu'à réaliser (*decree, order; promulgate*)

decriminalization (*n*): ⟨Jur⟩ la **dépénalisation** des petits délits

decriminalize (*v*): ⟨Jur⟩ on parle de **dépénaliser** l'abus de stupéfiants; en Espagne, la consommation des stupéfiants est **dépénalisée**

deduct (*v*): **décompter** le nombre de jours de congé qu'il reste à prendre; il a fallu **défalquer** les 2.000 voix 'suspectes'; ⟨Fisc⟩ on peut **déduire** ses revenus professionnels de ses impôts (*deduct*); l'impôt sur le revenu est **prélevé à la source** par l'employeur (*deduct at source*); les pertes **se retranchent** des revenus imposables (*be deducted*)

deductible (*adj*): ⟨Fisc⟩ la **déductibilité** des dépenses de parrainage et de mécénat (*being deductible [esp. for taxation purposes]*); SEE ALSO **tax-deductible**

deduction (*n*): après **déduction** (*f*) des frais (*deduction*); après **défalcation** (*f*) des voix frauduleuses (*deduction, subtraction*); ⟨Fisc⟩ les **retenues** (*f*) pour la Sécurité sociale étaient de 6,5% (*deduction, stoppage*); une **retenue à la source** par l'employeur sur tous les salaires (*deduction/ stoppage at source*); les **prélèvements** (*m*) **sociaux** retranchés du revenu (*social security deductions*); SEE ALSO **contribution, stoppage**

deed (*n*): ⟨Jur⟩ la rédaction d'**actes** (*m*) est réservée aux professionnels compétents (*deed; legal document*); la loi oblige à passer par **acte notarié** les contrats portant sur des immeubles (*deed executed by notary*)

56

de-escalate (*v*): leur libération aida à **décrisper la situation** (*de-escalate/ defuse a situation*)

de-escalation (*n*): encore un signe de la nouvelle **décrispation** sino-soviétique; Irak-Koweït: la **désescalade** se poursuit (*de-escalation; reduction of tension*)

defamation (*n*): ⟨Jur⟩ la **diffamation** et l'injure sont des délits; SEE ALSO **libel, slander**

defamatory (*adj*): des propos **diffamants**; SEE ALSO **libellous**

default (*n*): ⟨Comm⟩ les exportateurs, assurés contre les **défauts** (*m*) **de paiement** (*default on payment*); **en cessation** (*f*) **de paiements,** la firme dépose son bilan (*in default on payment, unable to pay its debts*)

default (*v*): ⟨Comm⟩ l'affaire périclitant, la société **se trouve en cessation** (*f*) **de paiements** (*default on payments*)

defaulter (*n*): ⟨Fin⟩ un droit de gage sur la propriété d'un **débiteur défaillant** (*defaulter; person defaulting on payment*)

defaulting (*adj*): ⟨Comm⟩ un client **défaillant**; SEE ALSO **defaulter**

defeat (*n*): ⟨Pol⟩ la spectaculaire **déconfiture** du gouvernement battu; ce premier **désaveu** enregistré par le gouvernement; les **échecs** (*m*) subis par les Travaillistes; le **rejet** de la motion de censure

defeat (*v*): ⟨Mil⟩ pour **venir à bout** des milices nationalistes (*defeat*); ⟨Pol⟩ le ministre a **fait échec** (*m*) à l'amendement socialiste (*defeat, block*); le gouvernement a été **mis en échec** par cette explosion sociale (*defeat, bring down*); **être mis en minorité** (*f*) sur une motion de censure (*be defeated*)

defect (*n*): des **malfaçons** (*f*) imputables à la négligence (*defect, fault [due to bad workmanship]*); une garantie contre les **défauts** (*m*) **de fabrication** (*manufacturing defect*); rechercher des solutions aux **dys-fonctionnements** (*m*) de la justice pénale (*defect, malfunctioning*); SEE ALSO **drawback, flaw, shortcoming**

defect (*v*): **faire défection** (*f*) et demander le droit d'asile

defection (*n*): la **défection** d'une partie de son électorat; déjà des **défections** du nouveau gouvernement italien! (*defection; desertion*)

defector (*n*): un **transfuge** (*m*) du parti socialiste

defence (*n*): ⟨Jur⟩ les détenus n'ont pas pu rencontrer leurs **défenseurs** (*m*); l'**avocat** (*m*) **de l'accusé** plaida la légitime défense (*defence lawyer; counsel for the defence*); la **défense** se pourvoit en appel contre le verdict (*defence*); être requis comme **témoin** (*m*) **à décharge** (*defence witness*); le parti peut arguer **à sa décharge** l'énorme travail accompli (*in its defence*)

defendant (*n*): ⟨Jur⟩ l'**accusé** (*m*) nie avoir été mêlé à un trafic de faux papiers; tout **prévenu** (*m*) est présumé innocent (*defendant; person charged with a crime*); le **défendeur** ou la personne contre laquelle un procès est engagé (*defendant in civil action*)

defer (*v*): **différer** d'une semaine la discussion du projet (*defer, postpone, put back*); SEE ALSO **postpone, defer**

deferment (*n*): ⟨Mil⟩ un **report d'incorporation** (*f*) pour cause d'études supérieures; les jeunes Français peuvent bénéficier d'un **sursis d'incorporation** (*deferment of military service*)

deferred (*adj*): ⟨Mil⟩ en tant que **sursitaire** (*m*), il fera son service militaire plus tard (*deferred conscript*)

deficit (*n*): ⟨Econ/Fin⟩ l'aggravation du **déficit**; un audit révèle un **passif** de 18 milliards de francs; combler le **trou** du financement du logement social; le **solde négatif** n'était que de 13 millions en 1986 (*deficit*); **déficitaire** depuis 1980, la société a dégagé un bénéfice en 1992 (*in deficit*); la balance industrielle **affiche une ardoise** de deux milliards en juin (*show a deficit*); SEE ALSO **budget**

deflate (*v*): ⟨Econ⟩ une politique qui équivaut à **provoquer une récession économique par la déflation** (*deflate the economy*)

deflation (*n*): ⟨Econ⟩ la **déflation**, ou une diminution durable et forte des prix

deflationary (*adj*): ⟨Econ⟩ les **mesures** (*f*) **déflationnistes** annoncées dans le budget

defraud (*v*): les contribuables salariés ne pourront plus **frauder** le fisc

defrauding (*n*): être poursuivi pour travail clandestin et **escroquerie** (*f*) aux ASSEDIC

defray (*v*): la maison lui **rembourse ses frais** (*mpl*) (*defray expenses*)

defunct (*adj*): la **défunte** fédération yougoslave

defuse (*v*): on a tout fait pour **désamorcer** la tension; aider à **décrisper** la situation entre les anciennes superpuissances

defusing (*n*): un nouveau signe de la **décrispation** Est-Ouest (*defusing of tension; improvement of relations*)

defy (*v*): les députés votent la loi, **passant outre au** véto du gouvernement (*defy, flout*)

degenerate (*v*): le mouvement risque de **basculer dans** des affrontements violents; une dispute qui **dégénère en** bataille rangée (*degenerate, turn into*); l'origine des troubles, une manifestation qui a **mal tourné** (*degenerate, go wrong*)

degeneration (*n*): autant de signes de la **dégénérescence** des sociétés occidentales (*degeneration; degeneracy*)

delay (*n*): achever les travaux **sans retard** (*m*); il faut aller de l'avant **sans tarder** (*without delay*)

delay (*v*): si on **tarde** à négocier avec les mineurs (*delay; be slow in doing sth*); une victoire qui ne fait que **retarder** l'échéance (*delay, put off*); SEE ALSO **hold up**

delayed (*adj*): ⟨Comm⟩ conséquence de la grève: activité ralentie, courrier **en souffrance** (*delayed, held up*); un **retard de livraison** (*f*) très ennuyeux (*delayed delivery*); SEE ALSO **hold up**

delaying (*adj*): cette décision peut être interprétée comme une **manœuvre de retardement** (*m*) (*delaying tactic*)

delegate (*n*): deux **délégués** (*m*) représentent le personnel auprès de la direction; SEE ALSO **representative**

delegate (*v*): les États ont accepté de **déléguer** leurs pouvoirs à Bruxelles

delegation (*n*): une **délégation** de patrons de PME s'est entretenue avec le ministre (*delegation*); ⟨Admin⟩ la **délégation** du pouvoir (*delegation/delegating [esp. of power/responsibility]*)

deliberate (*adj*): le choix **intentionnel** de cette date (*deliberate, intentional*); des actes de détérioration **volontaire**; avoir la volonté **délibérée** de nuire (*deliberate, wilful*)

deliberate (*v*): le conseil **délibérera** sur la question (*deliberate; confer*)

deliberately (*adv*): lancé avec un profil **volontairement** bas; certains armateurs boycottent **sciemment** les ports français (*deliberately, on purpose*)

deliberation (*n*): ⟨Jur⟩ les **délibérations** (*f*) du tribunal avant jugement; le **délibéré** précède le prononcé de la sentence

delinquency (*n*): ⟨Jur⟩ la **délinquance juvénile** ne fait que s'aggraver (*juvenile delinquency/crime*)

delinquent (*n*): ⟨Jur⟩ un **délinquant** ou une personne ayant commis un délit

deliver (*v*): ⟨Comm⟩ **livrer** la marchandise en fin de mois

delivery (*n*): dans l'espoir d'un **arrivage** de nourriture (*delivery, consignment*); ⟨Econ⟩ les Douze vont financer la **livraison** de blé hongrois à Tirana (*delivery; supply*); la **livraison à domicile** est gratuite (*home delivery*); envoyer son courrier en recommandé avec **accusé** (*m*) **de réception** (*proof of delivery*)

delude (*v*): on ne peut longtemps **tromper** le consommateur (*delude, deceive*); le gouvernement **se leurre** s'il croit encore à la victoire; **se faire des illusions** (*f*) quant à la popularité de son programme (*delude/deceive o.s.*)

delusion (*n*): la citoyenneté européenne est une **leurre** (*delusion, illusion*)

demand (*n*): cette **exigence** fut rejetée par le conseil de Sécurité (*demand*); ⟨Pol⟩ les **revendications** (*f*) **d'indépendance** des Albanais du Kosovo (*demand for independence*); la Syrie renonce à ses **revendications territoriales** (*territorial demand*); ⟨Econ⟩ l'offre n'arrive pas à rattraper la **demande**; SEE ALSO **supply**

demand (*v*): les nationalistes **réclament** le statut de république; les ouvriers **revendiquent** de nouvelles hausses de salaire (*demand*); ⟨Fisc⟩ le fisc lui **réclame** 5,3 milliards de dollars (*issue a [tax] demand*); ⟨Jur⟩ **requérir** une peine de prison de dix ans (*demand, ask for [esp. in court of law]*)

democracy (*n*): la **démocratie** sort amoindrie de ce simulacre d'élection

democrat (*n*/*adj*): ⟨Pol⟩ la victoire est revenue aux **Démocrates** (*m*); le Congrès américain, où le parti **démocrate** domine

democratic (*adj*): ⟨Pol⟩ la conception que nous avons du **jeu démocratique** (*democratic process*)

democratically (*adv*): le gouvernement n'a pas été **démocratiquement** élu

demonstrate (*v*): ⟨Pol⟩ une centaine de personnes **manifestent** devant le consulat; SEE ALSO **display**

demonstration (*n*): un appel à la **manifestation** lancé sur les ondes; débrayages et **manifestations** hier à l'usine de Sochaux

demonstrator (*n*): affrontement sanglant entre police et **manifestants** (*m*)

demote (*v*): ⟨Admin⟩ plusieurs préfets sont **rétrogradés**

demotion (*n*): ⟨Admin⟩ ces **rétrogradations** (*f*) ont surpris, les intéressés ayant toujours été bien notés

denationalization (*n*): ⟨Econ⟩ 1986 vit le début des **dénationalisations** (*f*)

denationalize (*v*): ⟨Pol/Econ⟩ la droite promet de **dénationaliser** le secteur bancaire; partout on cherche à **désétatiser** un secteur public tentaculaire; SEE ALSO **privatize**

denial (*n*): apporter un **démenti** aux rumeurs de désunion; leurs **dénégations** (*f*) pèsent peu face aux expertises

deny (*v*): il **dément** avoir eu des contacts avec les Iraniens en 1980; il a **dénié** qu'il y ait eu des violations des droits de l'homme (*deny*); **se défendre** de brader l'héritage économique du pays (*deny a charge; deny*); **réfuter** les accusations de dumping; **opposer un démenti formel** à ces assertions (*deny/reject completely*); **dénier à** l'opposition son droit d'amender le texte (*deny, deprive*)

department (*n*): ⟨Admin⟩ la **direction** du développement urbain de la ville d'Argenteuil (*department*); travailler au **service des contentieux** (*legal department*)

departmental (*adj*): ⟨Pol⟩ une enquête au niveau **départemental**; lors du prochain **conseil général** (*meeting of departmental council*/conseil général); SEE ALSO **council**

depend (*v*): une force d'intervention rapide qui **relèverait de** l'OTAN (*depend on; come under the control of*); la progression des transports **est tributaire de** l'évolution de la conjoncture (*depend on*)

dependant (*n*): ⟨Fisc/Soc⟩ il avait déclaré deux **personnes** (*f*) **à charge**; cette pension ne peut être attribuée qu'à l'assuré, à l'exclusion de ses **ayants droit** (*m*) (*dependant; dependent relative*)

dependent (*adj*): ⟨Econ⟩ une économie totalement **tributaire** de l'aide internationale (*dependent on*); ⟨Soc/Fisc⟩ les frais de garde d'un vieux **parent à charge** (*f*) (*dependent relative*); la CGT réclame 200F par mois par **enfant** (*m*) **à charge** (*dependent child*)

deploy (*v*): ⟨Mil⟩ le dispositif naval **mis en place** en Méditerranée (*deploy*); l'immense activité qui **se déploie** actuellement en océan Indien (*be deployed*)

deployment (*n*): ⟨Mil⟩ un **déploiement** de forces sans précédent

depose (*v*): ⟨Pol⟩ le Conseil d'État l'ayant **destitué**, il fit appel au Conseil constitutionnel; les militaires qui ont **démis** le président

deposit (*n*): ⟨Comm⟩ verser un **acompte** de 30% du prix d'achat (*deposit; down payment*); la **caution** de l'acheteur s'élève à 10% du prix de vente; le **dépôt** est au maximum de 25% (*deposit*); **verser des arrhes** (*fpl*) pour l'achat d'une maison (*pay/put down a deposit*); SEE ALSO **down payment**

deposit (*v*): ⟨Fin⟩ **déposer** une forte somme sur un compte bancaire en Suisse (*deposit, pay in*)

depositing (*n*): le **dépôt** des ordures ménagères en vrac sur la voie publique

deposition (*n*): ⟨Pol⟩ la **destitution** du chef de l'État (*deposition, deposing*); ⟨Jur⟩ la **déposition** du témoin fut accablante (*deposition, testimony*); SEE ALSO **statement**

depositor (*n*): ⟨Comm⟩ un krach ne toucherait pas les **petits déposants** (*m*) (*small depositor/saver*)

depreciate (*v*): ⟨Fin⟩ voir ses biens **se déprécier** en un an (*depreciate, lose value*); le titre a **perdu** 13% en dix mois (*depreciate in value, lose*)

depreciation (*n*): ⟨Econ⟩ la **perte de valeur** (*f*) subie par le troupeau; compte tenu de l'**amortissement** (*m*), elle ne vaut plus que 5.000F (*depreciation*); ⟨Fin⟩ le PNB, diminué des **amortissements** (*mpl*) et des impôts indirects (*sums set aside to cover depreciation*)

depress (*v*): ⟨Comm⟩ la hausse des prix **déprime** l'activité économique (*depress*); ⟨Fin⟩ le nouveau reflux du dollar **déprime** le franc (*depress; reduce in value*)

depressed (*adj*): ⟨Econ⟩ un marché **déprimé** (*depressed*); après cinq années **moroses**, le marché a bondi en 1993; le yen s'effondre, la bourse **déprime** (*be in a depressed state*); des restrictions budgétaires dues à la **morosité économique** actuelle (*depressed state of the economy*)

depression (*n*): ⟨Econ⟩ le **marasme** actuel du marché; la grande **crise économique** et ses conséquences sociales; au pire de la **dépression** du début des années 1980 (*[economic] depression; slump*); la Bourse a eu un nouvel accès de **déprime** (*f*) mercredi (*depression, gloom*); la **morosité** persiste (*depression; depressed trading conditions*); SEE ALSO **slump**

deprivation (*n*): une violence qui se nourrit de la **misère** et du chômage (*deprivation, [extreme] poverty*)

deprive (*v*): les Russophones seront **privés** du droit de vote; ⟨Jur⟩ le militant nationaliste a **été déchu de** sa nationalité soviétique (*be deprived of*)

deprived (*adj*): aider les pauvres, les **déshérités** (*m*) de notre société (*deprived person*)

61

deputation (*n*): une **délégation** représentant le personnel; une **députation** des agriculteurs de la région (*deputation*); ⟨Pol⟩ candidat à la **députation** (*deputation; office of parliamentary député*); SEE ALSO **delegation**

deputize (*v*): **assurer l'intérim** (*m*) de la direction financière (*deputize; hold office in a temporary capacity*)

deputy (*adj/m*): ⟨Pol⟩ les **adjoints** (*m*) **au maire** font le gros du travail (*deputy mayor*); élu **député** (*m*), il représenta sa circonscription pendant 25 ans (*deputy; elected member of* Assemblée); membre du parti socialiste, et **député-maire** (*m*) de sa ville (*deputy and mayor*)

deregulate (*v*): SEE **decontrol**

deregulation (*n*): ⟨Econ⟩ prendre position sur le marché britannique en vue de sa prochaine **dérégulation** (*f*); grâce à la **déréglementation** et à la globalisation financière; la **suppression du contrôle de l'État** sur les lignes aériennes (*deregulation, removal of controls*)

derelict (*adj*): les **friches** (*f*) **industrielles** des régions en perte de vitesse (*derelict industrial land*)

description (*n*): des affichettes portant les photos et **signalement** (*m*) des malfaiteurs (*description*); un **descriptif des lieux** proposés en location (*description, descriptive document*)

desert (*v*): ⟨Mil⟩ des milliers de soldats **désertent** vers Djibouti (*desert, abscond*)

desertion (*n*): ⟨Mil⟩ de nombreuses **désertions** (*f*) de soldats gouvernementaux; ⟨Jur⟩ coupable d'**abandon** (*m*) **du foyer conjugal** (*desertion [esp. of one's spouse or children]*)

designate (*v*): un quartier **désigné** zone d'aménagement concerté [ZAC]; SEE ALSO **select**

design (*n*): la **conception** et le financement du projet (*design, designing*); SEE ALSO **aim**

designation (*n*): SEE **selection**

despair (*n*): ⟨Soc⟩ l'insécurité et la **désespérance** des cités (*feeling of despair/hopelessness*)

despair (*v*): face à la montée de la violence, il y a de quoi **se désespérer** (*despair, lose hope*)

destitute (*n/adj*): ⟨Soc⟩ le relogement des plus **démunis** (*m*) (*destitute*); même **les indigents** (*m*) seront tenus de payer le nouvel impôt (*the destitute*)

destitution (*n*): vivre dans le **dénuement** le plus complet (*destitution, deprivation*)

detach (*v*): il a été **détaché** à Athènes après la guerre (*detach to; send on detachment*)

detachment (*n*): ⟨Mil⟩ un **détachement** militaire y a été envoyé (*detachment*); ⟨Admin⟩ pendant son **détachement** dans une filiale à l'étranger

62

(*detachment, posting*); le personnel français **détaché** à l'étranger (*on detachment; on detached service*)

detail (*n*): donner des **précisions** (*f*) supplémentaires sur l'opération (*detail*); le ministre **détaille** les axes de sa réforme (*give details of*); sur l'écran s'affichent les **coordonnées** (*fpl*) de votre correspondant (*personal details*)

detailed (*adj*): un rapport extrêmement **fouillé** (*very detailed; thorough*); un **examen approfondi** des propositions soviétiques (*detailed examination/ study*)

detain (*v*): ⟨Jur⟩ la police pourra **détenir** tout suspect pendant une durée de sept jours (*detain, hold*); il a été **placé en détention** (*f*) **provisoire** d'avril à octobre (*detain in police custody awaiting trial*)

detained (*n/adj*): ⟨Jur⟩ le nombre de **détenus** (*m*) s'élève à 50.000 (*detained person; person held in detention*)

detainee (*n*): ⟨Jur⟩ des **personnes** (*f*) **gardées à vue** sans inculpation ni procès (*detainee [esp. for political reasons]*)

detaining (*n*): SEE **detention, questioning**

détente (*n*): ⟨Pol⟩ la **détente** en cours entre les deux super-puissances

detention (*n*): sa **détention** n'a duré que six mois (*detention, imprisonment*); la police peut procéder à des **gardes** (*f*) **à vue** de 45 jours renouvelables (*detention without charge*)

deter (*v*): la peine de mort peut **exercer un effet de dissuasion** (*f*) (*deter; be a form of deterrence*); SEE ALSO **deterrent**

deteriorate (*v*): le conflit risque de **s'aggraver**; le climat politique **se détériore** au fil des jours; la situation risque de **s'exacerber**; l'emploi continue à **se dégrader**; comment peut-on laisser **pourrir** une telle situation?; SEE ALSO **decline, worsen**

deterioration (*n*): la **détérioration** de leurs relations avec Israël; dans un contexte de **dégradation** (*f*) du climat social; face à l'**aggravation** (*f*) de leurs conditions de vie; ces affrontements illustrent le **pourrissement** de la situation; SEE ALSO **worsening**

determination (*n*): ce **volontarisme** n'a fait que s'accentuer (*determination, determined/ambitious attitude*)

determined (*adj*): ⟨Pol⟩ une Europe **volontariste**, capable de se lancer dans de grands projets (*determined, energetic*); SEE ALSO **decisive, vigorous**

deterrent (*n/adj*): ⟨Pol/Mil⟩ la **dissuasion nucléaire** nous a mis à l'abri de la guerre (*nuclear deterrent/deterrence*); mais l'**effet** (*m*) **dissuasif** demeure limité (*deterrent effect*)

devalue (*v*): ⟨Fin⟩ on **dévalua** le franc à trois reprises (*devalue*); le métier d'enseignant **se dévalorise** au fil des ans (*be devalued; lose prestige*)

devaluing (*n*): la progression du nombre des enseignants a facilité la **dévalorisation** de leur traitement (*devaluing, fall in value*)

develop (*v*): on vient de **mettre au point** une thérapeutique contre le sida (*develop, perfect*); la situation **évolue**, mais très lentement (*develop, evolve*); **aménager** une zone industrielle (*develop, equip*)

developer (*n*): ⟨Comm⟩ le **maître d'ouvrage** confie la réalisation des travaux au maître d'œuvre

developing (*adj*): venir en aide aux **pays en voie** (*f*) **de développement** (*developing countries*)

development (*n*): l'**évolution** (*f*) de la situation (*development*); nouveau **rebondissement** (*m*) dans le dossier du financement occulte des partis (*[unexpected] development*); ⟨Comm⟩ la **mise au point** de produits ou procédés de fabrication coûteux (*development, perfecting*); ⟨Fin⟩ cette région bénéficie d'une **prime d'aménagement** (*m*) **du territoire** (*special development grant*); les incitations fiscales attachées aux **zones** (*f*) **d'entreprise** (*special development area*)

deviate (*v*): ⟨Pol⟩ **s'écarter** de la ligne officielle du parti

deviation (*n*): toute **inflexion** (*f*) de la politique de rigueur compromettrait la reprise (*deviation/shift from*)

device (*n*): l'**engin** (*m*) a explosé, faisant deux morts (*[explosive] device*)

devolution (*n*): ⟨Pol/Admin⟩ des **dévolutions** (*f*) de souveraineté au profit d'institutions internationales (*devolution, devolving*); partisans de la 'dévolution', c'est-à-dire une large décentralisation administrative, politique et économique; l'institution d'une **autonomie limitée** (*devolution [esp. in GB]*); les thèses **girondines** commencent à s'imposer (*in favour of devolution/devolved government*)

devolve (*v*): une responsabilité qui **incombe** plutôt au Premier ministre (*devolve to*); SEE ALSO **decentralize**

devote (*v*): quelle part du produit national le gouvernement entend-il **affecter** à la défense?; SEE ALSO **allot**

diagram (*n*): le **schéma** illustre clairement la structure de l'entreprise

dialogue (*n*): une large **concertation** franco-espagnole sur la sécurité européenne (*dialogue, consultation*)

diary (*n*): cette visite, inscrite sur l'**agenda** (*m*) du ministre (*diary; timetable*)

die down (*v*): la tension en Cisjordanie semble **s'apaiser** (*die down, subside*); le conflit scolaire semble **en voie d'apaisement** (*m*) (*to be dying down/subsiding*)

difference (*n*): ⟨Pol⟩ **divergences** (*fpl*) entre écologistes et agriculteurs; le **différend** russo-ukrainien sur les armes nucléaires tactiques (*difference of opinion*); SEE ALSO **disagreement**

differential (*n*): ⟨Econ⟩ les **écarts** (*m*) de revenus s'accroissent (*differential, disparity*); l'**écart de prix** peut aller du simple au double (*price differential*); la **fourchette des rémunérations** a été jusqu'ici très étroite (*wage differentials*)

dilapidated (*adj*): compte tenu de l'**état de délabrement** (*m*) de l'économie (*dilapidated/run-down state; state of decay*)

dimension (*n*): les grands groupes industriels d'**envergure** (*f*) européenne (*dimension, scale*); SEE ALSO **size**

dip (*v*): ⟨Econ⟩ la courbe d'activité des femmes **accuse un fléchissement** entre 25 et 40 ans (*dip, fall*)

direct (*v*): ⟨Educ⟩ on **oriente** trop d'élèves vers certains baccalauréats; **infléchir** la publicité dans le sens de la sécurité routière; SEE ALSO **manage**

direction (*n*): ⟨Pol⟩ donner un nouveau **tournant** aux relations franco-allemandes (*direction, course*); le **virage** de 1983 explique la défaite de 1986 (*change of direction*); définir les **grandes orientations** (*f*) de sa politique extérieure (*main directions*)

directive (*n*): ⟨Admin/Pol⟩ Education: une **directive** sur l'enseignement de l'histoire de l'URSS; une **directive** récente pour le traitement des eaux urbaines (*directive, instruction*)

director (*n*): ⟨Admin⟩ deux **dirigeants** (*m*) de la société ont été arrêtés; les **administrateurs** (*m*) de la société (*[company] director*); SEE ALSO **board**, **directorate**

directorate (*n*): ⟨Admin⟩ nommé président du **directoire** (*directorate, executive board*); SEE ALSO **board**

directory (*n*): consulter les pages bleues de l'**annuaire** (*m*) (*directory [esp. telephone]*)

disability (*n*): ⟨Ind⟩ accident de travail: **inaptitude** (*f*) physique (*disability*); un salarié atteint d'une **invalidité** le rendant inapte à exercer une activité (*disability, handicap*); une rente d'**incapacité** (*f*) **permanente** (*permanent disability*)

disagree (*v*): les deux pays **sont en plein désaccord** (*m*) à ce sujet (*disagree; be in total disagreement*)

disagreement (*n*): le **désaccord** entre les Douze sur l'avenir politique de la Communauté; il donna sa démission après son éclatant **différend** (*m*) avec le Premier ministre; les **divergences** (*f*) Élysée-Matignon (*disagreement, difference of opinion*); Paris-Alger: la **brouille** persiste (*disagreement, quarrel*); SEE ALSO **difference**, **relation**

disappointment (*n*): son échec fut une cruelle **déception** pour les centristes; c'est une **déconvenue** pour le président socialiste

disarray (*n*): après le sommet raté, c'est le **désarroi** dans le camp occidental (*disarray, confusion*); pour éviter une **débandade** lors des prochaines élections (*disarray; rout*)

disaster (*n*): le bassin, **sinistré** par la fermeture des houillères (*disaster-stricken; badly hit*); la commune a été déclarée **zone** (*f*) **sinistrée** (*disaster area*)

disburse (v): ⟨Fin⟩ l'État devra **débourser** plus de 1,6 milliard (*disburse, pay out*)

disbursement (n): ⟨Fin⟩ les **débours** (m) ou les sorties d'argent (*disbursement, expenditure*)

discharge (n): ⟨Jur⟩ la demande de **remise** (f) **en liberté** fut rejetée; la **libération** des prisonniers ne saurait tarder (*discharge, release*); bénéficier d'une **libération conditionnelle** (*conditional discharge*); la **relaxe** des mutins de la prison des Baumettes (*discharge, acquittal*); SEE ALSO **freeing, release**

discharge (v): ⟨Jur⟩ il sera **libéré** lundi prochain; la cour d'appel l'a **relaxé** au bénéfice du doute (*discharge, release*); le juge d'instruction **rend une ordonnance de non-lieu** (*discharge; dismiss case for lack of evidence*); ⟨Econ⟩ **débaucher** du personnel (*discharge, lay off*); SEE ALSO **lay off, redundant**

disclaim (v): ils **déclinent** toute responsabilité pour les avaries

discontent (n): la **contestation** étudiante reprend de plus belle; nouvelle **grogne** (f) au pays Basque; les grèves et autres manifestations de **mécontentement** (m); SEE ALSO **dissatisfaction**

discord (n): le parti, agité par de profondes **dissensions** (f); provoquant des **divisions** (f) au sein de l'équipe; **semer la division** dans les rangs de l'opposition; un diviseur qui **crée la zizanie** au sein du parti (*spread discord, create disharmony/division*)

discount (n): ⟨Comm⟩ un **rabais** de 20% sur le montant de la facture; consentir aux adhérents des **remises** (f) importantes; une **réduction** de 15% sur les commandes reçues avant le 31 mai (*discount, reduction, rebate*); **faire un escompte** de 4% pour tout paiement au comptant (*give a discount*); le groupe se renforce dans l'habillement **discount** (m) (*discount*); vendre **à des prix discount** (*at discount prices*)

discount (v): ⟨Comm⟩ **vendre au rabais** des fins de série (*discount; sell at reduced price*)

discriminate (v): des mesures qui **défavorisent** les petites entreprises (*discriminate against, put at a disadvantage; handicap*)

discrimination (n): il y avait **discrimination** (f) illégale (*discrimination*); dénoncer d'éventuelles **pratiques** (f) **discriminatoires** (*discrimination [esp. racial]*); un **traitement de faveur** injustifié (*[positive] discrimination, preferential treatment*); SEE ALSO **preferential**

discuss (v): le conseil municipal a **délibéré** les points suivants (*discuss, debate*); **s'entretenir de** la question avec son homologue français (*discuss/ have discussions on*); l'opposition est prête à **dialoguer** avec le gouvernement (*discuss; open a dialogue*)

discussion (n): un **entretien** entre le ministre et son homologue français (*discussion, talks*); organiser une **tribune** sur les questions sociales (*discussion, forum, debate*)

disengagement (*n*): ⟨Pol⟩ le **désengagement** américain de la région; ⟨Econ⟩ le **désengagement** de l'État fait l'affaire du secteur privé; SEE ALSO **withdrawal**

disengage (*v*): SEE **withdraw**

dishonest (*adj*): des fonds détournés par des intermédiaires **indélicats** (*dishonest*); les contrevenants en matière de **publicité** (*f*) **mensongère** (*dishonest advertising*)

dishonesty (*n*): accusé d'**indélicatesse** (*f*), il fut démis de ses fonctions

dismiss (*v*): ⟨Pol⟩ le ministre a été **démissionné** par le Président; **démettre** son ministre de ses fonctions (*dismiss from office/post*); ⟨Ind⟩ **licencier** sans préavis 55 employés (*dismiss, sack*); quinze journalistes vont **être remerciés** (*be dismissed/sacked*); ⟨Jur⟩ le juge a **rendu un arrêt de non-lieu** (*m*) (*dismiss a charge*); **être débouté** de son recours (*have a case/appeal dismissed*); SEE ALSO **sack**

dismissal (*n*): des fautes sanctionnées par mutations ou **mises** (*fpl*) **à l'écart**; le **licenciement** de la moitié des effectifs; SEE ALSO **removal, sacking**

disobedience (*n*): SEE **civil**

disobey (*v*): SEE **infringe**

disparity (*n*): on observe de grandes **disparités** (*f*) d'un département à l'autre; des **écarts** (*m*) importants existent entre Paris et la province; l'**inégalité** (*f*) de l'offre et de la demande (*disparity; difference*)

dispatch (*n*): ⟨Comm⟩ l'**expédition** (*f*) des marchandises; le service responsable de l'**acheminement** du courrier (*dispatch, dispatching*)

dispatch (*v*): la décision française de **dépêcher** dans la région des chasseurs de mines; SEE ALSO **forward**

dispensation (*n*): ces pays bénéficient d'une **dérogation** jusqu'en 1998; le **régime dérogatoire** actuel est supprimé (*special dispensation/arrangements*); un droit qui lui a été accordé **par dérogation** (*as a special dispensation, exceptionally*); SEE ALSO **exception**

display (*v*): côté français, on **affiche** une complète satisfaction (*display, exhibit*); il appelle au public de **faire preuve** (*f*) de vigilance (*display, show*)

displease (*v*): le nouveau découpage de l'année scolaire **mécontente** les professionnels du tourisme; les propositions de Moscou **mécontentent** les dirigeants baltes

displeasure (*n*): SEE **dissatisfaction**

disposable (*adj*): ⟨Econ⟩ le **revenu disponible** après paiement des impôts directs (*disposable income*); ⟨Fisc⟩ les prestations représentent plus de 20% du **revenu disponible brut des ménages** (*disposable domestic income/revenue*)

disposal (*n*): la **cession** de leurs intérêts miniers (*disposal, selling off*); les moyens que la France peut **mettre à sa disposition** (*put at the disposal of*)

dispose

dispose (*v*): ⟨Comm⟩ le groupe va **se séparer de** ses opérations financières; la firme va licencier du personnel et **céder** certaines activités; les Polonais ont du mal à **écouler** leur production (*dispose of, sell off*); SEE ALSO **sell**

disposing (*n*): la **cession** de leurs activités minières (*disposing of; selling off*); SEE ALSO **sale**

dispute (*n*): ⟨Pol⟩ il n'y a aucune **contestation** sur le fond du problème; les **désaccords** (*m*) opposant les particuliers et l'administration (*dispute*); rechercher une issue au **contentieux** communautaire; les **démêlés** (*m*) perpétuels du Caire avec Washington (*dispute, disagreement*); ⟨Jur⟩ une des principales sources de **chicane** (*f*) dans les copropriétés; le **litige** opposant les salariés à leurs employeurs (*dispute, contention*); un locataire **en litige** avec son propriétaire (*in dispute/litigation*); SEE ALSO **labour**

disputed (*adj*): ⟨Pol/Mil⟩ les deux zones encore **litigieuses** (*disputed; contentious*)

disquiet (*n*): les Européens ne cachent pas leur **inquiétude** (*f*) (*disquiet*); ce serait un sujet de **grave inquiétude** pour la France (*grave disquiet, dismay*); l'Égypte **s'inquiète** de la situation des travailleurs égyptiens en Irak (*express disquiet*)

disrupt (*v*): les services des Finances **perturbés** par des arrêts de travail

disruption (*n*): il y aura de nouvelles **perturbations** (*f*) dans le trafic aérien

dissatisfaction (*n*): une population en proie à un **mécontentement** croissant (*dissatisfaction*); le ministre a exprimé son **insatisfaction** (*f*) devant la parité actuelle du yen (*dissatisfaction; displeasure*); SEE ALSO **discontent**

disseminate (*v*): SEE **broadcast**

dissemination (*n*): des activités liées à la **diffusion** de l'information

dissociate (*v*): ⟨Pol⟩ son souci a été de **se démarquer** de ses ministres; **se désolidariser** de ses collègues du conseil municipal; **prendre leurs distances** (*f*) par rapport aux indépendantistes (*dissociate/distance o.s.*)

dissolution (*n*): pacte de Varsovie: **dissolution** (*f*) des structures militaires (*dissolution; breaking up, dismantling*); ⟨Pol⟩ la **dissolution du Parlement** et la tenue d'élections législatives (*dissolution of Parliament*)

dissolve (*v*): ⟨Pol⟩ le Président menace de **dissoudre** le Parlement

dissuasion (*n*): notre concept de **dissuasion** (*f*) s'est révélé inefficace et inadapté (*dissuasion, deterrence*); SEE ALSO **deterrent**

dissuasive (*adj*): une surveillance feutrée, une présence **dissuasive** (*dissuasive; deterrent*)

distraint (*n*): ⟨Jur⟩ obtenir une **saisie-arrêt** sur les comptes bancaires de la société pour factures impayées

distribute (*v*): son portrait, **diffusé** dans les ports et dans les aéroports (*distribute, circulate*)

distribution (*n*): une **répartition** très inégale de la population (*distribution, spread*); le **partage** de la richesse nationale (*distribution, sharing out*); ⟨Journ⟩ des journaux dont on a bloqué la **diffusion** locale; SEE ALSO **sharing out, spread**

district (*n*): ⟨Pol/Admin⟩ un **quartier** défavorisé de la banlieue nord (*district*); un **canton** de l'Isère particulièrement sensible; un des **arrondissements** de Paris les plus touchés par ce phénomène (*administrative district*)

distrust (*n*): la **défiance** socialiste à l'égard de l'argent; une certaine **méfiance** de l'opinion face aux syndicats

disturbance (*n*): **mouvements** (*m*) **d'humeur** et manifestations hier à Alger; alors que des **troubles** (*m*) avaient éclaté à Madrid (*disturbance, unrest*); on ne peut leur reprocher directement un **trouble de l'ordre public** (*disturbance of the peace*); le **tapage nocturne** et d'autres troubles de voisinage sont sévèrement réprimés (*disturbance of the peace at night*)

disturbed (*adj*): ⟨Soc⟩ une vie familiale très **perturbée** (*disturbed*); en échec scolaire, et **issu d'un milieu familial perturbé** (*product of a broken family; from a disturbed family background*)

disused (*adj*): la reconversion des sites **désaffectés** (*disused, abandoned*)

diversification (*n*): ⟨Econ⟩ devant la chute des commandes, la société envisage un **redéploiement** industriel (*diversification [into other industry/activity]*)

diversify (*v*): ⟨Econ⟩ la crise conduit la région à **diversifier ses activités** (*f*); la société cherche à **se diversifier** activement dans l'électronique (*diversify, move into a new area of activity*)

divide (*n*): SEE **division**

divide (*v*): se mettre d'accord pour **partager** le marché (*divide; share*)

divided (*adj*): le Congrès américain reste très **partagé** sur la question (*divided; in disagreement*); les avis sont presque **également partagés** (*equally divided*)

dividend (*n*): ⟨Fin⟩ la rémunération d'une action s'appelle le **dividende**

dividing (*n*): la **répartition** des pouvoirs s'est faite sans difficultés (*dividing, division, sharing out*)

division (*n*): le **partage** de la Corse en deux départements (*division, partition*); la décentralisation dépasse les **clivages** (*m*) **politiques** (*political divisions*); ⟨Agric⟩ le remembrement a résolu les problèmes causés par le **morcellement des terres** (*division of land into small lots*); SEE ALSO **split**

divorce (*n*): ⟨Jur⟩ le **divorce** par consentement mutuel (*divorce*); former une **demande en divorce** (*divorce petition*)

divorce (*v*): ⟨Jur⟩ **divorcer** pour cause de rupture de vie commune; une Française sur trois finit par **divorcer** (*divorce; obtain a divorce*)

dock (*n*): ⟨Jur⟩ Israël **en accusation** (*f*) devant les Nations unies (*in the dock*); Iran **mis au banc des accusés** par un tribunal de Genève; **faire le procès** du PC soviétique (*put in the dock*)

doctrinaire (*adj*): les méfaits du libéralisme **systématique** (*doctrinaire, unbending*)

domestic (*adj*): ⟨Pol⟩ les **affaires** (*f*) **intérieures** du pays (*domestic affairs/ politics*); une affaire **franco-française** (*domestic/internal [Fr]*); ⟨Écon⟩ un quart du taux de croissance était expliqué par la **demande intérieure** (*domestic demand*); la **consommation nationale** se tasse (*domestic consumption*); la forte demande du **marché intérieur** (*domestic market*); la croissance du **produit intérieur brut** aux États-Unis (*Gross Domestic Product*); ⟨Soc⟩ l'**aide** (*f*) **ménagère à domicile** à laquelle ont droit les +65 ans (*domestic/home help*); SEE ALSO home

dominance (*n*): ⟨Pol⟩ la **prépondérance** internationale des États-Unis (*dominance; supremacy*); mettre tout en œuvre pour renforcer leur **hégémonie** (*f*) (*dominance, ascendancy*); SEE ALSO **domination**

dominant (*adj*): ⟨Pol⟩ leur position **prédominante** pourrait être remise en cause; ⟨Comm⟩ une situation de **position** (*f*) **dominante** qui porte atteinte à la concurrence (*dominant trading position; semi-monopoly position*); le groupe tente de **verrouiller le marché** de l'informatique (*gain a dominant position*)

domination (*n*): ⟨Pol⟩ la crainte d'une **hégémonie** soviétique n'existe plus; un pays centralisé et marqué par la **prépondérance** serbe (*domination, hegemony*); SEE ALSO **dominance**

donation (*n*): ⟨Fin⟩ faire un **don** à une organisation caritative; des **contributions** (*f*) pour financer la campagne électorale

dormitory (*n*): un **grand ensemble dortoir** (*m*) pour les usines automobiles (*dormitory estate/suburb*)

doubt (*n*): malgré les **réticences** (*f*) exprimées par certains militaires (*doubt, misgiving*)

doubt (*v*): on peut **s'interroger** sur le bien-fondé de cette décision (*doubt; have doubts/misgivings*)

dove (*n*): ⟨Pol⟩ les anciens faucons jouent les **colombes** (*f*)

down payment (*n*): ⟨Comm⟩ verser un **acompte** de 30% du prix achat; un crédit immobilier classique: un emprunt de 20 ans, avec 20% d'**apport** (*m*) (*down payment, deposit*)

downturn (*n*): ⟨Écon⟩ **baisse** (*f*) de l'activité économique au premier trimestre; le **repli** sensible dans la production de voitures de luxe (*downturn, fall*); **tassement** (*m*) des ventes aux États-Unis (*downturn, slowing down*)

draft (*n/adj*): un **brouillon**, plein de ratures et de surcharges (*[rough] draft [esp. of letter]*); ⟨Admin⟩ en présentant les premières **esquisses** (*f*) du Xe Plan (*draft, outline*); ⟨Pol⟩ le **projet de budget** pour 1993–4 (*draft budget*); un **avant-projet de loi** fixe le cadre de la réforme (*draft bill*)

draft (*v*): faire **rédiger** un acte par un notaire (*draft, draw up*); ⟨Mil⟩ **être incorporé** dans un régiment d'infanterie (*be drafted/called up*); SEE ALSO draw up

drafter (*n*): les **rédacteurs** (*m*) du traité; dans l'esprit des **rédacteurs** du projet

drainage (*n*): le service d'**assainissement** (*m*) comprend aussi le service des eaux usées; des bidonvilles privés de tout système de **drainage** (*m*); SEE ALSO **sewerage**

drastic (*adj*): coupes **drastiques** dans les effectifs des chantiers navals

drastically (*adv*): les prix garantis seront **drastiquement** réduits (*drastically*); **amputer** les salaires des fonctionnaires (*cut/reduce drastically*)

draw (*v*): ⟨Fin⟩ **tirer un chèque** sur son compte (*draw/make out/write a cheque*); payer avec un chèque **tiré sur** une banque italienne (*drawn on*)

drawback (*n*): c'est là le **défaut** majeur de ces propositions (*drawback, defect*); ces réformes cumulent trois sortes d'**inconvénient** (*m*) (*drawback, disadvantage*)

drawer (*n*): ⟨Fin⟩ le **tireur** d'un chèque

draw up (*v*): **dresser** une liste de candidats au poste (*draw up*); les plans ont été **établis** par un architecte (*draw up, draft*); SEE ALSO **draft**

drawing up (*n*): la **rédaction** du contrat d'assurance (*drawing up, drafting*)

drift (*n*): il faut empêcher une **dérive** terroriste de l'islamisme (*drift, drift towards*); ⟨Econ⟩ la **désertification des campagnes** menace le Limousin tout entier; l'**exode** (*m*) **rural** vers les villes s'accentue (*drift from the land; rural depopulation*)

drive (*n*): ⟨Comm⟩ une vigoureuse **campagne** pour promouvoir les produits 'verts' (*drive, campaign*); SEE ALSO **publicity**

drive (*v*): ⟨Econ⟩ désormais la demande intérieure **tire** la croissance

driving force (*n*): ⟨Econ⟩ le secteur privé a été la **locomotive** de la croissance; l'exportation n'est plus le **moteur** de l'expansion (*driving force, mainspring*)

drop (*n*): ⟨Econ/Comm⟩ Acier: **recul** (*m*) de la production; Japon: **recul** des ventes des grands magasins; SEE ALSO **fall**, **decline**

drop (*v*): ⟨Comm⟩ les ventes ont **baissé** de 12%; SEE ALSO **decline**, **fall**

drop out (*n*): ⟨Soc⟩ un refuge de **marginaux** (*mpl*) et de délinquants

drought (*n*): intervenir en faveur des victimes de la **sécheresse**; une mauvaise récolte due à une longue **sécheresse**

drug (*n*): la législation draconienne sur les **stupéfiants** (*m*) (*drugs*); l'affaire a été confiée à la **brigade des stupéfiants** (*drug squad*)

dual-carriageway (*n*): la construction d'une nouvelle **route à 2 × 2 voies**; la **quatre-voies** qui va de Chartres à Dreux

due (*adj*): ⟨Fin⟩ restituer la **somme due** (*sum due/owing*); l'**échéance** (*f*), ou le terme d'un délai (*falling due [esp. of payment]*); le premier règlement **échoit** le 31 du mois (*fall due*); ⟨Jur⟩ prévoir un contrat de travail **en bonne [et due] forme** (*in due form*)

dues (*npl*) la **cotisation** des adhérents seule permet au syndicat de survivre (*dues, membership fee, contribution*); s'acquitter de sa **cotisation syndicale** (*union dues*)

dull (*adj*): ⟨Fin⟩ un marché aussi **terne** que le marché parisien (*dull, lacklustre*); **morosité** (*f*) à la Bourse de Paris (*dull trading conditions*)

duly (*adv*): ⟨Admin⟩ retourner un formulaire **dûment** rempli et signé

dumping (*n*): l'incinération et la **mise en décharge** (*f*) des déchets (*dumping/ tipping of refuse*); ⟨Comm/Econ⟩ vendre ainsi moins cher à l'étranger équivaut à pratiquer du **dumping**

duplicate (*n*): ⟨Admin/Jur⟩ en aucun cas il ne sera délivré de **duplicata** (*m*); un **duplicata** du bon de commande (*duplicate, copy*)

durable (*n/adj*): ⟨Econ⟩ hausse des commandes de **biens** (*mpl*) **durables** (*durables, durable goods*)

duty (*n*): ⟨Fisc⟩ des **droits** (*m*) **de douane** qui frappent les produits d'exportation (*duty, customs duty*); ⟨Admin⟩ en exécution de la **mission** qui lui avait été confiée (*duties*); les bureaux **assurant la permanence** des dimanches et jours fériés (*on duty; manned, open*); SEE ALSO **excise**

duty-free (*adj*): ⟨Fisc⟩ l'admission **en franchise** (*f*) des véhicules automobiles; on peut importer ces articles **en franchise de droits** (*m*) (*duty/tax-free*)

dwell (*v*): le domicile n'est pas nécessairement un lieu où on **habite**

dwelling (*n*): l'**habitation** (*f*) comprend aussi des dépendances; la location d'une **maison d'habitation** (*dwelling house*)

E

earlier (*adj*): ⟨Econ⟩ les entreprises situées **en amont** dans la chaîne de production (*earler, at an earlier stage*)

early (*adj*): ⟨Pol⟩ on annonce des **élections** (*f*) **anticipées** pour le 18 juin (*early elections*); ⟨Jur⟩ il peut espérer une **libération** (*f*) **anticipée** (*early release from captivity*); cette activité n'est en France qu'aux **balbutiements** (*m*) (*at an early stage of development; in its infancy*); SEE ALSO **retirement**

earmark (*v*): doublement du budget **affecté** à l'environnement (*earmark*); **affecter des sommes** (*f*) à l'amélioration des installations (*earmark funds/money*)

earn (*v*): **gagner** à peine plus que le SMIC (*earn, be paid*); activités qui pourraient lui **valoir** une peine de prison (*earn, cost*)

earnings (*n*): le **gain** horaire moyen des ouvriers; une baisse des **rémunérations** (*f*) dans le secteur des assurances; réduction du temps de travail sans **perte** (*f*) **de revenu** (*loss of earnings*)

ease (*v*): ⟨Econ⟩ la législation visant à **libérer** le commerce des céréales (*ease restrictions on*); ⟨Fin⟩ l'indice boursier **a fléchi** légèrement hier (*ease, fall slightly*); l'activité **a baissé** hier (*ease off, fall slightly*)

easing (*n*): ⟨Econ/Fin⟩ un **relâchement** de la politique monétaire française; un nouvel **assouplissement du crédit** (*easing of credit*); SEE ALSO **relaxing**

ecological (*adj*): SEE **green**

ecology (*n*): ⟨Pol⟩ l'arrivée d'un nouveau courant, l'**écologisme** (*m*) (*the ecology movement*)

economic (*adj*): ⟨Econ/Educ⟩ la **planification** soviétique était de conception assez rigide (*economic planning*); le ralentissement de la **conjoncture** (*general economic situation*); l'amélioration que les **conjoncturistes** (*m*) annoncent pour 1994 (*economic specialist*)

economics (*npl*): ⟨Econ/Educ⟩ l'**économie** (*f*) **politique**, la filière la plus suivie; la **[science] économique** n'est pas une science exacte

economy (*n*): ⟨Econ⟩ l'**économie** (*f*) du pays en dépend (*economy*); permettant des **économies d'échelle** (*f*) significatives (*economies of scale*)

edict (*n*): ⟨Pol⟩ le salaire minimum a été augmenté par **décret** (*m*) sur décision du gouvernement; SEE ALSO **decree**

editing (*n*): la **rédaction** de tracts électoraux (*editing, writing*); la **mise au point** d'un texte (*editing*)

editor (*n*): ⟨Journ⟩ ancien **rédacteur** (*m*) **en chef** du quotidien (*chief editor*); après quinze ans comme **rédacteur politique** de la revue (*political editor*)

editorial (*n*): ⟨Journ⟩ *Le Monde* consacra son **article** (*m*) **de tête** à l'Algérie (*editorial, leader, leading article*); dans les **rédactions** (*f*) des chaînes publiques (*editorial office*); (*adj*) il assure la direction **rédactionnelle** de l'hebdomadaire (*editorial*)

educate (*v*): le lycée **scolarise** la population la plus aisée (*educate, provide education/schooling for*)

education (*n*): ⟨Educ⟩ le délabrement de notre **système** (*m*) **éducatif** (*education system*); la rénovation des **formations** (*f*) universitaires (*education/training; course of study*); ⟨Educ/Ind⟩ proposer au personnel des cours de **formation permanente** (*continuing education*)

educational (*adj*): la création d'une **chaîne éducative** (*educational channel [TV]*)

effect (*n*): l'industrie subit le **contrecoup** d'un quasi-doublement de la TVA; avoir de lourdes **incidences** (*f*) sur la rentabilité de l'opération (*effect, impact*); la Constitution est annulée, **à compter du** 23 juin (*with effect* *from*); l'**entrée** (*f*) **en vigueur** du cessez-le-feu (*coming into effect*); la réforme est **entrée en vigueur** lundi dernier (*come into effect*); une mesure qui **prend effet** (*m*) à partir de 1995 (*come/be put into effect*); les accords **entrent en application** (*f*) tout de suite (*come into effect/ operation*); pour **concrétiser** ces bonnes intentions (*put into effect*); la **mise en place** de ces mesures serait très coûteuse (*putting into effect*); SEE ALSO **implement, implementation**

effect (*v*): le transfert de fonds **s'est opéré** à l'insu des autorités (*be effected/ carried out*)

effective (*adj*): les précautions ne sont pas **efficaces** à 100%; les mesures **entrent en vigueur** dès lundi prochain (*become effective*)

efficiency (*n*): l'**efficacité** (*f*) du système n'est plus à démontrer; garder un niveau d'**efficience** (*f*) équivalent; la fatigue **réduit les performances** (*f*) (*impair efficiency*); ⟨Econ⟩ le système des **primes** (*f*) **de rendement** (*efficiency bonus*)

efficient (*adj*): ⟨Econ⟩ les 20 entreprises les plus **performantes**; un des secteurs les plus **performants** de l'économie (*efficient, dynamic*)

efficiently (*adv*): gérer **efficacement** son budget

elect (*v*): ⟨Pol⟩ **élire** un député (*elect*); **être élu** à une majorité écrasante (*be elected*); les militants socialistes l'ont **plébiscité** (*elect with overwhelming majority*)

elected (*adj*): ⟨Pol⟩ un référendum sur la création d'une présidence **élective** (*elected*); les **élus** (*m*) et les responsables économiques de la région (*elected representative*)

election (*n*): ⟨Pol⟩ lors de l'**élection** (*f*) du maire; l'échec de la majorité lors des **consultations** (*f*) cantonales; la prochaine **échéance électorale** en mars

electioneering (*n*): la **campagne électorale** est à peine commencée (*electioneering, election campaign*); son discours constitue de la **propagande électorale** pour le parti (*electioneering, electoral propaganda*)

elector (*n*): ⟨Pol⟩ l'**électeur** (*m*) se rend aux urnes deux fois par an, en moyenne; apprécié par toutes les **électrices** (*f*)

electoral (*adj*): ⟨Pol⟩ le projet de **redécoupage** (*m*) **électoral** (*redrawing of electoral boundaries*); un scrutin marqué par une forte **participation** (*electoral turnout*); la deuxième **circonscription** [électorale] du Mans (*electoral ward/constituency*); SEE ALSO **constituency, fraud**

electorate (*n*): ⟨Pol⟩ le **corps électoral** est appelé à nouveau à se prononcer; un **électorat** majoritairement de gauche; les **électeurs** (*m*) ont boudé la consultation (*electorate, the electors*)

elementary (*adj*): ⟨Educ⟩ l'**enseignement** (*m*) **primaire**, gratuit et obligatoire (*elementary education*); à l'**école** (*f*) **primaire** du quartier (*elementary school*)

eligibility (*n*): ⟨Pol⟩ obtenir le droit de vote et l'**éligibilité** (*f*) (*eligibility; entitlement to stand for election*)

eligible (*adj*): ⟨Pol⟩ les ressortissants sont électeurs et **éligibles** (*eligible to vote*); **avoir droit** (*m*) **à** la retraite à partir de 60 ans; **avoir droit à** remboursement de frais (*be eligible/qualify for*); avoir pour effet de réduire le nombre d'**ayants droit** (*m*) (*person eligible [esp. for benefit]*)

embargo (*n*): ⟨Pol/Comm⟩ assouplir l'**embargo** (*m*) pétrolier vis-à-vis de Téhéran; **placer sous embargo** l'énergie, importante source de devises (*put an embargo upon*); les Douze décident de **lever l'embargo** sur les investissements dans ces pays (*lift the embargo*)

embezzle (*v*): ⟨Fin/Comm⟩ l'argent du contribuable n'a pas été **détourné**; **détourner frauduleusement** au moins 450 millions de livres des fonds de retraite; SEE ALSO **misappropriate**

embezzlement (*n*): ⟨Fin/Comm⟩ les **détournements** (*m*) **de fonds** s'élèvent à une dizaine de milliers de francs; des accusations de corruption et de **malversation** (*f*); SEE ALSO **misappropriation**

embitter (*v*): la question des minorités **envenime** les relations entre les deux pays

emerge (*v*): le parti **en est sorti** renforcé (*emerge, come out*); deux tendances **se dégagent** de l'étude de l'OCDE; c'est ce qui **ressort** du rapport établi par les enquêteurs (*emerge, be revealed*)

emergence (*n*): ⟨Pol⟩ la **sortie** de la dictature (*emergence from; end of*); ⟨Econ⟩ la **sortie de récession** (*f*) en Grande-Bretagne (*emergence from recession*)

emergency (*n*): ⟨Pol⟩ une **réunion de crise** (*f*) des ministres des Affaires étrangères (*emergency meeting*); mise en place d'une **cellule d'urgence** (*f*) (*emergency cabinet*); levée de l'**état** (*m*) **d'urgence** au Natal (*state of emergency*); une **aide d'urgence** octroyée par la CEE (*emergency aid/help*)

emoluments (*npl*): le total des **rémunérations** (*f*) versées

emphasize (*v*): **mettre en avant** les avantages du projet; **insister sur** la signification historique de leur rencontre (*emphasize, point out*); l'échec du vote de censure **met en évidence** (*f*) les divisions de l'opposition; ces graphiques **mettent en relief** (*m*) l'importance du phénomène (*emphasize, bring out*); la région cherche à **valoriser** son rôle de communication (*emphasize, draw attention to; exploit*)

employ (*v*): on l'**emploie** comme homme à tout faire; SEE ALSO **use**

employable (*adj*): ⟨Ind⟩ les titulaires du brevet professionnel sont directement **opérationnels**; le groupe restant, les moins **aptes à l'emploi** (*m*)

employed (*n/adj*): le nombre d'**actifs** (*m*) **occupés** a sensiblement augmenté (*employed person*); les petits commerçants et les **artisans** (*m*) sont les plus nombreux (*self-employed*); le grand parti des **indépendants** (*m*) et des paysans (*self-employed tradesman*)

employee (*n*): un **salarié** de chez Peugeot; les **employés** (*m*) de l'entreprise; SEE ALSO **share ownership**

employer (*n*): cette cotisation est à la charge de l'**employeur** (*m*); le **patronat** est hostile à l'idée; les **milieux** (*m*) **patronaux** ne semblent pas convaincus (*the employers/bosses*); deux propositions faites par l'organisation **patronale** (*employer, employers'*); ⟨Fisc⟩ la baisse des **charges** (*f*) **patronales** (*employers' social security contributions*)

employing (*n*): le projet initial prévoit l'**embauche** (*f*) de trente salariés; le relèvement du salaire minimum ne freinera pas l'**embauche** (*employing/ taking on of labour*); SEE ALSO **employment**

employment (*n*): ⟨Econ⟩ la politique de l'**emploi** (*m*) (*employment*); les conditions de travail et d'**embauche** (*f*) (*employment, taking on/hiring labour*); la croissance de l'**activité** (*f*) féminine (*employment, work*); être en âge d'**entrer dans la vie active** (*seek employment*); les salariés de 40 ans et plus **se reclassent** difficilement (*refind employment*); les offres d'emploi qui arrivent au **bureau de placement** (*m*) (*employment agency/ office*); SEE ALSO **full employment**

empower (*v*): ⟨Pol/Admin⟩ seul le Congrès est **habilité** à le démettre; la seule structure européenne **habilitée** à traiter des problèmes de défense; SEE ALSO **entitle**

enact (*v*): ⟨Pol/Jur⟩ de nouvelles législations ont été **promulguées**; SEE ALSO **promulgate**

enclose (*v*): **joindre** une attestation de prise en charge

enclosed (*adj*): le prospectus **ci-joint** contient tous les détails nécessaires

enclosure (*n*): renvoyez la déclaration de revenus et les [pièces] **annexes** (*f*)

encounter (*v*): la réforme **se heurte** à l'hostilité des syndicats (*encounter, come up against*)

encroach (*v*): on estime que le Premier ministre **empiète** sur le terrain présidentiel

end (*n*): à l'**issue** (*f*) de leur entretien (*end, completion*); la France souhaite l'**aboutissement** (*m*) des négociations (*end, successful conclusion*); l'alliance **a vécu** (*be at an end/finished*); PS: **haro sur** les privatisations (*a call for an end to/of*)

end (*v*): l'exercice qui vient de **se clôturer**; le congrès **s'achève** lundi à Luxembourg (*end, close*); **mettre fin** (*f*) au conflit; **mettre un terme** à la discrimination (*end, put an end to*)

endanger (*v*): cette agitation va **remettre en cause** la croissance de l'économie; ceci avait un temps **hypothéqué** la stratégie d'Israël; **porter atteinte** (*f*) à la sécurité de l'État (*endanger, threaten*); **mettant en péril** (*m*) ainsi la sécurité de l'État (*endanger, imperil*); SEE ALSO **jeopardize**

endeavour (*n*): SEE **attempt**

endeavour (*v*): Moscou **s'emploie** à resserrer ses liens avec Téhéran; SEE ALSO **attempt**

endorse (*v*): le Conseil constitutionnel doit **avaliser** le découpage électoral (*endorse, approve*); faire **endosser** par Washington le projet d'élections dans les territoires occupés; ⟨Fin⟩ **endosser** un chèque au profit d'un tiers

endorsement (*n*): Washington donne son **aval** (*m*) à l'accord (*endorsement, approval*); ⟨Fin⟩ une lettre de change peut être transmise à un tiers par **endossement** (*m*) (*endorsement [of cheque/bill]*)

energy (*n*): veiller à l'indépendance **énergétique** du pays; le plan **énergétique** pour les vingt ans à venir (*relating to energy resources*)

enhance (*v*): **revaloriser** le rôle des conseils généraux; SEE ALSO **increase, value, importance**

enjoy (*v*): ce type de placement **bénéficie** d'une déduction fiscale; l'Algérie **jouissait** du statut départemental; le Labour **dispose** du soutien des syndicats

enlarge (*v*): SEE **expand**

enlargement (*n*): intransigeant en ce qui concerne l'**élargissement** (*m*) de l'Europe

enlist (*v*): ⟨Mil⟩ **s'engager** à vingt ans (*enlist in armed forces*); l'armée a besoin chaque année de 14.000 **engagés** (*m*) (*enlisted soldier*)

enlistment (*n*): ⟨Mil⟩ avant la date d'**incorporation** (*f*) (*enlistment [into armed forces]*)

enquiry (*n*): ⟨Jur⟩ le parquet **ouvrit une information** après la fin de l'enquête de la police (*open/set up a [judicial] enquiry*); l'**enquête** (*f*) **préalable à la déclaration d'utilité publique** commencera jeudi (*public enquiry [GB]*); SEE ALSO **judicial**

enrol (*v*): **s'inscrire** dans un club de tir (*enrol, register*)

enrolment (*n*): ⟨Educ⟩ l'école a un **effectif** de 1.300 élèves (*enrolment; total numbers*); les **inscriptions** (*f*) s'ouvrent début octobre (*enrolment, registration*)

ensure (*v*): **assurer** provisoirement la direction du pays (*ensure, provide*); la force d'intervention a pour rôle d'**assurer** le maintien de la paix (*ensure, maintain*)

enter (*v*): le Canada **s'engage** dans la récession (*enter, go into*); **intégrer** la fonction publique (*enter, go into, join*)

entering (*n*): il dénonce l'**engagement** (*m*) français dans une aventure inconsidérée; un pas vers l'**engagement** de l'Allemagne dans la crise (*entering, involvement in*)

enthusiasm (*n*): accueillir une proposition avec **enthousiasme** (*m*) (*enthusiasm*); malgré un **engouement** des épargnants pour les SICAV (*enthusiasm, fad, passing craze*)

entire (*adj*): l'**intégralité** (*f*) **de la somme** a été remboursée (*entire/whole amount*); le **programme en son entier** reviendrait à dix milliards (*the entire programme*); SEE ALSO **totality, whole**

entitle (*v*): tout l'**autorise** à être confiant (*entitle, permit*); les lois **habilitent** le gouvernement à recourir aux ordonnances; ⟨Fin/Fisc⟩ les dépenses immobilières **donnent droit** (*m*) à des réductions d'impôt; des cotisations qui **ouvrent droit** à certaines prestations (*entitle; give entitlement to*)

entitlement (*n*): ⟨Fin/Soc⟩ l'**ouverture** (*f*) **des droits** est liée au versement des contributions au régime de sécurité sociale; les **conditions** (*f*) **d'accès** à ces différentes aides

entrance (*n*): ⟨Educ⟩ l'**examen** (*m*) **d'entrée** à l'ENA; ⟨Admin⟩ passer un **concours de recrutement** (*m*) (*entrance examination*); SEE ALSO **admission, examination**

entrant (*n*): ⟨Educ⟩ les **candidats** (*m*) reçus au baccalauréat (*entrant, candidate*)

entrenchment (*n*): ⟨Pol⟩ l'**ancrage** (*m*) du parti socialiste en Picardie reste fort (*entrenchment; [electoral] base*)

entry (*n*): ⟨Fin⟩ condamné à 30.000F d'amende pour fraude fiscale et omission d'**écritures** (*fpl*) (*book-keeping entry*)

environment (*n*): dans un **paysage** socio-économique profondément remanié; la dégradation du **cadre de vie** causée par une concentration urbaine excessive (*[living] environment*)

envisage (*v*): on n'**envisage** pas de hausse des taux d'intérêt (*envisage, plan*); les propositions **prévoyant** une liquidation totale des armes nucléaires tactiques (*envisage, provide for*)

equal (*adj*): ⟨Jur⟩ une directive sur l'**égalité** (*f*) **de traitement** entre les hommes et les femmes (*equal treatment*); garantir aux femmes des **droits** (*m*) **égaux à ceux des hommes** (*equal rights with men*); ⟨Admin⟩ une gestion **paritaire** patronat-syndicats (*with equal representation on both sides*); les trois actionnaires seront **à parité** (*f*) (*on an equal footing*); SEE ALSO **equal pay**

equality (*n*): la justice sociale et l'**égalité** (*f*) **des chances pour tous** (*equality of opportunity*)

equally (*adv*): la cotisation versée **à parts** (*fpl*) **égales** par les employeurs et les salariés; financé **à parité** (*f*) par l'État et les collectivités locales; répartir la somme **à égalité** (*f*) entre eux

equal pay (*n*): ⟨Econ/Jur⟩ les femmes demandent l'**égalité** (*f*) **devant le salaire**; à travail égal, **salaire** (*m*) **égal** (*equal pay*); le principe de l'**égalité de rémunération pour les travaux de valeur égale** (*equal work for equal pay*)

equanimity (*n*): la décision a été acceptée avec **sérénité** (*f*) par le gouvernement

equip (*v*): les locaux seront **aménagés** pour accueillir les nouveaux élèves; **doter** l'Europe d'une législation sociale commune (*equip*); les onze pays ont décidé de **se doter** d'armées indépendantes (*equip o.s. with*); la plupart des ménages **disposent du** téléphone à domicile (*be equipped with*)

equipment (*n*): une commande importante de **matériel** (*m*) **agricole**; SEE ALSO **plant**

equipped (*adj*): des missiles **dotés** de charges conventionnelles; la France est à cet égard la moins bien **lotie** (*equipped*); les pays baltes, **mal lotis** en ressources énergétiques (*poorly equipped/supplied*)

equipping (*n*): de l'aide pour l'**équipement** (*m*) et le chauffage d'un nouveau local

equitable (*adj*): une **équitable** partition des terres (*equitable, fair*)

equity (*n*): ⟨Com/Fin⟩ le **capital social** apporté par les associés; ⟨Jur⟩ conforme à l'**équité** (*f*) et à la justice naturelle; SEE ALSO **stocks**

erode (*v*): ⟨Fin⟩ les monnaies **s'effritent** vis-à-vis du dollar (*be eroded, decline in value*)

erosion (*n*): ⟨Pol⟩ nouvel **effritement** (*m*) des voix socialistes; ⟨Fin⟩ **effritement** des cours hier à la Bourse de Paris

escalate (*v*): ⟨Mil⟩ les combats **s'intensifient** (*escalate*); ⟨Comm⟩ les cours des matières premières **montent en flèche** (*f*) (*escalate [esp. costs/prices]*)

escalating (*adj*): ⟨Econ⟩ l'**escalade** (*f*) **des prix** pénalise toutes les couches socio-économiques (*escalating prices*)

escalation (*n*): une nouvelle **escalade** dans la violence; l'**escalade** de l'intégrisme dans cette région du monde

escape (*n*): il n'y a plus d'**échappatoire** (*f*) pour notre pays (*escape, way out*); insérer une **clause de sauvegarde** (*f*) dans le texte de l'accord (*escape clause*)

essential (*adj*): l'unité militaire de l'Europe **s'impose** (*be essential*)

establish (*v*): on a pu **établir** sa participation à l'attentat (*establish, prove*); ⟨Admin⟩ **être titularisé** dans ses fonctions (*be established/confirmed*); ⟨Econ⟩ la société **est implantée** dans la région depuis vingt ans (*be established*)

establishing (*n*): faciliter l'**établissement** (*m*) d'un dialogue entre producteurs et consommateurs (*establishing, setting up*); ⟨Pol⟩ l'**instauration** (*f*) à Alger de l'état d'urgence (*establishing, setting up*)

establishment (*n*): ⟨Pol⟩ l'**avènement** (*m*) de la Ve République (*establishment; advent*); les **milieux** (*m*) **dirigeants** britanniques; cet **establishment** (*m*) qui détient le pouvoir et veille au maintien de l'ordre établi (*the Establishment*)

estate (*n*): ⟨Admin/Jur⟩ éviter le morcellement des **propriétés** (*f*) (*estate, property, land*); le **partage des biens** (*m*) à la suite du décès du possesseur (*division of estate/possessions*); SEE ALSO **property**

79

estimate (*n*): ces **estimations** (*f*) sont contestées (*estimate*); ⟨Comm⟩ faire établir un **devis**; le **devis estimatif** des travaux (*estimate, quotation*); ⟨Fin/Econ⟩ les **prévisions** (*f*) ont été révisées en baisse (*estimate; forecast*)

estimate (*v*): **chiffrer** à 2.500 le nombre de morts

ethical (*adj*): cette solution poserait de graves problèmes **déontologiques** (*ethical, of ethics*)

ethics (*npl*): chaque manquement [supposé] à la **déontologie** policière (*ethics, code of ethics*); SEE ALSO **code**

evaluate (*v*): on **évalue** sa fortune à plus du double; **évaluer** à 500F le préjudice financier subi (*evaluate, estimate*)

evaluation (*n*): il aurait fallu procéder à des **expertises** (*f*) (*expert evaluation, appraisal*)

evasion (*n*): SEE **tax evasion**

event (*n*): une série de **manifestations** (*f*) réuniront hommes politiques et intellectuels polonais (*event, occasion*)

eventual (*adj*): des **bénéfices** (*m*) **éventuels** (*any eventual profits*)

eventuality (*n*): un autre **cas de figure** étant alors envisagé (*eventuality, situation*); la direction écarte complètement l'**éventualité** (*f*) de suppressions d'emplois (*eventuality, possibility*)

eventually (*adv*): avoir des chances de trouver un emploi **à terme** (*eventually, in the end, in the long run*)

evict (*v*): aucun locataire ne pourra être **expulsé** sans bénéficier d'une aide financière; des familles **expropriées** pour défaut de paiement (*evict from house/home*); ⟨Pol⟩ l'ancien parti unique, pratiquement **évincé du pouvoir** (*evict/oust from power*)

eviction (*n*): entraînant l'**éviction** (*f*) des actionnaires minoritaires; cette indemnité d'**éviction**, est-elle imposable? (*eviction, ousting*); le propriétaire transmet à son avocat une **demande d'expulsion** (*f*); l'huissier transmet au locataire un **commandement de vider les lieux** (*eviction order*)

evidence (*n*): ⟨Jur⟩ de nouveaux **témoignages** (*m*) sur les circonstances de sa mort (*evidence*); la police ne dispose d'aucun **indice** (*m*) sérieux (*piece of evidence; clue*); des **preuves** (*f*) manquent (*evidence; proof*); aveux extorqués par la violence, **dépositions** (*f*) trafiquées (*evidence, deposition*); refuser de **déposer** devant la commission enquêtant sur l'affaire; **témoigner** devant la cour d'assises (*give evidence*); SEE ALSO **testify**

examination (*n*): un **examen** approfondi (*examination, inspection*); ⟨Educ⟩ le concours d'entrée est **sur épreuves** (*fpl*) (*by examination*); ⟨Admin⟩ recruter par **concours** (*m*) (*competitive examination*); ⟨Jur⟩ lors des **auditions** (*f*) **de témoins** (*examination/questioning of a witness*)

examine (*v*): le tribunal des prud'hommes va **se pencher** sur ce train de licenciements; le Sénat va **se saisir** à son tour du dossier (*examine, study*); le ministre propose de **mettre à plat** ce dossier difficile (*examine thoroughly*); les experts **épluchent** les données économiques (*examine closely, dissect*); ⟨Jur⟩ le juge avait **instruit** de nombreux dossiers liés au terrorisme (*examine [esp. a criminal case]; conduct an investigation into*)

exceed (*v*): les médecins peuvent **dépasser** ces tarifs pour certains soins; la production du brut **outrepasse** la demande; l'armée fédérale aurait **dépassé** les ordres reçus (*exceed, go beyond*)

exceeding (*n*): ⟨Econ⟩ les pénalités pour **dépassement** (*m*) de quotas laitiers

except (*prep*): **hormis** trois millions de logements sociaux; la population active [**hors** agriculture] dépasse les 14 millions (*except; excluding*); SEE ALSO **excluding**

except (*v*): on a voulu **exclure** les immigrés de ces catégories de personnel; la loi **fait exception** (*f*) des immigrés de la deuxième génération (*except; exclude*)

excepted (*adj*): le Laos **mis à part**, la situation demeure bloquée dans l'ancienne Indochine

exception (*n*): une **dérogation** au principe de fermeture des magasins le dimanche (*exception; special dispensation*); ce serait **déroger aux règles** fixées par le protocole d'accord (*make an exception to/waive a rule*); SEE ALSO **dispensation, waiver**

exceptional (*adj*): le régime **dérogatoire** actuel est supprimé (*exceptional*); certaines monnaies ont aujourd'hui des **régimes** (*m*) **dérogatoires** (*exceptional arrangement*)

exceptionally (*adv*): une dérogation accordée **à titre d'exception** (*f*); droit qui lui a été accordé **par dérogation** (*f*) (*as a special dispensation; exceptionally*)

excess (*adj*): le reclassement des ouvriers **en sureffectifs** (*mpl*); les emplois **en surnombre** (*m*), très importants dans ce secteur (*excess; supernumerary*); se défaire du **personnel en surnombre** (*excess staff*)

excess (*n*): sous l'effet d'un **excès** des décès sur les naissances (*excess, surplus*); ⟨Econ⟩ réduire une **surcapacité** de 20% (*excess capacity*); ⟨Ins⟩ en cas de sinistre, une **franchise** de 10% de la prime restera à la charge de l'assuré (*insurance premium excess*)

excessive (*adj*): ⟨Pol⟩ la militarisation **à outrance** (*f*) du pays; maintenir l'ordre par l'usage **abusif** de la force; faire preuve d'un nationalisme **exacerbé** (*excessive*); ⟨Comm⟩ les taux pratiqués ne sont pas **excessifs**; des charges **exorbitantes** (*excessive, exorbitant*); une mise en garde contre les **dérapages** (*m*) **salariaux** (*excessive wage settlement*)

excessively (*adv*): le parti dramatisa **à outrance** (*f*) la situation sociale

exchange (*n*): ⟨Fin⟩ les variations des **taux** (*m*) **de change** (*exchange rate*); un démantèlement du **contrôle des changes** (*m*) (*exchange controls*);

⟨Econ⟩ des échanges franco-soviétiques sur la base du **troc** (*exchange, barter deal*); le revenu versé **en contrepartie** (*f*) **du** travail fourni (*in exchange/payment/return for*)

excise (*n*): ⟨Fisc⟩ des **droits** (*m*) **d'accises** qui frappent l'alcool et le tabac (*excise duty*)

excite (*v*): en dépit de l'émotion que **soulève** cette affaire

excitement (*n*): l'**émoi** (*m*) suscité par sa défaite était encore vif

exclude (*v*): elle n'**écarte** pas une hausse de cotisations; cette décision visait à **écarter** un homme trop ambitieux; les enquêteurs n'**excluent** aucune hypothèse (*exclude, rule out*); SEE ALSO **rule out**

excluding (*prep*): 14% des effectifs industriels **hors** BTP; **non compris** les intérêts (*excluding, not counting*); SEE ALSO **except**

exclusion (*n*): le parti veut éviter toute **exclusion** (*f*), tout esprit de chapelle (*exclusion, debarment; exclusiveness*)

exclusive (*adj*): ⟨Comm⟩ on lui a confié l'**exclusivité** (*f*) des exportations de diamants (*exclusive rights*)

exculpate (*v*): SEE **exonerate**

execute (*v*): SEE **carry out**

execution (*n*): dans l'**exercice** (*m*) de ses fonctions; SEE ALSO **carrying out**

executive (*n*): ⟨Pol⟩ la Commission de Bruxelles, l'**exécutif** (*m*) des Douze (*executive body/branch*); le nouvel **organisme exécutif** de l'union (*executive body*); partager le **[pouvoir] exécutif** (*executive power*); ⟨Admin⟩ les **cadres** (*m*) **supérieurs** qui assument la fonction patronale (*senior executive*); quatre autres membres du **comité de direction** (*f*) (*executive/management board*)

exempt (*adj*): ⟨Fin⟩ les loyers sont **exempts** de tout impôt (*exempt [esp. from tax]*); SEE ALSO **tax-free**

exempt (*v*): ⟨Mil⟩ 8% des jeunes **sont dispensés** du service militaire (*be exempt/excused*); ⟨Fisc⟩ **être exempté** de tout impôt; sont **exonérés [d'impôts]** les producteurs s'engageant à faire geler 15% de leurs terres (*be exempted from paying tax*); l'État peut **détaxer** la partie du revenu consacrée à l'épargne (*exempt/remove tax or duty*)

exemption (*n*): ⟨Fisc⟩ l'**exonération** (*f*) des charges sociales (*exemption*); la **gratuité** pour les enfants et les personnes âgées (*exemption from charge*); SEE ALSO **free**

exercise (*n*): le libre **exercice** du droit syndical; un **exercice** licite du droit de grève (*exercise, exercising*); SEE ALSO **carrying out**

exercise (*v*): la ville **exerça** son droit de préemption pour l'achat du terrain; le Labour perd ainsi un pouvoir qu'il **exerçait** depuis 16 ans (*exercise/wield [esp. power/right]*)

exonerate (*v*): ⟨Jur⟩ le président est **blanchi** au bénéfice du doute (*exonerate, clear*); sortir du tribunal **innocenté**; un communiqué de Paris semble **disculper** Bagdad; SEE ALSO **clear**, **innocent**

exoneration (*n*): SEE **clearing**

exorbitant (*adj*): ⟨Comm⟩ les **prix** (*m*) **exorbitants** qui se pratiquent sur la Côte (*exorbitant prices*); SEE ALSO **excessive**

expand (*v*): ⟨Econ/Comm⟩ le groupe japonais **agrandit** son usine alsacienne (*expand, develop*); Laforge **se renforce** en Amérique du Nord; la firme belge **s'étend** en Amérique du Sud (*expand operations*)

expanding (*adj*): l'économie britannique était alors **en plein essor** (*m*) (*rapidly expanding/developing*)

expansion (*n*): ⟨Econ⟩ l'**expansion** (*f*) est marquée par un essor général des affaires (*[economic] expansion*); le **gonflement** de la demande suivra obligatoirement

expatriate (*n/adj*): la relève des travailleurs **expatriés** par des nationaux

expect (*v*): ils **prévoient** de réduire leur production de 14% (*expect, hope*); les personnes dont il **escompait** la coopération; les experts **tablent sur** une baisse des prix des denrées de base (*expect, count on*)

expectancy (*n*): l'**espérance** (*f*) **de vie** se situe désormais à 73 ans pour les hommes (*life expectancy*); l'allongement de la **durée de la vie** (*life expectancy; longevity*)

expectation (*n*): les **attentes** (*f*) politiques des Français sont plus sobres

expected (*adj*): loin d'avoir l'effet **escompté**; les résultats **attendus** tardent à venir (*expected, anticipated*); un ralentissement plus fort que **prévu** (*expected; forecast*)

expel (*v*): Pékin **expulse** un journaliste anglais (*expel*); un journaliste **exclu** du parti communiste bulgare (*expelled*)

expenditure (*n*): les **dépenses** (*f*) de santé (*expenditure, outgoings*); ⟨Pol/Fin⟩ un contrôle rigoureux de la **dépense publique** (*public expenditure/ spending*); SEE ALSO **capital expenditure**, **spending**

expense (*n*): les **coûts** (*m*) de la reconstruction pèseront sur l'économie du pays (*expense, cost*); le salaire inclut une prime de 500F pour les **frais** (*m*) **professionnels** (*professional expenses*); SEE ALSO **cost**

expensive (*adj*): ⟨Econ⟩ le futur métro, jugé trop **onéreux**; il est plus **coûteux** de vivre à Tokyo (*expensive, costly*)

experience (*n*): avoir eu une longue **pratique** de la vie commerciale (*experience*); prendre en compte les **acquis** (*m*) **professionnels** (*[professional] experience*); parlementaire **expérimenté**, il fut plusieurs fois à la tête d'un ministère (*with long experience, experienced*)

experience (*v*): le pays a **connu** bien des crises (*experience, endure*); ce pays **vit** sa plus longue récession depuis la guerre (*experience, live through*)

experiment (*n*): l'**expérience** (*f*) n'étant pas concluante, le projet a été abandonné

experiment (*v*): SEE **try**

83

experimental (*adj*): des **réalisations** (*f*) **pilotes** d'habitat social (*experimental scheme*); mettre en place une **expérience-pilote** (*experimental/pilot scheme*)

expert (*adj*): des **expertises** (*f*) truquées, utilisées contre des innocents (*expert findings*)

expert (*n*): le **rapport d'expert** (*m*) portant sur l'accident du 14 avril; le **rapport d'expertise** (*f*) est formel (*expert's/valuer's report*); ⟨Pol⟩ le rapport de la **commission des sages** (*m*) sur le code de la nationalité (*committee of experts*)

expire (*v*): un grand nombre de baux **parviennent à échéance** (*f*) cette année; le délai de livraison vient d'**échoir**; le délai **expire** bientôt pour les squatters; son mandat **arrive à expiration** (*f*) au printemps prochain (*expire, run out*); SEE ALSO **lapse**

expiry (*n*): lors de l'**expiration** (*f*) de l'actuelle charte de la BBC; la date prévue pour l'**échéance** (*f*) d'un contrat à durée déterminée

exploit (*v*): ⟨Pol⟩ **exploiter** leur victoire électorale (*exploit, capitalize on*); ⟨Econ⟩ la région est bien décidée à mieux **tirer parti** (*m*) de ses atouts naturels; ⟨Comm⟩ Total espère y **mettre en valeur** (*f*) les ressources en hydrocarbures; **valoriser** en Limousin la filière bois (*exploit, make the most of*)

exploitation (*n*): ⟨Econ⟩ la **valorisation** de notre technologie (*exploitation; promotion*); ⟨Pol⟩ ils dénoncent l'**exploitation** (*f*) de ce meurtre à des fins racistes (*exploitation*); on craignait une **récupération politique** de la mort du jeune Maghrébin (*political exploitation*)

export (*n/adj*): ⟨Comm⟩ les **exportations** (*f*) sont en baisse (*exports*); l'impact de la crise sur les **commandes** (*f*) **à l'exportation** (*export order*); les **recettes** (*f*) **d'exportation** liées à cette activité (*export revenue*)

export (*v*): ⟨Comm⟩ les pays **exportant** plus qu'ils n'importent

exporter (*n*): ⟨Comm⟩ pays traditionnellement **exportateur** (*m*) de matières premières; les **pays** (*m*) **exportateurs** de viande de bœuf

expose (*v*): le Polisario **dénonce** un nouveau raid de l'aviation marocaine (*expose, reveal; denounce*)

ex-prisoner (*n*): un **repris de justice** recherché par la police (*ex-prisoner; person with a previous conviction*)

expulsion (*n*): le **renvoi** des clandestins; l'**expulsion** (*f*) ne peut aboutir qu'au terme d'une longue procédure; ⟨Pol⟩ les clandestins risquent la **reconduite à la frontière** (*expulsion*); former un recours contre un **arrêté d'expulsion** (*f*) (*expulsion order*); SEE ALSO **eviction**

extend (*v*): **élargir** les catégories d'étrangers bénéficiant de la carte de résident; un projet visant à **étendre** cette mesure des communes aux départements (*extend*); **reconduire** une action de grève (*extend, continue*); le contrat peut être **prorogé** avec l'accord des parties; **prolonger** un bail par tacite reconduction (*extend, renew*); ⟨Comm⟩

Total va **se redéployer** dans la chimie (*extend [esp. commercial/ manufacturing operation]*)

extendable (*adj*): une grève **reconductible** en cas d'échec des négociations (*extendable, renewable*)

extension (*n*): l'**élargissement** (*m*) du collège de cinq à huit membres; revendiquer une **rallonge** à l'accord salarial signé l'année dernière; chaque **prolongation** (*f*) est accordée au plus pour trois mois; demander un **sursis** pour le remboursement de la dette; SEE ALSO **renewal**

extent (*n*): l'**étendue** (*f*) des pratiques religieuses (*extent, scale*); un programme que l'État finance **à hauteur** (*f*) **de** près de 3 milliards (*to the extent/tune of*)

extenuating (*adj*): ⟨Jur⟩ bénéficier de **circonstances** (*fpl*) **atténuantes** (*extenuating/mitigating circumstances*)

external (*adj*): ⟨Pol⟩ les frontières **extérieures** des États; les **relations** (*f*) **extérieures** priment sur la politique intérieure (*external relations*); SEE ALSO **foreign trade**

extortion (*n*): ⟨Fin⟩ ils accusent le commissaire d'**extorsion** (*f*) **de fonds** (*extortion [of money]*); des entreprises contrôlées ou **racketées** par les Mafias (*subject to extortion*); les sommes **racketées** (*extort, obtain by extortion*)

extra (*adj*): ⟨Comm/Fin⟩ le **surcoût** sera très important pour les petites entreprises; un **surcoût** acceptable, si l'affaire marche (*extra cost*)

extradite (*v*): ⟨Pol⟩ un ressortissant turc **extradé** des Pays-Bas

extradition (*n*): ⟨Pol⟩ demander l'**extradition** (*f*) des immigrés clandestins; l'**extradition** vers un pays neutre

extravagance (*n*): les **dépenses** (*f*) **excessives** du conseil municipal; accusé de **gaspillage** (*m*), d'avoir dilapidé une fortune; SEE ALSO **waste**

extravagant (*adj*): les Français sont parmi les plus **dépensiers** pour leur santé (*extravagant, spendthrift*)

extreme (*adj*): on déplorait son discours **outrancier**; un nationalisme **exacerbé** partagé par la majorité de la population (*extreme; excessive*)

extremism (*n*): ils risquent de payer cher leur **jusqu'au-boutisme** (*m*); ⟨Pol⟩ la montée de l'**intégrisme** (*m*) au sein de la communauté algérienne (*extremism [esp. religious]*); SEE ALSO **fundamentalism**

extremist (*n/adj*): ⟨Pol⟩ un parti d'**extrémistes** (*m*) de droite; l'opposition, divisée entre **ultras** (*mpl*) et libéraux; les **jusqu'au-boutistes** (*m*) du mouvement islamiste; connus pour ses opinions **jusqu'au-boutistes**

F

fabric (n): la cohésion du **tissu social** (*social fabric*); ce projet va permettre de revitaliser le **tissu économique** (*economic fabric*)

fabricate (v): des 'preuves' **inventées de toutes pièces** (f) (*fabricate, invent*)

fabrication (n): les prétendus documents authentiques étaient en fait des **supercheries** (f) (*fabrication; hoax*)

face (v): le pays **affronte** une sérieuse crise politique; toutes ces branches sont **confrontées** à de difficiles adaptations

facet (n): le deuxième **volet** de ce dossier sensible (*facet, chapter*)

facility (n): un ensemble de **facilités** (f) à usage commun; ⟨Econ⟩ une remise à neuf des **installations** (f) (*[industrial] facilities; plant*); les **équipements** (mpl) touristiques de la région sont insuffisants (*facilities, amenities*); préserver un équilibre entre emploi, logements et **équipements collectifs** (*community facilities*); SEE ALSO **amenity**

facsimile (n): recevoir par **télécopie** (f) confirmation de sa réservation (*facsimile, FAX*)

faction (n): ⟨Mil/Pol⟩ le parti se divise en **factions** (fpl) (*faction, [warring] group*); désarmer les **factions combattantes** (*warring factions*)

factory (n): une **usine** de textile; une petite **fabrique** dans la zone artisanale (*factory*); une note de service adressée à l'encadrement et aux **ouvriers** (m) [d'usine] (*[factory] worker*); déposer une plainte auprès de l'**inspecteur** (m) **du travail** (*factory inspector*)

fail (v): la CEE a **échoué** dans sa tentative de médiation (*fail*); toutes les solutions ont **fait faillite** (f) (*fail, end in failure*)

failed (adj): le putsch **manqué** de 1991; la candidature **avortée** du député écologiste; SEE ALSO **abortive**

failing (n): **à défaut**, l'offre sera retirée par la direction (*failing this; in the absence of which*); SEE ALSO **shortcoming**

failure (n): **échec** (m) des négociations (*failure, breakdown*); en dépit de l'**insuccès** (m) de sa démonstration; le **taux d'échec** à l'Université (*failure rate*); interpellé pour **défaut** (m) de port de ceinture de sécurité (*failure/failing to*); le principal grief des usagers, c'est le **non-respect** des horaires (*failure to adhere/keep to*)

faint (adj): un **faible** espoir subsiste (*faint, slight*)

fair (adj): un financement plus **équitable** de la protection sociale (*fair, equitable*); ⟨Comm⟩ la **vérité des prix** (mpl), jusqu'alors fixés de manière arbitraire (*fair/realistic prices*)

fairly (adv): tous seront traités **équitablement** devant la loi

fairness (n): on juge un impôt sur son **équité** (f) et sur son efficacité (*fairness, equity*); l'**impartialité** (f) des juges a été plusieurs fois mise en cause (*fairness, impartiality*)

faith (*n*): SEE **promise**

fake (*n/adj*): un document **falsifié**; SEE ALSO **forged**

fake (*v*): **falsifier** une signature; SEE ALSO **forge**

fall (*n*): ⟨Econ/Fin⟩ nouvel **affaissement** (*m*) des cours à Wall Street; nette **baisse** (*f*) de la production (*fall*); la **dégringolade** du marché (*fall, collapse*); la **décote** du titre atteint 28% (*fall in value*); un **recul** des bénéfices; nouveau **reflux** (*m*) du dollar; nette **régression** (*f*) des valeurs minières à la Bourse; de très forts **replis** (*m*) sur les produits pétroliers; SEE ALSO **decline, decrease**

fall (*v*): les prix **baissent** et les taux suivent; le chômage n'a cessé de **décroître** depuis 1974; le nombre des sans-travail **fléchit** pour la deuxième année consécutive; le chiffre d'affaires **s'est infléchi** de 18% durant cette période (*fall*); le coût chute de 20%, **revenant à** 15 milliards (*fall, come down to*); sa cote de popularité **dégringole**; la mortalité **est en forte diminution** (*f*) (*fall sharply*)

fall back (*n*): prévoir un scénario de **repli** (*m*) (*fall back*); déjà, on songe à des **positions** (*f*) **de repli** (*fall-back position*)

falling (*adj*): ⟨Comm⟩ les vins d'Alsace **à la baisse**; ⟨Fin⟩ le dollar reste **orienté à la baisse** (*falling in value*)

falling behind (*n*): un **décrochage** international de l'industrie britannique; la **dévalorisation** des traitements des enseignants

fall-off (*n*): le **tassement** des voix socialistes (*fall-off, downturn*)

fall off (*v*): la demande **recule** cette année (*fall off, decline*)

false (*adj*): faire une **fausse** déclaration; une attestation **mensongère** (*false; untrue*); ⟨Jur⟩ le **faux témoignage** est sévèrement réprimé (*false evidence, perjury*)

falsehood (*n*): dire des **contre-vérités** (*f*) (*falsehood, lie*)

falsify (*v*): ⟨Fin⟩ présenter en toute régularité des **comptes** (*m*) **truqués** (*falsified accounts*)

family (*n*): les **ménages** (*m*) les plus modestes (*family, household*); des réductions pour **familles** (*f*) **nombreuses** (*large family*); les **allocations** (*f*) **familiales** sont dues à partir du deuxième enfant à charge (*family allowance; child benefit*); ⟨Comm⟩ une **entreprise familiale** créée au début du siècle (*family concern/firm*)

family planning (*n*): ⟨Soc⟩ la **planification des naissances** s'avère de plus en plus incontournable (*family planning; birth control*)

fare (*n*): les compagnies baissent leurs **tarifs** (*m*) (*fare; scale of charges*); le **relèvement des tarifs** de la SNCF (*fare increase*)

farm (*n*): ⟨Agric⟩ 80% des aides vont à 20% des **exploitations** (*f*) [agricoles] (*farm [unit]*); les **grandes exploitations** dominent dans la Beauce (*large farm [unit]*); ⟨Econ⟩ les **aides** (*f*) **à l'agriculture** (*farm support grant*); un éleveur dans le Limousin qui paie 38.000F de **fermage** (*m*) (*[farm] rent*)

farm (*v*): ⟨Agric⟩ **exploiter** 270 hectares dans la Beauce

farmer (*n*): ⟨Agric⟩ leur solidarité avec les **agriculteurs** (*m*) du Larzac; un **cultivateur** de la Dordogne; les **fermiers** (*m*) du Bocage normand; un **exploitant agricole** qui est aussi producteur et négociant (*farmer*); des dizaines de **petits exploitants** menacés d'expropriation; le gouvernement ne peut trahir les **paysans** (*m*) (*small farmers*)

farming (*n*): ⟨Agric⟩ l'**agriculture** (*f*) domine dans cette région (*farming, agriculture*); les **collectivités** (*f*) **rurales** sont les plus menacées (*farming/ agricultural community*)

farm-owner (*n*): ⟨Agric⟩ 40% des **chefs** (*m*) **d'exploitation** ont plus de 55 ans

fault (*n*): le **défaut** majeur de ces propositions, c'est leur coût; un autre **vice** du système actuel (*fault, defect*); dû à un **vice de construction** (*f*) (*construction fault*)

faulty (*adj*): des pièces **défectueuses** en raison d'un défaut de fabrication (*faulty, defective*)

favour (*n*): **être acquis à** un projet (*be in favour of, favour*); il s'est déclaré **partisan** de la peine de mort (*in favour of*); le maire est **en délicatesse** (*f*) avec son parti (*out of favour*); la **désaffection** qui menace la Maison Blanche (*loss of favour/popularity*)

favour (*v*): un découpage des circonscriptions qui **privilégie** les zones rurales (*favour*); les communistes **sont partisans** (*m*) de voter la censure; **préconiser** l'abandon de l'alliance; un tiers des écoles **prônent** la semaine de quatre jours (*favour, be in favour of*); **se prononcer pour** une augmentation des impôts directs (*come out in favour of; favour*); SEE ALSO **prefer**

favourable (*adj*): une conjoncture mondiale exceptionnellement **faste** (*favourable, prosperous*)

fax (*n*): SEE **facsimile**

fear (*n*): les **craintes** (*f*) des agriculteurs restent grandes (*fear*); les Croates vivent dans la **hantise** d'une intervention de l'armée fédérale (*[obsessive] fear*)

fear (*v*): les salariés **redoutent** des baisses de commandes en 1992; **craindre** une recrudescence de la violence

feasibility (*n*): il lui reste de régler de sérieux problèmes de **faisabilité** (*f*); la Banque mondiale va financer une **étude de faisabilité** (*feasibility study*)

feasible (*adj*): militairement **faisable** mais politiquement désastreux

federal (*adj*): ⟨Pol⟩ la construction d'une Europe **fédérale** (*federal*); une partition du pays en régions autonomes **fédérées** (*federal, federated*)

federalism (*n*): ⟨Pol⟩ le **fédéralisme** a ses chauds partisans; les **thèses** (*f*) **féderales** commencent à s'imposer

federate (*v*): ⟨Pol⟩ une alliance qui **fédère** tous les mécontents (*federate, bring together*); SEE ALSO **federal**

federation (*n*): la **fédération** socialiste des Bouches-du-Rhône

fee (*n*): la **redevance** initiale forfaitaire, relativement modeste (*fee, dues*); ⟨Fin⟩ les **honoraires** (*mpl*) des médecins généralistes (*[professional] fee, fees, honorarium*)

female (*adj*): un personnel en majorité **féminin** et rural

field (*n*): c'est **sur le terrain** des droits de l'homme que cette mesure est critiquable; **dans le domaine** économique et financier (*in the field/area of*)

fierce (*adj*): l'un des opposants les plus **farouches** au président (*fierce, unshakeable*); ⟨Comm⟩ la concurrence de plus en plus **vive** en Europe (*fierce [esp. competition]*); SEE ALSO **unconditional**

fiercely (*adv*): la volonté **farouchement** libérale du gouvernement

fight (*n*): la **lutte** contre le tabagisme et l'alcoolisme

fight (*v*): il **milite** pour le maintien d'un certain centralisme; **se battre** pour les minorités opprimées; **lutter** contre les inégalités qui pèsent sur les femmes

figure (*n*): ⟨Econ⟩ le **chiffre** (*m*) est une estimation; les **données** (*f*) mensuelles sur la main-d'œuvre (*figures, statistics, data*)

file (*n*): ⟨Admin⟩ 13.000 **dossiers** (*m*) ont été déposés par des demandeurs d'emploi (*file, dossier*); avoir accès à un **fichier** national (*file; catalogue*); la réglementation relative au **fichage informatique** (*putting on computer file/record*)

file (*v*): ⟨Admin⟩ **classer** des documents (*file, file away*); ⟨Comm⟩ la firme a **déposé son bilan** hier (*file bankruptcy proceedings*); ⟨Jur⟩ **intenter un procès à** son voisin (*file a suit against*); SEE ALSO **bankruptcy, court, sue**

fill (*v*): cinquante places sont à **pourvoir** (*fill [esp. of place, position, seat]*)

fill in (*v*): tout demandeur devra **remplir un formulaire de demande** (*f*) (*fill in/out an application*)

filling in (*n*): le **remplissage** d'un questionnaire

fillip (*n*): pour **donner un coup de fouet** à l'industrie française (*give a fillip*); SEE ALSO **boost, stimulate**

final (*adj*): mais l'**ultime** séance de négociations n'a rien donné; la signature du contrat **définitif** devant notaire (*final, definitive*)

finalize (*v*): il faudra **boucler** le dossier avant la fin avril; ⟨Comm⟩ on pourra **mettre au point** le protocole d'accord au sommet de janvier

finance (*n*): ⟨Fin⟩ la recherche de **financements** (*mpl*) pour le projet (*finance, financing*); ⟨Pol⟩ la réunion des **grands argentiers** (*m*) des pays de la CEE (*finance minister*)

finance (*v*): ⟨Fin⟩ pour **se financer**, l'État emprunte sur les marchés financiers (*finance/fund itself*); ⟨Pol⟩ **commanditer** une tentative d'assassinat (*finance, pay for*)

financial (*adj*): assurer ainsi la sécurité **pécuniaire** des victimes (*financial*); dans les **milieux** (*m*) **financiers**, on redoute une reprise de l'inflation (*financial community/circles*); ⟨Pol/Fin⟩ l'identité des **commanditaires** (*m*) de l'opération est connue; les **bailleurs** (*m*) **de fonds** étrangers qui lui apportent leur aide (*financial backer*)

financial year (*n*): approuver les comptes de l'**exercice** (*m*) **fiscal**; le début du dernier **exercice financier** (*financial/fiscal year*)

financing (*n*): ⟨Fin⟩ les discussions risquent d'achopper sur le **financement**; recevoir 2 milliards de francs de **dotations** (*f*) publiques (*financing; funds; grant*)

find (*v*): ⟨Jur⟩ le tribunal a **donné raison** au plaignant (*find for/in favour of*); la Cour européenne **donne tort** à la France (*find against*); SEE ALSO **rule**

finding (*n*): ⟨Jur⟩ le **verdict** de la Cour est sans appel; ⟨Jur⟩ les **conclusions** (*f*) du juge étaient claires; SEE ALSO **report**

fine (*n*): ⟨Jur⟩ une condamnation à une **amende** de 5.000F; à ce niveau, les **peines** (*f*) **d'amendes** sont la règle; une **contravention** pour stationnement interdit; SEE ALSO **penalty**

fine (*v*): ⟨Jur⟩ le maire **condamné à une amende** de 20.000F

fire (*v*): **limogé** en 1987 de son poste; le chef d'état-major brésilien **viré** pour avoir trop parlé (*fire, sack, dismiss*); SEE ALSO **dismiss**

firm (*adj*): l'offre d'embauches **fermes** augmente sensiblement (*firm, definite*); ⟨Comm⟩ les compagnies aériennes ont **passé commande** (*f*) **ferme** de 277 appareils (*place a firm order*)

firm (*n*): ⟨Comm⟩ la **firme** du Havre est un des leaders sur le marché français; l'amélioration de l'emploi dans les petits **établissements** (*m*) (*firm, business*)

firmness (*n*): il recommande la **fermeté** vis-à-vis les Américains; ⟨Fin⟩ encouragé par la **fermeté** de la place new-yorkaise

fiscal (*f*) ⟨Fisc⟩ un **conseiller fiscal** vous aidera à établir votre déclaration de revenus (*fiscal/tax adviser*); au cours de l'**exercice** (*m*) **fiscal** 1992 (*fiscal year*)

fitness (*n*): nul ne conteste ses **aptitudes** (*f*) pour le poste à pourvoir (*fitness, aptitude, suitability*)

five-year (*adj*): ⟨Econ⟩ Ottawa lance un **plan quinquennal** de réduction de dépenses (*five-year plan*)

fix (*v*): **arrêter** une série de mesures d'urgence (*fix, decide; finalize*); après avoir **institué** l'âge de la retraite à 60 ans (*fix, set*); ⟨Comm⟩ les trois firmes, soupçonnées de **s'entendre sur les prix** pour fausser la concurrence (*fix prices, agree on price-fixing*)

fixed (*adj*): moyennant le paiement d'une somme **forfaitaire** de 300F (*fixed*); ⟨Comm⟩ le **forfait** comprend le prix d'achat et d'éventuelles réparations (*fixed/all-in price*); un contrat **à prix** (*m*) **fixe** (*fixed-price*); SEE ALSO **flat rate**

fixed assets (*npl*): ⟨Econ⟩ les **actifs** (*m*) **immobilisés** de l'entreprise; les biens acquis ou créés par l'entreprise pour être utilisés durablement, ou **immobilisations** (*fpl*)

fixed-term (*adj*): ⟨Econ⟩ le **contrat à durée** (*f*) **déterminée** devient la règle (*fixed-term contract*)

fixing (*n*): la **fixation** d'un seuil moins élevé (*fixing*); ⟨Econ⟩ l'**instauration** (*f*) de quotas (*fixing, setting*); ⟨Comm⟩ la **détermination** d'un prix de vente (*fixing, determining*)

fixture (*n*): ⟨Comm⟩ vendre une maison **avec toutes les installations** (*f*) (*with all fixtures and fittings*)

flag (*n*): un navire **sous pavillon** (*m*) **de complaisance** libérien (*flying a flag of convenience*)

flagrant (*adj*): les carences dans ce domaine sont **flagrantes**

flare-up (*n*): à chaque **flambée** (*f*) de violences dans les banlieues (*flare-up, outbreak*)

flare up (*v*): la révolte qui **éclata** en 1991

flat rate (*n/adj*): payer un **forfait** trimestriel pour le gaz (*flat rate, fixed sum*); la pension **forfaitaire** est d'un montant modeste (*flat-rate; fixed*); SEE ALSO **fixed**

flaw (*n*): les principales **failles** (*f*) de l'accord (*flaw, weakness*); ⟨Jur⟩ casser un jugement pour **vice** (*m*) **de forme** (*on a legal flaw/irregularity*)

flexibility (*n*): la **souplesse** dans les horaires d'abord

flexible (*adj*): se montrer plus **souple** dans la négociation (*flexible*); il veut **assouplir** la réforme de son prédécesseur (*make more flexible*); la France est prête à **assouplir sa position** (*adopt a more flexible position*); ⟨Mil⟩ la stratégie de la **riposte graduée** (*flexible response*)

flexible working (*n*): ⟨Econ⟩ la mise en place d'**horaires** (*mpl*) **flexibles**; pratiquer l'**horaire variable ou mobile** pour fidéliser le personnel (*flexible working practices; flexitime working*)

float (*v*): ⟨Fin⟩ **émettre un emprunt** de 40 milliards de francs (*float/issue a loan*); la livre **flotte** depuis six mois déjà (*float [esp. money exchange rates]*)

floating (*adj*): ⟨Pol⟩ les **électorats** (*m*) **flottants** décident des élections (*floating voter*); ⟨Fin⟩ partisan des **taux** (*m*) **[de change] flottants** (*floating exchange rates*)

flood (*n*): à la suite d'**inondations** (*fpl*) et de sécheresse (*flood, flooding*); la **crue** atteignait parfois un mètre de hauteur (*flood water [esp. of river]*); la protection contre les **dégâts** (*m*) **des eaux** (*flood damage, flooding*); l'**afflux** (*m*) des réfugiés mozambicains (*flood, influx*)

flood (*v*): les réfugiés **affluent en** Allemagne (*flood into*); ⟨Fin⟩ les investissements étrangers qui **affluent** en ce moment (*flood in*)

floor (*n*): ⟨Fin⟩ le Franc tombe près de son **cours plancher** (*floor, bottom rate*)

flotation (*n*): ⟨Fin⟩ **émission** (*f*) d'un emprunt en ECU (*flotation [esp. of a loan]*)

flourish (*v*): les intermédiaires en tous genres y **prospèrent**; partout les marchés noirs **fleurissent** (*flourish; do good business*)

flourishing (*adj*): ⟨Comm⟩ **florissant** trafic d'armes dans l'ex-URSS; un tourisme **florissant** dans un pays en guerre; un marché noir très **prospère** (*flourishing, thriving*)

flout (*v*): **passer outre** à une interdiction; **bafouer** la souveraineté nationale sri-lankaise (*flout, ignore*); ⟨Jur⟩ s'ils **passent outre**, ils sont passibles d'une amende (*flout [esp. law/regulation]*)

flow (*n*): réduire le **débit** du pétrole exporté par oléoduc

fluctuate (*v*): ⟨Fin⟩ les cours **fluctuent** au gré des événements dans l'ex-Union soviétique

fluctuation (*n*): ⟨Fin⟩ les **fluctuations** (*f*) des taux de change (*fluctuation, movement*)

focus (*v*): les reproches **se focalisent sur** la plus criante des injustices; les conversations vont **porter sur** les problèmes de l'Afrique australe (*focus on*)

foil (*v*): **déjouer** une tentative de coup d'État militaire; **faire échouer** un attentat

following (*prep*): hausse des prix **consécutive à** des augmentations de salaires (*following*); **suite à** la suppression des contrôles douaniers (*following, in the aftermath of; as a consequence of*)

follow-up (*n*): la mise en chantier et le **suivi** des travaux (*follow-up, supervision*); ⟨Soc/Med⟩ le **suivi** au sortir de l'hôpital est capital dans ce type de chirurgie (*follow-up; after-care*)

foment (*v*): **attiser** les discordes et compliquer la tâche des négociateurs (*foment, stir up*); **entretenir des troubles** (*m*) dans le nord du pays (*foment unrest*)

food (*n*): ⟨Ecol⟩ l'**alimentation** (*f*) ne représente plus que 16% du budget; une forte hausse des **prix** (*m*) **alimentaires** (*food prices*); la **pénurie alimentaire** est due à un problème de distribution (*food shortage; famine*)

footing (*n*): les relations franco-marocaines restent **au beau fixe** (*on a good footing*)

forbid (*v*): **se voir interdire de** quitter le pays (*be forbidden to*); leur statut leur **interdit** de faire grève (*forbid; prevent, preclude*); SEE ALSO **ban**

forbidden (*adj*): le divorce y est actuellement **interdit** (*forbidden; illegal*)

forbidding (*n*): SEE **banning**

force (*n*): la France renforce son **dispositif** naval dans cette zone (*force, presence*); les taux de cotisation **en vigueur** en 1991 (*in force, current*); la loi **entrera en vigueur** dès 1993; la réforme doit **entrer en application** partout en 1994 (*come into force/effect*)

force (*v*): votre propriétaire peut vous y **contraindre**; pour **astreindre** Jérusalem à négocier (*force, compel, oblige*); la concurrence féroce l'**accule à** la faillite (*force/drive to the brink of*); SEE ALSO **oblige**

forcible entry (*n*): la police opérait une **perquisition** chez l'accusé (*forcible entry; search of premises*); **entrés par effraction** (*f*), les cambrioleurs ont été pris en flagrant délit (*making forcible entry; breaking and entering*)

fore (*n*): **se mettre en évidence** (*f*) lors du débat sur l'affaire Greenpeace (*come to the fore*)

forecast (*adj*): ⟨Comm⟩ des **pertes** (*f*) **prévisionnelles** de 2 MF (*forecast/expected losses*)

forecast (*n*): le recul de la production a été inférieur aux **prévisions** (*f*); la guerre du Golfe a déjoué les **pronostics** (*m*) de nombreux experts

forecast (*v*): il **pronostique** une augmentation des cotisations; la Sécurité civile **prévoit** une aggravation dans les 72 heures (*forecast, predict; expect*)

forecasting (*n*): ⟨Pol⟩ les erreurs de **prévision** (*f*) des instituts de sondages

forefront (*n*): **au tout premier rang** de ses préoccupations politiques; la Hongrie, **à la pointe** des réformes économiques à l'Est (*in the forefront*)

foreign (*adj*): des commandes émanant de l'**étranger** (*m*) (*foreign countries; abroad*); l'**étranger** risque de mal interpréter nos motivations (*foreign countries; people abroad, the foreigner*); SEE ALSO **currency**

foreign aid (*n*): ⟨Pol/Econ⟩ sur une **aide à l'étranger** d'un montant total de 14 milliards de dollars

foreign debt (*n*): la **dette extérieure**, ou l'ensemble des dettes vis-à-vis de créanciers étrangers; l'**endettement** (*m*) **extérieur** de la France inquiète le gouvernement (*foreign/external debt*)

foreign exchange (*n*): les **cambistes** (*m*) se sont accordé hier une journée de trêve (*foreign exchange dealer*)

foreign minister (*n*): ⟨Pol⟩ la démission surprise du **chef de la diplomatie** allemande (*foreign minister, Minister of Foreign Affairs*)

foreign ministry (*n*): ⟨Pol⟩ les **chancelleries** (*f*) se taisent au nom du réalisme; celui qui l'a remplacé à la tête de la **diplomatie** soviétique (*foreign ministry*)

foreign relations (*n*): ⟨Pol⟩ entretenir de **bonnes relations** (*f*) **avec l'extérieur** (*good foreign relations*)

foreign trade (*n*): ⟨Comm⟩ malgré un mauvais résultat du **commerce extérieur**; un pays qui dépend pour son développement des **échanges** (*m*) **internationaux** (*foreign/external trade*)

foreman (*n*): les cadres de même que les **chefs** (*m*) **d'équipe**; un **contremaître** licencié poursuit en justice ses employeurs (*foreman; supervisor*)

foresee (*v*): SEE **forecast**

foreseeable (*adj*): en fonction de l'évolution **prévisible**; ceci a peu de chances de se produire **dans un avenir prévisible** (*in the foreseeable future*)

foresight (*n*): par manque de **prévoyance** (*f*); l'**imprévision** (*f*) du gouvernement en matière d'enseignement supérieur (*lack of foresight*); SEE ALSO **improvidence**

forge (*v*): **contrefaire** une signature ou un document (*forge; counterfeit*)

forged (*adj*): l'affaire des **faux** passeports défraya la chronique (*forged, false*); la détection de **faux documents** (*m*) (*forged documents*); ⟨Jur⟩ inculpé de **faux** (*mpl*) **et d'usage de faux** (*issuing and use of forged documents*)

forger (*n*): la loi qui sanctionne les **auteurs** (*m*) **de contrefaçons** de peines lourdes

forgery (*n*): les documents présentés étaient des **faux** (*m*); une loi qui punit sévèrement les **contrefaçons** (*f*) de grandes marques (*forgery, copy*)

form (*n*): un **formulaire** d'inscription dûment rempli (*form, application form*); le **bordereau** annuel de renouvellement d'adhésion (*form, slip*); soit sur un **imprimé** spécial, soit sur papier blanc (*[printed] form*)

form (*v*): ⟨Pol⟩ chargé de **constituer un gouvernement**; disposer de dix jours pour **former un gouvernement** (*form a government*); les ministres qui **composent** le cabinet (*form, make up*)

formality (*n*): il faut accomplir certaines **formalités** (*f*) à la mairie

formation (*n*): ⟨Pol⟩ lors de la **constitution** de son dernier gouvernement; la **mise en place** du nouveau cabinet (*formation, setting up*)

former (*adj*): dans **ce qui fut** l'URSS (*the former*); le rôle de l'**ancien** ministre de l'Intérieur (*former*); ⟨Educ⟩ les **anciens** (*m*) des grandes Écoles prestigieuses (*former student*)

forming (*n*): la **constitution** de la future équipe présidentielle; l'autorisation de la **formation** de partis politiques; SEE ALSO **setting up**

fortune (*n*): ⟨Fisc⟩ les gros **patrimoines** (*m*) seraient davantage taxés par le biais des droits de succession (*personal fortune; estate*)

forward (*v*): la SNCF n'**achemine** que 18% des conteneurs du port (*forward, dispatch; transport*)

forward (*adv*): une volonté d'**aller de l'avant** (*go forward, progress*)

forwarding (*n*): la Poste ne s'occupe pas que de l'**acheminement** (*m*) du courrier (*forwarding, dispatch*)

foster (*adj*): ⟨Soc⟩ envoyer un enfant battu dans une **famille d'accueil** (*m*) (*foster parents*); **le placement familial des enfants** est la meilleure solution (*placing of children in foster homes*)

foster (*v*): ⟨Soc⟩ **prendre en nourrice** (*f*) les enfants abandonnés; SEE ALSO **adopt**

foundation (*n*): les accusations sont absolument **sans fondement** (*m*) (*without foundation, groundless*); il faut **jeter les bases** (*f*) de nouvelles relations soviéto-américaines (*lay the foundations for*); SEE ALSO **unfounded**

founding (*n*): la **fondation** d'écoles pour immigrés islamiques; lors de la **fondation** de l'État d'Israël (*founding, setting up*)

framework (*n*): l'Europe orientale, sans **cadre** (*m*) **légal** approprié (*legal framework*); **dans le cadre** de la lutte contre la délinquance (*in the framework/context*); une réforme **s'inscrivant dans le cadre de** la politique française en Méditerranée (*come within the framework/scope of*)

franchise (*n*): ⟨Econ⟩ les premiers **contrats de franchise** (*f*), arrivés ces jours-ci à échéance (*franchise/franchising agreement*); les risques encourus par le **franchisé** (*person holding a franchise*)

fraud (*n*): ⟨Jur⟩ dans l'**escroquerie** (*f*) c'est la notion de tromperie qui est essentielle (*fraud*); ⟨Fin/Comm⟩ le problème des **fraudes** (*f*) sur les subventions communautaires (*fraud, cheating*); découvrir à temps la **supercherie** (*fraud, deception*); détenir le record des **fraudes électorales** (*electoral fraud*); SEE ALSO **deception**

fraudulent (*adj*): mis en cause pour son implication dans les actions **frauduleuses** de l'ancien maire (*fraudulent, dishonest*)

fraudulently (*adv*): importé **frauduleusement**, et revendu à prix d'or; obtenir des prêts **par des moyens** (*m*) **frauduleux** (*fraudulently; under false pretences*)

free (*adj*): avoir droit à la **gratuité des transports en commun** à Paris (*free public transport*); toucher à la **gratuité des soins** (*m*) **médicaux** (*free medical treatment*); conseillé **bénévolement** par des experts; le bulletin est envoyé **gracieusement**; il sera envoyé **gratuitement** à tout abonné (*free of charge*); ⟨Econ⟩ la **libre concurrence** en vigueur ailleurs dans la CEE (*free competition*); les entraves à la **libre entreprise** (*free enterprise*)

free (*v*): ⟨Jur⟩ **élargir** un détenu ayant purgé la moitié de sa peine (*free, release*); interpellés, interrogés, puis **relâchés** (*free*); **recouvrer la liberté** après deux mois de détention (*be freed/released*)

freedom (*n*): retrouver enfin la **liberté** (*freedom; being free*); l'évolution de la **liberté d'expression** (*f*) en Algérie; revendiquer la **liberté d'opinion** (*f*); les atteintes au **libre discours**; donner enfin aux Khmers le **droit de s'exprimer librement** (*freedom of speech/expression*); ⟨Journ⟩ pour la **liberté d'informer** (*freedom of information; freedom to inform*)

free-for-all (*n*): un marché mondial aux allures de **foire** (*f*) **d'empoigne**

freehold (*n*): l'achat **en pleine propriété** (*f*) d'un appartement ou d'une maison; Eurodisney conserve la **pleine propriété** des hôtels (*freehold*); une maison d'habitation dont il **avait la pleine propriété** (*own the freehold*)

free of tax (*adj*): ⟨Fisc⟩ on peut transmettre jusqu'à 100.000F **en franchise** (*f*) **d'impôt**; SEE ALSO **tax-free**

free trade (*n*): ⟨Comm⟩ l'**accord** (*m*) **de libre-échange** avec le Mexique (*free-trade agreement*); accord sur la création d'une **zone de libre-échange** (*m*) (*free-trade area*)

freeze (*n*): ⟨Econ/Pol⟩ le **blocage des loyers** (*m*) institué par la loi (*rent freeze*); SEE ALSO **wage freeze**

freeze (*v*): ⟨Econ⟩ il faudrait **bloquer** les pensions pendant trois années consécutives; Bruxelles veut **geler** les prix agricoles

freight (*n*): ⟨Comm⟩ le coût du **fret** multiplie nos prix par deux (*freight, carriage*)

fringe (*n*): ⟨Soc⟩ être repoussé vers la **marginalité sociale** (*fringes of society*); ⟨Econ⟩ les **avantages** (*m*) **en nature** que reçoit le personnel; des **compensations** (*f*) accordées pour fidéliser les employés (*fringe benefit, perk*)

frontier (*n*): à la **frontière** est du pays; (*adj*) un incident **frontalier** a fait dix morts (*frontier*); ce **différend frontalier** est vieux de dix ans; après cinquante ans de **querelle** (*f*) **frontalière** (*frontier/boundary dispute*)

fruitless (*adj*): après deux séances d'entretiens **infructueux**

fruition (*n*) la première fois que se **concrétise** un tel projet sur le sol français (*come to fruition, be carried out/implemented*)

full (*adj*): devenir **membre** (*m*) **à part entière** (*full member*); la région est désormais une collectivité territoriale **de plein exercice** (*m*) (*full; fully-fledged*); une offensive **de grande envergure** (*f*) (*full-scale; all-out*)

full employment (*n*): ⟨Econ⟩ un retour enfin au **plein emploi**; une croissance soutenue a mené l'économie au **plein emploi**

full-time (*adj*): les salariés **à temps** (*m*) **plein**; ⟨Educ⟩ une formation **à temps complet** en un an; ⟨Admin/Pol/Ind⟩ un **permanent** du syndicat; les **permanents** du parti (*full-time official*); SEE ALSO **official**

function (*n*): en sa **qualité** de juge (*function, role*); l'université doit repenser ses **finalités** (*f*) (*function, purpose, aim*); SEE ALSO **purpose**

functionary (*n*): seuls les enseignants dans le secteur public sont des **fonctionnaires** (*m*); SEE ALSO **civil servant**

functioning (*n*): un droit d'information sur la **marche** des entreprises (*functioning, running, working*); est-il capable d'assurer la **bonne marche** de l'entreprise? (*efficient functioning/operation*)

fund (*n*): ⟨Fin⟩ un **fonds** de solidarité (*fund*); la Commission gère les **fonds** de la CEE (*funds*); les **moyens** (*m*) **financiers** prêtés par les créanciers (*funds, finance*); la firme possède près de 30 milliards de **disponibilités** (*fpl*) (*disposable funds/assets*); une baisse de sa **trésorerie** lui a fait perdre la confiance de ses banquiers (*funds, cash, liquidities*); la bonne gestion des **deniers** (*m*) **publics** (*public funds*)

fund (*v*): ⟨Fin⟩ pour **financer** son programme d'expansion (*fund, finance*)

fundamental (*adj*): engager des réformes **de fond** (*m*)

fundamentalism (*n*): ⟨Rel⟩ le danger que représente l'**intégrisme** (*m*) musulman (*[religious esp. Muslim] fundamentalism*)

fundamentalist (*n/adj*): ⟨Rel/Pol⟩ l'intransigeance des **intégristes** (*m*), qui n'admettent aucun compromis (*[religious esp. Muslim] fundamentalist*)

funding (*n*) ⟨Fin⟩ la dernière estimation du **financement** nécessaire; SEE ALSO **fund**

fund-raising (*n*): à la tête d'une entreprise de **récolte** (*f*) **de fonds**; la **collecte des dons** (*m*) auprès des entreprises et des citoyens

further (*adv*): ⟨Jur⟩ le parquet décidera des **suites** (*f*) à **donner** (*further action/measures*)

fuse (*v*): SEE **amalgamate**

future (*n*): le long terme, clé du **devenir** industriel de la France (*future*); l'embargo ne sera pas levé **prochainement** (*in the near/immediate future*); les médecins s'interrogent sur leurs **perspectives** (*f*) **d'avenir** (*future; future prospects*); des **lendemains** (*m*) **incertains** pour El Salvador (*uncertain future*)

future (*adj*): une certaine prudence quant aux ventes **à venir**; un **futur** Premier ministre; un **éventuel** gouvernement travailliste ne sera pas lié par le programme du parti (*future, possible*)

G

gain (*n*): le principal **acquis** de ce conflit (*gain, achievement*); ⟨Pol⟩ **gains** (*mpl*) substantiels pour les Centristes

gain (*v*): l'opposition a **remporté** une majorité des sièges (*gain, win*)

gaol (*n*): évasion de la **prison** de Mons; la **centrale** de Colmar paralysée par une grève des gardiens; SEE ALSO **prison**

gaol (*v*): SEE **imprison**

gap (*n*): l'**écart** (*m*) croissant entre les minimas professionnels et le SMIC; l'**inadéquation** (*f*) entre l'offre et la demande (*gap; difference*)

general (*adj*): ⟨Admin/Comm⟩ **gérant** (*m*) d'une moyenne entreprise (*general manager/director of a company*); ⟨Med⟩ les [médecins] **généralistes** (*m*) se plaignent de leur nouveau statut (*general medical practitioner*)

generalization (*n*): le risque de **banalisation** (*f*) du travail de nuit des femmes (*generalization, spread*)

generalize (*v*): il faut se garder de **schématiser**; il ne faut ni dramatiser ni **généraliser**

generate (v): ⟨Comm⟩ les cessions sont un moyen efficace de **générer** du cash; une stratégie susceptible de **générer** des emplois durables (*generate, create*)

gift (n): ⟨Fisc⟩ recevoir un bien en héritage ou **en donation** (f) (*as a gift*); la **donation-partage**, une solution avantageuse sur le plan fiscal (*gift/ settlement made during life of donor*)

gilt-edged (*adj*): ⟨Fin⟩ placer ses économies dans des **valeurs** (f) **de père de famille** (*gilt-edged stock/securities*); SEE ALSO **blue-chip**

giro (n): ⟨Fin⟩ par chèque bancaire ou par **chèque** (m) **postal** (*giro cheque*)

give in (v): il n'est pas prêt à **céder** sur ce point crucial (*give in; give way*); SEE ALSO **concede**, **submit**

give up (v): ⟨Jur⟩ les malfaiteurs ont été **livrés** à la police (*give up, hand over*); les lycéens ne **désarment** pas (*give up the fight*); SEE ALSO **abandon**, **surrender**, **renounce**

giving up (n): la campagne contre les **abandons** (m) de souveraineté nationale; SEE ALSO **abandonment**

gloom (n): la vague de **morosité** qui avait submergé les patrons; ⟨Comm⟩ les restrictions dues à la **morosité** économique actuelle

glut (n): ⟨Econ⟩ les investisseurs redoutent un **engorgement** du marché

go-ahead (n): **feu** (m) **vert** à la reprise de la société par le groupe scandinave (*go-ahead; permission*)

goal (n): travailler en vue d'**objectifs** (*mpl*) **communs** (*shared goals/objectives*)

go-between (n): les agents de change et autres **intermédiaires** (m)

gold (n): ⟨Fin⟩ le **métal jaune**, une valeur refuge incomparable

good (n): ⟨Comm⟩ le transport des **marchandises** (f) par camion (*goods*); ⟨Econ⟩ les importations de **biens** (*mpl*) **et services** devraient encore progresser de plus de 5% (*goods and services*)

go-slow (n): ⟨Ind⟩ des **grèves** (f) **perlées** paralysaient la production; **débrayages** (m) des personnels de la RATP hier

go slow (v): ⟨Ind⟩ les ouvriers **débrayent** pendant une heure en signe de protestation

govern (v): ⟨Admin⟩ les nouvelles règles qui **régissent** son fonctionnement (*govern*); la profession **est régie par** la loi de 1977; les anciens immeubles encore **soumis à** la loi de 1948 (*be governed by*); SEE ALSO **control**, **manage**

governing (*adj*): ⟨Admin⟩ le **conseil d'administration** de la BBC; les **instances** (f) **dirigeantes** du parti (*governing body*); ⟨Pol⟩ les membres de l'ancienne **majorité** (f) se représentent à nouveau (*governing party; party in government/majority*)

government (n): ⟨Pol⟩ le **pouvoir** s'est ressaisi après l'agitation dans les rues; les **pouvoirs publics** n'appuient pas cette initiative privée (*government*);

l'incapacité des **gouvernants** (*m*) à réduire les inégalités (*people in government*); les ministres **au banc du gouvernement** (*on the government bench*); les **cercles** (*m*) **dirigeants** américains (*government circles*)

grade (*n*): ⟨Admin⟩ au dernier **échelon**, elle n'a plus de promotion à attendre (*grade, echelon*); toutes les **catégories** (*f*) du personnel sont concernées (*grade, category*)

graduate (*n*): ⟨Educ⟩ **licencié** (*m*), il prépare un doctorat; **diplômé** (*m*) d'une école supérieure de commerce

graduate (*v*): ⟨Educ⟩ espérer **obtenir son diplôme** après trois années d'études universitaires (*graduate*); **frais émoulu** de l'université de Princeton (*freshly/recently graduated*)

grant (*n*): ⟨Fin⟩ les travailleurs sans emploi ne bénéficient d'aucun **subside** (*m*) (*grant, subsidy*); la Communauté réduit de 30% les **subventions** (*f*) aux agriculteurs; l'annonce des **dotations** (*f*) aux entreprises les plus nécessiteuses (*[central government] grant/subsidy*); ⟨Educ⟩ bénéficier d'**aides** (*fpl*) **financières** durant les études; les conditions d'accès aux **bourses** (*f*) **d'enseignement** (*education grant*); SEE ALSO **bursary**

grant (*v*): ⟨Fin⟩ la somme que l'État **alloue** aux musées nationaux; une prime de fin d'année, **octroyée** à tout le personnel; ⟨Educ⟩ le titre est **décerné** après trois ans d'études de haut niveau (*grant, award*)

granting (*n*): l'**attribution** (*f*) à la CEI d'un statut d'associé spécial auprès du FMI; l'**octroi** (*m*) d'un passeport à chaque Soviétique; **octroi** de larges pouvoirs aux Républiques

graph (*n*): le **graphique** permet de se faire une idée de l'évolution des dépenses; c'est ce qu'illustre le **graphique** ci-dessous

grass roots (*n*): ⟨Ind/Pol⟩ on a décidé de consulter la **base** (*grass-roots opinion; the rank and file members*)

greed (*n*): la brutalité et l'**avidité** (*f*) des grands propriétaires terriens

green (*adj*): la nécessité d'une **ceinture verte** autour des grandes villes (*'green belt'*); ⟨Pol⟩ le **parti Vert** a recueilli 14% des voix (*Green/Ecology Party*); Bruxelles, qui vient de présenter un **Livre vert**, souhaite déréglementer le marché européen des satellites (*Green paper; policy proposals document*)

grievance (*n*): le délégué fait part au patron des **griefs** (*m*) du personnel; leurs **doléances** (*fpl*) portent essentiellement sur l'augmentation du coût de la vie

gross (*adj*): ⟨Fin/Fisc⟩ le **salaire brut** recouvre les versements aux salariés et les cotisations et autres retenues (*gross salary*); ⟨Econ⟩ le PIB **[produit intérieur brut]**, c'est l'ensemble des biens et services produits sur le territoire national (*Gross Domestic Product*); le **produit national brut** [PNB] va baisser de 1% cette année (*Gross National Product*)

ground (*n*): un **terrain** propice à une poussée écologiste (*ground, terrain*); ⟨Jur⟩ l'abandon du domicile conjugal peut être un **cas de divorce** (*ground/grounds for*)

groundless (*adj*): des accusations absolument **sans fondement** (*m*); SEE ALSO **unfounded**

groundswell (*n*): une véritable **lame de fond** pourrait encore le porter à la présidence (*groundswell [esp. of opinion]*)

group (*n*): un petit **contingent** d'ouvriers; ⟨Pol⟩ les autres **formations** (*f*) de l'opposition (*group, party*); un **groupuscule** d'extrême-droite (*small group*); se rencontrer **en petit comité** (*m*) (*in a small group*)

group (*v*): tous les autres candidats avaient **fait bloc** (*m*) contre lui (*group together*); SEE ALSO **unite**

grow (*v*): le nombre des emplois **s'est accru** en 12 ans de 12 millions; le décalage entre les deux partis **s'accuse** (*grow, increase*); l'exode de la population kurde **s'amplifie** (*grow in scale*); les bénéfices **croissent** régulièrement cette année (*grow, increase*); SEE ALSO **increase, rise**

growing (*adj*): dans un climat d'insécurité **croissante** (*growing*); ⟨Econ⟩ le **creusement du déficit** français des échanges de marchandises (*growing/worsening deficit*); SEE ALSO **increasing, rising**

growth (*n*): l'**accroissement** (*m*) du déficit budgétaire s'accélère; la **croissance** japonaise continue (*growth*); les entreprises **à forte croissance** (*showing vigorous growth*); il faudrait maîtriser l'**évolution** (*f*) des dépenses de l'Assurance maladie; la **progression** des ventes à l'export a été nulle (*growth, increase*); face à la **recrudescence** des accidents du travail (*growth, increasing number*); la création de **pôles** (*mpl*) **de croissance** dans les régions plus excentriques (*growth centre*); SEE ALSO **increase, rise**

guarantee (*n*): ⟨Pol⟩ Moscou donne des **gages** (*m*) aux conservateurs; ⟨Fin⟩ le créancier demande des **sûretés** (*f*), des garanties supplémentaires (*guarantee, assurance*); le **cautionnement** constitue une sorte de dépôt de garantie (*guarantee, deposit*); **verser une caution** de 250F (*put down/pay a guarantee/security*)

guarantee (*v*): le système **assure** une retraite complémentaire aux salariés; ⟨Fin⟩ son pays emprunterait des dollars, **gagés** sur ses avoirs à l'étranger; SEE ALSO **secure**

guaranteed (*adj*): ⟨Econ⟩ le maintien des **prix** (*m*) **garantis** à leur niveau de l'année dernière (*guaranteed prices*)

guarantor (*n*): ⟨Jur/Fin⟩ le **répondant** est responsable sur tout son patrimoine (*guarantor*); ⟨Pol⟩ Washington **se porte garant** (*m*) d'un référendum en Érythrée (*be a guarantor*)

guard (*v*): **prévenir** ainsi toute augmentation excessive des prix (*guard against, prevent*)

guardian (*n*): ⟨Jur/Soc⟩ le **tuteur** a sur son pupille les pouvoirs et devoirs d'un parent

guardianship (*n*): ⟨Jur/Soc⟩ la mise sous **tutelle** (*f*) provisoire d'un enfant

guideline (*n*): ⟨Pol⟩ le gouvernement va publier des **directives** (*f*) (*guidelines*); une **loi d'orientation** (*f*) sur l'Éducation (*law containing guidelines for* *further action*); une réunion pour **jeter les bases** (*f*) d'une politique de l'emploi (*set/work out guidelines*)

guilt (*n*): ⟨Jur⟩ sa **culpabilité** n'est plus à démontrer; une inculpation a tendance à impliquer la **culpabilité** de la personne inculpée

guilty (*adj*): ⟨Jur⟩ **condamné** pour fraude, il est allé en appel; le délit dont il a été **reconnu coupable** (*find guilty*); les **fautifs** (*m*) payeront de fortes amendes (*guilty party; person found guilty*)

gulf (*n*): le **fossé** qui sépare les deux communautés; un véritable **gouffre** psychologique les sépare; le **grand écart** entre les intentions affichées et leur mise en œuvre sur le terrain

H

habit (*n*): les **mœurs** (*f*) politiques très particulières de ce pays (*habit, custom*); les **us** (*m*) **et coutumes** du pays (*habits and customs*)

habitual (*adj*): ⟨Soc/Jur⟩ un **récidiviste** qu'on eut tort de laisser en liberté sous caution (*habitual offender*); SEE ALSO **second**

haggle (*v*): **marchander** chaque concession; **chicaner sur le prix**, c'est de bonne guerre

haggling (*n*): ⟨Comm⟩ un prix fixe marqué [pas de **marchandage**] (*m*); ces **marchandages** parlementaires nuisent à l'image du parti (*haggling, bargaining*)

half (*n*): partagé **pour moitié** (*f*) entre l'élevage et les céréales (*half and half, equally*); un volume de ventes **moitié moindre** (*half as large*); bénéficier de taux **inférieurs de moitié** à ceux dont disposent nos entreprises (*half as high; twice as low*); produire **moitié moins** d'ingénieurs que l'Allemagne (*half as much/many*)

half year (*n*): ⟨Fin⟩ les résultats pour le **semestre** en cours s'annoncent bons (*half year, six-month period*)

half-yearly (*adj/adv*): ⟨Fin/Comm⟩ les bénéfices **semestriels** ont baissé de 8% (*half-year, half-yearly*); l'annonce de **résultats** (*m*) **semestriels** des grandes sociétés (*half-yearly figures/profits*)

halve (*v*): le chômage a été **réduit de moitié** (*f*) en trois ans

halving (*n*): la **réduction de moitié** (*f*) de la taxe sur la vente de voitures neuves

hand (*n*): ⟨Pol⟩ la loi fut votée à l'unanimité et **à mains** (*fpl*) **levées** (*by a show of hands*)

hand (*v*): **remettre** leurs armes à l'armée régulière (*hand in/over*); **livrer** les malfaiteurs à la police (*hand over; give up*)

harassment (*n*): les opposants, souvent persécutés, **brimés** (*subjected to harassment*); SEE ALSO **sexual**

hard (*adj*): ⟨Jur⟩ condamner à deux ans de **travaux** (*mpl*) **forcés** (*hard labour*); ⟨Comm⟩ grâce à une **promotion agressive**, les stocks ont pu être écoulés (*hard sell, aggressive selling*); ⟨Fin⟩ se faire payer **en espèces** (*fpl*) (*in hard cash*); des **devises** (*f*) **fortes**, comme le dollar et le mark (*hard currency*)

hard core (*n*): appartenir au **noyau dur** du parti (*hard core*); les **inconditionnels** (*m*) de la politique de la gauche (*hard-core supporter*)

harden (*v*): ils sont prêts à **durcir** le blocus (*harden*); le gouvernement **durcit le ton** (*harden its attitude*); plus on l'attaque, plus il **se radicalise** (*harden one's position*); ⟨Soc/Jur⟩ le **criminel endurci**, qui passe le plus clair de sa vie en prison (*hardened criminal*)

hardening (*n*): un **durcissement** de l'attitude des Américains (*hardening*); un certain **raidissement** se produit dans l'attitude des négociateurs

hard-hit (*adj*): ⟨Comm⟩ les compagnies aériennes, **durement éprouvées** par la crise; **durement touché** par le ralentissement économique

hardline (*adj*): ⟨Pol⟩ les rigueurs du communisme **pur et dur** (*hardline*); partisans de la **ligne dure** (*hardline attitude*); l'homme de la **tendance dure** du parti (*hardline faction/element*)

hardliner (*n*): ⟨Pol⟩ les **durs** (*m*) ont imposé leur ligne militante; les **tenants** (*m*) **de la ligne dure** sont majoritaires au Congrès

hardship (*n*): connaître une **gêne financière** (*financial hardship*)

harm (*n*): leur capacité de **nuisance** (*f*) envers qui se montrerait inamical (*doing harm*); ⟨Jur⟩ inculpé de **coups** (*mpl*) **et blessures** (*[inflicting] grievous bodily harm*)

harm (*v*): des erreurs de gestion qui **portent atteinte** (*f*) à la crédibilité du parti (*harm*); toute augmentation du salaire minimum **nuirait** à l'emploi (*harm, be harmful/detrimental to*)

harmful (*adj*): les conséquences **néfastes** d'une monnaie surévaluée (*harmful, undesirable*); souvent **dommageable** sur le plan de la vie familiale (*harmful, prejudicial*); les **effets** (*m*) **pervers** de la loi-littoral sont dénoncés par des maires bretons; la lutte contre les **nuisances** (*f*) écologiques (*harmful effect*)

harmless (*adj*): les produits **sans nuisance** (*f*) pour l'environnement

harsh (*adj*): l'ampleur des **exactions** (*f*) commises par les troupes (*harsh treatment; atrocity*)

haven (*n*): ⟨Pol⟩ un **havre** en Allemagne pour les demandeurs d'asile (*[safe] haven*); la France, **terre** (*f*) **d'accueil** des minorités opprimées (*haven; land of welcome*)

hawk (*n*): ⟨Pol⟩ **faucons** (*mpl*) contre colombes: le Congrès américain reste très partagé (*'hawk', hardliner*)

head (*n*): ⟨Admin⟩ avoir son **siège social** à Lyon (*head office*); ⟨Pol⟩ **chef** (*m*) **de l'État** d'une république bananière (*head of state*); SEE ALSO **headquarters**

102

head (*v*): ⟨Admin⟩ **être à la tête** d'une société nationalisée; **chapeauter** l'enseignement en Région parisienne (*head, be at the head of; run*)

headhunt (*v*): ⟨Comm⟩ choisi pour **recruter les cadres** (*m*) **dirigeants**

headhunter (*n*): ⟨Comm⟩ **chasseur** (*m*) **de têtes** pour le compte d'une grande société américaine

headline (*n*): la défaillance de la société a **défrayé la chronique** (*f*) (*be headline news*); Le Figaro **titrait**: ... (*run a headline*); sa visite **fait la une** de tous les journaux (*make the headlines/front page*); **ravir la vedette** (*f*) dans la presse régionale (*steal the headlines*)

headquarters (*npl*): ⟨Admin⟩ les grandes institutions financières y ont leur **siège** (*m*) **principal**; les **quartiers** (*m*) **généraux** de sociétés étrangères en France; ⟨Mil⟩ dans l'**état-major** (*m*) allié; SEE ALSO **head**

health (*n*): de nouvelles **règles** (*f*) **sanitaires** pour les fruits et légumes (*health/ sanitary regulations*); ⟨Pol/Soc⟩ l'État transfère à la Région 80% de l'**action** (*f*) **sanitaire et sociale**; le domaine de la **Santé et de l'action sociale** (*health and social services*); ⟨Econ/Fin⟩ le groupe est **en voie** (*f*) **d'assainissement** (*returning to health, becoming healthier*)

healthy (*adj*): ⟨Econ⟩ le secteur le plus **performant** (*healthy, sound*); la banque **se porte bien** malgré la conjoncture difficile (*be healthy/in good health*); le marché du logement privatif **reprend de la vigueur** (*become more healthy*); ⟨Fin⟩ la **bonne tenue** du franc suisse (*healthy state*)

hear (*v*): ⟨Jur⟩ l'**affaire** (*f*) **sera plaidée** devant le tribunal de grande instance de Tours (*hear a court case*)

hearing (*n*): ⟨Jur⟩ une **audience** consacrée à l'audition des témoins (*hearing; session*); au premier jour des **auditions** (*f*) publiques (*hearing of court case*); l'**audition des témoins** a occupé toute la matinée (*hearing of witnesses*); lors du **délibéré**, il y eut des révélations fracassantes (*private hearing by a judge*)

heavy (*adj*): ⟨Comm⟩ **lourdes pertes** (*fpl*) pour la Banque populaire suisse (*heavy losses*); un commerçant qui **subit une perte considérable** (*make a heavy loss*); ⟨Econ⟩ dans le domaine de l'**industrie** (*f*) **lourde** (*heavy industry*)

height (*n*): être **au zénith** de sa popularité (*at the height/peak/zenith*)

heir (*n*): ⟨Fisc⟩ 80% des **héritiers** (*m*) ne paient aucun droit de succession; ⟨Pol⟩ le chef de l'État choisit son **dauphin** (*heir*); il est de l'avis de tous l'**héritier naturel** (*rightful heir*)

help (*n*): ⟨Pol/Fin⟩ avec le **concours** de la Ville (*help; assistance*); chômage partiel: **coup** (*m*) **de pouce** aux entreprises (*help [esp. from government]*); il leur faut l'**assistance** (*f*) d'un avocat (*help, assistance*); SEE ALSO **aid**

help (*v*): les pays occidentaux enfin **viennent au secours** des Kurdes; envoyer ses troupes pour **prêter main-forte** au gouvernement (*help, come to the help of*); il y a 2.000 personnes officiellement **secourues** (*in receipt of help/aid*)

103

heritage (*n*): la mise en valeur du **patrimoine** et de l'environnement (*heritage*); **patrimoine**: protéger les monuments historiques (*heritage [esp. architectural/natural]*); SEE ALSO **inheritance**

hiding (*n*): le chef des rebelles, depuis **en clandestinité** (*f*) (*in hiding*); SEE ALSO **underground**

hierarchy (*n*): la notion de **hiérarchie** (*f*) est moins répandue qu'autrefois; la **hiérarchie** administrative; SEE ALSO **command**

high (*adj*): ⟨Econ⟩ les exportations de pétrole restent **élevées** (*high, at a high level*); une indemnité que la **cherté des prix** a vite dévorée (*high prices*); des rencontres **à haut niveau** (*m*) (*high-level*); SEE ALSO **cost**

higher (*adj*): pertes **supérieures aux prévisions** (*f*) (*higher than forecast*); ⟨Fin/ Comm⟩ préparer une **surenchère** à l'offre de l'industriel australien (*higher bid*)

highest (*adj*): la Commission reste l'organe **suprême** de décision en vertu du traité de Rome (*highest, supreme*)

highlight (*v*): son intention: **mettre en avant** les réalisations du gouvernement; ce qui **met en lumière** le retard des économies de l'Est (*highlight, emphasize*)

highly (*adv*): les pays **hautement** industrialisés

high-ranking (*adj*): un diplomate **de haut rang** (*m*); une commission composée de six officiers **de haut rang**

high-tech (*n/adj*): ⟨Econ⟩ le défi des **secteurs** (*m*) **de pointe** (*high-tech sector*); l'essor d'industries **de pointe** (*f*) au Canada (*high-tech, leading-edge*)

highway (*n*): le camion-benne de la **voirie** municipale; la **voirie** municipale a dégagé les routes (*roads and highways department*)

hijack (*n*): Algérie: tentative de **détournement** (*m*) **d'avion**; **détournement** avorté du vol Rome-Tunis (*hijack [esp. of plane]*)

hijack (*v*): un pirate de l'air tente de **détourner** un DC9 d'Alitalia

hinterland (*n*): un **arrière-pays** riche en petites industries

hire (*n*): la **location** d'un appartement (*hire, renting*); le bail ou l'**engagement** (*m*) **à location** (*hire/rental agreement*)

hire (*v*): SEE **recruit**

hire purchase (*n*): ⟨Comm⟩ **acheter à tempérament** est le moyen le moins onéreux (*hire purchase*); signer un **contrat d'achat** (*m*) **à crédit** (*hire purchase agreement*)

hit (*v*): le secteur le plus **touché** par la crise; la sécheresse **frappant** l'Afrique australe; les exportations françaises sont plus **affectées** que celles de l'Espagne (*hit, affect*); ⟨Mil⟩ une croisière **touchée** par un missile libyen (*hit, strike*); SEE ALSO **affect**, **stricken**

hitch (*n*): un nouvel **accroc** dans la cohabitation Élysée-Matignon (*hitch, difficulty*)

hold (*n*): la **mainmise** cléricale sur la vie publique polonaise (*tight hold/grip*); Liban: la Syrie renforce son **emprise** (*f*) (*hold; control*)

hold (*v*): l'État **détient** dorénavant 50% des actions (*hold, possess*); ⟨Jur⟩ un suspect peut être **détenu** pendant trois jours (*hold, detain*); la réunion **se tient** dimanche à Nice (*be held, take place*)

holder (*n*): les **détenteurs** (*m*) de visas seuls peuvent y aller; les **porteurs** (*m*) Eurocard; **titulaire** (*m*) **de** la double nationalité (*holder, person in possession of*)

holding (*n*): la **tenue** d'une conférence sur le Moyen-Orient (*holding*); ⟨Fin/ Comm⟩ le gel partiel des **avoirs** (*m*) chinois en France (*holdings, assets*); le groupe va prendre la forme juridique d'un **holding** (*holding company*); ⟨Pol/Admin⟩ la **rétention** en zone internationale de transit des demandeurs d'asile (*holding, detention*)

hold-up (*n*): **attaque** (*f*) **à main armée** sur un fourgon des Postes; **braquage** (*m*) dans une bijouterie parisienne; tentative de **hold-up** (*m*) dans une banque de Honfleur

hold up (*v*): un taxi **braqué** par un ripou (*hold up*); ⟨Comm⟩ le marché **s'est mieux tenu** que prévu (*hold up, resist*); des livraisons **retardées** par une grève des camionneurs (*hold up, delay*); SEE ALSO **delayed**

holiday (*n*): s'aligner sur les **congés** (*m*) des fournisseurs et des clients (*holiday; leave*); avoir droit à des **congés payés** (*paid holiday*); des jours **fériés** [fêtes civiles ou religieuses]; la fête **est chômée** en France (*be designated an official holiday*); SEE ALSO **stagger**

home (*n*): ⟨Pol⟩ les rapports des insulaires avec la **métropole** (*home country*); ⟨Econ⟩ l'importance du **marché intérieur**; ouvrir le **marché domestique** aux concurrents étrangers (*home/domestic market*); ⟨Soc⟩ l'**aide** (*f*) **ménagère** est accordée après enquête sociale; les services d'**aide à domicile**; la somme est versée à l'association employant la **garde à domicile** (*home/domestic help*)

homeland (*n*): ⟨Pol⟩ la **patrie** de ses ancêtres; un **foyer** pour le peuple juif

homeless (*n/adj*): plus d'un million de **sans-abri** (*m*) à Khartoum; le problème des sans-emploi et des **sans-toit** (*m*)

home loan (*n*): ⟨Fin⟩ un **prêt immobilier** pour l'accession à la propriété d'un logement

home-owner (*n*): le rêve d'**être propriétaire** (*m*) **de sa maison** (*be a home-owner/householder*); les ménages modestes ne peuvent pas espérer pouvoir **accéder à la propriété** (*become a home-owner*)

home ownership (*n*): bientôt l'**accession** (*f*) **à la propriété** sera à la portée de tous; promouvoir l'**accès** (*m*) **à la propriété** des locataires de logements sociaux

home rule (*n*): ⟨Pol⟩ certains Bretons aspirent à l'**autonomie** (*f*) (*home rule; autonomy*)

host (*n/adj*): ⟨Pol⟩ dans le **pays d'accueil** (*m*) (*host country*)

105

hostage (*n*): six morts dans une **prise d'otage** (*m*) (*taking of hostages*); un commando **prend en otage** six Palestiniens en Cisjordanie (*take hostage*); les terroristes **preneurs** (*m*) **d'otages** (*hostage-taker*)

hostel (*n*): les immigrés logés dans des **foyers** (*m*) ou des hôtels meublés

hostile (*adj*): être **réticent à** l'idée; les Britanniques, **adversaires** (*m*) **déclarés** de l'Europe sociale (*hostile to*); **s'opposer** au principe d'une défense européenne (*be hostile to, oppose*); ⟨Comm⟩ une **OPA [offre publique d'achat] inamicale** lancée sur la société nantaise (*hostile take-over bid*)

hostility (*n*): le projet suscite la **défiance** de 59% des interrogés; il **s'est attiré les foudres** (*m*) des associations locales (*attract the hostility of*); un projet qui **fait l'unanimité** (*f*) **contre lui** (*encounter general hostility*); SEE ALSO **suspicion**

hour (*n*): pendant les **heures** (*f*) **de bureau** (*office hours*)

hourly (*adj*): ⟨Fin⟩ une revalorisation du **taux de salaire horaire** (*hourly rate [of pay]*); (*adv*) des ouvriers **payés à l'heure** (*f*) (*paid hourly/by the hour*)

house (*n*): ⟨Pol⟩ la **Chambre haute** dans un système bicaméral (*Upper House [esp. of Parliament]*); SEE ALSO **upper**

house (*v*): les HLM **logent** un Français sur quatre (*house*); on a pu **héberger** les réfugiés chez l'habitant (*house, accommodate*)

house arrest (*n*): une mise en **résidence** (*f*) **surveillée** de l'ancien chef des rebelles; quatre **assignations** (*f*) **à domicile** après le coup manqué (*house arrest*); le chef de l'État **assigné à domicile** (*m*) après le putsch militaire (*put under house arrest*)

household (*n*): les **ménages** (*m*) les plus modestes; des centaines de **foyers** (*m*) privés d'électricité (*household*); ⟨Econ⟩ la **consommation des ménages** est en progression de 2,9% (*household consumption*)

householder (*n*): le **locataire** doit notifier son intention au propriétaire (*householder, tenant*); les réparations relèvent du **propriétaire** (*householder, owner*); l'imprimé lui est adressé, en tant que **chef** (*m*) **de famille** (*householder, head of the household*)

housewife (*n*): le panier de la **ménagère** (*housewife*); d'abord **femme** (*f*) **au foyer** puis infirmière (*housewife [as opposed to career woman]*)

housing (*n*): le marché de l'**habitat** (*m*) continue de flamber (*housing*); baisse des ventes de **logements** (*m*) **neufs** (*new housing*); en raison du marasme de l'**immobilier** (*m*) (*housing market/sector*); ⟨Pol⟩ définir une **politique du logement** (*housing policy*); ⟨Soc/Fisc⟩ bénéficier d'une **aide au logement** (*housing benefit*)

humanitarian (*adj*): l'action d'**organismes** (*m*) **humanitaires** sur place (*humanitarian organization*)

human rights (*npl*): ⟨Pol⟩ insister sur le respect des **droits** (*m*) **de l'homme**; de graves violations des **droits de l'homme**

hunger strike (*n*): ⟨Pol⟩ la **grève de la faim** des prisonniers républicains

hush up (*v*): Matignon a **étouffé** l'affaire; afin d'**étouffer** une affaire de drogue et de trafic d'armes; SEE ALSO **cover up**

hypothesis (*n*): c'est une **hypothèse** qui semble assez peu probable (*hypothesis, theory*)

hypothetical (*adj*): en attendant une **hypothétique** reprise de la croissance

I

idea (*n*): favorable aux **thèses** (*f*) des séparatistes basques (*idea, argument, thesis*)

identification (*n*): une **fiche signalétique** aussi précise que possible (*identification card*)

identity (*n*): muni de faux **papiers** (*m*) **d'identité** (*[identity] papers*)

idle (*adj*): ⟨Econ⟩ 2.000 ouvriers **réduits au chômage** par la récession (*make idle*)

idleness (*n*): le chômage, l'échec scolaire, le **désœuvrement** sont ici le lot quotidien de beaucoup d'adultes; ⟨Econ⟩ les jours d'**inemploi** (*m*) ne sont plus garantis par une caisse nationale (*[enforced] idleness*)

ignorance (*n*): la **méconnaissance** des principes qu'elles veulent défendre; la **méconnaissance** des mécanismes de l'économie

ignore (*v*): le Sénat **passe outre** au véto que le Président a promis d'apporter au texte (*ignore, disregard*); **passer sous silence** (*m*) la question la plus importante (*ignore, pass over*); sur le papier, les chiffres paraissent **incontournables** (*impossible to ignore*)

ill-conceived (*adj*): un projet **mal-conçu**, et mal rédigé

illegal (*adj*): le cumul **illicite** d'un revenu salarié et d'une allocation-chômage; ⟨Pol/Admin⟩ la majorité des immigrés **illégaux** (*illegal*); lutter contre les **entrées** (*f*) **clandestines** (*illegal entry/immigration*); la reconduite à la frontière des **clandestins** (*m*) (*illegal entrant*); ⟨Econ⟩ une amende infligée aux deux firmes pour **entente** (*f*) **illicite** (*illegal agreement/arrangement*); SEE ALSO **illicit, unauthorized**

illegally (*adv*): **en toute illégalité** (*f*), et sans permis de construire (*illegally*); un hôtelier qui hébergeait **clandestinement** des étrangers en situation irrégulière (*illegally; without declaring officially*)

illegitimate (*adj*): ⟨Soc⟩ l'augmentation régulière des **naissances** (*f*) **hors mariage** (*illegitimate birth*); un **enfant naturel**, ou né en dehors du mariage; être **enfant illégitime** n'est plus une tare (*illegitimate child*)

illicit (*adj*): la résorption du travail **clandestin** (*illicit, illegal, underground*)

ill-suited (*adj*): les programmes de prévention y demeurent **mal adaptés** à la situation; une solution tout à fait **inadaptée** (*ill-suited, unsuitable*)

107

ill-treat (*v*): ⟨Soc⟩ enfants abandonnés ou **maltraités** (*ill-treated; battered*)

ill-treatment (*n*): ⟨Soc⟩ signe quasi absolu de **maltraitance** (*f*) (*ill-treatment, cruelty*); plusieurs détenus ont subi des **sévices** (*mpl*), selon leurs avocats (*ill-treatment; torture*)

image (*n*): ⟨Comm⟩ améliorer son **image** (*f*) **de marque**; les hommes politiques soignent leur **image de marque** (*brand/ corporate image*)

imbalance (*n*): ⟨Econ⟩ l'**inadéquation** (*f*) entre l'offre et la demande; les principaux **déséquilibres** (*m*) dont souffre la région

immediately (*adv*): suspendre **sans délai** (*m*) toute importation de matériels de guerre

immigration (*n*): de nouvelles lois restreignant et contrôlant l'**immigration** (*f*) (*immigration*); tout pays a le droit de contrôler le **flux migratoire**; un **solde migratoire** estimé en 1992 à 80.000 personnes (*movement of population [esp. immigration]*)

imminent (*adj*): en raison du **prochain** départ de la compagnie UTA (*imminent*); des restructurations **s'annoncent** (*be imminent*)

imminently (*adv*): une demande pourrait leur être adressée **très prochainement**

impact (*n*): la **portée** et l'efficacité d'une grève (*impact, effectiveness; scope*); demander une **étude d'impact** (*m*) préalable (*impact study*)

impair (*v*): cette crise risque d'**altérer** les relations entre Londres et Dublin; une défaite **entamerait** largement sa crédibilité (*impair, affect, spoil*)

impeach (*v*): ⟨Pol⟩ la possibilité pour le Congrès de **destituer** le président des États-Unis; SEE ALSO **dismiss**, **depose**

impeachment (*n*): ⟨Pol⟩ le président menacé d'une procédure de **destitution** (*f*); recommander la **mise en accusation** (*f*) du président; SEE ALSO **deposition**

imperil (*v*): ces conflits pourraient **remettre en cause** (*f*) l'expansion prévue (*imperil, jeopardize*)

impetus (*n*): créer une **dynamique** unitaire; donner un nouvel **élan** au développement économique local; donner une nouvelle **impulsion** à la machine économique (*impetus, boost, momentum*); la **relance** du processus de paix (*giving fresh impetus*); SEE ALSO **boost**, **momentum**

implacable (*adj*): l'opposition **irréductible** de plusieurs députés libéraux

implement (*v*): **mettre en œuvre** le plan de licenciements prévu; la politique de transparence **mise en œuvre** récemment (*implement, put into effect/ operation*); pour **mettre à exécution** (*f*) son programme (*implement, carry out*)

implementation (*n*): l'impact qu'a eu l'**entrée** (*f*) **en application** du grand marché européen; il faudra surveiller la **mise en œuvre** du cessez-le-feu (*implementation*); incertitude sur les **modalités** (*f*) du cessez-le-feu (*[details of the] implementation*); SEE ALSO **effect**

implicate (*v*): un scandale **impliquant** une banque japonaise; l'enquête risque de **mettre en cause** (*f*) des personnalités connues (*implicate, involve*); un marchand d'armes **lié à** l'attentat (*be implicated/involved in*); SEE ALSO **involve, mix up**

implication (*n*): considérer les **implications** (*f*) politiques et diplomatiques (*implication, consequence*); l'**implication** directe de membres du gouvernement dans les délits de trafic d'influence (*implication, involvement*)

import (*n*): ⟨Econ⟩ une fiscalité qui pénalise les **importations** (*f*) (*imports, importing*)

import (*v*): ⟨Econ⟩ les **produits** (*m*) **importés**, frappés de droits de douane (*imported goods*)

importance (*n*): il faut **revaloriser** le rôle du Parlement (*give greater importance to*); SEE ALSO **enhance**

impose (*v*): l'amnistie **fixe** des conditions pour son exil

imposition (*n*): la Commission a annoncé l'**imposition** (*f*) de taxes antidumping; SEE ALSO **levy**

impotence (*n*): les Douze, conscients de l'**impuissance** (*f*) de leurs initiatives de politique étrangère

impotent (*adj*): SEE **powerless**

impoverish (*v*): des guerres incessantes ont **appauvri** ce pays

impoverished (*adj*): le Vietnam, très **appauvri** par le régime communiste; 3,6 millions de Bulgares **économiquement faibles**; SEE ALSO **deprived**

impoverishment (*n*): ⟨Agric⟩ le problème de l'**appauvrissement** (*m*) des sols (*impoverishment*); ⟨Econ⟩ la **paupérisation** et la marginalisation des paysans (*impoverishment, pauperization*)

imprison (*v*): ⟨Jur⟩ trop jeune pour être **mis en prison** (*f*); un policier **écroué** pour extorsion de fonds; inculpé et **incarcéré** à la centrale de Saverne; la Cour d'assises l'a **renvoyé derrière les barreaux** (*m*) (*imprison, send to prison*); SEE ALSO **bar**

imprisonment (*n*): ⟨Jur⟩ une mesure alternative à l'**incarcération** (*f*); cinq ans d'**emprisonnement** (*m*); une peine de 20 ans de **réclusion** (*f*) **criminelle** (*imprisonment*); des **conditions** (*f*) **carcérales** déplorables (*conditions of imprisonment*); SEE ALSO **detention**

improper (*adj*): l'**utilisation** (*f*) **abusive** de la procédure; un **usage abusif** de son autorité parentale (*improper use, misuse*)

improve (*v*): la position de l'Auvergne **s'est améliorée** depuis; les choses pourront **s'arranger**; ⟨Econ⟩ la situation des entreprises **s'est assainie** depuis lors; la situation semble aujourd'hui **se redresser**

improvement (*n*): une **amélioration** des voies de communication; ⟨Econ⟩ signes d'**assainissement** (*m*) de l'économie; une **embellie** dans la situation économique; avec un léger **mieux** en 1994; la **progression** par rapport à 1994 est de 19,8% (*improvement*); ils demandent une **revalorisation** de leur statut (*improvement; revaluation*); la municipalité propose des **primes à l'aménagement** (*m*) **de l'habitat** (*[property] improvement grant*)

improvidence (*n*): ⟨Pol/Fin⟩ il dénonce l'**imprévoyance** (*f*) de la gestion socialiste; SEE ALSO **foresight**

improvident (*adj*): une gestion **imprévoyante** (*improvident; lacking in foresight*)

inability (*n*): l'**incapacité** (*f*) des Douze à élaborer une politique autonome commune (*inability*); ⟨Fin⟩ pour résoudre d'éventuelles **incapacités** (*f*) **de remboursement** d'un prêt immobilier (*inability to make repayments*); SEE ALSO **incapacity**

inaccessible (*adj*): une région complètement **enclavée**, mal desservie par la route comme par le rail (*inaccessible, enclosed, cut off*)

inaccessibility (*n*): un des problèmes de l'Auvergne, c'est son **enclavement** (*m*) (*inaccessibility*); la région tente de mettre fin à son **enclavement routier** (*inaccessibility by road*)

inaccurate (*adj*): il est **inexact** de dire qu'il a menti (*inaccurate, incorrect*)

inactivity (*n*): l'**inaction** (*f*) et les erreurs du gouvernement (*inactivity, lack of initiative*)

inadequacy (*n*): on déplore l'**insuffisance** (*f*) des salaires

inadequate (*adj*): des moyens de lutte **insuffisants**; les mesures annoncées sont jugées **insuffisantes**

inadmissible (*adj*): ⟨Jur⟩ déclarer **irrecevable** une requête

inadmissibility (*n*): ⟨Pol⟩ par l'exercice d'**irrecevabilité** (*f*), on affirme que le texte proposé est anticonstitutionnel

inappropriate (*adj*): cette médiation est jugée **inopportune** par Washington; SEE ALSO **unsuitable**

incapable (*adj*): leurs dirigeants semblent **inaptes** à comprendre le monde de l'après-guerre froide (*incapable, unable*)

incapacity (*n*): l'**impuissance** (*f*) des gouvernements à réduire le chômage; SEE ALSO **inability, powerlessness**

incentive (*n*): préférer l'**incitation** (*f*) à la contrainte; les **mesures** (*f*) **incitatives** semblent quelque peu légères (*incentive*); des **incitations** (*f*) **fiscales**, tels des abattements à 80% (*tax incentive*); ⟨Econ⟩ la mise en place de **programmes** (*m*) **d'incitation au travail** (*work incentive scheme*); des **primes** (*f*) **de rendement** pour améliorer la productivité de la main-d'œuvre (*incentive payment*)

incident (*n*): à l'issue de brefs **incidents** (*m*), on comptait 43 interpellés; des **accrochages** (*m*) opposant manifestants et forces de l'ordre (*incident, clash*); ⟨Pol⟩ les **péripéties** (*f*) de la campagne électorale (*incident, episode*)

incite (*v*): il estimait que les forces de l'ordre **poussaient** à la violence

incitement (*n*): coupable d'**incitation** (*f*) à la haine raciale; un **appel à la révolte** diffusé par la radio (*incitement/call to rebel*)

include (*v*): **inclure** dans le texte une clause spéciale; ces projets doivent **englober** les autres pays européens; le prix forfaitaire **comprend** matériels et frais de transport

including (*prep*): 14 inculpations, **dont** celle d'un policier; les inculpés, **y compris** un mineur de 13 ans; un loyer, **charges** (*fpl*) **comprises** (*including charges*)

inclusion (*n*): la CGT exige l'**intégration** (*f*) des primes dans le salaire (*inclusion, including*)

incoherent (*adj*): les décisions **incohérentes** de ministres successifs; la politique africaine **décousue** pratiquée par le gouvernement

income (*n*): 3,5 milliards de **recettes** (*f*) nouvelles; les dépenses étaient inférieures aux **rentrées** (*f*); avec leurs 15.000F de **revenus** (*m*) nets mensuels (*income, receipts*); le **revenu agricole** est globalement en régression (*agricultural income*); ⟨Soc⟩ un **supplément de revenu** (*m*) accordé aux plus de seize ans (*income support grant/payment*)

income tax (*n*): l'assiette de l'**impôt** (*m*) **sur le revenu** est devenue trop étroite (*income tax*); le fait d'**être imposé sur le revenu** (*pay/be liable to income tax*)

inconsistency (*n*): un risque croissant d'**incohérence** (*f*) dans le domaine de la défense; l'inspecteur du fisc a décelé quelques **incohérences** dans la déclaration; SEE ALSO **incoherent**

inconsistent (*adj*): la fiscalité lourde, complexe et **incohérente** (*inconsistent; incoherent*)

inconvenience (*n*): les **désagréments** (*m*) que la grève va entraîner (*inconvenience, annoyance*)

inconvenient (*adj*): le moment est **mal choisi**; l'arrivée **inopportune** du ministre (*inconvenient; ill-chosen*); un refus américain aurait été particulièrement **mal venu** (*inconvenient, inappropriate*)

increase (*n*): l'**accroissement** (*m*) du travail féminin; imposer aux enseignants un **alourdissement** de leurs charges; un **gain** de pouvoir d'achat; des **hausses** (*f*) de tarif de 10 à 15%; un **renforcement** des aides et une réforme des quotas (*increase*); la **multiplication** des tarifs réduits pour familles nombreuses (*increase in the number of*); SEE ALSO **rise**

increase (*v*): la Chine veut **accroître** son influence sur la gestion de Hongkong; le nombre de chômeurs **s'accroît** au fil des mois; si le terrorisme continuait à **s'amplifier** (*increase*); des attentats contre les personnels militaires **se multiplient** (*increase in number; become more frequent*); SEE ALSO **grow, raise, rise**

increased (*adj*): une coopération internationale **accrue** (*increased*); des accords d'intéressement fondés sur des **gains** (*m*) **de production** (*increased productivity*)

111

increasing (*adj*): une activité occupant une place **croissante** dans l'économie; l'importance **grandissante** de ce secteur de la vie économique (*increasing, growing*); un pourcentage qui est **en augmentation** (*f*) (*increasing, on the increase*); la **multiplication** des faillites (*increasing number*)

incriminate (*v*): ⟨Jur⟩ le témoignage de ses associés **met en cause** l'homme d'affaires belge

incriminating (*adj*): ⟨Jur⟩ un document **compromettant** (*incriminating, compromising*); on a pu examiner à loisir la **pièce à conviction** (*incriminating evidence/document*)

incur (*v*): ⟨Jur⟩ **encourir** une peine totale de 125 ans de prison; SEE ALSO **risk**

indebtedness (*n*): ⟨Econ⟩ **endettement** (*m*) ne signifie pas nécessairement mauvaise gestion; l'**endettement** total du groupe s'élevait à 34MF (*indebtedness, debt*); SEE ALSO **debt**

indecency (*n*): ⟨Jur⟩ inculpé d'**outrage** (*m*) **aux bonnnes mœurs**

indecent (*adj*): ⟨Jur⟩ la prostitution est un **outrage public à la pudeur** (*indecent behaviour*); le juge l'a inculpé d'**attentat** (*m*) **à la pudeur** sur un mineur de treize ans (*indecent assault*)

indecisive (*adj*): il est assez **velléitaire** sur cette question où il aurait fallu déjà agir

indefinite (*adj*): un préavis de grève d'une durée **indéterminée**

indefinitely (*adv*): **reporter** *sine die* les élections; le sommet a été **reporté à une date indéterminée** (*postpone/put off indefinitely*)

indemnification (*n*): ⟨Ins⟩ instaurer l'**indemnisation** (*f*) à 100% pour les chômeurs de longue durée

indemnify (*v*): ⟨Ins⟩ le transporteur doit alors vous **indemniser**; le nombre de chômeurs **indemnisés** a légèrement baissé; SEE ALSO **compensate**

indemnity (*n*): verser un gros **dédommagement** en guise de récompense; SEE ALSO **compensation**

independence (*n*): ⟨Admin⟩ l'**autonomie** (*f*) de la Poste et de France Télécom (*independence, autonomy*); ⟨Pol⟩ la Namibie a pu **accéder à l'indépendance** (*f*) (*gain/win independence*); dès son **accession** (*f*) **à l'indépendance** en 1961 (*achieving independence*); cette région **s'est proclamée autonome** (*declare its independence*); SEE ALSO **autonomy**

independent (*n/adj*): ⟨Pol⟩ une liste centriste **autonome** aux élections européennes; le sénateur **non-inscrit**, maire de Caen (*independent*); comment voteront les **non-inscrits** (*m*)? (*independent member of parliament*/député)

in-depth (*adj*): une **étude approfondie** de la question; une **réflexion en profondeur** (*f*) sur l'efficacité d'ensemble de l'éducation (*in-depth study/examination*)

index (*n*): ⟨Econ⟩ l'**indice** (*m*) du coût de la construction; ⟨Fin⟩ des prestations **indexées** sur le coût de la vie (*index-linked*); SEE ALSO **Stock Exchange**

index (*v*): ⟨Fin⟩ **indexer** les retraites sur le coût de la vie

indexing (*n*): ⟨Econ⟩ l'**indexation** (*f*) des salaires sur les prix

indicate (*v*): les traitements nets **font ressortir** une baisse du pouvoir d'achat; ceci **témoigne de** l'importance qu'on lui accorde; SEE ALSO **show**

indict (*v*): SEE **accuse**

indictable (*adj*): ⟨Jur⟩ la moitié des **affaires** (*f*) **sérieuses** confiées à la police (*indictable offence*); par leur contenu, elles **tombent sous le coup de la loi** (*be an indictable offence*)

indictment (*n*): un véritable **réquisitoire** contre la politique de son prédécesseur (*indictment, attack*); ⟨Jur⟩ ne pas confondre **inculpation** (*f*) et culpabilité; un **chef d'inculpation** qui pourrait lui valoir la détention à vie (*indictment, charge*); SEE ALSO **charge**

indignant (*adj*): **s'indigner de** l'attitude du ministre (*be indignant about, express indignation about*)

indignation (*n*): le président **s'est ému** des propos tenus par son homologue allemand; Paris **s'en indigne** (*express indignation*)

indirect (*adj*): ⟨Fisc⟩ vers un rapprochement des **fiscalités** (*f*) **indirectes** (*indirect taxation/taxes*)

individual (*n*): les mesures concernent les **particuliers** (*m*) et les entreprises

individual (*adj*): multiplier les réformes **ponctuelles** (*individual, isolated, limited*)

individuality (*n*): ⟨Pol⟩ affirmer sa **spécificité**; le **pbrticularisme** des provinces est un des fondements du fédéralisme (*separate identity, individuality*)

individually (*adv*): ces situations se négocient **au cas par cas** (*individually, case by case*)

induce (*v*): ces résultats n'**inclinent** pas à l'optimisme (*induce, inspire*)

inducement (*n*): ⟨Fisc⟩ des abattements et autres **incitations** (*f*) **fiscales** (*tax inducement*); ⟨Comm⟩ une publicité tapageuse qui **incite à l'achat** (*m*) (*be an inducement to buy*)

industrial (*adj*): ⟨Econ⟩ devant la chute des commandes, on envisage un **redéploiement industriel** (*industrial redeployment*); une petite entreprise de la **zone industrielle** Est (*industrial park/estate*); SEE ALSO **tribunal**

industry (*n*): ⟨Econ⟩ une région de petites et moyennes **industries** (*f*) (*industry*); ministre du Commerce et de l'**Artisanat** (*m*) (*small [esp. independent] industry*); SEE ALSO **cottage industry**

ineffective (*adj*): des solutions parfaitement **inefficaces** (*ineffective*); une infrastructure **inopérante**, et une administration déficitaire (*ineffective, inefficient*)

ineffectiveness (*n*): le rapport dénonce l'**inefficacité** (*f*) de certains programmes d'aide; SEE ALSO **inefficiency**

113

inefficiency (*n*): l'**inefficacité** (*f*) flagrante du système (*inefficiency*); ⟨Econ⟩ la **faible productivité** de la compagnie publique des transports (*inefficiency, inefficient production*); SEE ALSO **productivity**

inefficient (*adj*): ⟨Econ⟩ un dispositif totalement **inefficient**; la machine bureaucratique, lourde et **inefficace**; des industriels trop **peu performants** (*inefficient; ineffective*)

inequality (*n*): les **inégalités** (*f*) s'accentuent, et les revendications demeurent; des textes visant à réduire les **inégalités**

inescapable (*adj*): l'OLP est un élément **incontournable** dans la recherche d'un règlement pacifique (*inescapable, essential*); SEE ALSO **ignore**

inevitable (*adj*): une hausse des prélèvements sociaux n'est pas **inéluctable** (*inevitable, unavoidable*)

inevitably (*adv*): **inévitablement** c'est l'usager qui en fera les frais; **fatalement**, ces augmentations seront impopulaires

inexperience (*n*): son **inexpérience** (*f*) des affaires l'a desservi dans ce poste (*inexperience, lack of experience*)

inexperienced (*adj*): des enseignants souvent jeunes et **inexpérimentés**

infiltrate (*v*): ⟨Pol⟩ **noyauter** un parti pour en prendre la direction

infiltration (*f*): ⟨Pol⟩ le **noyautage** de l'armée par des éléments de l'opposition

inflation (*n*): ⟨Econ⟩ après la récession, le spectre de l'**inflation** (*f*) (*inflation*); le revenu moyen **en francs** (*m*) **constants** des agriculteurs s'est accru de 1,3% (*inflation-adjusted*)

inflexibility (*n*): cette **rigidité** doctrinaire rend la négociation difficile; malgré la **crispation** dogmatique de leurs dirigeants

inflexible (*adj*): une manière plus ou moins **rigoriste** ou laxiste d'appliquer les règlements (*inflexible, rigid*)

influx (*n*): un **afflux** massif d'aides et de capitaux (*influx, inflow*); SEE ALSO **flood**

inform (*v*): en **avisant** le fisc, on évite des désagréments; SEE ALSO **advise**, **notify**

informal (*adj*): ⟨Pol⟩ Panama: **accord** (*m*) **à l'amiable** avec Washington (*informal agreement*); ⟨Jur⟩ arriver à un **accord à l'amiable** (*informal/ out-of-court agreement*)

information (*n*): une demande de **renseignements** (*mpl*) (*information*); les chiffres sont donnés **à titre indicatif** (*for information only*)

infrastructure (*n*): les villes du tiers-monde aux **infrastructures** (*f*) dégradées ou inexistantes

infringe (*v*): **contrevenir aux** règles en la matière (*infringe, break*); **enfreindre la législation sur** l'ouverture dominicale (*infringe/contravene the law*); ⟨Jur⟩ **tomber sous le coup des lois** (*f*) contre la diffamation (*infringe a rule/law*); SEE ALSO **contravene**

infringement (*n*): une **atteinte** au monopole de la distribution du courrier; une **entorse** aux règlements; condamné pour **infraction** (*f*) à la législation sur les stupéfiants; un **manquement** au code de déontologie médicale (*infringement, breach of*); SEE ALSO **breach, breaking**

inherit (*v*): il a **hérité** d'une belle propriété dans la Somme

inheritance (*n*): comment payer moins d'impôts à la suite d'un **héritage**; les démarches à accomplir pour régler une **succession**; ⟨Fisc⟩ une fiscalité qui frappe lourdement le **patrimoine** (*inheritance, legacy*); 80% des héritiers ne paient aucun **droit** (*m*) **de succession**; des mesures concernant la **fiscalité du patrimoine** dans le prochain budget (*inheritance tax*)

initiate (*v*): la Chine **amorce** un rapprochement avec ses voisins (*initiate*); le déclin **amorcé** en 1992 se poursuit; **entamer** une procédure de naturalisation (*initiate, begin*)

initiative (*n*): ⟨Pol⟩ des **démarches** (*f*) pour sauvegarder la paix (*initiative, step, move*); ⟨Pol/Soc⟩ un programme d'**actions** (*fpl*) visant à l'insertion professionnelle des jeunes (*initiative, policy*)

injunction (*n*): la Ville lui envoya une **sommation** de quitter les lieux; ⟨Jur⟩ l'huissier envoit un **commandement** vous enjoignant de payer; un avertissement, puis une **mise en demeure** en bonne et due forme (*injunction, order*); **obtenir un arrêt du tribunal** interdisant la publication de l'article (*obtain a [legal] injunction*)

innocent (*adj*): ⟨Jur⟩ l'accusé, présumé **innocent**, tant qu'il n'a pas été jugé coupable (*innocent*); il a été **innocenté** par la Cour d'appel; les prévenus furent **relaxés** (*find/declare innocent*); SEE ALSO **clear**

innovate (*v*): en **innovant** sans cesse, ils conservent leur avance sur la concurrence; la loi de 1992 **innove** sur un point essentiel (*innovate; break new ground*)

innovation (*n*): une **innovation** qui leur permet de garder le leadership sur ce créneau

innovative (*adj*): une entreprise dynamique et **innovante**; une entreprise des plus **novatrices** (*innovative*); deux villes-**pilotes** en matière de transports en commun (*innovative, forward-looking; experimental*)

input (*n*): l'**apport** (*m*) du tourisme étranger (*input, contribution*)

insecurity (*n*): le climat d'**insécurité** (*f*) qui règne dans la capitale

insert (*n*): ⟨Jour⟩ un **encart publicitaire** inséré dans trois journaux régionaux (*publicity insert*)

insert (*v*): ⟨Soc⟩ il n'est pas facile de **caser** un jeune Maghrébin (*insert/place in employment*)

insertion (*n*): ⟨Soc⟩ faciliter l'**insertion** (*f*) des jeunes dans la vie active

in-service (*adj*): ⟨Educ⟩ une **formation au sein de l'entreprise** offerte aux jeunes; ⟨Econ⟩ faire un stage de **formation professionnelle continue** (*in-service training*)

insider (*n*): ⟨Fin⟩ lors du rachat de la firme, des **initiés** (*m*) ont gagné des millions de dollars (*insider*); enquêter pour voir s'il y a eu **délit** (*m*) **d'initié** (*insider dealing*)

insoluble (*adj*): la situation pour l'instant semble **bloquée**

insolvency (*n*): ⟨Comm⟩ l'**insolvabilité** (*f*) peut être un délit (*insolvency*); la **procédure de redressement** (*m*) **judiciaire** a été ouverte à leur égard (*insolvency/bankruptcy proceedings*)

insolvent (*adj*): ⟨Comm⟩ en état d'**insolvabilité** (*f*) notoire; en **cessation** (*f*) **de paiements** depuis un mois, la société a déposé son bilan (*insolvent, unable to pay one's debts*)

inspect (*v*): le Brésil accepte qu'on **contrôle** ses matériels nucléaires (*inspect, check*); le juge fit **arraisonner** le bateau (*stop and inspect*)

inspection (*n*): un **contrôle** effectué par les inspecteurs de l'ONU (*inspection, checking*); ⟨Fin⟩ une **vérification** des comptes révéla l'existence de fausses factures (*inspection, examination*)

inspector (*n*): ⟨Educ⟩ l'**inspecteur** (*m*) **d'académie** a décidé de fermer le collège (*regional education inspector*)

inspectorate (*n*): ⟨Admin⟩ un rapport fait par l'**inspection** (*f*) des Finances (*inspectorate*); ⟨Educ⟩ s'adresser à l'**inspection** académique (*[school] inspectorate*)

install (*v*): le dispositif **mis en place** par la gendarmerie s'est révélé efficace (*install, set up*)

instalment (*n*): ⟨Fin/Comm⟩ la France payera par **versements** (*mpl*) **échelonnés**; ils pourront également payer en trois **règlements** (*m*) **échelonnés** (*instalment*); les **échéances** (*f*) **mensuelles** d'un remboursement (*monthly instalment/loan repayment*)

institute (*v*): ⟨Jur⟩ il **intenta un procès** contre les autorités françaises (*institute proceedings*)

institution (*n*): l'anniversaire de l'**instauration** (*f*) de la République (*institution, setting-up, founding*); ⟨Educ⟩ plusieurs **établissements** (*m*) **scolaires** (*institution; school*); ⟨Jur⟩ un **établissement pénitentiaire** dans le 12e arrondissement (*penal institution; prison*)

instruct (*v*): **mettre en demeure** les autorités d'agir sans délai (*instruct, order*)

instruction (*n*): ⟨Admin⟩ une **mise en demeure** leur a été adressée par l'administration (*instruction, order*); SEE ALSO **injunction**

insufficient (*adj*): se plaindre de l'**insuffisance** (*f*) de ses frais de mission (*insufficient/inadequate level*)

insult (*n*): une nouvelle **avanie** infligée à la France (*insult, snub*); ⟨Jur⟩ elle l'attaque pour **injure** (*f*), et non pour diffamation (*insult, abuse*); inculpé d'**outrage** (*m*) **à agent** (*insulting behaviour to an officer*); **rébellion** (*f*) **à agent** dans l'exercice de ses fonctions (*insulting behaviour to an officer [carrying out his duty]*)

insult (*v*): ⟨Jur⟩ lorsqu'on vous **injurie**, vous pouvez porter plainte (*insult, abuse*); la présence de l'armée indienne **bafoue** la souveraineté nationale sri-lankaise (*insult, ridicule*)

insurance (*n*): ⟨Ins⟩ le fret et les **assurances** (*f*) (*insurance*); souscrire une **police d'assurance** tous risques; vérifier que votre **contrat** (*m*) **d'assurance** vous couvre (*insurance policy*); **contracter une assurance** contre l'incendie (*take out an insurance policy*); un formulaire de **déclaration** (*f*) **de sinistre** (*insurance claim*)

insure (*v*): ⟨Ins/Comm⟩ **assurer** son habitation (*insure*); **prendre une assurance-vie** par précaution (*insure one's life, take out life insurance*)

insured (*adj*): ⟨Ins⟩ le courtier, défenseur de l'**assuré** (*m*) (*person insured; policy-holder*)

insurgent (*n*): SEE **rebel**

insurrection (*n*): ⟨Mil/Pol⟩ la **fronde** dégénère en révolte; lors de l'**insurrection** (*f*) populaire de 1989; le **soulèvement** fut durement réprimé

integral (*adj*): une **partie intégrante** de la sécurité européenne (*integral part*); ce concept **s'intègre dans** un vaste projet à l'échelon de la région (*be an integral part*)

integrate (*v*): arriver à **s'intégrer** professionnellement; les nouveaux **s'y sont intégrés** parfaitement dès leur arrivée (*integrate, settle in*)

integrated (*adj*): ⟨Mil⟩ création d'une **force intégrée** (*integrated force*)

integration (*n*): ⟨Soc⟩ les rapatriés ont parfaitement réussi leur **intégration** (*f*); l'**insertion** (*f*) **sociale** des anciens détenus pose problème (*social integration*)

integrity (*n*): veiller à la **probité** et à la moralité de la profession médicale (*integrity, probity*); ⟨Pol⟩ préserver l'**intégrité** (*f*) de la république balte; la restauration de l'**intégrité territoriale** du Liban (*territorial integrity*)

intelligence (*n*): la recherche spatiale à des fins de **renseignements** (*mpl*); un organisme chargé du **renseignement** et de l'action à l'extérieur (*intelligence gathering; spying*); SEE ALSO **information**

intention (*n*): il déplore les **visées** (*f*) expansionnistes d'Israël (*intention; aim, ambition*)

intentional (*adj*): ⟨Jur⟩ inculpé de coups et blessures **volontaires** (*intentional; with intent*)

interest (*n*): ⟨Fin/Comm⟩ détenir une **participation majoritaire** dans la société (*controlling interest/share*); le montant des **intérêts** (*m*) **des prêts** contractés (*interest on a loan; loan interest*); l'annonce d'une baisse des **taux** (*m*) **d'intérêts** (*interest rates*)

interested (*adj*): cette perspective fut bien accueillie par les **intéressés** (*m*) eux-mêmes (*interested party*)

interest group (*n*): ⟨Pol/Comm⟩ lutter contre les grandes **féodalités** (*f*) au moyen de législations anti-trust; SEE ALSO **association**

interfere (*v*): **s'immiscer** dans les affaires d'un autre pays; évitant de **s'ingérer** dans le 'domaine réservé' français; SEE ALSO **meddle**

interference (*n*): ce refus d'**ingérence** (*f*) dans les affaires intérieures du pays; l'**immixtion** (*f*) du pouvoir législatif dans le champ du judiciaire (*interference, meddling*); une atteinte au principe de **non-ingérence** (*f*) (*non-interference*)

interim (*adj*): ⟨Pol⟩ le gouvernement **intérimaire** de la résistance afghane; la formation d'un gouvernement **par intérim** (*m*) (*interim*); ⟨Fin⟩ fixer le **dividende intérimaire** à 75 pence (*interim dividend*); ⟨Fisc⟩ le **tiers provisionnel**, un acompte sur l'impôt sur le revenu (*interim tax payment*)

intermediary (*n*): il s'est proposé pour servir d'**intermédiaire** (*m*) (*intermediary*); l'État exerce sa tutelle **par le truchement du** Préfet (*through the intermediary/agency of*); SEE ALSO **mediator**, **middleman**

internal (*adj*): ⟨Pol⟩ une coalition en proie à des dissensions **internes** (*internal*); des difficultés **internes** de tous ordres (*internal, domestic*); faire étalage de ses petites **querelles** (*f*) **de chapelle**; des **querelles intestines** déchirent le parti (*internal squabbles*); ⟨Pol/Jur⟩ l'ordre public et la **sécurité interne** (*internal security*)

intervene (*v*): la police **est intervenue** pour disperser les manifestants; les troupes soviétiques **interviennent** en Lituanie (*intervene*); ⟨Pol⟩ le **devoir d'ingérence** (*f*) est maintenant admis par l'ONU (*duty to intervene in the internal affairs of another state for humanitarian reasons*)

intervention (*n*): ⟨Econ⟩ les **interventions** (*f*) de l'État dans l'économie; l'**intervention**, ou le rachat à prix garantis de la production; ⟨Admin/Jur⟩ l'**interposition** (*f*) d'un médiateur dans un conflit (*intervention*); ⟨Mil⟩ la **force d'interposition** pourrait intervenir par voie terrestre (*intervention force*); ⟨Pol⟩ prôner l'**ingérence** (*f*) des pays occidentaux en Yougoslavie (*intervention [esp. to protect civilians]*)

interventionist (*adj*): ⟨Econ⟩ un gouvernement, qu'il soit libéral ou **dirigiste**

intractable (*adj*): se montrer **inflexible**; être **intraitable** sur ce point fondamental (*intractable*); un problème **insoluble** (*intractable, insoluble*)

intransigence (*n*): venir à bout de l'**intransigeance** (*f*) des deux parties

intransigent (*adj*): Pékin **campe ses ses positions** (*f*) (*remain intransigent*)

intrigue (*n*): les **agissements** (*m*) de quelques fauteurs de trouble; ils ont été accusés de **menées** (*f*) illégales (*intrigue, manœuvre*)

introduce (*v*): la réforme devrait être **mise en œuvre** à partir de la rentrée (*introduce, implement*); l'augmentation sera **étalée dans le temps** (*introduce gradually/in stages*)

introduction (*n*): la **mise en œuvre** de la réforme risque d'être délicate; SEE ALSO **implementation**

invalid (*adj*): un billet d'entrée **périmé** (*invalid, out of date*); ⟨Jur⟩ une déclaration déclarée **irrecevable** (*invalid, inadmissible*)

invalidate (*v*): ⟨Jur⟩ des restrictions **invalidées** par les tribunaux

inventory (*n*): un **état** détaillé des forces armées des pays concernés (*inventory*); faire établir l'**état des lieux** (*inventory of fixtures and fittings*); s'occuper de la **gestion des stocks** (*m*) (*inventory control*)

invest (*v*): ⟨Pol⟩ **investir** un ministre de pouvoirs extraordinaires (*invest; grant*); ⟨Fin⟩ **investir** toutes ses économies dans une affaire; **placer ses capitaux** (*m*) dans l'immobilier (*invest capital*)

investigate (*v*): la commission qui **enquête** sur cette affaire (*investigate, inquire into*); ⟨Jur⟩ le juge d'instruction qui va **instruire le dossier** (*investigate a case; carry out a judicial investigation*)

investigation (*n*): ⟨Jur⟩ la police ouvre une **enquête** (*investigation*); le procureur ouvre une **information judiciaire** (*[preliminary] investigation*); confier l'**instruction** (*f*) du dossier à un juge de Rennes (*judicial investigation*)

investment (*n*): ⟨Fin⟩ un gros effort d'**investissement** (*m*) doit être fait; un **placement** sûr (*investment*); les actionnaires ne sont responsables des dettes que dans la mesure de leurs **apports** (*m*) (*investment, stake*); la gestion des **immeubles** (*m*) **de rapport** (*investment property*)

investor (*n*): ⟨Fin⟩ les **investisseurs** (*m*) étrangers; l'**épargnant** (*m*) peut gagner gros sur le long terme (*investor*); des titres achetés par des **petits souscripteurs** (*m*); le nombre des **petits porteurs** (*m*) a quadruplé en dix ans (*small investor*)

inviolability (*n*): ⟨Pol/Jur⟩ les conventions internationales sur l'**intangibilité** (*f*) des frontières; son intégrité territoriale et l'**inviolabilité** (*f*) de ses frontières

inviolable (*adj*): ⟨Jur/Pol⟩ les libertés publiques que les neuf sages considèrent comme **intangibles** (*inviolable, sacred*)

invitation (*n*): SEE **bid**, **tender**

invite (*v*): ils sont **conviés** à Paris pour une réflexion commune; SEE ALSO **tender**

invoice (*n*): ⟨Fin⟩ établir une **facture** de 3.000 dollars; la **facture** du gaz sibérien sera lourde (*invoice, bill*)

invoice (*v*): ⟨Fin⟩ les importations de brut sont **facturées** en fin de mois (*invoice, bill*)

invoicing (*n*): ⟨Fin⟩ un système informatisé de **facturation** (*f*) des clients (*invoicing, billing*); la société servant de plaque tournante à des **facturations fictives** (*false invoicing; invoicing for fictitious services*)

involve (*v*): des initiatives **associant** la population (*involve, bring together*); les grandes puissances ont intérêt à ne pas **s'en mêler** (*get involved*); deux officiers de police **mêlés à** un trafic de devises (*be involved/implicated in*); il pourrait avoir **trempé dans** l'assassinat (*be involved in; have a hand in*); SEE ALSO **implicate, mix up**

involvement (*n*): son **engagement** (*m*) personnel dans la lutte contre la drogue (*involvement, commitment*); ils nient leur **participation** (*f*) dans l'affaire (*involvement/participation*); connus pour leur **implication** (*f*) **dans** le milieu des jeux (*involvement, implication in*); SEE ALSO **interference**

irregular (*adj*): SEE **illegal**

irregularity (*n*): ⟨Jur⟩ le jugement fut cassé pour **vice** (*m*) **de procédure**; SEE ALSO **flaw**

isolated (*adj*): traiter les problèmes au cas par cas, par petites réformes **ponctuelles** (*isolated; individual*)

isolation (*n*): l'autoroute mettra fin à l'**enclavement** (*m*) de la région (*isolation; inaccessibility*); **désenclaver** la région (*end the isolation/ inaccessibility of*); SEE ALSO **inaccessibility**

issue (*n*): les **questions** (*f*) relatives à la sécurité (*issue, question*); ⟨Admin⟩ la **délivrance** d'une carte de séjour (*issue, issuing*); ⟨Fin⟩ l'**émission** (*f*) de nouvelles actions (*issue, issuing*); SEE ALSO **capital**

issue (*v*): la Poste **émet** une nouvelle série de timbres; ⟨Fin⟩ Londres pourrait **émettre** des obligations en ECUs lourds

item (*n*): ⟨Comm⟩ cet **article** (*m*) ne figure pas dans le catalogue (*item; article*)

itemize (*v*): il importe de **détailler** les dépenses déjà encourues; **répertorier** les 270 personnes portées disparues (*itemize; list*)

J

jargon (*n*): le **jargon** de l'administration; utiliser une **langue de bois** impénétrable pour les profanes

jeopardize (*v*): la crise pourrait **mettre en péril** (*m*) la rencontre au sommet; **hypothéquer** ainsi les chances électorales de l'opposition (*jeopardize, put in jeopardy*); SEE ALSO **endanger**

job (*n*): ⟨Ind⟩ le secteur industriel a perdu 1.000 **postes** (*m*) **de travail** (*job, post*); d'après le **profil du poste** (*job description*); lors d'un **entretien d'embauche** (*f*) (*job interview*); vivre de **petits boulots** (*m*) sans avenir (*small/dead-end job*); la **formation sur le tas** par l'apprentissage (*on-the-job training*)

job centre (*n*): se renseigner dans les **agences** (*f*) **pour l'emploi**

job creation (*n*): ⟨Econ⟩ la reprise aura un effet rapide sur la **création d'emplois**; ⟨Soc⟩ des jeunes employés dans des **programmes** (*m*) **de**

création d'emplois; les **aides** (*f*) **à l'insertion** des jeunes (*job-creation scheme*)

job experience (*n*): proposer aux jeunes une **première expérience de l'emploi**

jobless (*n*): le taux des **sans-travail** (*m*) avoisine les 13% sur l'ensemble du département; SEE ALSO **unemployed, out-of-work**

job loss (*n*): les **pertes** (*f*) **d'emplois** ont été beaucoup plus modérées en décembre; les créations de postes seront loin de compenser les **réductions** (*f*) **d'effectif** (*job loss, redundancy*)

job market (*n*): les chiffres pour avril confirment l'amélioration du **marché de travail**

job mobility (*n*): un fonds créé pour encourager la **mobilité des employés** (*m*) (*job mobility*); indemnités de changement de résidence et **allocations** (*f*) **de mobilité** (*job-mobility allowance*)

job security (*n*): la **sécurité de l'emploi** (*m*) sera un enjeu dans ces élections (*job security*); l'**insécurité** (*f*) **de l'emploi**, accentuée par la crise économique; le **travail précaire**, un sujet maudit pour les partenaires sociaux (*lack of job security/security of employment*)

job-seeker (*n*): 22.000 **demandeurs** (*m*) **d'emplois [non-satisfaits]** ont été recensés

job-sharing (*n*): ⟨Econ⟩ selon lui, le **partage du travail** est illusoire et pernicieux

job-shedding (*n*): ⟨Econ⟩ l'heure est aux restructurations, c'est-à-dire à l'**allégement** (*m*) **du personnel**!

job-training (*n*): ⟨Econ⟩ la mise en place de **programmes** (*m*) **de formation professionnelle** (*job-training scheme*)

job vacancy (*n*): deux **postes** (*m*) **à pourvoir** dans le service comptabilité; on compte au total 120.000 **demandes** (*f*) **d'emploi non satisfaites**

join (*v*): ⟨Pol⟩ il **adhéra** au parti en 1937; les pays voulant **intégrer** la CEE; **s'affilier** à une association; la livre sterling a enfin **rejoint** le SME (*join*); refuser de **s'associer à** une démarche (*join in/be associated with*)

joining (*n*): son **adhésion** (*f*) au parti remonte à la guerre; son **ralliement** à l'Association France Plus (*joining, coming over to*)

joint (*adj*): le développement **conjoint** de gisements de gaz en Extrême-Orient soviétique (*joint*); ⟨Fin⟩ les cotitulaires d'un **compte joint** (*joint bank/ savings account*); ⟨Pol⟩ la **liste d'entente** (*f*) de la majorité sortante (*joint electoral list*)

joint committee (*n*): une **commission paritaire** patronat-ouvriers

jointly (*adv*): ils lancent **conjointement** un appel au calme; ⟨Comm⟩ les associés sont **solidairement** responsables des dettes sociales (*jointly*); création d'une **filiale commune à 50–50** (*jointly-owned subsidiary*)

joint management (*n*): ⟨Econ⟩ une loi de 1976 impose la **cogestion** dans les sociétés de plus de 2.000 personnes

joint-stock company (*n*): SEE **limited**

joint venture (*n*): ⟨Econ⟩ les étrangers créant des **sociétés** (*f*) **mixtes** sont exemptés d'impôt; les principaux actionnaires de cette **joint-venture** (*joint venture*); Gillette **signe un accord de joint-venture**; Allied Lyons **s'associe** à Carlsberg (*sign a joint-venture agreement*)

journey (*n*): au cours d'un **voyage** en Inde; au terme d'un **déplacement** de 48 heures au Moyen-Orient (*journey, trip*)

judge (*n*): ⟨Jur⟩ le **juge** instruit et tranche les conflits en rendant des jugements et des ordonnances (*judge*); les juges forment la **magistrature assise** ou du siège (*judges of the bench, the Bench*)

judgement (*n*): des mesures laissées à l'**appréciation** (*f*) de chaque gouvernement (*judgement, assessment*)

judgment (*n*): ⟨Jur⟩ le **jugement** a été rendu hier; le Conseil d'État a rendu son **avis** (*m*); les magistrats ont rendu leur **arrêt** (*m*) (*judgment, verdict*); le juge, après interrogatoire des parties, **rend la décision** (*hand down a judgment/verdict/decision*); SEE ALSO **pronounce**

judicial (*adj*): ⟨Jur⟩ la nécessité de la **réforme juridique** (*judicial reform*); l'ouverture d'**informations** (*fpl*) **judiciaires** contre des clubs de football (*judicial inquiry*); menacer d'**entamer des poursuites** (*f*) **judiciaires** (*institute judicial proceedings*)

judiciary (*n*): ⟨Jur⟩ en vertu de la séparation des pouvoirs, le **[pouvoir] judiciaire** est indépendant (*judiciary*); la **justice** américaine indemnise les communes françaises sinistrées (*judiciary; the courts*)

junior (*n/adj*): des emplois **subalternes** (*junior, low-grade*)

junk (*n*): ⟨Fin⟩ des obligations à forts taux d'intérêts et à risques élevés, appelées **junk bonds** (*junk bond*); des brochures et autres **prospectus** (*m*) **publicitaires sans intérêt** (*junk mail*)

jurisdiction (*n*): ⟨Jur⟩ la plus haute **juridiction** irlandaise (*jurisdiction, court*); SEE ALSO **court**

jurisprudence (*n*): ⟨Jur⟩ une **jurisprudence** en pleine évolution; SEE ALSO **case**, **precedent**

juror (*n*): ⟨Jur⟩ pour être **juré** (*m*) il faut être de nationalité française

jury (*n*): ⟨Jur⟩ les affaires criminelles sont jugées par trois juges et un **jury** qui comprend neuf citoyens tirés au sort

justice (*n*): rétablir l'**équité** (*f*) fiscale (*fairness, justice*); ⟨Jur⟩ **rendre la justice** est une fonction essentielle de l'État (*dispense justice*); Justice: la **chancellerie** joue la transparence (*Ministry of Justice*)

justification (*n*): tous ne sont pas convaincus du **bien-fondé** de sa démarche (*justification; merits*)

justified (*adj*): le service militaire apparaît moins **justifié** de nos jours (*justified, justifiable*); les bruits qui courent sont-ils **fondés**? (*justified, well-founded*)

122

justify (*v*): voilà qui vient **conforter** les craintes du gouvernement (*justify; confirm*)

K

keep down (*v*): ⟨Econ⟩ **restreindre** les dépenses publiques (*keep down*); **maintenir les prix** (*m*) **bas** et relancer la demande; une politique qui vise à **empêcher la hausse des prix** (*keep prices down/low*); SEE ALSO **restrict**

key (*adj*): ces trois **domaines-clef** (*m*) de la reconstruction du pays (*key area*); un **personnage-clef** de l'administration (*key member*); ils tiennent les **postes-clés** (*m*) (*key position*)

keystone (*n*): ces bases sont la **clef de voûte** de la stratégie alliée en Extrême-Orient; SEE ALSO **corner-stone**

kidnap (*v*): Colombie: libération des journalistes **enlevés** par la guérilla

kidnapper (*n*): refuser de négocier avec les **ravisseurs** (*m*)

kidnapping (*n*): un **enlèvement** d'enfant suscite toujours un émoi tout particulier; le **rapt** et le viol d'une jeune fille

knock down (*v*): ⟨Comm⟩ la négociation des prix permet d'**abattre** de 40% le tarif théorique (*knock down [esp. prices]*)

knock-down (*adj*): ⟨Comm⟩ tout le stock bradé **à vil prix** (*m*) (*at a knock-down price*)

know-how (*n*): on leur exporte aussi bien le **savoir-faire** que les équipements (*know-how; skills*)

L

label (*n*): des gens répondant à cette **appellation** (*label, name*); ⟨Pol⟩ les **étiquettes** (*f*) politiques ont peu d'importance ici; ⟨Comm⟩ les **labels** (*m*) et autres certificats de qualité (*label, trademark*)

labour (*n*): ⟨Econ⟩ il faut baisser le **coût du travail** (*labour costs*); la concurrence croissante des pays **à faible coût de main-d'œuvre** (*with low labour costs*); pour les industries **de forte main-d'œuvre** (*f*) (*labour-intensive*); ⟨Jur⟩ condamné à une peine de douze années de **travaux** (*mpl*) **forcés** (*hard labour*)

labourer (*n*): ⟨Econ⟩ la disparition des postes de **manœuvre** (*m*) et d'ouvrier spécialisé (*labourer; manual worker*)

labour force (*n*): ⟨Ind⟩ la formation et la qualité de la **main-d'œuvre**; SEE ALSO **work-force**

labour relations (*npl*): ⟨Ind⟩ une amélioration des **relations** (*f*) **entre employeurs et employés**

lack (*n*): le **manque** chronique de main-d'œuvre; un **défaut** de consensus (*lack, absence*); les chantiers navals licencient, **faute de** commandes (*for lack of*)

lack (*v*): cette région **manque de** dynamisme; le Japon importe les matières premières qui **lui font défaut** (*m*) (*lack, be without*); le Tchad, pour lequel les statistiques récentes **font défaut** (*lack, be lacking/missing*)

lag behind (*v*): **être à la traîne** des autres pays européens; les salaires, **à la traîne** depuis trois ans (*lagging behind*)

land (*n*): ⟨Agric⟩ s'acheter une **terre** dans le bocage vendéen (*piece of land*); leur petit **lopin** (*m*), leur seule ressource (*small piece of land*); ⟨Econ⟩ une nouvelle politique **foncière** (*land; pertaining to use of land*); SEE ALSO **consolidation**, **estate**, **property**

landlord (*n*): sauf accord du **propriétaire**; faire des travaux sans l'accord écrit du **bailleur** (*landlord; owner*); SEE ALSO **lessor**

landowner (*n*): le nouveau conseil général, où les **propriétaires** (*m*) **fonciers** dominent

land register (*n*): ⟨Admin⟩ réévaluer le **cadastre** pour pouvoir rétablir l'équité fiscale (*land register, cadastre*)

landslide (*n*): ⟨Pol⟩ **raz-de-marée** (*m*) socialiste aux élections cantonales

lapse (*v*): l'ordonnance d'expropriation est **devenue caduque** hier; son abonnement **est venu à expiration** (*f*) (*lapse, expire*); SEE ALSO **expire**

larceny (*n*): ⟨Jur⟩ inculpé de **vol** (*m*) et écroué (*larceny, petty theft*); SEE ALSO **theft**

large-scale (*adj*): Washington craint une intervention **d'envergure** (*f*) de l'armée yougoslave (*large-scale*); une opération humanitaire **de grande envergure** (*on a very large scale*); la militarisation **à outrance** (*f*) du Nicaragua (*large-scale; excessive*)

last (*adj*): la date **butoir** est reportée à la fin du mois prochain; mais l'**ultime** séance de négociations n'a rien donné (*last, final*)

last (*v*): une récession qui devra **se prolonger** jusqu'en 1995 (*last, continue*)

lasting (*adj*): l'espoir d'une paix **durable** (*lasting, durable*)

late (*adj*): la crise a eu des effets **tardifs** dans le Nord (*late; delayed*); aviser un fournisseur d'un **retard de livraison** (*f*) (*late delivery*)

late (*adv*): des marchandises qui arriveraient **très tardivement** (*very late, belatedly*)

later (*adv*): il est possible de le modifier **ultérieurement** (*later; at a later date*)

launch (*n*): ⟨Comm⟩ le **lancement** d'un nouveau produit (*launch, launching*)

launch (*v*): Washington **lance** une nouvelle initiative de paix

launder (*v*): ⟨Fin⟩ **blanchir** des narcodollars; soupçonnés d'avoir **blanchi** des capitaux pour le compte de l'ETA

laundering (*n*): ⟨Fin⟩ le **blanchiment** des capitaux du crime organisé; le **lessivage** de l'argent sale

law (*n*): ⟨Jur⟩ un concept très important du **droit** britannique (*law; legal system*); les **lois** (*f*) et les décrets (*law, legislation*); transmettre le dossier à la **justice** (*law; the courts*); la **règle de droit** s'applique à tous (*rule of law*); une réforme de la **réglementation** communautaire (*law, legislation*); être en droit de **saisir la justice** (*go to law/the courts*); ⟨Jur/Pol⟩ l'**ordre** (*m*) et la répression sont des thèmes préférés de la Droite (*law and order*); le Préfet demeure chargé du **maintien de l'ordre** dans le département (*maintaining law and order*)

law firm (*n*): ⟨Jur⟩ les **cabinets** (*m*) **juridiques** s'internationalisent de plus en plus

lawful (*adj*): ⟨Jur⟩ c'est **légal**, car conforme à la loi; un exercice **licite** du droit de grève (*lawful, licit*)

lawlessness (*n*): ⟨Soc⟩ la vague d'**incivisme** (*m*) qui sévit dans les banlieues des grandes villes; la lutte contre l'**insécurité** (*f*) a permis de réduire la délinquance

lawsuit (*n*): ⟨Jur⟩ un **procès** intenté contre les auteurs (*lawsuit*); il se dit prêt à le **poursuivre en justice** (*file a lawsuit against*); il finit par **obtenir gain de cause** dans son action contre son propriétaire (*win a lawsuit/case*)

lawyer (*n*): ⟨Jur⟩ **juriste** (*m*) par profession (*lawyer*); la possibilité pour un détenu de **s'entretenir avec un avocat** (*consult/have access to a lawyer*); SEE ALSO **solicitor, barrister**

lax (*adj*): quand une société est **laxiste**, tout est possible pour les délinquants (*lax, permissive*)

laxity (*n*): l'instabilité politique et le **laxisme** financier (*laxity, being lax/permissive*)

lay (*adj*): ⟨Pol/Rel⟩ la **laïcité** de l'enseignement (*the lay/secular ethos*); le rôle accru de l'apostolat des **laïcs** (*m*) (*lay person; laity*)

laying off (*n*): ⟨Ind⟩ un **dégraissage** des effectifs; la crise se traduit par d'importants **délestages** (*m*) **de main-d'œuvre**; le directeur menace les salariés d'une **mise en chômage** (*m*) **technique** (*laying off of labour*); SEE ALSO **redundancy**

layman (*n*): le **profane** a peu de chances de comprendre ces querelles byzantines

lay-off (*n*): ⟨Ind⟩ le nombre de **mises en chômage** (*m*) **technique** augmente sans cesse; les demandeurs d'emploi pour cause de **licenciement** (*m*) **économique** (*lay-off, redundancy*)

lay off (*v*): ⟨Ind⟩ **débaucher**, quitte à réembaucher massivement plus tard (*lay off*); **mettre au chômage technique** de nombreux salariés (*lay off, make redundant*); **dégraisser** les effectifs (*lay off, slim down*); les entreprises commencent à **licencier du personnel** (*lay off staff; trim the work-force*)

lead (*n*): l'**avance** (*f*) des Travaillistes dans les sondages (*lead*); la droite **prend une avance** certaine (*go into the lead; take the lead*)

lead (*v*): ⟨Pol⟩ sondage: le Labour **devance** les Tories; les communistes **distancés** par les socialistes (*lead, outstrip*); une insurrection **animée** par des communistes (*lead, inspire*)

leader (*n*): ⟨Pol⟩ l'un des **chefs** (*m*) **de file** des radicaux; le député écoutait les revendications d'un **dirigeant** paysan; les principaux **ténors** (*m*) du parti; ⟨Econ/Comm⟩ les entreprises **leader** (*m*) sur leur marché

leadership (*n*): abandonner la **direction** du parti; le double langage de la **direction** du parti; ⟨Comm⟩ pour conserver son **leadership** européen dans les produits de la mer

leading (*adj*): il joua un rôle **moteur** dans la réforme des institutions; conserver un rôle **prépondérant** dans les négociations européennes sur l'UEM (*leading*); ⟨Journ⟩ un **article de fond** dans Le Figaro (*leading article, leader*)

leaflet (*n*): un **dépliant** illustré et en couleurs

lease (*n*): ⟨Jur⟩ un **bail de location** (*f*) de six ans; concéder un **bail de jouissance** (*f*) à d'autres occupants; les **baux** (*mpl*) **locatifs** sont souvent de vingt ans

lease (*v*): ⟨Jur⟩ **prendre un bail** sur une propriété en bord de mer (*lease, take out a lease*); le leaseholder peut occuper les lieux ou **concéder à bail** à un ou plusieurs occupants (*lease out*)

leasehold (*n*): ⟨Jur⟩ une **propriété louée à bail** (*m*); la jouissance d'une propriété **en location** (*f*) **à bail**

leaseholder (*n*): ⟨Jur⟩ tout occupant, qu'il soit propriétaire ou **locataire** (*m*); SEE ALSO **tenant**

leasing (*n*): ⟨Fin/Comm⟩ une société spécialisée dans le **crédit-bail** (*leasing*); ouvrir une succursale de **leasing** (*m*) **de voitures** (*car leasing*)

leave (*n*): ⟨Mil⟩ les **permissions** (*f*) des policiers ont été supprimées (*leave [of absence]*); ⟨Soc⟩ être **en arrêt** (*m*) **de maladie** (*on sick leave*); toute femme enceinte a droit à un **congé de maternité** (*maternity leave*); les **congés sans solde** (*f*) de la mère pour l'éducation d'un enfant (*unpaid leave*)

leave (*v*): SEE **quit**

legacy (*n*): recevoir des dons et **legs** (*mpl*) en franchise de droit de mutation (*legacy*); une propriété qu'il a reçue **par héritage** (*m*) (*by legacy*); léguer au futur gouvernement un **héritage** particulièrement difficile à gérer; SEE ALSO **bequest, inheritance**

legal (*adj*): ⟨Jur⟩ être soumis à un régime **juridique** particulier; une entreprise commerciale n'a pas d'existence **juridique** (*legal, juridical*); engager des **poursuites** (*f*) **judiciaires** pour factures non-réglées (*legal/court proceedings*); il annonça qu'il **intenterait un procès** s'il n'était pas remboursé dans les dix jours (*take legal action*); SEE ALSO lawful

legal aid (*n*): ⟨Jur⟩ bénéficier de l'**aide** (*f*) **juridictionnelle**

legal document (*n*): ⟨Jur⟩ les actes notariés et autres **actes** (*m*) **authentiques** (*legal document, instrument*)

legal expert (*n*): ⟨Jur⟩ un cabinet de **conseil** (*m*) **juridique** s'installe dans cette ville allemande (*legal adviser/expert*)

legality (*n*): ⟨Jur⟩ le Conseil constitutionnel est chargé de contrôler la **régularité** des élections

legalization (*n*): ⟨Jur⟩ la **légalisation** de l'avortement souhaitée par Bruxelles

legalize (*v*): ⟨Jur⟩ les pays où l'IVG est **légalisée** (*legalized, permitted*)

legatee (*n*): ⟨Jur⟩ les **légataires** (*m*) doivent payer des droits de succession (*legatee, inheritor*)

legislate (*v*): ⟨Pol⟩ le Parlement **légifère**; comment **légiférer** dans un domaine si sensible? (*legislate, make laws*)

legislation (*n*): la **législation** est de plus en plus contraignante; la **réglementation** ici est assez protectionniste (*legislation, laws*); une **loi** visant à réduire les pouvoirs du Président (*law; piece of legislation*)

legislator (*n*): le **législateur** a fait preuve d'initiative et d'imagination (*legislator, law-maker*)

legislature (*n*): ⟨Pol⟩ le **corps législatif** avait trop de pouvoir face à l'exécutif (*legislature, legislative body*)

leisure (*n*): ⟨Soc⟩ le manque d'**équipements** (*mpl*) **de loisir**; des **équipements socioculturels** seront également implantés (*leisure amenities; community cultural and recreational facilities*)

lend (*v*): ⟨Fin⟩ la banque **prête** aux particuliers, mais à de gros intérêts

lender (*n/adj*): ⟨Fin⟩ la dette de l'emprunteur envers le **prêteur** (*lender*); l'organisme **prêteur** était maître de la situation (*lender, lending*); SEE ALSO **creditor**

lengthen (*v*): des accords récents **allongent** le temps de travail (*lengthen*); **allonger** la scolarité, ce serait remédier au chômage (*lengthen, prolong*)

lengthening (*n*): vers un **allongement** concerté de la durée du travail; un **étalement** de certains programmes militaires; l'**étalement dans le temps** de leur programme d'investissement; SEE ALSO **extension**

less (*adj*): les chèques d'un montant **inférieur à** 100F seront refusés (*less/lower than; under, below*)

lessee (*n*): la loi fixe dorénavant les rapports entre bailleur et **locataire** (*m*) (*lessee; tenant*)

lessen (*v*): **atténuer** la portée de la retraite à soixante ans; SEE ALSO **reduce**

lesson (*n*): le Premier ministre a d'abord souligné les **enseignements** (*m*) politiques de la guerre (*lesson*); le Labour saura **tirer les enseignements** de son échec (*learn/draw a lesson*)

lessor (*n*): ⟨Fin/Comm⟩ dans le leasing, le **loueur** reste propriétaire de son bien (*lessor, hirer*); une réforme s'impose dans les relations entre **bailleurs** (*m*) et locataires; le **bailleur** peut demander une indemnité égale à 8% des loyers impayés (*lessor; landlord*)

level (*n*): ⟨Admin⟩ des émissions locales, **à l'échelon** (*m*) **de** la région (*at the level of*); des négociations **au niveau régional** (*at regional level*); le **seuil** critique de tolérance a été atteint (*level, threshold*); les résultats ne sont pas **à la hauteur** des espoirs (*on a level/on a par with*); le **nivellement** des rémunérations sera long à obtenir (*bringing to the same level*)

level (*adj*): la France et l'Allemagne sont **à égalité** (*f*) (*level, on a level/par*)

level off (*v*): les prix de l'immobilier en région parisienne ont **plafonné** en 1991 (*level off; reach a plateau*)

levelling (*n*): il y aura certainement un **nivellement par le bas** (*levelling downwards*); le **plafonnement** des recettes publicitaires (*levelling off*)

levy (*n*): ⟨Fisc⟩ ces communes subiront un double **prélèvement**; SEE ALSO **tax**

levy (*v*): ⟨Fisc⟩ la fiscalité qui **frappe** le patrimoine des Français (*be levied upon*)

levying (*n*): ⟨Fisc⟩ la **levée** d'un nouvel impôt

liabilities (*npl*): ⟨Comm/Fin⟩ le **passif** atteint 38 millions de francs; l'État a repris à sa charge le **passif** de la société (*liabilities; debt*); SEE ALSO **debt**

liable (*adj*): ⟨Fisc⟩ le cadre expatrié est alors **redevable de** l'impôt français; les contribuables **soumis à** l'impôt sur les grandes fortunes; une taxe à laquelle sont **assujetties** les entreprises (*be liable to, be subject to*); ⟨Jur⟩ **encourir** la peine de mort; le contrevenant **s'expose à** une forte amende (*be liable to; risk*)

libel (*n*): ⟨Jur⟩ **assigner en diffamation** (*f*) le directeur d'un journal (*sue for libel*); une **plainte en diffamation** de quatre policiers contre France Soir; gagner un **procès** (*m*) **en diffamation** (*libel suit/action*); SEE ALSO **defamation, slander**

libel (*v*): ⟨Jur⟩ estimant que le journaliste l'avait **diffamé**, il porta plainte

libellous (*adj*): des propos qu'il jugeait **diffamatoires**

liberal (*n/adj*): ⟨Pol⟩ la politique **libérale** dans ce domaine est un peu floue (*liberal; pertaining to the Liberal Party*); les **Libéraux** (*m*) sont partisans de la représentation proportionnelle (*Liberal*)

liberalization (*n*): ⟨Pol/Econ⟩ le dernier pays d'Europe de l'Est à entamer sa **libéralisation**; la **libéralisation** d'une économie encore trop étatisée et protectionniste

liberalize (*v*): ⟨Econ⟩ il s'agit aussi de **libéraliser** les échanges de produits textiles; ⟨Pol⟩ **libéraliser** la politique de l'immigration

licence (*n*): payer une **redevance** pour l'utilisation du brevet; la **redevance** TV augmenta de 15% en 1991 (*licence fee*); ⟨Comm⟩ produire des articles **sous licence** (*f*) (*under licence*); des **autorisations** (*f*) d'importation; accorder un **permis** (*licence*); l'octroi d'un **permis d'exporter** (*export licence*)

life (*adj*): ⟨Pol⟩ sénateur **inamovible**, il occupa son fauteuil sénatorial pendant 35 ans (*life; for life*)

life annuity (*n*): ⟨Fin⟩ percevoir une **rente viagère** en vertu d'une clause de réversion (*life annuity*); si on achète un bien **en viager** (*m*), on doit payer la rente jusqu'au décès du vendeur (*as a life annuity*); **vendre en viager**, moyennant une rente (*sell in exchange for a life annuity*)

life expectancy (*n*): le gain d'**espérance** (*f*) **de vie** ne cesse d'augmenter; l'allongement de la **durée de vie moyenne** (*[average] life expectancy*)

life insurance (*n*): ⟨Ins⟩ l'avantage de **souscrire un contrat d'assurance-vie** (*f*) (*take out life insurance*)

life sentence (*n*): ⟨Jur⟩ condamné à prison **à perpétuité** (*f*) (*for a life sentence*)

life style (*n*): ⟨Soc⟩ l'évolution des **modes** (*m*) **de vie**

lift (*v*): la direction refuse de **lever** les mesures de blocage des salaires (*lift, remove; suspend*); ⟨Pol⟩ promettre de **lever les sanctions** (*f*) (*lift/remove sanctions*)

lifting (*n*): malgré la **levée** de leur mot d'ordre de grève; la **levée** des sanctions (*lifting, suspension*)

light (*adj*): un appareil administratif très **léger** (*light, lightweight*); dans le secteur de l'**industrie** (*f*) **légère** (*light industry*)

lighten (*v*): le désir du gouvernement d'**alléger les impôts** (*m*) (*lighten the tax burden*)

lightening (*n*): un **allégement** des contrôles aux frontières (*lightening; reduction*)

limit (*n*): ⟨Fisc⟩ une majoration **jusqu'à concurrence** (*f*) de 2.000F pour les enfants à charge (*up to a limit of*); inférieur de 0,35 point au **plancher** légal (*lower limit; minimum*); ⟨Econ⟩ des mesures de **contingentement** (*m*) des importations (*setting limits/quotas*); SEE ALSO **ceiling**, **quota**

limit (*v*): la France **se cantonne** dans un rôle de gendarme; pour **s'en tenir** à la période 1988-90 (*limit/restrict oneself*); SEE ALSO **curb**, **restrict**, **ration**

limited (*adj*): un nombre assez **réduit** d'articles; s'adresser à un public assez **restreint** (*limited, small*); ⟨Econ⟩ les sociétés de capitaux, dont la **société anonyme** (*[public] limited company*); il n'y a pas de conseil d'administration dans une **société à responsabilité limitée** (*limited liability company*)

line (*n*): le salaire minimum **s'aligne** automatiquement sur l'inflation (*keep in line/step*); on devra **aligner** la pratique ici sur les dispositions en vigueur en France (*bring into line*)

link (*n*): Bangkok renforce ses **liens** (*m*) avec le Laos (*link; connection*); des **relations** (*f*) **culturelles** rapprochent les pays de l'ancienne Communauté (*cultural links*); la nouvelle **liaison** Sarre-Moselle (*link [esp. road/rail]*)

link-up (*n*): ⟨Comm⟩ US Air et Air Canada préparent une **alliance**; un éventuel **rapprochement** Renault-Volvo (*commercial link-up; alliance*)

link up (*v*): ⟨Econ⟩ les deux groupes **s'associent** pour la reprise de la firme britannique

liquid assets (*npl*): ⟨Fin⟩ le marché regorge de **liquidités** (*fpl*) prêtes à s'investir; la firme dispose encore de 80 milliards de **disponibilités** (*fpl*) (*liquid assets; cash reserves*)

liquidation (*n*): ⟨Comm⟩ après son dépôt de bilan, la firme est menacée d'une **liquidation** (*f*) pure et simple (*liquidation*); la société est près de **déposer son bilan** (*go into voluntary liquidation*); l'entreprise est **en règlement** (*m*) **judiciaire** (*facing compulsory liquidation*)

liquidator (*n*): ⟨Comm⟩ un **liquidateur** devrait être désigné dans la semaine (*liquidator; receiver*)

list (*n*): ⟨Pol⟩ la **liste** de la majorité l'a emporté (*list*); refuser de figurer sur la **liste d'union** (*joint electoral list*)

list (*v*): SEE **itemize**

listing (*n*): ⟨Fin⟩ la firme demandera une **cotation** à la Bourse de Paris

litigant (*n*): ⟨Jur⟩ le **plaideur** peut se défendre sans l'assistance d'un avocat

litigation (*n*): obligé de **prendre les mesures** (*fpl*) **contentieuses** qui s'imposaient (*have recourse to litigation*); SEE ALSO **lawsuit**

live (*v*): **vivre** de journalisme (*live, make a living*); ⟨Soc⟩ décider de **vivre ensemble** (*live together*); les bénéficiaires **vivent plus vieux** (*live longer*); SEE ALSO **cohabit**

living (*n*): un accroissement général du **niveau de vie** (*living standards*); le **mal de vivre** dans les grands ensembles (*poor living conditions*)

loan (*n*): ⟨Fin⟩ solliciter un **prêt** pour l'achat d'une résidence secondaire (*loan*); moins de subventions, plus de **crédits** (*mpl*) (*loan, credit*); le remboursement d'**emprunts** (*mpl*) peut être une charge onéreuse

loan (*v*): SEE **lend**

lobby (*n*): ⟨Pol⟩ un **lobby** homogène et puissant (*lobby*); le puissant **groupe de pression** (*f*) juif à Washington (*lobby, pressure group*)

lobby (*v*): la communauté juive **fait pression** (*f*) sur les membres du congrès

local (*adj*): ⟨Fisc⟩ exonéré des **impôts** (*m*) **locaux** (*local taxes/taxation*); ⟨Comm⟩ l'absence de **commerces** (*mpl*) **de proximité** dans les cités; on délaisse les **commerces de quartier** (*local business/shop*); SEE ALSO **neighbourhood**

local authority (*n*): ⟨Admin⟩ le produit de l'impôt sera reversé aux **collectivités** (*f*) **locales**

130

local government (*n*): ⟨Admin⟩ l'**administration** (*f*) **locale** a eu un regain de vie depuis 1982; la nouvelle organisation de l'**administration territoriale** (*local government/administration*)

locate (*v*): ⟨Comm⟩ Michelin **implante** une usine dans l'Ouest (*locate, site*); l'institut, **sis** rue de Bruxelles (*located, situated*)

lock-out (*n*): ⟨Ind⟩ une **grève patronale** ou 'lock-out'

lock up (*v*): SEE **imprison**

lodge (*v*): **héberger** les réfugiés chez l'habitant (*lodge, put up, give shelter*); ⟨Jur⟩ **déposer un recours** devant la juridiction compétente (*lodge an appeal*); décider de **se pourvoir en cassation** (*f*) (*lodge an appeal against conviction*); SEE ALSO **appeal**

lodging (*n*): ⟨Soc⟩ pour l'immigré se pose le problème du **logement**; les frais d'**hébergement** (*m*) et de nourriture (*lodging, accommodation*); ⟨Jur⟩ après le **dépôt** de plusieurs plaintes pour escroquerie (*lodging [esp. of a complaint]*)

long-established (*adj*): ⟨Comm⟩ une entreprise familiale **établie depuis longtemps** dans la région

long-standing (*adj*): son antagonisme **de longue date** (*f*) contre l'ex-URSS

long-term (*adj*): ⟨Econ⟩ développement du chômage **de longue durée** (*f*) (*long-term*); il entrevoit **à long terme** (*m*) une européanisation de l'industrie militaire (*in the long term*)

loophole (*n*): **tourner** l'embargo vers le golfe Persique (*find a loophole in, get round*); **tourner la loi** sur l'embauche des stagiaires (*find a loophole in the law/legislation*)

loose (*adj*): ⟨Comm⟩ vendu **en vrac** (*m*) ou emballé (*loose; unpackaged*)

lose (*v*): ⟨Fin⟩ le titre **cède** 15 pence, soit 15% de sa valeur (*lose*); toutes les monnaies **s'effritent** vis-à-vis de la devise allemande (*lose ground, fall in value*); l'entreprise **perd de l'argent** (*m*) (*lose money*)

loser (*n*): les Bruxellois sont les premiers **perdants** (*m*) dans cette affaire; l'Italie **sort perdante** de cet accord communautaire (*emerge as the loser; lose out*)

loss (*n*): ⟨Fin⟩ les **pertes** (*f*) se sont élevées à 70.000F (*loss*); ⟨Fin/Comm⟩ la firme **subit des pertes** continues depuis 1988 (*make losses*); **subir une moins-value** de 22 MF (*make a loss*); un **manque à gagner** de 2.000F (*loss of earnings/revenue*); vendre **à perte** (*f*) (*at a loss*)

loss-making (*adj*): ⟨Fin/Comm⟩ la société est **déficitaire** depuis deux ans déjà (*loss-making; operating at a loss*)

low (*adj*): ⟨Econ⟩ le **faible** niveau des ventes (*low*); la **faiblesse de l'épargne** (*f*) en France (*low level of savings*); justifier son désir de partir par la **faiblesse des salaires** (*m*) (*low salary/pay*); des concurrents redoutables par le **bas coût de la main-d'œuvre** (*low labour costs*); un pays **à inflation** (*f*) **faible** (*with a low inflation rate*); ⟨Pol⟩ **faible participation** (*f*) aux élections municipales (*low electoral turn-out*)

lower (*adj*): ⟨Comm⟩ Mobil: bénéfices **en baisse** (*f*) (*lower, falling*); qui dit concurrence dit **baisse des prix** (*lower/falling prices*); recul **moindre que prévu** (*lower/smaller than expected*); ⟨Pol⟩ la Diète, la **Chambre basse** polonaise (*Lower House*)

lower (*v*): on promet d'**abaisser** les taux d'intérêt; la négociation des prix permet d'**abattre** de 20% le tarif; **faire baisser** le niveau de chômage (*lower, reduce*); SEE ALSO **reduce**

lowering (*n*): ⟨Econ⟩ l'**abaissement** (*m*) des coûts; la relance de l'économie par la **baisse** des taux d'intérêt (*lowering, reduction; bringing down*)

lowest (*adj*): ⟨Comm⟩ le fournisseur le **moins-disant** (*lowest/most competitive [esp. bidder]*)

low-income (*adj*): ⟨Fin/Soc⟩ des familles **aux faibles revenus** (*m*); cette aide est accordée à toutes les personnes **à revenus modestes**

lucrative (*adj*): ⟨Fin/Comm⟩ préférer les cultures les plus hautement **rémunératrices**; des contrats **juteux** (*lucrative*); un contrat qui représente un véritable **pactole** pour la firme française (*lucrative business; gold-mine*)

lukewarm (*adj*): un accueil **tiède**; réaction **peu enthousiaste** de la part des syndicats

lump sum (*n*): ⟨Fin⟩ à sa retraite, on lui versera une **allocation forfaitaire**

luxury (*n*): un hôtel **de grand standing** (*m*) (*luxury*); taxé comme un **produit de luxe** (*m*) (*luxury good/item*)

M

machine (*n*): ⟨Pol⟩ l'**appareil** (*m*) qui gouvernait depuis 70 ans a été abattu; l'**appareil du parti** démocrate (*[party] machine*); ⟨Admin⟩ l'**appareil administratif** est grippé (*administrative machine, machine of government*)

magistracy (*n*): ⟨Jur⟩ faire carrière dans la **magistrature**; la **magistrature**, ou le corps des magistrats de l'ordre judiciaire (*magistracy, magistrature*)

magistrate (*n*): ⟨Jur⟩ il a été présenté au **magistrat instructeur**; l'affaire fut confiée à un **juge d'instruction** (*f*) d'Évreux (*examining magistrate*); le **tribunal correctionnel** statue sur les délits; comparaître au **tribunal de grande instance** (*f*) (*magistrate's court*)

magnitude (*n*): en raison de l'**ampleur** (*f*) des dégâts (*magnitude, scale*); son statut de puissance militaire **de première grandeur** (*f*) (*of the first magnitude*); SEE ALSO **scale**

mail order (*n*): ⟨Comm⟩ tous les majors de la **vente par correspondance** (*mail-order sales*)

mainland (*n*): les rapports tendus que les Corses entretenaient avec la **métropole** (*mainland France*); (*adj*): le premier maire noir d'une commune **métropolitaine** (*of/in/on mainland France*)

main lines (*npl*): les trois **axes** (*m*) de la politique algérienne; les **principaux axes** de notre politique de l'emploi

maintain (*v*): **entretenir** la voirie départementale (*maintain*); construit à la va-vite, et **mal entretenu** faute de crédits (*poorly maintained*)

maintaining (*n*): le gouvernement prévoit un simple **maintien** du pouvoir d'achat du salaire horaire

maintenance (*n*): l'**entretien** (*m*) de la voirie relève du maire; la **maintenance**, ou le maintien en état de fonctionnement (*maintenance, servicing*); SEE ALSO **alimony**

major (*adj*): un **important** cabinet juridique de Montréal; jouer un rôle **de premier plan** (*m*) (*major, important*); les **gros** travaux annuels de rénovation; une réforme fiscale **d'envergure** (*f*) (*major, large-scale*); SEE ALSO **large-scale**

major (*n*): ⟨Jur/Soc⟩ être **majeur** (*m*) ou émancipé (*major, having reached the age of majority*); SEE ALSO **majority**

majority (*n/adj*): ⟨Pol⟩ la **majorité** des électeurs se sont prononcés clairement (*majority*); la gauche est **majoritaire** en France (*in the majority, the majority party*); le **gouvernement par la majorité** bientôt en Afrique du Sud? (*majority government*); ⟨Fin⟩ racheter une **part majoritaire** d'une autre société (*majority stake/holding*); **prendre la majorité** dans le capital d'une société (*take/acquire a majority holding*); ⟨Jur⟩ la **majorité** était de 21 ans (*[age of] majority*); un verdict rendu **à la majorité** (*by a majority verdict*)

make out (*v*): ⟨Fin⟩ **établir un chèque** à l'ordre de quelqu'un (*make out/write a cheque*)

make-up (*n*): la **composition** du nouveau cabinet sera annoncée lundi

make up (*v*): pour **combler** le déficit de l'assurance-maladie (*make up*); une indemnité destinée à **combler** partiellement le manque à gagner (*make up for*); son but, **pallier le déficit** en formations de haut niveau (*make up/make good a deficiency/shortage*)

maladministration (*n*): les **erreurs** (*f*) **de gestion** de la gauche expliquent sa défaite

malfunctioning (*n*): une table ronde sur le **dysfonctionnement** de l'économie

malpractice (*n*): une sombre histoire de **tripatouillage** (*m*) électoral

manage (*v*): ⟨Admin⟩ **gérer** une affaire avec compétence et dynamisme

management (*n*): confier la **gestion** à un entrepreneur du privé (*management, day-to-day running*); **direction** (*f*) et syndicats se sont rencontrés; l'**encadrement** (*m*) de la société en a informé le personnel (*management*); le conseil exécutif, ou **conseil de gérance** (*f*) (*board of* *management*); lors du **comité directeur** de lundi (*[meeting of]* *management committee*); ⟨Econ/Fin⟩ une **prise de contrôle de la société par sa direction** (*management buy-out*)

manager (*n*): le **directeur** de l'agence de Francfort; exploitants privés, ou **gérants** (*m*) de fermes d'État (*manager*); un maire, **gestionnaire** (*m*) des intérêts locaux (*manager, administrator, person in charge*)

managerial (*adj*): une PMI exige des **qualités de gestionnaire** (*m*) mais aussi de psychologue (*managerial qualities*); l'ensemble des **cadres** (*m*) (*managerial staff/personnel*); ceci limite leur évolution et les prive de **responsabilités** (*fpl*) **d'encadrement** (*managerial responsibility*)

managing director (*n*): le **directeur-général** d'une grande entreprise; l'**administrateur-gérant** (*m*) du consortium européen

mandate (*n*): ⟨Pol⟩ son **mandat** est de cinq ans (*mandate, period of office*); il décide de renoncer à sa **délégation** (*mandate, commission*)

mandate (*v*): ⟨Admin⟩ le mandataire, ou la personne à qui on **donne procuration** (*f*) (*mandate, give a mandate to*); leur député, **mandaté** pour les représenter à Paris (*mandated, holding a mandate*); SEE ALSO **elect**

manœuvre (*n*): on dispose d'une certaine **marge de manœuvre** (*f*) (*room for manœuvre*); en les accusant de **menées** (*f*) illégales (*manœuvre, ploy*); toutes les **manœuvres électorales** sont bonnes (*electoral manœuvres/ intrigues*)

manpower (*n*): ⟨Ind⟩ l'agriculture manque de **bras** (*mpl*) et d'engrais; au prix d'une diminution de l'**effectif** (*m*) (*manpower*); l'importance de la **gestion de ressources** (*f*) **humaines** (*manpower resource management*); SEE ALSO **labour**

manslaughter (*n*): ⟨Jur⟩ condamné à deux ans de prison pour **homicide** (*m*) **involontaire**; il risque une peine de prison pour **coups** (*mpl*) **et blessures volontaires ayant entraîné la mort sans intention de la donner**

manual (*adj*): la disparition progressive des postes de **manœuvre** (*m*); les ouvriers, travailleurs manuels ou **cols** (*mpl*) **bleus** (*manual worker*)

manufacture (*n*): le pétrole entre dans la **fabrication** de tellement de produits

manufacture (*v*): ⟨Comm⟩ Daimler-Benz menace d'aller **produire** aux États-Unis (*manufacture, carry out production*); pays exportateur de **biens** (*mpl*) **fabriqués** (*manufactured goods*)

manufacturer (*n*): la guerre des prix entre les **fabricants** (*m*) de pneumatiques (*manufacturer, maker, producer*); réduction de 10% sur le **prix conseillé** (*manufacturer's recommended price*)

manufacturing (*n/adj*): ⟨Comm⟩ la firme annonce la fin de ses activités de **fabrication** (*f*) en Chine (*manufacturing*); les **industries** (*f*) **manufacturières** ont été les plus touchées (*manufacturing industry*); le seul moyen, c'est en réduisant les **coûts** (*m*) **de production** (*manufacturing/production costs*)

march (*n*): le grand **défilé** organisé à Paris le 28 mars (*march, demonstration*)

march (*v*): ⟨Pol/Ind⟩ les organisateurs espèrent voir **défiler** plus de 120.000 agriculteurs (*march, demonstrate*)

margin (*n*): ⟨Comm⟩ calculer les **marges** (*f*) au plus juste; SEE ALSO **profit margin**

marginal (*adj*): une existence **précaire**; ⟨Pol⟩ plusieurs **sièges** (*m*) **disputés** font la différence au deuxième tour (*marginal seat*)

market (*n*): ⟨Comm⟩ la France perd des **marchés** (*m*) (*market*); l'industrie continue à perdre des **parts** (*f*) **de marché** à l'étranger (*market share*); des **créneaux** (*m*) spécifiques, des modèles compétitifs (*market sector/ niche*); les techniques habituelles d'**études** (*f*) **de marché** (*market research*); ⟨Econ⟩ abandonner le socialisme, et retourner à une **économie de marché** (*market economy*); l'État reste en dehors du **jeu des marchés** (*market forces; free play of market forces*); SEE ALSO **black market, outlet**

market (*v*): ⟨Econ⟩ une société créée pour **commercialiser** des véhicules utilitaires aux États-Unis; elles seront **commercialisées** à partir de 1995 (*market, sell*)

marketing (*n*): ⟨Econ⟩ un contrat pour la **mise sur le marché** d'antennes paraboliques; l'ère de la **mercatique**; la conception et la réalisation d'un produit, ou le **marketing**

mass (*adj*): des désertions **en masse** (*f*) (*mass, widespread*); ⟨Comm⟩ le **publipostage** et d'autres techniques publicitaires (*mass mailing*); un produit **grand public** ne peut pas s'imposer sans publicité; conquérir des **marchés** (*m*) **de masse** (*mass market*); les techniques de la **grande distribution** (*mass marketing*); la **fabrication en série** (*f*) n'est pas prévue avant 1994 (*mass production*); le nouveau modèle sera **fabriqué en série** à partir de 1995 (*mass-produced*); le rôle des nouveaux **moyens** (*m*) **de communication de masse** sur la vie des Français (*mass media*)

material (*n*): SEE **raw material**

materialize (*v*): si le plan **se concrétise**, ce sera la fin du parti (*materialize, take shape*)

mature (*v*): ⟨Fin⟩ un grand nombre de baux **parviennent à échéance** (*f*) cette année; des traites qui **viennent à échéance** dans six mois (*mature*); le montant payable **à échéance** (*on maturing*)

maturity (*n*): ⟨Fin⟩ 1995, l'année de l'**échéance** (*f*) des bons (*date of maturity*)

maverick (*n/adj*): ⟨Mil/Pol⟩ quelques **francs-tireurs** (*m*) centristes voulaient ainsi marquer leur indépendance; certains critiquent l'esprit **franc-tireur** de la capitale régionale

mayor (*n*): ⟨Pol⟩ le **maire** sortant; le **premier magistrat** (*m*) de Nice

mayoral (*adj*): le maire sortant a gardé son **écharpe** (*f*) (*mayoral sash; mayoral office [Fr]*)

mayoress (*n*): la politique engagée par la **maîresse** de cette cité allemande

135

meagre (*adj*): inaccessible au **maigre** budget d'un maire

means (*npl*): ⟨Soc/Fisc⟩ une aide accordée aux personnes aux **ressources** (*f*) insuffisantes (*means of support; resources*); l'allocation est **attribuée sous condition de ressources**; des prestations **liées à des conditions** (*f*) **de ressources** (*means-tested*); SEE ALSO **resource**

measure (*n*): un certain nombre de **dispositifs** (*m*) pour réhabiliter les quartiers en difficulté (*measure, step*); la police a pris les **dispositions** (*f*) nécessaires (*measure, precaution*); l'entrée en vigueur d'un **train de mesures** (*f*) d'austérité économique (*series/batch of measures*); SEE ALSO **series**

measure (*v*): une étude qui permet de **prendre la mesure** du phénomène en France

meddle (*v*): ⟨Pol⟩ la France refuse que d'autres pays **s'immiscent** dans ses affaires; **s'ingérer** dans les affaires intérieures d'un autre État; SEE ALSO **interfere**

meddling (*n*): ⟨Pol⟩ l'**ingérence** (*f*) dans les affaires d'un autre pays (*meddling, interference*)

media (*npl*): ⟨Journ⟩ les **médias** (*m*) se sont emparés de l'affaire; le gouvernement veut contrôler les **moyens** (*m*) **d'information** (*the media*); jamais une maladie n'a été tant **médiatisée** (*cover by the media*); l'exploitation **médiatique** de l'affaire (*media, by/in the media*); SEE ALSO **coverage, mass**

mediate (*v*): ⟨Jur/Ind⟩ nommé pour **être le médiateur** entre le gouvernement et les acteurs socio-économiques; les pays occidentaux essaient de **jouer un rôle de médiation** (*f*) (*mediate, be a mediator*)

mediation (*n*): ⟨Jur/Ind⟩ après l'échec de la conciliation, puis de la **médiation**; Israël et l'OLP amorcent un dialogue **par l'entremise** (*f*) des États-Unis (*with the mediation of*)

mediator (*n*): ⟨Jur/Ind⟩ il espérait servir d'**intermédiaire** (*m*) entre les deux parties; le **médiateur** intervient après l'échec de la conciliation; l'Égypte s'était posée en **médiatrice** (*f*); SEE ALSO **intermediary**

medium (*adj*): ⟨Econ⟩ l'État encourage l'expansion des **PME-PMI** (*f*) pour faire contrepoids aux grands groupes (*small or medium-sized company or industry*); sur le long et le **moyen-terme** (*medium-term*)

medium (*n*): ⟨Journ⟩ le message fut diffusé **par voie** (*f*) **de presse** (*through the medium of the press*)

meet (*v*): l'OPEP va **se réunir** en mars prochain (*meet, assemble*); il risque de **se heurter à** un mur de refus (*meet, encounter, come up against*)

meeting (*n*): une **réunion** du bureau politique de l'UDF (*meeting*); un grand **rassemblement** des partisans de l'Europe (*[public] meeting; assembly*); ⟨Comm⟩ lors de la prochaine **assemblée générale des actionnaires** (*m*) (*shareholders' annual general meeting*)

member (*n*): il est demandé aux **adhérents** (*m*) de respecter cette consigne (*member*); **sociétaire** (*m*) de l'association sportive du Mans (*member of* *club/society*); ⟨Pol⟩ la coopération des **États membres** (*m*) de la CEE (*member state*); une délégation d'**élus** (*m*) lorrains (*elected member/ representative*)

membership (*n*): l'**adhésion** (*f*) du Portugal au Marché commun; l'**appartenance** (*f*) de la Livre sterling au SME (*membership*); les **adhésions** se font au rythme de 2.000 par an actuellement (*taking out of membership*)

memorandum (*n*): ⟨Comm⟩ communiqué au personnel au moyen d'une **note de service** (*internal memorandum*)

merchandise (*n*): ⟨Comm⟩ les **marchandises** (*f*) furent livrées en containeur

merchant (*n*): SEE **dealer**

merge (*v*): ⟨Econ⟩ conclure un accord pour **fusionner** leurs deux groupes (*merge, amalgamate*)

merger (*n*): ⟨Econ⟩ cette **fusion** entraînera des suppressions d'emplois; le service qui contrôle les **fusions et acquisitions** (*f*); partout, l'heure est aux **regroupements** (*m*); Presse: enquête sur les **concentrations** (*f*) [des entreprises] en Suisse

merging (*n*): la **fusion** de leurs deux mouvements (*merging, combining; uniting*)

merit (*n*): la promotion se fera **au mérite** (*by/on merit*); la société est à la première place du **palmarès** de l'agro-alimentaire (*table of merit*)

method (*n*): ⟨Fin⟩ les **modalités** (*f*) du remboursement de frais sont les suivantes; différents **modes** (*m*) **de paiement** (*method/mode of payment*)

metropolis (*n*): des **métropoles** (*f*) comme Paris, Londres et Tokyo

metropolitan (*adj*): en Afrique du nord et en France **métropolitaine** (*metropolitan, mainland*)

middle class (*n*): ⟨Soc⟩ les **classes** (*f*) **moyennes** y dominent

middleman (*n*): ⟨Comm⟩ les ventes d'armes dégagent des commissions énormes pour les **intermédiaires** (*m*)

middle-management (*n*): **cadre** (*m*) **moyen** dans une grosse entreprise

middle-sized (*adj*): ⟨Econ⟩ le PDG d'une **moyenne entreprise** (*middle-sized company*)

migrant (*n*): on a eu recours à la **main-d'œuvre itinérante** (*migrant labour*)

migration (*n*): le difficile contrôle des **flux** (*m*) **migratoires** entre l'Est et l'Ouest

militancy (*n*): ⟨Pol⟩ la crise du **militantisme** et le déclin des idéologies (*militancy, political activism*)

militant (*n/adj*): ⟨Pol⟩ un **militant** (*m*) du parti communiste (*militant, political activist*); les 'durs' ont imposé leur ligne **militante** au congrès (*militant*); l'étudiant qui **militait** jadis au parti communiste (*be a militant activist*); SEE ALSO **activist**

137

minimal (*adj*): partisan d'une dose **minimale** de proportionnelle; une **faible** présence hors de l'Hexagone

minimize (*v*): Time Warner **minimise** l'importance de ses dettes

minimum (*n/adj*): ⟨Ind⟩ les syndicats demandent la suppression des **minima** (*f*) (*minimum [esp. wage]*); il fallait se battre pour un **salaire minimum** à 2.000F (*national minimum wage*); (*Fam*) les **smicards** (*m*) ont leur salaire indexé sur l'évolution des prix (*[Fr] person in receipt of national minimum wage*)

minister (*n*): ⟨Pol⟩ nommé **ministre** (*m*) des Affaires étrangères

ministerial (*adj*): ⟨Pol⟩ un **arrêté ministériel**, une décision émanant d'un ministre (*ministerial decree/order*); un **maroquin** ou portefeuille ministériel (*ministerial office*); sur le **banc des ministres** (*ministerial benches*)

ministry (*n*): ⟨Pol⟩ la Gendarmerie mobile relève du **ministère** des Armées (*ministry*); il n'a pas été capable de **former un gouvernement** (*form a ministry*); SEE ALSO **cabinet**

minor (*n/adj*): ⟨Jur⟩ dès treize ans, un **mineur** est jugé responsable de ses actes (*minor, under-age person*); il s'agit d'une simple **contravention** (*minor offence*); SEE ALSO **abduction**

minority (*n/adj*): ⟨Pol⟩ les Kurdes, une **minorité** opprimée dans ce pays (*minority*); un **gouvernement minoritaire** qui ne comprend aucun communiste (*minority government*); ⟨Comm⟩ acheter une **part minoritaire** d'une autre société (*minority stake/shareholding*)

minute (*n*): ⟨Admin⟩ le **compte rendu** des séances doit être affiché dans les huit jours; le **procès-verbal** de la séance précédente (*minute[s]*)

minute (*v*): ⟨Admin⟩ on a **pris note** (*f*) de leur opposition au projet

misappropriate (*v*): 90 MF ont été **détournés** par des associés indélicats (*misappropriate [esp. money/funds]*); SEE ALSO **embezzle**

misappropriation (*n*): ⟨Fin⟩ des **détournements** (*m*) **de fonds** s'élevant à $20.000 (*misappropriation of funds*); la **dilapidation** des fonds publics (*misappropriation; waste, squandering*); une **concussion** digne des républiques bananières (*misappropriation of public funds*); SEE ALSO **embezzlement**

miscalculation (*n*): un **mauvais calcul** qui lui a coûté cher (*miscalculation*); ultime **mécompte** (*m*) pour les services financiers de la Poste (*miscalculation; disappointment*)

miscarriage (*n*): ⟨Jur⟩ l'**erreur** (*f*) **judiciaire** n'est pas si rare (*miscarriage of justice*)

misdemeanour (*n*): le moindre **écart de conduite** (*f*) est lourdement sanctionné (*misdemeanour*); ⟨Jur⟩ un **délit**, ou une contravention plus ou moins grave à la loi (*misdemeanour, [minor] offence*)

misgiving (*n*): il ne cache pas ses **réticences** (*f*) vis-à-vis de l'Europe; malgré les **états-d'âme** (*m*) de certains députés, le texte fut voté en l'état (*misgiving, doubt*)

mismanagement (*n*): la **mauvaise gestion** fut à l'origine de la défaillance de l'entreprise

miss (*v*): ⟨Comm⟩ **rater** ses objectifs de vente (*miss, fail to attain*); **rater une occasion** de faire une bonne affaire (*miss a good opportunity*); **rater le coche** de la modernisation (*miss out on*)

mission (*n*): ⟨Pol⟩ une éventuelle **mission** permanente serait créée sur place (*mission, embassy*); l'envoi d'une **mission diplomatique** dans cette région sensible (*diplomatic mission*)

missing (*adj*): ⟨Fin⟩ retrouver les millions **manquants**

mistrust (*n*): les Japonais manifestent leur **défiance** (*f*) à l'égard des États-Unis; la **méfiance** de l'Église envers les sciences (*mistrust, distrust*)

mistrust (*v*): l'Europe a raison de **se méfier de** Pékin (*mistrust, distrust*)

misunderstanding (*n*): le **malentendu** entre Paris et Londres (*misunderstanding*); **lever les équivoques** (*f*) entre Paris et le nouveau pouvoir (*remove/resolve a misunderstanding*)

misuse (*v*): il **abuse d**'un droit que lui accorde la Constitution (*misuse, abuse*)

mitigating (*adj*): ⟨Jur⟩ des **circonstances** (*f*) **atténuantes** pourraient leur être reconnues (*mitigating circumstances*); SEE ALSO **extenuating**

mixed (*adj*): réaction **mitigée** à Washington (*mixed; reserved, lukewarm*); sa proposition a reçu un **accueil mitigé** dans les territoires occupés (*mixed reception*); ⟨Econ⟩ va-t-on vers l'**économie** (*f*) **mixte** en Pologne? (*mixed economy*); la **polyculture** prédomine dans cette région de petites exploitations (*mixed farming*); ⟨Educ⟩ la **mixité** dans les écoles (*mixed schools/schooling, coeducation*)

mix up (*v*): il s'est trouvé **mêlé** à une affaire de drogue (*mix up, involve*); SEE ALSO **implicate, involve**

mob (*n*): une **cohue** de manifestants ont investi le bâtiment (*mob*); les **émeutiers** (*m*) ont pris d'assaut le palais présidentiel (*mob; rioters*)

mobility (*n*): la **mobilité** accrue de la main-d'œuvre (*mobility*); un soutien à la **mobilité des personnels** (*worker mobility*); SEE ALSO **social mobility**

mode (*n*): les **modalités** (*f*) de calcul de la retraite (*mode, method*)

moderate (*adj*): les prix de gros progressent à un rythme plus **sage**; la France adopte une position plus **nuancée**; des revendications assez **modérées** (*moderate, reasonable*); ⟨Econ⟩ les experts attendent une **reprise modérée** (*modest recovery*)

moderately (*adv*): la publicité n'est que **moyennement** développée en France

moderation (*n*): ⟨Comm⟩ la **sagesse** de la consommation d'outre-Rhin; une centrale syndicale réputée pour sa **modération**

modest (*adj*): hausse **modérée** des ventes de détail en juillet; le bilan de l'action menée reste **mitigé** (*modest; moderate*); étant donné la **modicité** des sommes en jeu (*modest level*); la **modestie des résultats** obtenus en deux jours de grève (*modest/meagre results*)

modification (*n*): depuis les traités de Rome, des **aménagements** (*m*) ont été faits; refuser l'**infléchissement** (*m*) de la politique sociale demandé par les centristes (*modification, change*)

modify (*v*): tenter d'**aménager** le système existant (*modify, adapt*); dans quelle mesure la politique économique sera-t-elle **infléchie**? (*modify, reorientate*)

momentum (*n*): redonner à l'économie du pays l'**élan** (*m*) nécessaire (*momentum, impetus*); l'industrie manufacturière **en perte de vitesse** (*f*) (*losing momentum*); SEE ALSO **boost, impetus**

monetary (*adj*): ⟨Fin⟩ un resserrement de la **politique monétaire** (*monetary policy*)

money (*n*): ⟨Fin⟩ on prétend que des **fonds** (*m*) publics finançaient la campagne électorale (*money, funds*); ⟨Econ⟩ ce train de mesures ne manquera pas de gonfler la **masse monétaire** (*money in circulation, money supply*)

monitor (*v*): ⟨Soc⟩ une assistante sociale **suit** les familles en difficulté (*monitor, follow up, follow the progress of*)

monitoring (*n*): ⟨Soc⟩ la nécessité de créer un service de **suivi** (*m*) médico-social (*monitoring, following up*)

monopolize (*v*): ⟨Pol⟩ **confisquer** la politique extérieure (*monopolize, take sole command of*); **truster** toutes les premières places (*monopolize, take over*); **investir les postes clés** du service public; on **verrouille** de plus en plus au sein du comité central (*monopolize/take over key posts*)

monopoly (*n*): ⟨Econ⟩ l'État a le **monopole** des tabacs (*monopoly*); l'opération est actuellement sous les feux de la **commission antimonopoles** (*Monopolies Commission*); le **conseil de la concurrence** peut infliger des amendes (*[French] Monopolies Commission*); briser les **positions** (*f*) **de monopole** (*monopoly position*); elle aura en ce domaine un **quasimonopole** (*quasi/virtual monopoly*)

month (*n*): ⟨Fin⟩ la **mensualisation** des salaires se généralise (*payment of salaries by the month*); ceux qui **sont mensualisés** auront des situations sûres (*be paid by the month*)

monthly (*adj/adv*): salaire **mensuel**: 10.200 F (*monthly*); l'ampleur des fluctuations **au mois le mois** (*monthly, month by month*); ⟨Fin⟩ des emprunts bancaires, remboursables par **mensualités** (*f*) (*monthly instalments*); on voit constamment croître les **mensualités de remboursement** (*m*) (*monthly repayment/instalment*); les employés sont payés au mois, ou **mensualisés** (*paid monthly*)

mood (*n*): l'**ambiance** (*f*) est plutôt à la réconciliation (*general mood; atmosphere*)

moonlight (*v*): ⟨Econ⟩ réduit à **faire du travail au noir** pour arrondir ses fins de mois; des professionnels du bâtiment **travaillant au noir** (*moonlight, work on the side*)

140

moonlighting (*n*): ⟨Econ⟩ le **travail au noir** se généralise (*moonlighting, work[ing] on the side*)

moratorium (*n*): ⟨Pol⟩ adopter un **moratoire** sur le nucléaire

mortality (*n*): le **taux de mortalité** (*f*) infantile est le plus élevé en Grande-Bretagne (*mortality rate*)

mortgage (*n*): ⟨Fin⟩ ne pas avoir d'**hypothèque** (*f*) à rembourser; un **emprunt-logement** à un taux très avantageux; l'octroi d'un **prêt hypothécaire** (*mortgage loan*); baisse des taux du **crédit hypothécaire** en Grande-Bretagne (*mortgage lending*); de fortes hausses des **taux** (*m*) **d'intérêt hypothécaires** (*mortgage interest rate*)

mortgage (*v*): ⟨Fin⟩ **hypothéquer** les deux fermes et la maison

motion (*n*): ⟨Pol⟩ la **motion** a été adoptée à l'unanimité; la **proposition** du gouvernement sera examinée en commission (*motion, proposal*)

move (*n*): ils multiplient les **démarches** (*f*) pour sauvegarder la paix (*move, initiative*)

move (*v*): ⟨Pol/Admin⟩ **proposer** le renvoi à huitaine du débat (*move, propose [esp. a motion]*); notre système **s'achemine vers** le système américain de subventions (*move towards*); SEE ALSO **transfer**

movement (*n*): ⟨Econ⟩ l'**évolution** (*f*) des coûts salariaux y est plus favorable (*movement*); ⟨Pol⟩ des militants de la Voix noire, une **mouvance** radicale (*movement, body*); les accords sur la **libre circulation** des personnes (*free movement; freedom of movement*); SEE ALSO **tendency**

multi-party (*adj*): ⟨Pol⟩ les premières élections **pluralistes**; des élections libres et **multipartistes**; une nouvelle Constitution fondée sur le **multipartisme**; un régime démocratique fondé sur la **pluralité des partis** (*multi-party political system*)

multiple (*adj*): ⟨Pol/Admin⟩ seul le **cumul** avec un mandat local devrait être possible (*multiple office-holding*); le **pluralisme des candidatures** étant la règle (*multiple candidacy*)

multiply (*v*): le gouvernement **accumule** les mesures pénalisant la propriété; Londres **multiplie** les avertissements au régime des ayatollahs

multi-purpose (*adj*): une brigade d'intervention **polyvalente**; un local **polyvalent** permettra d'accueillir plus d'activités

municipal (*adj*): en vue des élections **municipales** de 1989

municipality (*n*): ⟨Pol⟩ la gauche a gagné la moitié des **municipalités** (*f*) dans le département

murder (*n*): ⟨Jur⟩ inculpé d'**homicide** (*m*) **volontaire** et écroué; **assassinat** (*m*) d'un Américain à Istanbul (*murder, unlawful killing*)

murderous (*adj*): les auteurs de l'embuscade **meurtrière**

mutineer (*n*): les **mutins** (*m*) réclamaient de meilleures conditions de détention

141

mutiny (*n*): **mutinerie** (*f*) dans un centre de détention en Argentine

mutiny (*v*): 400 prisonniers **se sont mutinés** en prenant une dizaine d'otages

mutual (*adj*): des contrôles et des vérifications **réciproques**; il insiste sur le respect **réciproque** des cultures (*mutual, reciprocal*); ⟨Jur/Comm⟩ résilier un contrat **d'un commun accord** (*by mutual agreement*); le recours peut être **amiable** ou judiciaire (*by mutual agreement, out of court*); Serbes et Croates **s'accusent mutuellement** (*make mutual accusations*); ⟨Soc⟩ le divorce par **consentement** (*m*) **mutuel** des époux (*mutual consent*)

mutual aid (*n*): ⟨Soc⟩ la notion d'**entraide** (*f*) et l'esprit de solidarité

mutual insurance (*n*): ⟨Ins/Fin⟩ de nombreux Français adhèrent à des **mutuelles** (*f*) (*mutual insurance scheme*); les représentants du patronat, des syndicats et de la **mutualité** (*mutual benefit insurance company*)

mutualist (*adj*): ⟨Ins/Fin⟩ l'action **mutualiste** s'est étendue à bien des domaines

mutually (*adv*): les deux pays s'estiment **mutuellement**

N

name (*n*): le Centre, région qui ne justifie guère son **appellation** (*f*) (*name*); des centaines de gens répondant à cette **appellation** (*name, title*); des personnes **nommément** désignées (*by name*)

name (*v*): ⟨Admin⟩ il a été **nommé** président; son successeur fut **désigné** le lendemain; un expert **désigné** par le tribunal (*name; choose*)

naming (*n*): la **désignation** d'un successeur ne saurait tarder (*naming; choosing*)

narrow (*adj*): **courte** victoire pour les Conservateurs (*narrow*); le gouvernement dispose encore d'une **courte majorité** au Knesset (*narrow majority*)

narrowing (*n*): le **resserrement des écarts** (*m*) entre conservateurs et travaillistes (*narrowing of gap*)

narrowly (*adv*): les élections remportées **de justesse** (*f*) par la droite

nation (*n*): ⟨Pol⟩ la **nation** a choisi son Président (*nation*); on voit l'**État-nation** se dissoudre dans l'espace européen (*nation state*)

national (*n*): les **ressortissants** (*m*) français dont les avoirs sont bloqués en Algérie (*national, citizen*); (*adj*): concourir **à l'échelon** (*m*) **national** (*at national level*); un problème qui se pose **à l'échelle** (*f*) **nationale** (*on a national scale*)

nationalist (*n/adj*): ⟨Pol⟩ les **autonomistes** (*m*) revendiquent l'attentat à la bombe; le parti **nationaliste** vainqueur aux élections; c'est l'œuvre de l'organisation **indépendantiste** basque

nationality (*n*): ⟨Pol⟩ la dissociation entre **nationalité** (*f*) et citoyenneté; la suppression du **droit du sol** en matière de nationalité (*nationality by virtue of birth in the country;* jus soli)

nationalization (*n*): ⟨Econ⟩ le PCF exige la **nationalisation** des filiales du groupe

nationalize (*v*): ⟨Econ⟩ le gouvernement va **étatiser** les grandes banques; la Gauche menace de **nationaliser** de grands noms de l'industrie française

nation-wide (*adj*): une question qu'il faudrait traiter **à l'échelle** (*f*) **du pays** (*on a nation-wide basis*); (*adv*) des manifestations se sont déroulées **à travers tout le pays** (*nation-wide*)

native (*n/adj*): les **autochtones** (*m*), parmi les plus défavorisés en général (*native; indigenous population*); il est **originaire** (*m*) **de** Mulhouse (*a native of*); utilisant les matières premières **indigènes** des pays en voie de développement (*native; indigenous*)

natural (*adj*): le médecin légiste a conclu à la **mort naturelle** (*death from natural causes*); SEE ALSO **wastage**

naturalization (*n*): muni d'une **déclaration de naturalisation** (*f*) (*naturalization papers*)

naturalize (*v*): **se faire naturaliser** Français (*to be naturalized*); chaque année 89.000 **naturalisés** (*m*) augmentent le nombre des Français (*naturalized person*)

nature (*n*): une Turquie bien armée et **volontiers** offensive (*by nature*)

necessary (*adj*): des réformes **incontournables** (*necessary, unavoidable*); la prudence **s'impose** plus que jamais (*be necessary/essential*)

necessity (*n*): l'**impératif** (*m*) d'économies budgétaires (*necessity, need*)

neediness (*n*): être dans le **dénuement** le plus complet (*neediness, poverty*)

needy (*n*): les sans-abri, les **indigents** (*m*), ceux qui sont dans le besoin; (*adj*) les familles **nécessiteuses**, vivant dans le dénuement le plus total

neglected (*adj*): ⟨Soc⟩ des enfants en bas âge, **laissés à l'abandon** (*m*) (*neglected*); un quartier de centre ville **laissé complètement à l'abandon** (*[completely] neglected*)

negligence (*n*): encore une preuve de l'**incurie** (*f*) des gestionnaires socialistes; un incendie dû à la **négligence** (*negligence, carelessness; omission*)

negligible (*adj*): à lire les statistiques, le chômage est **dérisoire** en Suisse (*negligible; nominal*)

negotiable (*adj*): ⟨Comm/Ind⟩ salaire **à débattre**

negotiate (*v*): prêt à **négocier** avec l'État hébreu (*negotiate*); les deux parties **sont en pourparlers** (*mpl*) (*negotiate; be in negotiation*)

negotiated (*adj*): ⟨Pol⟩ trouver une **solution négociée** au conflit afghan (*negotiated settlement*)

negotiation (*n*): des **pourparlers** (*m*) directs commenceront demain (*[preliminary] negotiations*); des **négociations** (*f*) sont en cours (*negotiations, talks*); après des mois de **tractations** (*f*), on arriva enfin à un accord (*laborious/difficult negotiations*)

neighbour (*n*): les **voisins** (*m*) du Bangladesh ont eux aussi ressenti les effets de la sécheresse (*neighbour*); les **États** (*m*) **voisins** se sentent concernés (*neighbour state*)

neighbourhood (*n*): dans les grandes agglomérations ou dans les petites **localités** (*f*) (*neighbourhood, small community*); une **police de proximité** (*f*), plus dissuasive que répressive (*neighbourhood police/policing*)

neighbouring (*adj*): les départements **limitrophes**; dans les Vosges **voisines**, le chômage est en recul (*neighbouring, adjacent*); les pays **riverains** ou voisins de la mer Noire (*neighbouring, bordering on*)

network (*n*): un vaste **réseau** de franchisés dans toutes les régions de France

neutral (*adj*): ⟨Pol⟩ le **statut de neutralité** (*f*) de l'Autriche (*neutral status*); les **puissances** (*f*) **neutres** ne se sentent pas concernées (*neutral power*)

neutrality (*n*): ⟨Pol⟩ la Suède voudra maintenir sa **neutralité**; la **politique de neutralité** à laquelle ce pays reste attaché (*policy of neutrality*)

neutralize (*v*): éliminer le dictateur en le **mettant hors d'état de nuire**

news (*n*): cette **information** (*f*) n'a pas été confirmée par la police (*[piece of] news*); un reportage dans le **bulletin d'actualités** (*f*) (*news bulletin*); ⟨Journ⟩ cette question **défraye la chronique** à nouveau (*be in the news*); le désastre en Iran a **ravi la vedette** aux victimes de l'accident (*steal the news headlines*)

newscast (*n*): le **bulletin d'actualités** de la BBC

newspaper (*n*): ⟨Journ⟩ le célèbre **quotidien** madrilène (*daily newspaper*)

next of kin (*n*): on est à la recherche du **plus proche parent** du défunt

night (*n*): ⟨Ind⟩ le **travail de nuit** est relativement mal payé (*night work*); ceux qui **sont de nuit** (*work a night shift*)

nineties (*npl*): la **décennie 90** a vu l'émergence d'un nouvel actionnariat (*the nineties*)

no-claim bonus (*n*): ⟨Ins⟩ le régime du **bonus-malus**, qui applique les réductions ou augmentations de primes selon les dommages subis par les véhicules; compte tenu de la **bonification pour non-sinistre**

no confidence (*n*): ⟨Pol⟩ le **vote de défiance** (*f*) à l'égard du gouvernement (*vote of no confidence*); **refuser la confiance** au gouvernement (*pass a vote of no confidence*); SEE ALSO **censure**

no-go area (*n*): ⟨Mil/Pol⟩ la bande frontalière a été déclarée **zone** (*f*) **interdite**

noise (*n*): mener une **campagne pour la lutte contre le bruit** (*noise-abatement campaign*); les **nuisances** (*f*) **sonores** que subissent les riverains d'aéroports (*noise pollution*)

144

noisy (*adj*): SEE **rowdy**

nominal (*adj*): il était chef de l'État **de nom** (*nominal, nominally*); il y habitait moyennant un **loyer insignifiant** (*nominal rent*)

nominate (*v*): ⟨Pol⟩ le président avait déjà été **nommé**; certains furent élus au comité, d'autres **désignés** (*nominate, appoint*); le seul nom **proposé** pour le poste vacant (*nominate [esp. for election/office]*)

nomination (*n*): ⟨Pol⟩ aucune **proposition** (*f*) **de candidat** n'a été reçue (*nomination*); **briguer l'investiture** (*f*) du parti en vue des élections (*seek nomination*)

nominee (*n*): ⟨Pol⟩ il est le **candidat agréé** des partis centristes

non-aggression (*n*): un **pacte de non-agression** (*f*) pourrait bientôt être signé (*non-aggression pact*)

non-aligned (*adj*): ⟨Pol⟩ une conférence des **pays** (*m*) **non-alignés**; le mouvement des **non-alignés** s'interroge sur son rôle (*non-aligned country/state*)

non-compliance (*n*): une plainte pour **non conformité** (*f*) au décret; en cas d'**inexécution** (*f*), une action en justice sera intentée (*non-compliance, failure to obey*)

non-contributory (*adj*): ⟨Fin⟩ une préférence pour les **régimes** (*m*) **de retraite à la charge de l'employeur**; il opta pour un **régime de retraite sans retenues ni cotisations** (*non-contributory pension scheme*)

non-custodial (*adj*): ⟨Jur⟩ les prisons sont pleines, il faut trouver des **peines** (*f*) **de substitution** (*non-custodial sentence*)

non-earning (*adj*): ⟨Econ⟩ des familles d'immigrés aux épouses **inactives**

non-existent (*adj*): autant de conditions **inexistantes** dans les sociétés du tiers-monde

non-fulfilment (*n*): la **non-exécution** de leurs obligations contractuelles

non-interference (*n*): ⟨Pol⟩ le sacro-saint principe de la **non-ingérence** dans les affaires intérieures des autres pays

non-intervention (*n*): SEE **non-interference**

non-observance (*n*): un cas flagrant d'**inobservation** (*f*) de la loi; un **manquement au respect des règles** (*f*) (*non-observance [esp. of law]*)

non-partisan (*adj*): certaines options politiques **non sectaires**

non-political (*adj*): ⟨Pol⟩ les Français dans leur ensemble sont de plus en plus **apolitiques** (*non-political; apolitical*); veiller à l'**apolitisme** (*m*) de ses propos (*non-political nature; political neutrality*)

non-profit-making (*adj*): une association **sans but lucratif** (*non-profit-making*); une **association régie par la loi de 1901** (*non-profit-making organization [Fr]*)

non-suit (*v*): ⟨Jur⟩ le tribunal le **débouta** de sa plainte (*non-suit a plaintiff*)

non-taxable (*adj*): ⟨Fisc⟩ ces gains sont **non-imposables**

non-union (*adj*): ⟨Ind⟩ le personnel **non-syndiqué** est majoritaire dans l'établissement

norm (*n*): avec les années, la formule **s'est généralisée** (*become the norm/ general rule*)

normalization (*n*): ⟨Pol⟩ cela devra permettre un **retour à la normale** en Irak

notary (*n*): SEE **solicitor**

note (*v*): les deux hommes ont **constaté** leur opposition à la neutralité allemande (*note, take note of; record*); le marché a **pris acte** (*m*) de l'augmentation des taxes sur les alcools (*note; register*)

notice (*n*): les locataires avaient **reçu congé** (*m*) du propriétaire (*receive notice to quit*); donner un **préavis de quinze jours** (*a fortnight's notice*); être en train de **faire son temps de préavis** (*work one's notice*); ⟨Ind⟩ **déposer un préavis de grève** (*f*) de 24 heures pour lundi (*give notice of a strike*)

notification (*n*): aucun **avis de réception** (*f*) n'a été présenté (*notification/ advice of receipt*); ⟨Jur⟩ la **signification** du jugement se fait par l'intermédiaire de l'huissier (*notification [esp. of court decision/ruling]*)

notify (*v*): on les **avisa** de la date choisie; ⟨Jur⟩ le juge a **signifié** quatorze inculpations dont celle d'un policier; SEE ALSO **advise**

notoriety (*n*): SEE **reputation**

null (*adj*): la décision a été déclarée **nulle et non avenue** (*null and void*); ⟨Jur⟩ circonstance qui **invalide** la décision du tribunal (*render null and void*)

nullify (*v*): ⟨Pol⟩ un texte qui **rendait caduc** le compromis de Luxembourg; le découpage cantonal du Loir-et-Cher est **annulé** (*nullify, cancel*)

nullity (*n*): ⟨Jur⟩ une **demande en nullité** (*f*) de mariage (*matrimonial nullity suit; application for marriage annulment*)

number (*n*): l'importance des **effectifs** (*m*) envoyés dans le Golfe (*numbers*); le **parc** des logements sociaux s'est accru de 12% en 15 ans (*total number*); des classes **à effectifs réduits** [25 élèves par classe] (*with small numbers*)

number (*v*): l'équipage **compte** 36 hommes; **être au nombre de** 650 (*number*); la ville **comptait** seize établissements scolaires (*number, possess, contain*)

nursery (*n*): ⟨Soc⟩ la création de **crèches** (*f*) pour la garde des enfants (*crèche, day nursery*); le manque de **garderies** (*f*) pour enfants en bas âge (*day nursery, day-care centre*); ⟨Educ⟩ envoyer un enfant à l'**école** (*f*) **maternelle** dès l'âge de trois ans (*nursery school*)

nursing home (*n*): ⟨Soc⟩ un long séjour en **maison** (*f*) **de repos**

O

oath (*n*): **prêter serment** (*m*) devant l'Assemblée (*take/swear an oath*); lors de la **prestation de serment** par le nouveau président (*taking an oath*); **assermenté** et tenu au secret (*on oath; having sworn an oath*); ⟨Jur⟩ il a témoigné **sous serment** à la barre du tribunal (*under oath*)

obey (*v*): les Républiques refusent de **se plier** à l'ultimatum de la présidence; ⟨Jur⟩ devant son refus d'**obtempérer**, l'agent l'arrêta (*obey, comply with*); l'accusé a refusé de **déférer à** la citation à comparaître (*obey [esp. a summons]*)

object (*n*): se trouver **en butte** (*f*) à l'hostilité de toute la droite; **sous le coup d'**une mesure d'expulsion (*the object of*)

object (*v*): ils **récusent** notamment le projet de réforme du mode de scrutin (*object to; challenge*); SEE ALSO **oppose**

objection (*n*): ne pas tenir compte des **réticences** (*f*) d'ordre politique; les **réticences** des Américains (*objections*); la mesure fait l'objet d'une vive **contestation** de la part des syndicats (*objection, opposition, resistance*)

obligation (*n*): **être tenu d'**assister à la cérémonie, de par sa position (*be under an obligation/obliged*)

oblige (*v*): la concurrence **impose** aussi de réduire les coûts (*oblige, compel, force*); l'employeur dans ce cas **est tenu** de rémunérer son employé (*be obliged*); SEE ALSO **force**

observance (*n*): ⟨Jur⟩ le **respect** des lois; ⟨Mil⟩ une force de paix chargée de surveiller le **respect** du cessez-le-feu

observe (*v*): faire **respecter** les règlements (*observe*); **adhérer à** un code de bonne conduite (*observe, adhere to*); SEE ALSO **non-compliance**, **respect**

observer (*n*): ⟨Pol⟩ assister aux entretiens en tant qu'**observateur** (*m*)

obstacle (*n*): la cherté du crédit est une **entrave** au commerce (*obstacle, hindrance*)

obstruct (*v*): **faire obstacle** (*m*) au processus de paix (*obstruct, block*); la CEE accusée d'**entraver** le commerce mondial (*obstruct, be an obstacle to*); **entraver un agent** dans l'exercice de ses fonctions (*obstruct the police*)

obstruction (*n*): une action en justice pour **entrave** (*f*) au droit syndical

obtain (*v*): les grandes sociétés peuvent **se procurer** des ressources financières (*obtain, procure*)

obtaining (*n*): l'**obtention** (*f*) d'une licence

occupancy (*n*): ⟨Comm⟩ le **taux d'occupation** (*f*) des hôtels ne cesse de baisser (*occupancy rate*); la baisse du **coefficient d'occupation** des avions (*seat occupancy rate*)

occupation (*n*): ⟨Mil/Pol⟩ l'**occupation** (*f*) par des colons juifs de maisons palestiniennes à Jérusalem-Est (*occupation*); ⟨Econ/Soc⟩ l'**insertion** (*f*)

professionnelle des jeunes (*placing in occupation*); SEE ALSO **trade**, **profession**

occupational (*adj*): ⟨Ind⟩ la législation sur les **accidents** (*m*) **du travail** (*occupational injury*); les décès sont bien dûs à une **maladie professionnelle** (*occupational/occupationally-linked disease*); ⟨Fin⟩ bénéficier d'une **pension d'entreprise** par capitalisation (*occupational pension scheme*)

occupier (*n*): une maison actuellement sans **occupant** (*m*) (*occupier*); le précédent **locataire** a vidé les lieux (*occupier; tenant*); ⟨Mil⟩ l'**occupant** s'est bien comporté (*occupier, occupying power*)

occupy (*v*): il **occupe** un poste intérimaire à la recette-perception (*occupy/ hold [esp. a job/position]*)

offence (*n*): ⟨Jur⟩ coupable du **délit** de recel (*offence*); un **délit grave** passible de prison (*serious offence*); une **infraction à** l'article 175 du Code pénal (*offence against, breach of*); un refus **est passible des tribunaux** (*m*) (*be an indictable offence*)

offend (*v*): pour ne pas **heurter** un électorat que l'on espère récupérer (*offend*); ⟨Jur⟩ **commettre un délit** expose le fautif à des poursuites (*offend, commit an offence*)

offender (*n*): ⟨Jur⟩ des amendes sont infligées aux **fautifs** (*m*); les sanctions prévues contre les **contrevenants** (*m*) (*offender*); un **délinquant**, une personne qui a commis un délit (*offender, law-breaker*); SEE ALSO **habitual**

offer (*n*): ⟨Comm⟩ la **proposition** peut difficilement être améliorée (*offer*); Boeing donne aux Européens un mois pour **améliorer leur proposition** (*improve/raise an offer*)

offer (*v*): **consentir** des avantages aux locataires (*offer, grant*); ⟨Fin⟩ les trois quarts des actions **mises en vente** (*f*) (*offer for sale*)

office (*n*): ⟨Admin⟩ le **bureau** de l'Immigration (*office, department*); le **poste** qu'il occupe; sa **charge** lui impose la discrétion (*office, position*); ⟨Pol⟩ le Président **prendra ses fonctions** (*f*) en janvier (*take office*); ⟨Econ⟩ créer des **emplois** (*m*) **de bureau** (*office job*); la construction de trois **immeubles** (*m*) **de bureaux** (*office block*); SEE ALSO **term**

officer (*n*): ⟨Admin⟩ élection de deux **membres** (*m*) **du comité directeur** (*officer [esp. of organization]*); le comité a désigné son **bureau** (*officers*)

official (*adj*): on l'a appris **de source** (*f*) **autorisée** (*from an official source*); dans des **milieux** (*mpl*) **autorisés** syriens (*official circles*); faire une demande **par voie** (*f*) **hiérarchique** (*through official channels*)

official (*n*): un **responsable** américain l'a confirmé (*official*); la visite d'un **haut responsable** politique français (*high-ranking official*); SEE ALSO **full-time**

officially (*adv*): SEE **approved**

offset (*v*): les créations d'emplois ne suffisent pas à **contrebalancer** la croissance démographique; pour **pallier** la pénurie d'emplois (*offset; compensate for*)

old (*adj*): ⟨Soc⟩ des logements pour les **personnes** (*f*) **âgées** (*old people; the elderly*); finir ses jours dans un **hospice de vieillards**; des lits en **maison** (*f*) **de retraite** ou en foyer-logement (*old-people's home; home for the elderly*); ⟨Fin/Ins⟩ la **vieillesse** coûte le plus cher à l'assurance maladie; l'un des deux éléments composant le **minimum vieillesse** (*[minimum] old-age retirement pension*)

ombudsman (*n*): ⟨Pol⟩ le ministre du Travail a nommé un **médiateur** pour régler le litige; SEE ALSO **mediate, mediator**

one (*adj*): l'annonce de mesures **ponctuelles** (*one-off, isolated*); par delà des **aides** (*f*) **ponctuelles** d'urgence (*one-off/selective grant*); ⟨Pol⟩ sous un régime **de parti** (*m*) **unique** (*one-party, single-party*)

onerous (*adj*): la fiscalité **s'est alourdie** au fil des années (*become more onerous*)

ongoing (*adj*): un processus multilatéral et **continu** de négociation

open (*adj*): son appui **affiché** au pouvoir en place (*open, overt*); **prêter le flanc** aux critiques de ses adversaires (*lay o.s. open to*); ⟨Mil⟩ en cas de **guerre** (*f*) **ouverte** dans le Golfe (*open warfare*)

open (*v*): le congrès doit bientôt **s'ouvrir** (*open, begin*); ⟨Comm⟩ l'Inde est prête à **s'ouvrir** aux exportateurs occidentaux (*open up*); l'essentiel, c'est d'**établir de nouveaux marchés** (*m*) pour nos produits (*open up new markets*); la nouvelle route permettra de **désenclaver** la région (*open up, bring out of isolation*)

opening (*n*): il demande l'**ouverture** (*f*) d'une enquête (*opening*); les lycéens qui ne sont pas informés des **débouchés** (*m*) des baccalauréats (*opening, job*); ⟨Econ/Comm⟩ adversaire d'une **ouverture** de la CEE trop large aux automobiles japonaises (*opening up*); ⟨Pol⟩ un gouvernement d'**ouverture** vers le centre (*opening; openness*); ⟨Fin⟩ l'**ouverture du capital de l'entreprise** à hauteur de 3% (*opening up share capital*)

openness (*n*): la polémique sur la **transparence** du financement des partis politiques; l'exigence de **transparence** du patrimoine des députés (*openness; openness to scrutiny*)

operate (*v*): ⟨Comm⟩ **exploiter** un petit fonds de commerce en centre ville (*operate [esp. a business]*); SEE ALSO **run**

operating (*n*): ⟨Comm⟩ une autorisation d'**exploitation** (*f*) de salles de jeux (*operating*); les **frais** (*m*) **de fonctionnement** montent vertigineusement (*operating costs*); un **résultat d'exploitation** supérieur aux prévisions (*operating profit*); beaucoup d'entreprises vont connaître un **déficit d'exploitation** en 1993 (*operating loss*)

operation (*n*): le **fonctionnement** des comptes bancaires en France; un droit de regard sur la bonne **marche** de la société (*operating, functioning*); ⟨Mil⟩ les **opérations** (*f*) **militaires** ont été menées à bonne fin (*military operation*); au milieu d'un impressionnant **dispositif de sécurité** (*f*) (*security operation*); SEE ALSO **implement**

operator (*n*): ⟨Comm⟩ l'**exploitant** (*m*) d'une décharge (*operator, manager*)

opinion poll (*n*): ⟨Pol⟩ lors d'une **enquête d'opinion** effectuée début mars; tous les **sondages** (*m*) **d'opinion** donnent le concurrent centriste gagnant (*opinion poll*)

opponent (*n*): farouche **adversaire** (*m*) du projet (*opponent*); ⟨Pol⟩ Tchad: trois morts lors d'arrestations d'**opposants** (*mpl*) (*opponent [esp. of political regime]*)

opportunity (*n*): les **opportunités** (*f*) qu'offre le marché unique européen

oppose (*v*): ⟨Pol⟩ les Travaillistes pouraient **s'opposer** au traité (*oppose*); il continue à **s'opposer aux réformes** (*f*) (*oppose reform*); ⟨Comm⟩ les créanciers peuvent **faire opposition** (*f*) au projet de fusion (*oppose, resist*)

opposing (*adj*): ⟨Jur⟩ les avocats de la **partie adverse** (*opposing party*)

opposite number (*n*): son **homologue** (*m*) allemand partage son point de vue

opposition (*n*): ⟨Pol⟩ les partis de l'**opposition** (*f*) ont fait bloc contre lui

optimal (*adj*): ceci leur impose une gestion **optimale** des ressources (*optimal, optimum*)

optimism (*n*): ⟨Comm⟩ les prévisions, marquées par l'**euphorie** (*f*) économique de l'époque (*optimism, confidence*)

optimistic (*adj*): il se montre **serein** pour l'avenir (*optimistic, confident*)

optimize (*v*): ⟨Comm⟩ **optimiser** les bénéfices (*optimize, maximize*)

optimum (*adj*): les **conditions** (*f*) **optima** pour une reprise de l'activité (*optimum conditions*)

option (*n*): ⟨Jur⟩ le propriétaire a la **faculté** de vendre son bien (*option, freedom*); ⟨Educ⟩ il prépare un Bac littéraire avec **option** (*f*) latin (*optional subject*); SEE ALSO **right**

optional (*adj*): l'heure de religion **facultative** dans les écoles; ⟨Educ⟩ choisir trois **matières** (*f*) **à option** parmi les vingt proposées (*optional subject*)

order (*n*): ⟨Comm⟩ les vins français: baisse des **commandes** (*f*) de l'étranger; les **prises** (*f*) **de commandes** ont été très flatteuses (*order*); ⟨Jur⟩ à la suite d'un **arrêté d'expulsion** (*deportation/expulsion order*); ⟨Pol⟩ le plan sera appliqué par **ordonnances** (*fpl*) gouvernementales (*[government] order, edict*); le Préfet est chargé du **maintien de l'ordre** (*m*) (*maintaining order*); SEE ALSO **decree, edict, law and order**

order (*v*): ⟨Pol⟩ la décision de **décréter** un embargo sur les livraisons d'armes; ⟨Pol/Mil⟩ il **ordonna** la cessation des combats (*order, decree*); ⟨Jur⟩ le tribunal peut **ordonner** la publication de sa décision (*order*); ⟨Comm⟩ Air France **passe commande** (*f*) de douze Airbus A320 (*order, place an order*)

order book (*n*): ⟨Comm⟩ le **carnet de commandes** (*f*) est en progression de 34%; baisse de son **plan de charge**, liée au ralentissement du programme nucléaire

organization (*n*): ⟨Pol/Admin⟩ gravir les échelons de l'**appareil** (*m*) du parti (*organization, [party] apparatus*); des **organismes** (*m*) régionaux et départementaux; la **structure** qu'il avait fondée en 1981 (*organization, body*); l'**organigramme** (*m*) de la société (*organization chart*)

organizing (*n*): ⟨Pol⟩ soupçonné d'avoir participé au **montage** de l'attentat (*organizing, organization*)

oust (*v*): ⟨Pol⟩ quatre ministres **évincés**

ousting (*n*): ⟨Pol⟩ la **mise à l'écart** du secrétaire-général du parti; la société dénonce son **évincement** (*m*) du marché britannique

out-and-out (*adj*): partisans d'un libéralisme **à tout crin**; l'opposition **irréductible** de certains députés de droite

outbid (*v*): SEE **overbid**

outbidding (*n*): SEE **overbidding**

outbreak (*n*): le **déchaînement** des querelles nationales bloque l'union; avec l'**éclatement** (*m*) de la crise méxicaine en 1982 (*outbreak*); une **recrudescence** de la violence interethnique (*further/more serious outbreak; upsurge*)

outcome (*n*): le **dénouement** inattendu de la prise d'otages; ce fut l'**aboutissement** (*m*) de longues négociations (*outcome, result, conclusion*)

outcry (*n*): ce fut un beau **tollé** de la part des petits commerçants (*outcry, protest*); **[crier] haro** sur les augmentations de prix (*raise an outcry against, rail against*)

outflow (*n*): ⟨Fin⟩ la crainte d'une **hémorragie** des capitaux (*massive outflow [esp. of capital]*)

outgoing (*adj*): ⟨Pol⟩ la victoire du chef de l'État **sortant**; l'équipe **sortante** comptait 49 membres

outgoings (*npl*): SEE **expenditure**

outlaw (*v*): ⟨Pol⟩ l'Égypte est **mise au ban** du monde arabe; SEE ALSO **ban**

outlawing (*n*): ⟨Pol⟩ depuis sa **mise hors la loi** par le nouveau régime; SEE ALSO **banning**

outlay (*n*): ⟨Fin⟩ une **mise de fonds** initiale de 500 milliards (*outlay, investment*)

outlet (*n*): ⟨Econ/Comm⟩ l'Europe constitue un excellent **débouché** pour les produits japonais; une crise aggravée par la perte de **débouchés** au Moyen-Orient (*outlet, market*); SEE ALSO **market, retail**

outline (*n/adj*): ⟨Admin⟩ présenter les premières **esquisses** (*f*) du Xième Plan (*outline, sketch*); la Ville de Paris débat du **schéma** d'aménagement de la ville (*outline plan*); échec de l'**accord-cadre** (*m*) conclu avec la Régie (*outline agreement*); esquisser les **grandes lignes** (*f*) de la proposition de paix (*[broad] outlines*)

out-of-court (*adj*): ⟨Jur⟩ un **règlement amiable** des litiges (*out-of-court settlement*); l'emprunteur pourra ainsi **arriver à un accord amiable** avec ses créanciers (*settle out-of-court, reach an out-of-court settlement*); SEE ALSO **amicable**

out-of-print (*adj*): avec un premier tirage à 8.000 exemplaires déjà **épuisé**

out-of-work (*n/adj*): 16 millions de **sans-emplois** (*m*) dans les pays de la CEE; le taux des **sans-travail** (*m*) augmente sans cesse; SEE ALSO **unemployed**

output (*n*): ⟨Comm⟩ en limitant le **volume des productions** (*f*), grâce à des systèmes de quotas; le **rendement** est passé à 50 millions en 1992 (*output, yield*); SEE **capacity**, **yield**

outskirts (*npl*): à Nanterre, dans la **banlieue** parisienne (*outskirts, suburbs*)

outstanding (*adj*): ⟨Fin/Comm⟩ la facture des **impayés** (*m*) s'élève à 3 milliards (*bill/debt outstanding*); le **montant dû** s'élève à 3.500F (*debt/sum outstanding*); le **solde débiteur** de la facture (*amount outstanding/unpaid*)

outstrip (*v*): les communistes ont **distancé** les socialistes dans cette circonscription

outvote (*v*): ⟨Pol⟩ **mis en minorité** (*f*), le ministre a démissionné; le projet fut **rejeté à la majorité des voix** (*outvote; defeat*)

overbid (*v*): ⟨Fin/Comm⟩ il fallait **surenchérir** ou renoncer à son OPA (*overbid; raise the bid*)

overbidding (*n*): ⟨Fin/Comm⟩ sa **surenchère** a toutes les chances de lui faire gagner la bataille (*overbidding; higher bid*); la CGT, dépassée par la **surenchère** de la base (*overbidding; excessive demands*)

overcharge (*v*): ⟨Comm⟩ **faire payer un prix excessif** à ses clients (*overcharge*); il a **payé un prix excessif** (*be overcharged*)

overcharging (*n*): ⟨Comm⟩ les **dépassements** (*m*) **de tarifs** sont passibles d'amendes

overcrowded (*adj*): un autre ghetto **surpeuplé** et insalubre

overcrowding (*n*): habitat insalubre, **surpeuplement** (*m*) notoire

overdraft (*n*): ⟨Fin⟩ l'octroi de **facilités** (*fpl*) **de caisse**; les conditions d'octroi d'un **découvert [bancaire]** (*bank overdraft facilities*)

overdraw (*v*): ⟨Fin⟩ ne pas **dépasser son crédit** (*overdraw*); en **mettant son compte à découvert**, on s'expose à des pénalités (*overdraw an account*)

overdrawn (*adj*): ⟨Fin⟩ un compte bancaire **non-approvisionné** (*overdrawn*); la banque accepte que le compte demeure **débiteur** (*overdrawn, in the red*); SEE ALSO **worthless**

overdue (*adj*): ⟨Fin/Comm⟩ un paiement **en retard** (*overdue*); en raison des **retards** (*m*) **de paiement** dûs à la pénurie de roubles (*overdue payment; delay in paying*)

overhaul (*n*): une **refonte complète** du système de crédit (*complete overhaul/overhauling*)

152

overhaul (*v*): **refondre** totalement la fiscalité (*overhaul, recast*)

overheads (*npl*): ⟨Comm⟩ les marges baissent et les **frais** (*m*) **généraux** sont toujours aussi élevés

overheating (*n*): ⟨Econ⟩ ces chiffres font renaître les risques de **surchauffe** (*f*); une **surchauffe** de l'économie suivie d'une reprise de l'inflation (*overheating [esp. of the economy]*)

overland (*adv*): expédier **par voie** (*f*) **terrestre**

overmanned (*adj*): l'administration **aux effectifs** (*mpl*) **pléthoriques** est aussi surpayée; le tiers des entreprises estiment être **en sureffectif**

overmanning (*n*): ⟨Ind⟩ il y a bien un problème de **sureffectif** (*m*) à la Sécurité sociale; SEE ALSO **overstaffing**

overpopulation (*n*): une **surpopulation** fruit d'une immigration massive; le **surpeuplement** menace cette ville qui ne cesse de s'étendre

overproduction (*n*): ⟨Econ⟩ la **surproduction** européenne et les importations massives des pays de l'Est; **surproduction** et chute des cours

override (*v*): ⟨Jur⟩ faire **prévaloir** le droit communautaire sur le droit national (*override, prevail*)

overriding (*adj*): vaincre l'inflation est **primordial** (*of overriding importance*)

oversee (*v*): c'est lui qui **chapeautait** l'aménagement du territoire en Auvergne; le même ministre **coiffe** les Finances et l'Économie (*oversee; be at the head of*)

overseeing (*adj*): l'autorité **de tutelle** (*f*) de la télévision privée (*overseeing, supervisory*)

overshooting (*n*): ⟨Comm⟩ les **dépassements** (*m*) constants des quotas laitiers

oversight (*n*): **par négligence** (*f*) ou imprudence (*by/through an oversight*)

overspend (*n*): ⟨Econ⟩ un **dépassement budgétaire** évalué à 10 milliards (*budget[ary] overspend*)

overstaffing (*n*): ⟨Econ⟩ un gros problème de **sureffectif** (*m*); des coupes claires dans les **effectifs** (*m*) **pléthoriques** du personnel municipal; SEE ALSO **overmanning**

overt (*adj*): SEE **open**

overtax (*v*): ⟨Fisc⟩ les économiquement faibles s'estiment **surimposés**

overtaxation (*n*): ⟨Fisc⟩ la **surimposition** de ces catégories est flagrante

overthrow (*n*): ⟨Pol⟩ la crise en Union soviétique après le **renversement** du régime

overthrow (*v*): ⟨Pol⟩ le gouvernement, **renversé** par le coup d'État, a pris la fuite

overtime (*n*): ⟨Ind⟩ les **heures** (*f*) **supplémentaires** sont rémunérées au même taux (*overtime*); le refus d'**effectuer des heures supplémentaires** (*do/work overtime*)

overture (*n*): les **ouvertures** (*f*) faites en direction de Pékin (*overture, approach*); le leader du RPR **tend la main** aux partis de l'opposition (*make overtures*)

overturn (*v*): ⟨Jur⟩ le verdict fut **cassé** par la Cour de cassation; la chambre d'accusation **infirma** le jugement (*overturn, quash*)

owe (*v*): ⟨Fin⟩ **devoir** des sommes énormes à des créanciers; **être redevable** d'une forte somme à ses parents

owings (*npl*): ⟨Fin⟩ les sinistrés réclament leur **dû** (*m*) à l'État (*[rightful] owings; amount/sum due*)

own (*v*): **être propriétaire** (*m*) [de son logement] plutôt que louer (*own, be a home-owner*)

owner (*n*): ⟨Jur⟩ la législation régissant les rapports entre **propriétaires** (*m*) et locataires (*owner*); ⟨Comm⟩ le **repreneur** connaît déjà ce secteur du marché (*new owner [esp. of a business]*)

owner-occupier (*n*): la plupart sont **propriétaires** (*m*) **de leur logement principal** (*owner-occupier*)

ownership (*n*): des litiges sur la **propriété** du sol (*ownership, possession*); ⟨Comm⟩ la firme italienne **change de propriétaire** (*m*) (*change ownership/owner*); l'**entrée** (*f*) **en jouissance** du nouveau propriétaire (*coming into ownership, taking possession*); SEE ALSO **home ownership, possession**

P

pacesetter (*n*): ⟨Econ⟩ cette entreprise, une des **locomotives** (*f*) du secteur

package (*n*): ⟨Econ⟩ le **train de mesures** (*f*) annoncées dans le budget; le **paquet de mesures** additionnelles en faveur de l'ex-RDA (*package of measures*)

package (*v*): ⟨Comm⟩ les peintures, **conditionnées** dans des pots de 2,5 litres (*package, pack, present*)

packaging (*n*): ⟨Comm⟩ le fabricant se charge du **conditionnement**; un projet de directive sur les **emballages** (*m*)

page (*n*): ⟨Journ⟩ il tient la **rubrique** des faits divers dans le journal régional (*page, column, item*)

paragraph (*n*): l'article 49, **alinéa** (*m*) 4 de la Constitution

pardon (*n*): ⟨Jur⟩ il a bénéficié d'une **grâce** présidentielle; SEE ALSO **amnesty**

pardon (*v*): ⟨Jur⟩ condamné à mort, il a été **gracié**

parent (*n*): ⟨Econ⟩ il a transféré ses pertes vers la **société mère** (*parent company*)

parity (*n*): **parité** (*f*) entre le statut des magistrats du siège et du parquet (*parity, equality*)

parliament (*n*): ⟨Pol⟩ la mère des **parlements** (*m*) (*parliament*); la durée actuelle d'une **législature** (*parliament, duration of a parliament*)

parliamentarian (*n*): ⟨Pol⟩ le traitement et les avantages en nature des **parlementaires** (*m*) (*parliamentarian; member of parliament*)

parliamentary (*adj*): ⟨Pol⟩ lors des **élections** (*f*) **législatives** de mars (*parliamentary/general elections*); il a retrouvé de justesse son **siège de député** (*parliamentary seat*)

parochialism (*n*): partout l'**esprit** (*m*) **de clocher** empêche que l'intérêt national soit pris en compte; mettre fin aux **querelles** (*f*) **de clocher** (*parochialism; local/parochial rivalry*)

parole (*n*): ⟨Jur⟩ il pourrait bénéficier d'une **libération conditionnelle** (*parole, release on parole*)

parole (*v*): ⟨Jur⟩ il fut **mis en liberté** (*f*) **conditionnelle**; ces détenus **bénéficient** d'une **mise en liberté sur parole** (*be paroled, be released/freed on parole*)

participation (*n*): ⟨Econ⟩ un système de **participation** (*f*) **du personnel** aux grandes orientations de l'entreprise (*worker participation/involvement*)

partisan (*adj*): la désaffection de l'électorat pour la **politique partisane** (*partisan/party politics*)

partition (*n*): ⟨Pol⟩ le jeune État tchèque, issu de la **partition** de la Tchécoslovaquie

partner (*n*): ⟨Comm⟩ il a remercié son ancien **associé** (*m*); une société anonyme suppose un minimum de sept **associés** (*partner; associate*)

partnership (*n*): un véritable **partenariat** entre municipalités et organismes d'HLM; un **partnership**, ou société en nom collectif (*partnership*); ⟨Comm⟩ le français Thomson **s'allie** avec British Aerospace (*form a partnership*)

part-time (*adj*): ⟨Ind⟩ le remplacement d'emplois stables par des emplois **à temps** (*m*) **partiel**; la même protection sociale pour les **emplois** (*m*) **atypiques** (*part-time/temporary/seasonal employment*)

party (*n*): ⟨Pol⟩ le **parti** conservateur a triomphé; les autres **formations** (*f*) préféraient s'abstenir (*party*); il adressa un ultimatum à toutes les **parties** (*f*) **prenantes** (*party to an agreement/dispute*); (*adj*) un sénateur dont l'affiliation **partisane** n'est pas révélée (*party-political*)

party politics (*npl*): ⟨Pol⟩ ils sont nombreux à refuser la **politique partisane**

pass (*v*): ⟨Pol⟩ très critiquée, la loi ne sera **votée** qu'en 1928; trente-deux lois **adoptées** (*pass; adopt [esp. parliamentary bill]*)

pass on (*v*): ⟨Comm⟩ le patronat s'engage à ne pas **répercuter** les augmentations sur les prix (*pass on*); une augmentation qu'on ne saurait **répercuter** sur le client (*pass on [esp. costs/price rise]*)

passing on (*n*): ⟨Comm⟩ la **répercussion** des mouvements du dollar sur les prix français (*passing on; repercussion, incidence*)

patent (*n*): payer une redevance pour l'utilisation des **brevets** (*m*) (*patent*); **faire breveter** un nouveau procédé (*take out a patent on*)

patent (*v*): **breveter** une invention

paternity (*n*): ⟨Jur⟩ la **paternité** est dite 'adoptive' lorsque l'enfant est adopté (*paternity*); engager une **action en recherche de paternité** (*paternity suit*)

path (*n*): ⟨Educ⟩ de nouvelles **filières** (*f*) sont ouvertes (*path; course, subject*)

pay (*n*): ⟨Econ⟩ le **gain** horaire net moyen; une pension égale à 70% de la dernière **rémunération** (*pay*); demander une **augmentation [de salaire]**; une **réévaluation des salaires** des infirmières (*pay rise*); le personnel va **être augmenté** de 1,75% (*receive a pay rise*); l'assuré doit fournir les trois dernières **feuilles** (*f*) **de paie** (*pay slip*); les hommes **à la solde de** l'IRA (*in the pay of*); SEE ALSO **equal**

pay (*v*): ⟨Econ⟩ **acquitter** une cotisation globale de 5% du salaire (*pay*); une formation **rémunérée** à 30% du SMIC (*be paid*); le contrevenant peut **régler** par un timbre amende (*pay, settle an account*); le vendeur **est redevable** d'une commission sur la vente (*have to pay, owe; be charged*); l'État **prend en charge** (*f*) les frais de déménagement (*pay for; reimburse*); c'est la France qui va **faire les frais** (*m*) **de** ce conflit (*pay the cost of*)

payable (*adj*): ⟨Fin⟩ acheter des avoirs **libellés** en dollars (*payable*); un chèque **à l'ordre de** notre société (*payable/made out to*); le coût des repas est **à la charge de** la famille (*payable by; chargeable to*)

payee (*n*): ⟨Fin⟩ indiquer le nom du **bénéficiaire** sur un chèque

pay in (*v*): ⟨Fin⟩ **déposer** cette somme sur un livret spécial (*pay in*); **alimenter** ou approvisionner un compte bancaire (*pay money into/deposit money in an account*)

paymaster (*n*): les tueurs présumés et leur **commanditaire** (*m*) syrien

payment (*n*): ⟨Fin⟩ une **rémunération** en espèces ou en nature (*payment*); ⟨Comm⟩ un chèque en **règlement** (*m*) d'achat est parfaitement légal; ⟨Fin⟩ les **versements** (*m*) peuvent s'effectuer dans toutes les succursales; SEE ALSO **remittance**

pay off (*v*): ⟨Fin⟩ le prêt sera **amorti** en cinq ans; les 14 milliards investis seront **amortis** dès l'an prochain (*pay off*); la Pologne a totalement **apuré sa dette**; il a dû débourser des millions pour **éponger ses dettes** (*pay off a debt*)

pay out (*v*): sans **débourser** un centime; il a **déboursé** 2.000F en frais de déplacement

peace (*n*): ⟨Pol⟩ le pouvoir fédéral accepte le **plan de paix** européen (*peace plan*)

peace-keeping (*adj*): ⟨Pol/Mil⟩ les missions de **maintien** (*m*) **de la paix** des Nations unies (*peace-keeping*); le commandant de la **force de maintien**

156

de la paix; une **force d'interposition** (*f*) doit se placer sur les lieux des combats (*peace-keeping force*)

peak (*n*): ⟨Fin⟩ après une **pointe**, le titre a fait marche arrière; le **pic** ayant été atteint en 1988, avec 36%

penal (*adj*): ⟨Jur⟩ l'administration **pénitentiaire** devra contenir ces mutineries (*penal*); le **système pénal** le plus antidémocratique qui soit (*penal system*)

penalize (*v*): **pénaliser** les plus démunis; ⟨Jur⟩ **sanctionner** les sociétés ne respectant pas la réglementation (*penalize; inflict a penalty*)

penalty (*n*): récupérer son épargne sans aucune **pénalité** (*f*); ⟨Jur⟩ la **sanction** des infractions aux règles de la navigation (*penalty*); partisan d'une **répression très forte** pour les chauffards (*heavy penalties*); ⟨Fin⟩ une **astreinte** de 100.000F par jour de retard constaté (*financial penalty, fine*)

pending (*adj*): son dossier demeure **en attente** (*f*); des dossiers **en instance** (*f*) s'empilent dans les bureaux

pension (*n*): une **pension** indexée sur le coût de la vie; le débat sur le système des **retraites** (*f*) (*[retirement] pension*); ils continuent d'acquérir des **droits** (*m*) **de retraite** jusqu'à soixante ans (*pension rights*)

pension fund (*n*): ⟨Fin⟩ des **fonds** (*m*) **de retraite** des employés

pension off (*v*): on va **mettre à la retraite** le personnel âgé; SEE ALSO **retire**

perfect (*v*): le système a été constamment **peaufiné**; on a **mis au point** un système sans faille (*perfect; develop*)

period (*n*): on dispose alors d'un **délai** de trente jours (*period*); dans le **laps de temps** qui lui reste (*period of time*); lier l'indemnisation à la **durée** de cotisation (*period, length of time*)

periodic (*adj*): ⟨Econ⟩ 300 emplois permanents, et 220 emplois **intermittents** (*periodic, occasional; irregular*)

perjury (*n*): ⟨Jur⟩ un **faux serment**, ou faux témoignage fait sous serment

perk (*n*): SEE **fringe**

permanency (*n*): des incidents qui prouvent la **pérennité** du sentiment raciste (*permanency; durability*)

permanent (*adj*): son dernier **emploi fixe** remonte à 1988; trouver un véritable **emploi à durée** (*f*) **indéterminée**; débouchant sur un emploi **stable et durable** (*permanent/stable job*)

permit (*n*): des **autorisations** (*f*) d'ouverture sont octroyées par les communes (*permit, authorization*); 125 **autorisations de permis** (*m*) **de construire** accordées cette année (*building permit*)

permit (*v*): la Syrie **autorise** la communauté juive à émigrer; SEE ALSO **allow**

personnel (*n*): grève du **personnel** navigant (*personnel, staff*); s'adresser au **service du personnel** (*personnel department*)

perspective (*n*): dans l'**optique** (*f*) du marché unique de 1993; dans l'**optique** américaine (*perspective, point of view*); chiffres qui doivent toutefois **être relativisés** (*put into [proper] perspective*); SEE ALSO **proportion**

pertaining (*adj*): les dépenses **afférentes à** l'habitation principale; l'ensemble des activités **se rapportant aux** services (*pertaining/relating to*)

pessimism (*n*): ⟨Comm⟩ les coûts du travail sont en partie responsables de la **sinistrose** sur le marché de l'emploi

pessimistic (*adj*): la Bourse de Londres avait de quoi **broyer du noir** (*be pessimistic*)

petition (*n*): une **pétition** contre la peine de mort

petition (*v*): ⟨Pol⟩ le droit pour chaque citoyen de **faire pression** (*f*) **sur** le gouvernement

petty (*adj*): ⟨Jur⟩ les faits relèvent de la simple **contravention** (*petty crime*)

piece-work (*n*): ⟨Ind⟩ les ouvriers **travaillent à la pièce** (*do/be on piece-work*); un **salaire aux pièces**, au rendement ou à la commission (*payment at piece-work rate*)

pilfer (*v*): il **chaparde** aux étalages ou dans les voitures

pilfering (*n*): petits larcins, **chapardage** (*m*) et autres petites infractions; commettre quelques **menus larcins** (*m*) (*pilfering, pilferage*); SEE ALSO **theft**

place (*n*): ⟨Ind⟩ des **postes** (*m*) pour trente maçons (*place, vacancy*); ⟨Educ⟩ **être admis** à faire anglais (*get a [Univ] place*); SEE ALSO **take place**

place (*v*): ⟨Ind⟩ il n'est pas facile de **caser** un jeune immigré (*place [esp. in employment]*); une vingtaine de salariés seront **reclassés** parmi les 36 nouveaux postes créés (*place; find a new placement for*)

placement (*n*): ⟨Soc⟩ une formation, un stage, un **placement** en foyer (*placement*); ⟨Ind⟩ la CGT demande le **reclassement** des partants dans des entreprises de la région (*finding of new placement/job*)

plaintiff (*n*): ⟨Jur⟩ le **demandeur** a obtenu gain de cause; la **partie plaignante** dans un procès (*plaintiff; petitioner*)

plan (*n*): faire des **projets** (*m*); un **projet** de taxe sur les carburants (*plan, project*); ⟨Econ⟩ le prochain **plan quinquennal** (*five-year plan*); SEE ALSO **planned**

plan (*v*): **prévoir de** créer six ou sept coopératives régionales (*plan, envisage*); **projeter** la construction d'un deuxième pont (*plan to/for*); l'explosion avait dû être **planifiée** longtemps à l'avance (*plan, prepare*)

planned (*adj*): la réforme **prévue** du Code civil (*planned*); le **projet de réduction** (*f*) des forces armées (*planned reduction/cuts*); SEE ALSO **projected**

planning (*n*): ⟨Econ⟩ un système de **planification** (*f*) démocratique et décentralisée (*[economic] planning]*; ⟨Pol/Econ⟩ l'**aménagement** (*m*) **du territoire** a aidé à remédier à ces déséquilibres (*regional planning*); ⟨Admin⟩ l'octroi d'un **permis de construire** (*planning permission*); SEE ALSO **family planning, town planning**

plant (*n*): ⟨Comm⟩ les clients pourront visiter les nouvelles **installations** (*f*) (*plant*); ⟨Econ⟩ une poussée des achats d'**équipement** (*m*) (*plant and* *machinery*); ⟨Fisc⟩ hostile à la taxation de l'**outil** (*m*) **de travail** (*plant and equipment*)

plea (*n*): un vibrant **plaidoyer** en faveur du désarmement (*plea*); la France **prône** la cohésion face à la crise yougoslave (*make a plea/appeal for*); ⟨Jur⟩ les juges interrogent les parties et entendent les **plaidoiries** (*f*) (*plea*)

plead (*v*): ⟨Jur⟩ **plaider** la légitime défense (*plead*); pris en flagrant délit, il ne lui restait plus qu'à **plaider coupable** (*plead guilty*)

pledge (*n*): il a fait les frais de ces **engagements** (*m*) **non tenus** (*broken pledge/promise*); SEE ALSO **promise**

pledge (*v*): SEE **promise**

plenary (*adj*): ⟨Pol⟩ la deuxième **session plénière** (*plenary session*); le Parlement **siège en séance** (*f*) **plénière** à Strasbourg (*meet in plenary session*)

pluralism (*n*): les uns admettent déjà le **pluralisme** syndical

point out (*v*): on **souligne** que ces mesures ne sont pas irréversibles (*point out, emphasize*); les adversaires **font valoir** l'énorme coût de la construction (*point out/to*); les prix y sont en baisse, **précise** l'enquête; SEE ALSO **show, indicate**

point to (*v*): la direction **met en avant** une diminution des agressions dans le Métro; SEE ALSO **point out, reveal**

polemic (*n*): la décision suscita de vives **polémiques** (*f*) en France (*polemics; heated debate*); il évite de **polémiquer** sur une question si délicate (*indulge in polemics*)

police (*n*): les **forces** (*f*) **de maintien de l'ordre** brillaient par leur absence (*police, forces of law and order*); 97 d'entre eux sont toujours **placés en garde** (*f*) **à vue** (*in police custody*); le **tribunal de police** juge les contraventions (*police court*)

police (*v*): les gardes champêtres **policent** les petites communes

policeman (*n*): un **agent**, fonctionnaire de police d'une grande ville (*policeman*); un simple **gardien de la paix** (*policeman, [police] constable*)

police record (*n*): la condamnation figure au **casier judiciaire**; à condition de ne pas avoir un **passé judiciaire** trop lourd; les inculpés, connus pour leurs **antécédents** (*mpl*) **judiciaires** (*police/criminal record*)

police station (*n*): opération commando contre un **poste de police**; porter plainte au **commissariat [de police]** de votre quartier (*police station*); devant la **gendarmerie** de Cagnes-sur-Mer (*police station [in countryside/small town]*)

policing (*n*): le **maintien de l'ordre** ici relève de la gendarmerie nationale (*policing, maintenance of law and order*); SEE ALSO **community policing**

policy (*n*): ⟨Ins⟩ une **police d'assurance** tous risques (*insurance policy*)

politics (*npl*): ⟨Pol⟩ la désaffection de l'opinion à l'égard de la **politique**; une vie toute entière consacrée à la **chose politique**

poll (*n*): ⟨Pol⟩ le **vote** aura lieu dimanche; la veille du **scrutin** (*poll, election, vote*); SEE ALSO **opinion**

poll (*v*): toutes les catégories de personnel ont été **sondées**

polling station (*n*): ⟨Pol⟩ dès la clôture des **bureaux** (*m*) **de vote**

pool (*v*): les fermiers **mettent en commun** leur matériel

pooling (*n*): la **mise en commun de moyens** (*mpl*) dans un même lieu de travail (*pooling of resources*)

poor (*n/adj*): même les **indigents** (*m*) seront tenus de s'acquitter du nouvel impôt; les ménages les plus **démunis** (*poor, deprived, impoverished*)

poorly (*adv*): les jeunes **faiblement qualifiés** (*poorly qualified*)

popular (*adj*): Tchécoslovaquie: le séparatisme **fait recette** (*f*) (*be popular*); la **presse à sensation** s'est emparée de l'affaire (*popular press*)

popularity (*n*): la **désaffection** qui menace la Maison Blanche; le **discrédit** des grandes formations politiques (*loss of popularity/favour*); SEE ALSO **unpopularity**

populate (*v*): une fédération **peuplée** de 17,5 millions d'habitants

population (*n*): ⟨Econ/Soc⟩ le problème de la **dénatalité** (*population decline; falling birth-rate*); les cantons ruraux, menacés par la **désertification** (*population drain*); pour contrebalancer la **croissance démographique** (*population increase*)

portfolio (*n*): ⟨Pol⟩ les deux vont partager le **portefeuille** de la Justice (*ministerial portfolio*); ⟨Fin⟩ un **portefeuille** de valeurs mobilières (*[share] portfolio*)

portion (*n*): ⟨Fisc⟩ la **part** départementale de la taxe d'habitation (*portion, fraction*)

position (*n*): sa **charge** l'oblige à la plus grande discrétion (*position, office, post*)

possess (*v*): son armée **dispose de** 4.000 chars; la plupart **disposent du** téléphone (*possess; have at one's disposal*)

possession (*n*): ⟨Jur⟩ tentative de vol de voiture et **détention** (*f*) de faux papiers (*possession*); condamné pour **détention d'armes** (*being in possession of arms*); l'entrée en **jouissance** (*f*) d'une propriété (*right of possession, [esp. on transfer of ownership]*)

possessor (*n*): le pays **détenteur** des plus vastes réserves de pétrole

possibility (*n*): sans écarter l'**éventualité** (*f*) de licenciements; il lui reste la **ressource** de tout vendre et de partir ailleurs (*possibility; expedient*)

possible (*adj*): une **éventuelle** adhésion des pays d'Europe de l'Est; d'**éventuelles** révisions du prix (*possible; future*)

possibly (*adv*): avant d'être **éventuellement** inculpé (*possibly, in the future*)

post (*n*): 〈Admin/Pol〉 il quittera ses **fonctions** (*f*) fin août (*post, office*); il devait **rester en fonction** jusqu'à juillet 1994 (*remain in post/office*); une **création d'emploi** (*m*), non pas un remplacement d'une personne partante (*new post*)

post (*v*): 〈Mil〉 les objecteurs de conscience sont souvent **affectés** dans une formation militaire non armée (*post, appoint*)

postal (*adj*): le paiement peut s'effectuer par **mandat** (*m*) **postal** (*postal money order*)

posting (*n*): 〈Mil〉 il a reçu son **affectation** (*f*) dans la réserve du service national

postpone (*v*): la Belgique **diffère** sa décision sur l'achat de l'avion français; on parle de **reculer** le scrutin jusqu'au 13 juin; on ne peut plus **renvoyer à plus tard** cette question cruciale; la discussion a été **reportée** à aujourd'hui; **repousser** à lundi la décision (*postpone, put off*); SEE ALSO **put back, defer, put off**

postponement (*n*): il a demandé le **renvoi** de la discussion à la semaine prochaine; le **report** d'un an d'élections prévues en 1992

potential (*n*): le **potentiel** économique de l'ex-RDA reste à évaluer; Taïwan, dont les **potentialités** (*f*) commerciales sont très intéressantes

poverty (*n*): la lutte contre la **pauvreté** dans les grandes villes (*poverty*); ils vivent en-dessous du **seuil de pauvreté** (*poverty threshold/line*); progression de la **misère** dans les pays pauvres (*extreme poverty*)

power (*n*): 〈Pol〉 il peut compter sur le soutien des **puissances** (*f*) **occidentales** (*Western powers*); leurs efforts pour dénoncer les **pouvoirs** (*m*) **en place** (*powers that be*); l'**accession** (*f*) **au pouvoir** du président (*coming to power*); les Douze veulent accroître les **prérogatives** (*f*) des institutions communautaires (*power, prerogative*)

powerful (*adj*): une **puissante** armée capable de les tenir en échec

powerless (*adj*): ce gouvernement semble tout aussi **impuissant à** juguler l'inflation (*powerless to; incapable of*)

powerlessness (*n*): l'**incapacité** (*f*) de la justice à faire appliquer ses propres décisions (*powerlessness; inability*)

power-sharing (*n*): 〈Pol〉 un **partage du pouvoir** avec les communistes; on envisage à Alger une nouvelle **cogestion** avec les islamistes (*power-sharing, sharing of power*)

practice (*n*): condamné en appel pour **exercice** (*m*) illégal de la médecine (*practice [esp. of a trade]*); un **cabinet médical** en centre ville (*medical practice*); **s'établir** comme avocat (*set up in practice*)

practise (*v*): **exercer** la profession d'avocat; **se livrer** au piratage et à la violation de copyright (*practise, carry out*)

precedence (*n*): ici la convention collective **prime** sur la loi (*take precedence*)

precedent (*n*): 〈Jur〉 la décision du juge constitue un **précédent** important (*precedent*); selon les juristes, l'arrêt pourrait **faire jurisprudence** (*f*) (*set* *a legal precedent*); une circonstance où la **jurisprudence fait défaut** (*be no legal precedent*)

pre-condition (*n*): l'amnistie reste un **préalable** à la normalisation entre Paris et Pékin; un cessez-le-feu est une **précondition** essentielle à un règlement pacifique

predominantly (*adv*): des régions à **prédominance** (*f*) tertiaire; le parti Inkatha, **à dominante** (*f*) zoulou

pre-empt (*v*): il pensait ainsi **désamorcer** d'éventuelles critiques (*pre-empt, forestall*)

prefer (*v*): **privilégier** le mandat présidentiel de sept ans (*prefer, have a preference for*); ⟨Jur⟩ le délit de vol **a été retenu** contre lui; sans qu'aucune **charge soit retenue** contre lui (*prefer charges*); SEE ALSO **favour, priority**

preferential (*adj*): le premier pays à bénéficier d'un tel **traitement de faveur** (*preferential/favourable treatment*); ⟨Fin⟩ des prêts **à taux** (*m*) **préférentiel** (*at preferential rates*)

preliminary (*adj*): les **pourparlers** (*mpl*) ont été inaugurés au plus haut niveau (*preliminary talks/discussions*)

premature (*adj*): il juge **prématurée** l'idée d'un parti unique de l'opposition

premier (*n*): ⟨Pol⟩ le troisième **Premier ministre** de la présidence Mitterrand

premiership (*n*): sous le **ministère** précédent (*premiership; ministry*)

premises (*npl*): un nouveau **local** servant de lieu de prière pour les Musulmans

premium (*n*): ⟨Ins⟩ le montant total des **primes** (*f*) **d'assurance** (*insurance premium*)

prerogative (*n*): la dissuasion nucléaire **est du domaine** du chef de l'État (*be the prerogative of*)

present (*adj*): l'**actuel** chef de l'exécutif (*present, current*)

present (*v*): le texte définitif sera **soumis** au Parlement à la mi-avril (*present, submit*); SEE ALSO **submit**

presidency (*n*): ⟨Pol⟩ il accéda à la **magistrature suprême** en 1981 (*highest office [esp. presidency]*); la **présidence tournante** échoit au Portugal (*revolving presidency/chairmanship*); SEE ALSO **chairmanship**

president (*n*): ⟨Pol⟩ élu **président** (*m*) en 1981

presidential (*adj*): ⟨Pol⟩ lors des [élections] (*f*) **présidentielles** (*presidential elections*); les **candidats** (*m*) **à l'Élysée** (*presidential candidate [French]*)

press (*n*): ⟨Journ⟩ un empire de la **presse écrite**

pressure (*n*): Pékin exerce de vigoureuses **pressions** (*f*) pour couler l'opération (*pressure*); Paris et Bruxelles **font pression sur** le président zaïrois (*put pressure on*)

pressure group (*n*): SEE **lobby**

presumed (*adj*): ⟨Jur⟩ Colmar: le meurtrier **présumé** sous les verrous

pre-tax (*adj*): ⟨Comm/Fisc⟩ le **bénéfice avant impôts** (*mpl*) du groupe a plongé de 38% (*pre-tax profits*)

prevail (*v*): le réalisme a fini par **l'emporter** (*prevail; win*); **avoir raison** (*f*) **de** l'inflexibilité de Moscou (*prevail over; defeat*)

prevailing (*adj*): les vols et violences **ambiants** qui caractérisent ces quartiers (*ambient, prevailing*)

prevent (*v*): des mesures destinées à **prévenir** un été 'chaud' dans les banlieues; comment **prévenir** la délinquance urbaine? (*prevent, avert, avoid*)

prevention (*n*): depuis des années, les politiques oscillent entre répression et **prévention** (*f*) (*prevention*); priorité à la **prévention routière** (*accident prevention*)

price (*n*): ⟨Comm⟩ les **cours** (*m*) des matières premières ont dégringolé (*price; market price*); la **flambée des prix** de cette année (*rocketing/soaring prices*); conséquence directe du **renchérissement** du gaz (*raising of the price; rise in price*)

price control (*n*): ⟨Econ⟩ il promet le **contrôle des prix** et des réformes politiques; recourir à une **réglementation des prix** (*price controls*)

price-fixing (*n*): ⟨Comm⟩ un système planifié de **fixation** (*f*) **de prix**

price freeze (*n*): ⟨Econ⟩ le gouvernement choisit un **blocage des prix** pour résoudre le problème

price index (*n*): ⟨Econ⟩ l'**indice** (*m*) **des prix** permet de constater l'évolution des prix

price list (*n*): ⟨Comm⟩ un **barème des prix** doit être affiché (*price list; scale of charges*)

price range (*n*): ⟨Comm⟩ dans une **fourchette de prix** allant de 100 à 750F

price rise (*n*): ⟨Comm⟩ décréter des **hausses** (*f*) **de prix** allant jusqu'à 240%; il n'y aura pas de **majorations** (*f*) **de prix**

price support (*n*): ⟨Comm⟩ les dépenses affectées au **soutien** de la production agricole (*[price] support*)

price war (*n*): ⟨Comm⟩ **guerre** (*f*) **des prix** dans les librairies britanniques

prime (*adj*): la France reste l'**élément** (*m*) **moteur** de la construction européenne (*prime mover*)

principal (*n*): ⟨Educ⟩ **directeur** (*m*) d'un établissement scolaire; le **proviseur** d'un lycée; **principal** (*m*) d'un collège technique

principality (*n*): ⟨Pol⟩ l'Andorre, la petite **principauté** pyrénéenne

print (*n*): seul *Le Monde* a un **tirage** supérieur à ce chiffre (*print run; circulation*)

print (*v*): *Le Figaro* **tire** à 500.000 exemplaires par jour (*print [esp. newspaper]; have a circulation of*); une édition en langue russe **tirée** à 50.000 exemplaires (*be printed*)

printed (*adj*): les **imprimés** (*m*) sont expédiés à un tarif réduit (*printed form/ paper*)

printing (*n*): ⟨Econ/Fin⟩ recourir à la **création monétaire** pour se tirer d'affaire; on a eu recours en Pologne à la **planche à billets** (*mpl*) (*printing of money*)

priority (*n*): tout est subordonné à cette **priorité**; maîtriser l'inflation reste notre **objectif** (*m*) **prioritaire** (*priority*); la compagnie aérienne va **privilégier** son activité charter; **valoriser** les projets rail-route (*give priority/preference to*)

prison (*adj*): ⟨Jur⟩ des conditions **carcérales** déplorables (*prison, penal*); pour certains délinquants, un traitement **pénitentiaire** s'impose (*prison, custodial*); la **population pénale** ne cesse de s'accroître (*prison population*)

prison (*n*): ⟨Jur⟩ écroué à la **maison d'arrêt** de Douai; la **prison** de Mons; Melun, célèbre pour sa **centrale pénitentiaire** (*prison*); arrêté et transféré au **dépôt** de Nanterre (*[holding] prison*)

prisoner (*n*): ⟨Jur⟩ le nombre de **détenus** (*m*) s'élevait à 50.000 personnes; le seul **inculpé** toujours détenu (*prisoner; person charged with/accused of a crime*)

private (*adj*): ces mesures concernent les **particuliers** (*m*) et les entreprises (*private person/individual*); la production de **voitures** (*f*) **particulières** est en baisse (*private car/automobile*)

private enterprise (*n*): ⟨Econ⟩ un projet financé par des **fonds** (*m*) **privés**

private sector (*n*): ⟨Econ⟩ les salariés du [secteur] **privé** ont été mieux lotis que ceux du public en 1992 (*private sector*); **céder au secteur privé** 17% de British Petroleum (*sell to the private sector; privatize*)

privatization (*n*): ⟨Econ⟩ la **vente au privé** des grands établissements étatiques; le programme de **privatisations** (*f*) des entreprises publiques

privatize (*v*): ⟨Econ⟩ British Telecom, **privatisée** en 1984 et dont l'État conserve 48%; SEE ALSO **denationalize**

probation (*n*): ⟨Jur⟩ le **sursis** simple laisse le délinquant sans soutien moral; un sursis avec **mise à l'épreuve surveillée** (*placing on probation; probationary period*); SEE ALSO **trial**

probationary (*adj*): la **période d'essai** (*m*) dure de trois à cinq ans; pour une **période probatoire** d'un an (*probationary/trial period*)

probationer (*n*): ⟨Comm⟩ des postes de **stagiaire** (*m*) réservés aux jeunes; SEE ALSO **trainee**

problem (*n*): l'aide **se heurte** sur place à de grands problèmes; les négociations **butent sur** le casse-tête de la vérification (*encounter/come* up *against a problem*); ⟨Soc⟩ s'occuper des **enfants à problème** (*m*) (*problem child*)

procedure (*n*): les **démarches** (*f*) à accomplir (*procedure, step*); les **modalités** (*f*) de remboursement des frais (*procedure, method, mode*)

proceed (*v*): les négociations **se poursuivent**; la normalisation du pays **suit son cours** (*proceed, continue*); la situation financière de la Jordanie l'empêche de **donner suite** (*f*) (*proceed, go further; respond*)

proceedings (*npl*): ⟨Jur⟩ treize **procédures** (*f*) ont déjà été engagées contre des fraudeurs (*legal proceedings/action*); **intenter un procès** contre les autorités françaises; **engager des poursuites** (*f*) [**judiciaires**] pour factures impayées (*institute legal proceedings*)

process (*n*): un **procédé** pour lequel il va déposer une demande de brevet

process (*v*): ⟨Fin⟩ **analyser** des chiffres; ⟨Comm⟩ **traiter** une déclaration de sinistre; **traiter** une commande (*process, deal with*)

processing (*n*): ⟨Comm⟩ le **traitement** des commandes reçues; la commande à destination de Tokyo est en cours de **traitement**

produce (*n*): ⟨Econ⟩ des excédents, principalement des **produits** (*m*) **agricoles** (*agricultural/farm produce*)

produce (*v*): la France en **produit** la moitié de la production européenne

producer (*n*): ⟨Econ⟩ un des principaux **producteurs** de pétrole du monde

product (*n*): ⟨Comm⟩ renouveler sa **gamme de produits** (*mpl*); un vaste **éventail de produits** (*product mix*); un élargissement de sa **gamme de fabrications** (*f*) (*product line/range*)

production (*n*): ⟨Ind⟩ l'usine **commença à tourner** l'année dernière (*start production*); la plus moderne de ses **unités** (*f*) **de fabrication** (*production unit; factory unit*); SEE ALSO **mass**

production line (*n*): ⟨Ind⟩ informatiser la **ligne de fabrication** (*f*); le passage du travail artisanal au **travail à la chaîne** [de production] (*production line work/methods*)

productive (*adj*): ⟨Econ⟩ une agriculture à la fois **productive** et rentable

productivity (*n*): ⟨Econ⟩ la **productivité**, c'est-à-dire l'efficacité dans la production (*productivity*); une **prime à la productivité** pour l'ensemble du personnel (*productivity bonus*); SEE ALSO **inefficiency**

profession (*n*): un journaliste tué dans l'exercice de sa **profession** (*profession*); notaire **de son état** (*m*) (*by profession*); SEE ALSO **trade**

professional (*n/adj*): ⟨Mil⟩ une **armée de métier** (*m*), forte de 48.000 hommes (*professional army*); fournir un renfort de **personnels** (*m*) **de métier** (*professional soldier*)

profit (*n*): ⟨Econ⟩ baisse des **résultats** (*m*) des constructeurs automobiles (*profits*); **dégager un bénéfice** de 2,2 millions de dollars (*make a profit*); ⟨Fin⟩ Michelin fait l'objet de quelques **prises** (*f*) **de bénéfices** (*profit-*

taking); le **compte de résultats** pour l'exercice 1994 (*profit and loss account*)

profitability (*n*): ⟨Econ⟩ la **rentabilité** de l'affaire est désormais assurée (*profitability*); le retour à la **profitabilité** (*profitability, profits*); les banques suisses **renouent avec les bénéfices** (*return to profitability/ profits*)

profitable (*adj*): ⟨Econ⟩ privilégier les cultures les plus **rémunératrices**; des activités hautement **rentables** (*profitable*); la sidérurgie sera **bénéficiaire** l'an prochain (*profitable; in profit*); il compte ainsi **rentabiliser** son investissement (*make profitable/cost-effective*); la stratégie se révèle **payante** (*profitable; which pays*); SEE ALSO **remunerative**

profit margin (*n*): ⟨Comm⟩ les **taux** (*m*) **de marge** des sociétés ont reculé de 15% (*profit margin*); appliquer des **marges** (*f*) **élevées** (*high profit margins*); rechercher un chiffre d'affaires élevé avec des **marges bénéficiaires réduites** (*small profit margins*)

profit-sharing (*n*): ⟨Ind⟩ les accords de 1991 sur les salaires et l'**intéressement** (*m*); un contrat d'**intéressement aux résultats de l'entreprise** a été signé (*profit-sharing*); il touche une **prime d'intéressement** (*profit-sharing bonus*)

programme (*n*): un **programme** de réinsertion des détenus; ⟨Pol⟩ appliquer la **plate-forme** socialiste lors de la campagne (*[electoral] programme*)

progress (*n*): l'absence de réelles **avancées** (*f*) sur ce dossier délicat; être informé de l'**avancement** (*m*) des négociations; les deux parties se sont félicitées des **progrès** (*m*) réalisés

progressive (*adj*): ⟨Pol⟩ le **parti du mouvement**, du progrès (*progressive party, party of progress*); les députés les plus **progressistes**, les plus réformateurs (*progressive, forward-looking*)

project (*n*): l'**opération** (*f*) coûtera 20 milliards de francs (*project*); une **entreprise** qui tarde à se concrétiser (*project, plan*); SEE ALSO **proposal**

projected (*adj*): du retard sur la date **prévue**; deux syndicats ont refusé les modifications **prévues** (*projected, proposed*); SEE ALSO **planned, proposed**

promise (*n*): le nouvel élu tient à honorer ses **engagements** (*m*) politiques (*promise*); il a **respecté sa promesse** (*carry out/keep a promise*); les **reniements** (*m*) de l'ancien maire (*broken promise*); capable de **revenir sur ses engagements** (*m*) (*break a promise/one's word*); SEE ALSO **breaking, commitment, pledge**

promise (*v*): la tâche du cabinet **s'annonce** difficile; la récolte **s'annonçait** abondante (*promise to be*)

promote (*v*): **promouvoir** une politique de progrès social; **relancer** le rôle politique de la France (*promote*); des propositions pour **faire avancer** l'Europe sociale (*promote, foster, further*); **être promu** premier secrétaire (*be promoted/upgraded to the rank of*); ⟨Comm⟩ **animer** les ventes dans les grandes surfaces (*promote, do a promotion*)

promotion (*n*): l'**avancement** (*m*) est à l'ancienneté; des exemples d'inégalité dans la **promotion** des hommes et des femmes (*promotion*); le candidat aura de réelles **perspectives** (*f*) **d'évolution** (*promotion prospects*); un poste passionnant et **évolutif** (*with promotion prospects*); assurer la **valorisation** de l'image de marque de la société (*promotion, promoting*)

promulgate (*v*): ⟨Pol⟩ la loi instaurant le multipartisme a été **promulguée** (*promulgate, enact [esp. a law/legal document]*); SEE ALSO **enact**

pronounce (*v*): un conseil national **statuera** sur l'avenir du syndicat (*pronounce on; decide, give a decision*)

pronounced (*adj*): la crise en France est beaucoup moins **prononcée** qu'à Londres (*pronounced, acute*); le décalage entre les deux partis **s'accuse** (*become more pronounced*)

proof (*n*): sur **justification** (*f*) de la qualité de salarié (*proof, evidence*); sur présentation de **pièces** (*f*) **justificatives**; gains au jeu: conservez vos **justificatifs** (*m*) (*documentary proof/evidence*); pouvoir **justifier** de ses ressources ou de l'absence de celles-ci (*furnish proof/evidence of; prove*); SEE ALSO **prove**

property (*adj*): en plein **boom** (*m*) **immobilier** des années 1970 (*property boom*); un **projet immobilier** qui menace l'environnement (*property development scheme*)

property (*n*): l'acquisition de **biens** (*m*) **immobiliers**; maisons, terrains ou autres **biens immeubles** ou fonciers (*property; real estate*); SEE ALSO **estate**

proportion (*n*): la **part** des hydrocarbures dans les exportations (*proportion, share*); le faible **taux** de population autochtone dans les Émirats (*proportion, part*); il faut **relativiser les choses** (*keep things in proportion/perspective*); SEE ALSO **perspective**

proportional (*adj*): ⟨Pol⟩ le **scrutin proportionnel** revient à la mode; la **représentation proportionnelle** a toujours des adeptes (*proportional representation; voting under PR system*)

proposal (*n*): Sénat: **propositions** (*f*) sur la nationalité (*proposal, proposition*); SEE ALSO **project**

propose (*v*): on a **proposé** un train de mesures sécuritaires

proposed (*adj*): une **proposition de réforme** du mode d'élection des sénateurs (*proposed reform*); SEE ALSO **planned, projected**

prosecute (*v*): ⟨Jur⟩ la possibilité d'**engager des poursuites** (*fpl*) (*prosecute, take s.o. to court*); **être poursuivi** pour abus de biens sociaux; il risque d'être **traduit en justice** (*f*) (*be prosecuted/brought before the courts*)

prosecution (*n*): ⟨Jur⟩ toute fausse déclaration peut entraîner des **poursuites** (*f*) **pénales** (*prosecution, legal proceedings*); l'**accusation** (*f*) s'appuie sur les documents fournis par la police (*prosecution; the prosecution case*); la déposition des **témoins** (*m*) **à charge** sera cruciale (*witness for the prosecution*)

prosecutor (*n*): ⟨Jur⟩ le **ministère public** a requis une peine de cinq ans; le **procureur** réclame l'application de la loi (*public prosecutor*)

prospect (*n*): sortir du système scolaire sans diplôme ni **perspectives** (*fpl*) (*prospects of employment*); ⟨Econ⟩ avec la **perspective** d'une reprise de l'activité avant l'été (*prospect, possibility*); SEE ALSO **promotion**

prospect (*v*): ⟨Comm⟩ il faudra diversifier nos services et **prospecter** le marché européen

prosperous (*adj*): les concessions fiscales accordées aux contribuables **aisés**; une élite intellectuelle et **fortunée** (*prosperous, wealthy*); par rapport aux autres salariés, ils sont des **nantis** (*m*) (*prosperous, privileged*); les pays les **moins nantis** pourront rattraper leur retard (*least prosperous*)

protectorate (*n*): ⟨Pol⟩ le Cambodge, ancien **protectorat** (*m*) français

protest (*n*): la décision provoqua un véritable **tollé** de la part du personnel (*protest, outcry*); ⟨Pol⟩ la violence et la **contestation** dans les cités noires; **manifestation** (*f*) houleuse devant l'ambassade des États-Unis (*protest demonstration*); au terme d'un **défilé de protestation** (*f*) (*protest march*); le **vote protestataire** ne faiblit pas (*protest vote*); ⟨Ind⟩ la journée a été marquée par des **mouvements** (*m*) **revendicatifs** (*protest action [esp. in support of claims]*)

protest (*v*): le secrétaire d'État **s'élève contre** ces procédés (*protest against*); ⟨Pol⟩ **manifester** dans les rues contre le nouvel impôt (*protest; demonstrate*)

protester (*n*): ⟨Pol⟩ échec des négociations entre gouvernement et **contestataires** (*m*)

prove (*v*): l'administration doit **faire la preuve** de la fraude (*prove*); si l'authenticité du document est **avérée** (*prove, confirm*); une reconversion qui **s'avère** lente et difficile (*prove to be*); SEE ALSO **proof**

provide (*v*): **prévoir** l'avenir et penser à sa retraite; l'accord **prévoit** la création d'une monnaie unique, l'écu (*provide/make provision for*)

provident (*adj*): ⟨Fin⟩ un **fonds de prévoyance** (*f*) (*provident fund*)

provider (*n*): un pays qui était un grand **pourvoyeur** de main-d'œuvre; l'industrie a cessé d'être une grande **pourvoyeuse** d'emplois; SEE ALSO **supplier**

province (*n*): **en province** (*f*), et non pas à Paris (*in the provinces*)

provision (*n*): ⟨Jur⟩ selon les **dispositions** (*f*) de l'article 142 du code de travail (*provision, clause*); **tomber sous le coup de la loi** sur les expropriations (*fall within the provisions of a law*); ⟨Admin⟩ la **mise en place** d'équipements socio-culturels; ⟨Comm⟩ la libre **prestation de services** (*provision/providing a service*); SEE ALSO **clause**

provoke (*v*): les exécutions **suscitent** l'indignation des pays occidentaux (*provoke, cause, arouse*)

proxy (*n*): ⟨Admin⟩ confier ses intérêts à un **mandataire** (*proxy*); autorisé à **signer par procuration** (*f*) (*sign by proxy*); ⟨Pol⟩ tous les **votes par**

public

procuration sont allés dans le même sens; donner sa **délégation de vote** à un collègue (*proxy vote*); SEE ALSO **attorney**

public (*adj*): dans un rapport **rendu public** hier (*make public, release*); l'interdiction de fumer dans les **lieux** (*m*) **à usage collectif**; interdit dans les **lieux publics** (*public area*); une bonne part de l'**opinion** (*f*) [publique] partage ses vues (*public opinion*); ⟨Fin⟩ se faire **coter en Bourse** (*f*); la compagnie vient d'**être cotée en Bourse** (*go public*)

public (*n*): les **usagers** (*m*) sont les premiers touchés par ces grèves (*public; member of the public*)

publication (*n*): la **publication** du livre blanc sur la précarité (*publication, coming out*); ⟨Journ⟩ sa **parution** a été interrompue (*publication*); la **sortie en librairie** est prévue pour mai (*publication date*)

publicity (*n*): on a fait un énorme **battage** autour de cette affaire (*publicity*); ⟨Comm⟩ une vigoureuse **campagne de publicité** (*f*) (*publicity drive*)

public sector (*n*): ⟨Econ⟩ il n'y a pas eu d'augmentations dans le **secteur public** (*public sector*); l'analyse des **déficits** (*m*) **publics** (*public sector deficit*)

publish (*v*): le Livre blanc sera **publié** demain; Amnesty International vient de **diffuser** son dernier rapport (*publish; release*)

publisher (*n*): l'**éditeur** (*m*) du bestseller de l'année; les **maisons** (*f*) **d'édition** broyent du noir

publishing (*n*): l'un des grands de l'**édition** (*f*) mondiale

punish (*v*): les électeurs ont **sanctionné** le gouvernement; des fautes qui ont été sévèrement **sanctionnées** par les autorités; ⟨Jur⟩ l'article 26 **réprime** l'offense au chef de l'État

punishable (*adj*): ⟨Jur⟩ un crime **passible** de la peine de mort; le taux d'alcoolémie pénalement **punissable** (*punishable*); toute infraction est **sanctionnée par les tribunaux** (*punishable by law*)

punishment (*n*): la **sanction** des infractions aux règles boursières (*punishment, penalty*); **écoper de** six mois de mise à pied (*receive a punishment/sentence*)

puppet (*adj*): ⟨Pol⟩ le gouvernement **fantoche** mis en place par l'Irak (*puppet*); le **régime fantoche** installé à Koweït par Bagdad (*puppet regime*)

purchase (*n*): ⟨Comm⟩ l'**achat** (*m*) d'une centrale nucléaire à la France; le montant global de l'**acquisition** (*f*) (*purchase*); le **prix d'achat** avoisine 2.000F (*purchase price*)

purchase (*v*): les titres peuvent **s'acquérir** aux guichets de la Poste (*be purchased/acquired*)

purchaser (*n*): la maison devrait trouver **acquéreur** (*m*) (*purchaser, buyer*); l'**acquéreur** peut alors décider de ne pas acheter la propriété (*[intending] purchaser/buyer*)

169

purchase tax (*n*): ⟨Fisc⟩ la **taxe d'achat** (*m*) a été remplacée par la TVA

purchasing (*n*): ⟨Econ⟩ les ménages profitent de gains de **pouvoir** (*m*) **d'achat** (*purchasing power*); ⟨Comm⟩ les grandes **centrales** (*f*) **d'achat** font chuter les prix (*central purchasing organization*)

purpose (*n*): l'impôt en question a une double **vocation** (*purpose, intention*); l'utilisation des postes militaires **à des fins** (*f*) **civiles** (*for civil purposes*); SEE ALSO **function**

purse (*n*): apportant ainsi d'abondantes recettes fiscales dans les **caisses** (*f*) de l'État (*purse, coffers*); le **Trésor public** finance ces acquisitions (*public purse; Treasury*)

put across (*v*): **véhiculer** un message publicitaire (*put across, convey*)

put back (*v*): **repousser** à vingt ans la limite d'âge; SEE ALSO **postpone**

put down (*v*): ⟨Mil⟩ l'armée **réprima** brutalement toute velléité de révolte (*put down, quell, suppress*); ⟨Fin⟩ **verser des arrhes** (*fpl*) pour la location de l'appartement (*put down a sum/deposit [to secure a property]*); SEE ALSO **repress**

put forward (*v*): chacun **mettait en avant** son argument (*put forward, offer, propose*)

put off (*v*): la décision est **renvoyée** à la semaine prochaine; cette réforme, trop longtemps **différée**; SEE ALSO **postpone, put back, defer**

Q

qualification (*n*): ⟨Educ⟩ quitter le système d'éducation, sans **titres** (*m*) et sans formation (*qualification, diploma*); ⟨Ind/Scol⟩ les ouvriers quadragénaires, **à bas niveau** (*m*) **de qualification** (*with poor qualifications; poorly qualified*)

qualified (*adj*): la France a répondu par un 'oui' **nuancé** (*qualified*); ⟨Pol⟩ le vote n'a pas donné la **majorité qualifiée** des deux tiers (*qualified majority*); ⟨Jur/Admin⟩ un huissier est **compétent** pour effectuer ce type de procédure (*qualified, competent, entitled*)

qualify (*v*): une prédiction qu'il convient toutefois de **relativiser**; on doit alors **nuancer** le discours soviétique (*qualify, relativize*); il pense pouvoir **prétendre** à cette allocation (*qualify for; claim*)

quality (*n*): ⟨Soc⟩ le **mal de vivre** suscite un sentiment d'insécurité (*poor quality of life*); ⟨Econ⟩ l'importance du **contrôle de qualité** (*quality control*)

quantity (*n*): ⟨Comm⟩ une remise est offerte pour les **achats en nombre** (*m*) (*quantity purchase*)

quarrel (*n*): normalisation après 12 années de **brouille** (*f*) entre les deux pays (*quarrel; bad relations*)

quarter (*n*): ⟨Fin⟩ à un **quart** de point de son plafond; ⟨Fisc⟩ le premier **trimestre** de l'exercice fiscal

quarterly (*adj*): un loyer **trimestriel** (*quarterly; three-monthly*); un **relevé trimestriel** est envoyé à chaque client (*quarterly statement of account*); (*adv*) payé tous les trois mois ou **trimestriellement** (*quarterly, at three-month intervals*)

quash (*v*): ⟨Jur/Pol⟩ le Conseil d'État **casse** le décret du ministre; le jugement **est infirmé** pas la cour de cassation (*be quashed*); le tribunal administratif **annule** l'arrêté préfectoral (*quash, annul*)

quashing (*n*): débrayage massif pour exiger l'**annulation** (*f*) des licenciements (*quashing, revoking*); ⟨Jur⟩ la **cassation** ne change rien à la culpabilité (*quashing/setting aside of a verdict*)

quell (*v*): SEE **put down, repress**

question (*n*): la réforme suscite bien des **interrogations** (*f*) (*question, doubt*); la CGT refuse toute **remise** (*f*) **en cause** du SMIC (*calling into question*); les syndicats sont divisés sur les grands **dossiers** (*m*) (*question, subject*); ⟨Pol⟩ une **interpellation** adressée au ministre (*question; request for clarification*); le retour au passé est tout à fait **exclu** (*out of the question*); SEE ALSO **exclude**

question (*v*): on peut **s'interroger** sur le bien-fondé de cette décision (*question; have doubts about*); **mettre en cause** les fondements mêmes de l'alliance (*question, challenge*); ⟨Pol⟩ le ministre a été **interpellé** sur la montée du chômage (*question, ask s.o. for clarification*); ⟨Jur⟩ il a été **entendu** et inculpé par le juge; la procédure permet d'**auditionner un témoin** en présence de ses conseils (*question a witness*)

questionable (*adj*): une affirmation pour le moins **discutable**

questioning (*n*): cette **mise en cause** de son honnêteté professionnelle (*questioning, doubting*); ⟨Jur⟩ elle a subi douze heures d'**interrogatoires** (*m*) (*police questioning; cross-examination*); une **garde à vue** de trois jours (*holding for questioning*); remettre en liberté après **audition** (*f*); **interpellé** hier à Paris et inculpé de trafic d'armes (*take in/detain for questioning*); il y a eu quinze **interpellations** (*f*) lors des manifestations (*stopping/detaining for questioning*)

questionnaire (*n*): une enquête d'opinion sous forme de **questionnaire** (*m*)

quit (*v*): ⟨Pol⟩ le président albanais **quitte le pouvoir** (*quit office, resign*); la Lituanie **prend congé** (*m*) **de** l'URSS (*quit, leave*); ⟨Jur⟩ le propriétaire **donna congé aux locataires** (*m*) du troisième (*give tenants notice to quit*)

quorum (*n*): la séance est reportée pour absence de **quorum** (*m*); le **quorum** n'a pas été atteint

quota (*n*): ⟨Admin/Pol⟩ la mise en place de **quotas** (*m*) raciaux ou ethniques dans les entreprises; chaque parti reçoit un **contingent** strict

171

d'invitations (*quota*); une sélection à l'entrée **contingente** effectivement le nombre de diplômés (*fix a quota, set a limit*); ⟨Econ⟩ tout **contingentement** (*m*) européen des ventes d'autos japonaises (*fixing/ setting quotas*); les **quotas** laitiers et la chute des cours de la viande bovin

quotation (*v*): ⟨Fin⟩ la société vient d'**être cotée en Bourse** (*receive a Stock Exchange quotation; go public*); SEE ALSO **public**

quote (*v*): ⟨Fin⟩ le mark **cotait** 3,46F hier (*be quoted at*)

R

race (*n*): ⟨Soc⟩ elle est de **race** (*f*) indienne (*race, stock, blood*); des questions de **race** compliquent la situation; ⟨Pol⟩ des **émeutes** (*f*) **raciales** ont ravagé Los Angeles (*race riots*)

racial (*adj*): ⟨Soc/Pol⟩ le problème de la **discrimination raciale** (*racial discrimination*); partisan de la **ségrégation raciale** (*racial segregation*); le respect des **minorités** (*f*) **raciales** (*racial minority*)

racialism (*n*): (*Soc/Pol*) la lutte contre le **racisme**; le **racisme** anti-Noirs aux États-Unis (*racialism, racism*); SEE ALSO **racist**

racialist (*n/adj*): SEE **racist**

racist (*n/adj*): ⟨Soc⟩ des arguments **racistes** (*racist*); un groupuscule imbu d'**attitudes** (*f*) **racistes** (*racist/racialist attitudes; racialism*)

racket (*n*): ⟨Comm⟩ le **trafic** des voitures volées; impliqué dans le **trafic de la drogue** (*drug racket*); SEE ALSO **traffic**

racketeering (*n*): céder au **racket** est toujours un délit (*racket, extortion*); face aux accusations d'**affairisme** (*m*) (*political racketeering*)

raid (*n*): **incursion** (*f*) des rebelles croates en Serbie (*raid, foray*); le juge ordonna une **rafle** de tous les établissements du quartier; une **descente** simultanée à Paris chez un autre revendeur (*raid [esp. by police]*)

raid (*v*): la police a **fait une rafle** dans les milieux de la drogue

raise (*v*): ⟨Pol⟩ la décision de **relever** de 2,4% le SMIC; **revaloriser** les prestations familiales (*raise, increase*); ⟨Fin⟩ Péchiney s'apprête à **lever** plus de 500MF (*raise [esp. capital/finance]*); ⟨Econ⟩ tous les producteurs **majorent leurs prix** (*m*) en janvier (*raise prices*); l'allocation **passe à** 770F; le montant de l'allocation **est porté à** 63F par jour (*be raised/put up to*); SEE ALSO **increase**

raising (*n*): l'**élévation** (*f*) du niveau des qualifications; la **revalorisation** des salaires; un **relèvement** du plafond de ressources à 4.400F (*raising*); le **relèvement des tarifs** de la SNCF (*raising of fares*); SEE ALSO **price**, **capital**

rally (*n*): **ralliement** (*m*) pour la défense des droits des harkis (*rally [esp. political/electoral]*)

rally (*v*): les voteurs indécis ont en majorité **rallié** la droite (*rally to; join*); les pays hésitants pourraient **se rallier à** la proposition turque (*rally to; be converted to; support*)

rallying (*n*): son récent **ralliement à** la motion socialiste (*rallying to; coming round to; going over to*); Espagne: **mobilisation** (*f*) contre la violence de l'ETA (*rallying, mobilization*)

range (*n*): les personnes d'un large **éventail** socio-économique (*range, spread*); SEE ALSO **product**

rank (*n*): obtenir le **statut** de contractuel (*rank, status, position*); il rejoint la Snecma **en qualité** (*f*) **de** directeur-général adjoint (*with the rank/ position of*); ⟨Mil⟩ porter le **grade** d'amiral ou de général

rank and file (*n*): ⟨Ind⟩ les syndicats vont consulter leur **base** (*f*) (*rank and file; membership*)

rape (*n*): ⟨Jur⟩ le **viol** est un crime (*rape*); une affaire de **viol collectif** (*collective/gang rape*)

rape (*v*): ⟨Jur⟩ **commettre un viol** sur un enfant constitue une circonstance aggravante (*rape, commit rape*)

rapist (*n*): ⟨Soc⟩ la police interpelle environ 2.500 **violeurs** (*m*) par an

rate (*n*): ⟨Ind⟩ le type de travail, la **cadence**, l'âge des salariés (*rate [esp. of work/assembly line]*); ⟨Econ/Comm⟩ le **rythme de l'inflation** a freiné les exportations (*rate of inflation*); on va diminuer les effectifs **à la cadence de** 8.000 par an; **à raison de** 39 heures par semaine (*at the rate of*)

rateable (*adj*): ⟨Fisc⟩ la **valeur locative imposable** est de £280 par an (*rateable value*)

ratepayer (*n*): SEE **taxpayer**

ratification (*n*): ⟨Pol⟩ la **ratification** des traités internationaux; SEE ALSO **endorsement**

ratify (*v*): ⟨Pol⟩ le Conseil constitutionnel doit **avaliser** le découpage électoral; les principes d'un règlement ont été **entérinés** le 20 juillet; un vote qui **sanctionne** la politique française au Proche-Orient (*ratify, confirm*)

rating (*n*): le ministre améliore sa **cote de popularité** (*f*) (*[popularity] rating*)

ration (*v*): ⟨Econ⟩ on s'apprête même à **rationner** le pain; SEE ALSO **limit, restrict**

rationing (*n*): ⟨Econ⟩ les pénuries et les tickets de **rationnement** (*m*); les biens de base, distribués par un **système de coupons** (*mpl*) (*rationing*); privations alimentaires, **restrictions** (*fpl*) de la consommation (*rationing, restrictions*)

raw material (*n*): ⟨Econ⟩ les cours des **matières** (*f*) **premières** n'ont cessé de baisser

reach (*v*): il faut que les femmes puissent **accéder** aux postes de responsabilité; Espagne: le taux de chômage **atteint** 17% (*reach, rise to, attain*)

read (*v*): le porte-parole du gouvernement **donna lecture** (*f*) du communiqué (*read, read out*)

readership (*n*): ⟨Journ⟩ un tirage de 200.000 exemplaires et une **audience** de 520.000 lecteurs

reading (*n*): une **lecture** stricte du texte de 1958 justifie cette interprétation (*reading, interpretation*); ⟨Pol⟩ le Sénat l'a adopté **en première lecture** (*at a first reading [esp. of parliamentary bill]*)

readjustment (*n*): ⟨Pol⟩ à la suite du **rééquilibrage** de la diplomatie égyptienne en faveur de la Syrie

real (*adj*): ⟨Econ⟩ les bénéfices ont été divisés par trois **en valeur** (*f*) **réelle** (*in real terms*); augmenter son bénéfice de 34% **en monnaie** (*f*) **constante** (*in real/inflation-adjusted terms*); SEE ALSO **inflation**

real estate (*n*): un secteur porteur, l'**immobilier** (*m*) (*real estate, the property business*); maisons, terrains et autres **biens** (*m*) **immeubles** ou biens fonciers (*real estate; landed property*)

realistic (*adj*): ⟨Comm⟩ le mot d'ordre est: **vérité** (*f*) **des prix** (*realistic/fair prices*)

realization (*n*): la **prise de conscience** (*f*) progressive de l'importance de cet événement (*realization*); ⟨Econ⟩ la **réalisation des actifs** et le paiement des créances (*realization of assets; conversion into cash*)

realize (*v*): l'Afrique a enfin **pris conscience** (*f*) **de** l'importance de l'enjeu

reappoint (*v*): le président sortant sera-t-il **reconduit dans ses fonctions?** (*reappoint; re-elect*); SEE ALSO **re-elect**

reappointment (*n*): sa **reconduction dans ses fonctions** a surpris les politologues (*reappointment; re-election*)

reason (*n*): le **motif** de la demande (*reason, motive*)

reasonable (*adj*): à des prix **abordables** pour les ménages à revenus modestes (*reasonable*); elle exige un salaire **correct** et de meilleures conditions de travail (*reasonable, fair*)

rebate (*n*): ⟨Comm⟩ la **ristourne** vise à récompenser la fidélité de l'acheteur; un **rabais** accordé par le fournisseur pour retard de livraison (*rebate; refund*)

rebel (*n*): ⟨Mil/Pol⟩ les **insurgés** (*m*) investissent le palais présidentiel (*rebel, insurgent*); une lutte pour le pouvoir au sein de la **rébellion** (*rebel movement, rebels*)

rebel (*v*): les Républiques **s'insurgent** contre le centre

rebellion (*n*): ⟨Pol⟩ nouvelle **fronde** (*f*) au Parlement: le projet de budget est rejeté; ⟨Mil⟩ il soutenait la **rébellion** des communistes grecs

rebellious (*adj*): la plus **frondeuse** des républiques s'apprête à quitter la fédération

rebuff (*n*): un cinglant **démenti** à l'adresse du pouvoir; le vote constitue un net **désaveu** du gouvernement socialiste (*rebuff; rejection, repudiation*)

recall (*n*): ⟨Pol⟩ Bonn annonce le **rappel** de son chargé d'affaires

recall (*v*): ⟨Pol⟩ les Douze **rappellent** leurs ambassadeurs

recapture (*n*): ⟨Mil⟩ les autorités ont annoncé la **reprise** de la ville hier matin

recapture (*v*): ⟨Mil⟩ les troupes ont pu **reprendre** la ville aux rebelles (*recapture, retake*)

receipt (*n*): ⟨Admin⟩ l'administration délivre un **récépissé**; une **quittance** de prime d'assurance (*receipt*); dès **réception** (*f*) du règlement (*receipt, receiving*); il a **accusé réception** du colis (*acknowledge/confirm receipt*); ⟨Comm⟩ une baisse des **recettes** (*f*) publicitaires (*receipts, revenue*); ⟨Soc⟩ le nombre d'**allocataires** (*m*) des ASSEDIC a fortement augmenté (*person in receipt of; beneficiary, recipient*); SEE ALSO **recipient**

receipt (*v*): ⟨Fin/Comm⟩ présenter une **facture acquittée** (*receipted bill*)

receive (*v*): ⟨Fin⟩ recevoir une rémunération modeste; **toucher** un salaire en contrepartie d'un travail fourni; **percevoir** les allocations de chômage (*receive, be paid*)

receiver (*n*): ⟨Jur/Comm⟩ les affaires en dépôt de bilan sont confiées à l'**administrateur** (*m*) **judiciaire** (*official receiver*); pour la reprise de la société en faillite, les **syndics** (*m*) se sont prononcés pour le groupe belge (*receivers*); le dépôt de bilan de l'entreprise, suivi de la **mise en redressement** (*m*) **judiciaire** (*calling in the receiver*); ⟨Comm⟩ le butin, retrouvé chez un **receleur** notoire (*receiver of stolen goods*)

receivership (*n*): ⟨Comm⟩ le **règlement** (*m*) **judiciaire**, s'il échoue, débouche sur une liquidation (*putting into receivership*)

receiving (*n*): impliqué dans une affaire de **recel** (*m*) (*receiving/possession [of stolen goods]*)

reception (*n*): ⟨Soc⟩ le ministre a visité quinze **structures** (*f*) **d'accueil** pour personnes âgées (*reception centre*); la pénurie d'**infrastructures** (*f*) **d'accueil** pour les tout-petits (*reception facilities*)

recession (*n*): ⟨Econ⟩ un simple ralentissement du rythme de croissance, que l'on qualifie de **récession** (*f*)

recidivism (*n*): ⟨Jur⟩ le taux de **récidive** (*f*) inquiétant des violeurs (*recidivism; committing of a further offence*)

recidivist (*n*): ⟨Jur⟩ **récidiviste** (*m*) notoire, il se vit refuser une libération sous caution; parmi eux, de nombreux **récidivistes**, fichés au commissariat de police (*recidivist; habitual offender*)

recipient (*n*): ce pays est le deuxième **bénéficiaire** de l'aide publique française (*recipient, beneficiary*); ⟨Soc⟩ 20.000 **allocataires** (*m*) du revenu

175

minimum d'insertion (*recipient [esp. of a social benefit]*); SEE ALSO **beneficiary**

reciprocal (*adj*): des **accords** (*m*) **de réciprocité** négociés entre la France et ses partenaires (*reciprocal agreement*)

recognition (*n*): ⟨Pol⟩ une **reconnaissance** par l'armée du pouvoir central (*recognition*); la **reconnaissance** des Républiques de l'ex-Yougoslavie n'a pas tardé (*official/diplomatic recognition*)

recognize (*v*): ⟨Pol⟩ **reconnaître** l'indépendance de la Slovénie (*recognize, give diplomatic recognition*)

recommend (*v*): il **préconise** l'intégration des étrangers (*recommend, be in favour of*)

recommendation (*n*): ⟨Jur⟩ les **réquisitions** (*f*) du substitut ne vont pas dans le sens de la clémence (*recommendation [esp. to judge/jury]*)

reconcile (*v*): le problème: **concilier** liberté et ordre; de nouvelles mesures permettant de **concilier** vie de famille et vie professionnelle

reconciliation (*n*): ⟨Pol⟩ France-Allemagne: le **rabibochage**; vers un **rapprochement** soviéto-japonais; on va vers une **réconciliation** entre Moscou et Pékin; après les **retrouvailles** (*fpl*) algéro-marocaines

reconsider (*v*): Paris prêt à **remettre en cause** ses engagements dans cette partie du monde; la direction n'entend pas **revenir sur** les mesures annoncées (*reconsider; go back upon*)

reconsideration (*n*): une **remise en question** de la stratégie nucléaire; la **remise en cause** des réformes initialement prévues (*re-examination, reconsideration*)

record (*n*): le **record** de la longévité (*record*); un **record d'affluence** (*f*) (*record attendance*); la réglementation relative au **fichage informatique** (*computer records*)

record (*v*): le chiffre le plus élevé jamais **enregistré**; plusieurs cas ont été **recensés** dans ce quartier (*record, report*); SEE ALSO **register**

recoup (*v*): ⟨Fin⟩ il faut 3.000 heures de vol pour **amortir** un appareil (*recoup the cost; amortize*)

recourse (*n*): l'État décidait de **recourir à** des capitaux privés; ⟨Pol⟩ **recourir à** l'ONU pour régler le conflit (*have recourse to; appeal to*); SEE ALSO **resort**

recover (*v*): le parti **se remet** peu à peu de son échec électoral (*recover from*); ⟨Fin⟩ le souscripteur peut à tout moment **récupérer** son épargne (*recover, get back*); ⟨Fin/Comm⟩ il est d'ores et déjà **rentré dans ses frais** (*m*) (*recover one's expenses*); SEE ALSO **regain**

recovery (*n*): le **relèvement** économique français des années 40; ⟨Econ⟩ l'économie est sur la voie du **redressement**; auteur du **renouveau** économique; la firme achève enfin son **rétablissement**; ⟨Fin⟩ Bourse de Paris: **reprise** (*f*) modérée

recovery plan (*n*): ⟨Econ⟩ le **plan de redressement** (*m*) impliquera 15.000 licenciements

recruit (*v*): ⟨Econ⟩ les chefs d'entreprise, moins que jamais enclins à **recruter** (*recruit, take on labour*)

recruitment (*n*): ⟨Econ⟩ encourager les petites entreprises à reprendre l'**embauchage** (*m*); une véritable crise de **recrutement** (*m*) des infirmières (*recruitment, recruiting*); son projet prévoit l'**embauche** (*f*) de 55 salariés (*recruitment, taking on, hiring*)

recycle (*v*): l'importance de **recycler** le verre; **récupérer** tout ce qui peut l'être, lutter contre le gaspillage

recycling (*n*): le **recyclage** des emballages sera obligatoire en Allemagne; ⟨Fin⟩ le **recyclage** de l'argent de la drogue

redeem (*v*): ⟨Fin⟩ le prêt hypothécaire une fois **remboursé**; il était loin de pouvoir **amortir** ses anciennes dettes (*redeem, repay, pay off*)

redemption (*n*): ⟨Fin⟩ l'**amortissement** (*m*) de la dette exigera de longues années (*redemption, repayment*)

redeploy (*v*): ⟨Ind⟩ une partie des effectifs sera **reclassée** (*redeploy, place in new employment*)

redeployment (*n*): un **reclassement** des partants dans des entreprises locales; les suppressions d'emplois se feront par départs en pré-retraite et **reconversions** (*f*) (*redeployment into new job/industry*)

redevelop (*v*): ces quartiers seront totalement **rénovés** (*redevelop, renovate*)

redevelopment (*n*): la **rénovation** des quartiers populaires de la ville (*redevelopment*); l'instauration d'une **zone de reconversion** (*f*); le projet a aussi reçu des soutiens accordés aux **pôles** (*m*) **de conversion** (*redevelopment zone/area*)

redrawing (*n*): ⟨Pol⟩ l'épineuse question du **redécoupage des frontières** (*redrawing frontiers*); un véritable **charcutage** de la carte électorale; un nouveau **découpage électoral** s'impose (*redrawing of electoral boundaries*)

redress (*n*): ⟨Jur⟩ porter plainte et obtenir **réparation** (*f*)

redress (*v*): **réparant le tort** qui leur avait été fait (*redress a grievance/wrong*)

reduce (*v*): les effectifs administratifs ont été **allégés**; ceci permettra de **faire baisser** le chômage; le montant des frais se trouve **minoré** d'autant (*reduce*); le Japon a su **résorber** les excédents (*bring down, reduce gradually*); peu à peu le chômage **se résorbe**; l'écart avec l'Allemagne **s'est ramené** à 0,4% en rythme annuel (*be reduced/brought down*); SEE ALSO **bring down**

reduced (*adj*): SNCF: trafic très **réduit** en région parisienne (*reduced*); ⟨Fisc/Fin⟩ soit au taux plein soit **au taux minoré** (*at the reduced rate*)

reduction (*n*): au prix d'une **diminution** des effectifs (*reduction, cutting*); l'**infléchissement** (*m*) du taux d'inflation (*reduction, bringing down*);

⟨Ind/Educ⟩ la réforme proposée entraînera un **allégement des horaires** (*reduction of working hours; timetable reduction*); ⟨Jur⟩ consentir des **remises** (*f*) **de peine** (*reduction of sentence; remission; pardon*)

redundancy (*n*): ⟨Ind⟩ 1.290 nouvelles **suppressions** (*f*) **d'emplois**; il n'y aura pas de **licenciements** (*m*) sans plan social (*redundancy, job loss*); les suppressions d'emplois comprendront 400 **licenciements secs** (*outright redundancy*); le bilan définitif des **départs** (*m*) **volontaires** (*voluntary redundancy*); licencié sans préavis ni **prime** (*f*) **de licenciement** (*redundancy/severance pay*); SEE ALSO **lay-off, laying off, severance**

redundancy plan (*n*): le **plan social** se traduit par 500 suppressions d'emplois

redundant (*adj*): ⟨Econ/Ind⟩ la firme vient de **licencier** 45 personnes (*make redundant*); aux **licenciés** (*m*) **économiques** sera versée une allocation spéciale pendant un an (*worker made redundant*); SEE ALSO **sack**

re-education (*n*): ⟨Soc⟩ hébergement, **réadaptation** (*f*) et réinsertion sociale (*re-education, rehabilitation [esp. of delinquent]*)

re-elect (*v*): ⟨Pol⟩ le comité central **reconduit** sa direction; il devrait **être reconduit** à son poste de président (*be re-elected*); SEE ALSO **reappoint**

re-election (*n*): ⟨Pol⟩ la **reconduction** de l'équipe sortante (*re-election, renewal*); le président sortant **candidat** (*m*) **à sa propre succession** (*standing for re-election*); SEE ALSO **reappointment**

re-emerge (*v*): la crainte de voir **resurgir** un empire tsariste russe (*re-emerge, reappear*)

re-emergence (*n*): on craignait la **résurgence** des nationalismes (*re-emergence, reappearance*)

re-employment (*n*): ⟨Econ⟩ les difficultés de la **réinsertion** des chômeurs de longue durée (*re-employment; finding a new job*)

re-examine (*v*): les industriels sont en train de **remettre à plat** toutes les alliances (*re-examine*); il somme Bruxelles de **remettre à plat** ce dossier épineux (*re-examine; send back to the drawing-board*)

refer (*v*): ⟨Pol⟩ la France va **saisir** le Conseil de sécurité (*refer a matter to a court/jurisdiction*); l'opposition **défère** la nouvelle loi au Conseil constitutionnel (*refer, submit*); ⟨Jur⟩ le dossier a été **renvoyé** devant la cour d'Angers (*refer, send*); avec ses complices, il fut **déféré au parquet** (*refer/send to court*)

referendum (*n*): ⟨Pol⟩ soumettre une question à un **référendum** (*referendum*); pendant le déroulement de la **campagne référendaire** (*referendum campaign*)

referral (*n*): ⟨Jur⟩ le **renvoi** devant une cour d'assises des six membres de la bande

reflate (*v*): ⟨Econ⟩ l'ONU demande aux pays riches de **relancer leurs économies** (*f*); **relancer** par l'augmentation de la masse monétaire (*reflate, reflate the economy*)

reflation (*n*): ⟨Econ⟩ la **relance de l'économie** se fait toujours attendre

reflationary (*adj*): ⟨Econ⟩ les **mesures** (*f*) **de relance** n'ont pas eu l'effet escompté (*reflationary measures*)

refloat (*v*): ⟨Fin/Econ⟩ l'État refuse de **renflouer** constamment les 'canards boiteux' (*refloat; rescue; bail out*)

refloating (*n*): ⟨Fin⟩ le **renflouement** de la Sécurité sociale ne sera pas chose aisée; des efforts méritoires de **remise** (*f*) **à flot** de l'économie; SEE ALSO **bailing out**

reform (*n*): un indispensable **assainissement** des finances publiques; une **réforme** de la procédure; une **rénovation** des institutions s'avérait urgente

reform (*v*): des décisions visant à **assainir** la trésorerie du régime local de la Sécurité sociale

reforming (*adj*): ⟨Pol⟩ fier de l'œuvre **réformatrice** de la Gauche

reformist (*adj*): ⟨Pol⟩ l'émergence d'un courant **réformateur** au sein de la communauté blanche

refresher course (*n*): ⟨Educ/Ind⟩ des formations de **remise** (*f*) **à niveau des connaissances** (*f*) sont nécessaires périodiquement (*refresher course*); la nécessité de **remettre ses compétences** (*f*) **à niveau** (*undergo a refresher course*)

refuge (*n*): cette **terre** (*f*) **d'accueil** des opprimés (*refuge; country of refuge*)

refugee (*n*): une importante colonie de **réfugiés** (*m*); bénéficier du statut de **réfugié** (*m*) **politique** (*political refugee*)

refusal (*n*): se heurter à un **refus** net et catégorique

refuse (*n*): les 20 millions de tonnes de **rebuts** (*m*) (*refuse*); fermeture prochaine de la **décharge municipale** (*council refuse dump*); dès la mise en place d'une **déchetterie** centrale (*refuse recycling plant*); le service traditionnel de **collecte** (*f*) ne prend pas en charge les objets encombrants (*refuse/rubbish collection*)

refuse (*v*): le président a **opposé son refus** à la réalisation de cet accord (*refuse; veto*); le ministre **exclut de** se démettre (*refuse; rule out*); le porte-parole **s'est refusé à tout commentaire**; le maire **s'interdit de commenter** les malheurs de son collègue (*refuse/decline to comment [on]*); ⟨Jur⟩ les quelque 100.000 demandeurs d'asile **déboutés** (*refuse; turn away*); les jeunes immigrés **boudent** les activités communautaires (*refuse to have anything to do with; stay away from*); **opposer une fin de non-recevoir** à tout projet d'augmentation des impôts (*refuse categorically*); SEE ALSO **reject**

179

regional

regional (*adj*): ⟨Pol/Econ⟩ Bruxelles multiplie les programmes d'**aide** (*f*) **aux régions** (*regional aid*); une politique d'**aménagement** (*m*) **du territoire** (*regional development*); des **primes** (*f*) **de développement régional**, allouées aux régions en difficulté (*regional development grant*); Nancy et Metz, réunies en une seule **métropole d'équilibre** (*regional growth centre*)

register (*n*): la **liste** des membres de l'association (*register*); inscrire un nom au **registre électoral** (*electoral register*)

register (*v*): Aérospatiale **enregistre** un effondrement de ses bénéfices en 1990 (*register, record*); les 700.000 entreprises **immatriculées** au Registre du commerce (*officially registered*); 14% des Français déclarent **être inscrits** dans une bibliothèque (*register, enrol*); SEE ALSO **record**

registered (*adj*): une **lettre recommandée** avec accusé de réception (*registered letter*)

registrar (*n*): ⟨Admin⟩ devant un **officier de l'état** (*m*) **civil** (*registrar of births and deaths*); ⟨Jur⟩ le **greffier** s'occupe de la délivrance des jugements et de la conservation des minutes (*registrar; Clerk to the Court*)

registration (*n*): les **droits** (*m*) **d'enregistrement** (*registration fees*); ⟨Educ⟩ les **inscriptions** (*f*) s'ouvrent le 30 septembre (*course registration*); un **droit d'inscription** de 390F (*registration/enrolment fee*); les **immatriculations** (*f*) devraient peu diminuer cette année (*registration [esp. of deed/ vehicle]*)

registry (*n*): ⟨Admin⟩ au **greffe** du tribunal de commerce; ⟨Jur⟩ déposer un dossier au **greffe** (*registry [esp. of court minutes/proceedings]; Clerk's Court*)

regrading (*n*): ⟨Admin⟩ les fonctionnaires exigent des **reclassements** (*m*) et un meilleur déroulement de carrière; la **reclassification** des agents en fonction de leur véritable métier; ils demandent une **revalorisation** de leur statut (*regrading, reclassifying*)

regulate (*v*): pour **réglementer** la présence des piquets de grève lors des conflits sociaux; la prostitution n'est ni interdite ni **réglementée** en France (*regulate, control*)

regulation (*n*): le **règlement** impose le port du casque en agglomération (*regulation, rule*); les **règles** (*f*) **de sécurité** sont draconiennes (*safety regulations*); la **réglementation** en la matière est très stricte (*regulations, rules; the law*)

rehabilitate (*v*): ⟨Soc⟩ une association qui aide à **réinsérer** les drogués (*rehabilitate*); les jeunes étrangers **se réinsèrent** plus difficilement (*be rehabilitated into society*)

rehabilitation (*n*): la **remise à niveau** des installations existantes (*rehabilitation, restoration*); ⟨Soc⟩ après sa sortie de prison, le problème de son **reclassement**; la **réinsertion** des anciens détenus dans la société (*rehabilitation [esp. of ex-prisoner into society]*)

rehouse (*v*): ⟨Soc⟩ un plan d'action pour **reloger** les personnes défavorisées

180

rehousing (*n*): ⟨Soc⟩ le **relogement** des squatters; ces familles attendent des garanties sur leur **relogement** définitif

reimburse (*v*): dans l'impossibilité de **rembourser** ses créditeurs (*reimburse, pay back*); **être défrayé** des dépenses engagées (*be reimbursed*); il sera **remboursé de ses frais** (*mpl*) (*have one's expenses/costs reimbursed*); SEE ALSO **repay**

reimbursement (*n*): assurer aux plus défavorisés une **prise en charge** de leur santé à 100% (*reimbursement of costs*); SEE ALSO **repayment**

reinstate (*v*): deux ministres déchus **réintégrés** dans le cabinet (*reinstate*); l'enseignant révisionniste **rétabli dans ses fonctions** (*fpl*) (*reinstated*)

reinstatement (*n*): la **réintégration** du personnel abusivement renvoyé

reinvest (*v*): ⟨Econ⟩ l'impôt est réduit lorsque les bénéfices sont **réinvestis** (*reinvest, plough back*)

reject (*n*): ⟨Soc⟩ les SDF et autres **laissés-pour-compte** (*m*) de notre société (*[social] reject, victim*); SEE ALSO **victim**

reject (*v*): les cheminots ont **rejeté** hier les propositions de la direction (*reject*); ⟨Pol⟩ deux ministres **ont été récusés** par le Sénat (*be rejected/refused*); ⟨Jur⟩ le recours des onze autres **a été repoussé** (*be rejected/dismissed/turned down*); SEE ALSO **refuse**

rejected (*adj*): les quelque 100.000 demandeurs d'emploi **déboutés** (*rejected, refused*)

rejection (*n*): le **rejet** par Washington du plan de paix soviétique; un **désaveu** pour le président (*rejection*); un cinglant **démenti** à l'adresse du gouvernement (*rejection, repudiation*)

rejoin (*v*): pas question pour la France de **réintégrer** l'OTAN militaire (*rejoin, re-enter*)

rejoining (*n*): la **réintégration** de la France dans l'OTAN est tout à fait exclue

relation (*n*): ⟨Pol⟩ rétablir des **relations** (*f*) **diplomatiques** (*diplomatic relations*); une normalisation, après des années de **brouille** (*f*) (*bad relations, being on bad terms*); SEE ALSO **relative**

relationship (*n*): les **relations** (*f*) **privilégiées** entre le Liban et la Syrie (*special relationship*)

relative (*n*): transmettre à un **proche** [parent] un capital qui ne sera pas soumis aux droits de succession (*relative, relation*)

relax (*v*): ⟨Econ/Fin⟩ **assouplir** l'embargo pétrolier; le Japon a pu **détendre** sa politique monétaire; SEE ALSO **slacken**

relaxation (*n*): l'**assouplissement** (*m*) des conditions de détention; SEE ALSO **relaxing**

relaxing (*n*): la **relaxation** des politiques fiscale et salariale; SEE ALSO **easing, slackening**

release (*n*): ⟨Fin/Econ⟩ le **déblocage des crédits** (*m*) destinés à des équipements de santé (*release/releasing of funds*); ⟨Jur⟩ l'**élargissement**

(*m*) puis l'expulsion des trois hommes; la **libération** des prisonniers politiques; la **mise** (*f*) **en liberté** d'un trafiquant d'armes (*release, freeing*); SEE ALSO **acquittal, discharge**

release (*v*): ⟨Econ⟩ l'État refuse de **débloquer des crédits** (*m*) pour la réfection des locaux (*release funds*); ⟨Jur⟩ interpellé, interrogé, puis **relâché** (*release*); il fut **mis en liberté sous caution** (*f*) (*release on bail, bail*); SEE ALSO **bail, parole**

relevant (*adj*): la demande sera examinée par la commission **adéquate**; en s'adressant aux autorités syriennes **compétentes** (*relevant, appropriate*)

reliability (*n*): s'interroger sur la **fiabilité** des statistiques

reliable (*adj*): un outil statistique **fiable**; les informations étaient apparemment **dignes de foi** (*f*) (*reliable, trustworthy*); en l'absence de **données** (*fpl*) **fiables**, on ne peut se prononcer (*reliable data*); les nouvelles techniques ont **fiabilisé** les transfusions (*make [more] reliable*)

relief (*n*): l'**allégement** (*m*) de la pauvreté en est une condition essentielle (*relief, reduction*); la mise en place d'un **programme de secours** (*m*) **d'urgence** (*urgent relief programme*); SEE ALSO **tax relief**

relieve (*v*): un moyen d'**alléger** le chômage (*relieve, ease*)

relocate (*v*): ⟨Comm⟩ les industriels qui **délocalisent** leur production hors France; on parlait déjà de **déménager** les Halles à Rungis; SEE ALSO **transfer**

relocation (*n*): le **déménagement** du siège social (*relocation*); ⟨Comm⟩ la **délocalisation** de la production vers l'Espagne (*relocation; transfer*)

reluctance (*n*): le ministre s'est heurté aux **réticences** (*f*) des députés socialistes; la **frilosité** des employeurs à l'embauche (*reluctance, resistance*)

reluctant (*adj*): ils sont **réticents à** s'engager plus avant (*reluctant*); certains pays **rechignent à** apporter leur contribution à un projet si coûteux; le gouvernement **renâcle à** subventionner les puits de mines (*be reluctant to; hesitate to*)

remainder (*n*): ⟨Comm/Fin⟩ le **solde** doit être réglé un an plus tard (*remainder, balance*); SEE ALSO **balance**

remand (*n*): ⟨Jur⟩ après deux mois de **détention** (*f*) **provisoire**; la **préventive**, ou la détention avant le jugement d'un inculpé (*remand in custody pending trial*)

remand (*v*): ⟨Jur⟩ il fut **laissé en liberté provisoire sous caution** (*f*) (*remand/ free on bail*); la décision de **mettre en détention** (*f*) **préventive** (*remand in custody pending trial*)

remedy (*n*): la fiscalité indirecte est le seul **remède** (*remedy*); comment **remédier au** surpeuplement dans les prisons? (*find a remedy/cure for*)

remedy (*v*): pour **remédier à** cette situation; il faut **remédier au** déficit de la Sécurité sociale (*remedy, put right; find a solution for*)

reminder (*n*): ⟨Comm⟩ un **rappel** adressé à un débiteur défaillant; l'envoi d'une **lettre de rappel** (*[letter of] reminder*)

remission (*n*): ⟨Econ/Fin⟩ la Pologne vient d'obtenir une **remise** de 50% de sa dette (*remission, reduction*); ⟨Jur⟩ plusieurs **remises de peine** (*f*) ont été prononcées; une **réduction de peine** pour ceux qui se livrent aux autorités (*remission/reduction of sentence*)

remit (*n*): ⟨Admin⟩ ils ont estimé que leur collègue **sortait de ses attributions** (*f*) (*exceed one's remit*)

remit (*v*): ⟨Fin/Comm⟩ veuillez nous **couvrir du** montant de la somme due (*remit*); **virer** la somme restant due (*remit; pay*); ⟨Jur⟩ **bénéficier d'une remise de peine** (*f*) (*have part of a sentence remitted*); SEE ALSO **remission**

remittance (*n*): ⟨Fin/Comm⟩ dès réception de votre **règlement** (*m*); une **somme** envoyée en règlement d'une facture; SEE ALSO **payment**

removal (*n*): valse des Préfets: quinze **révocations** (*f*) (*removal from office; sacking*); les **indemnités** (*f*) **de déplacement**, lors d'une mutation (*removal expenses*)

remove (*v*): ⟨Admin⟩ douze hauts fonctionnaires **révoqués** pour abus de pouvoir (*remove from office; sack*); **être écarté de** la direction du parti (*be removed/sacked [from]*); ⟨Pol⟩ les rebelles disent avoir **destitué** leur chef (*remove from power*)

remuneration (*n*): **en rémunération** (*f*) de ses services (*in remuneration/ payment*); SEE ALSO **pay, payment**

remunerative (*adj*): on a privilégié les cultures les plus **rémunératrices**; SEE ALSO **profitable**

renegade (*n*): le **transfuge** du parti socialiste, qu'il avait quitté en 1989

renew (*v*): Madagascar: l'état d'urgence a été **reconduit** pour deux semaines; le bailleur ne peut à l'issue du bail refuser de le **renouveler** (*renew, extend for a further period*); cet accord a été **actualisé** au mois de juin 1987 (*renew; update*)

renewable (*adj*): une grève **reconductible** de 24 heures a été déclenchée par la CGT (*renewable; extendable*)

renewal (*n*): une **reconduction** exacte des déductions appliquées en 1991; le **renouvellement** partiel du comité central (*renewal, renewing*); l'Ulster connaît un brusque **regain** de tension (*renewal, revival*); l'existence d'un droit pour le locataire à **renouvellement de son bail** (*renewal of lease*); SEE ALSO **extension**

renewed (*adj*): l'échec des pourparlers fait craindre une **relance** du terrorisme (*renewed outbreak*); un **regain de tension** (*f*) entre le Pérou et l'Équateur à propos d'un conflit frontalier (*renewed tension*); SEE ALSO **outbreak, upsurge**

renounce (*v*): ils ont **renoncé** à la lutte armée (*renounce, give up*)

renovate (*v*): **rénover** un local désaffecté; démolir certains logements, **remettre en état** (*m*) d'autres; SEE ALSO **redevelop**

renovation (*n*): une opération de **réhabilitation** (*f*) de logements sociaux; la **remise en état** (*m*) de 300 logements vacants; la nécessité d'une **rénovation** et d'une moralisation de la vie politique (*renovation, renewal*); SEE ALSO **rehabilitation**

rent (*n*): les **loyers** (*m*) montent moins vite à Paris (*rent*); l'**encadrement** (*m*) **des loyers** instauré à l'automne 1989; la **réglementation des loyers** instituée par la loi de 1988 (*rent control*); vers une **libération totale des loyers** (*abolition of rent controls*)

rent (*v*): acheter ou **louer** un appartement (*rent [esp. a property]*); habiter dans une maison ou la **donner en location** (*f*) (*rent, rent out*); SEE ALSO **rented**

rental (*n*): faire réduire le **montant du loyer**; il reçoit des **revenus** (*m*) **immobiliers** de source étrangère (*rental, rent*); le **revenu locatif** des immeubles (*rental, housing rent*); un bel appartement, **valeur** (*f*) **locative** 8.500F par mois (*rental value*)

rented (*adj*): l'aide au **logement locatif** en zone rurale (*rented accommodation*); choisir entre **être locataire** (*m*) et accéder à la propriété de sa résidence principale (*live in rented accommodation, rent a property*)

renting (*n*): la **location** du terrain et des locaux (*renting*); des problèmes **locatifs** ou de copropriété (*renting; pertaining to rented accommodation*); acheter de l'immobilier **à des fins** (*f*) **locatives** (*for renting*); le montant du loyer et les **charges** (*f*) **locatives** (*renting charges*); SEE ALSO **tenancy**

renunciation (*n*): cette **renonciation** à la violence a débloqué la situation

reoffend (*v*): ⟨Jur⟩ **récidiver** à la première occasion; beaucoup de prisonniers, une fois libérés, **récidivent** (*reoffend, commit a further offence*)

reorganization (*n*): ⟨Econ⟩ en raison de la **restructuration** de l'entreprise

reorganize (*v*): ⟨Econ⟩ la société va **restructurer** ses activités pharmaceutiques

reorientate (*v*): le ministre va-t-il **infléchir** son action dans ce sens?; SEE ALSO **modify**

reorientation (*n*): tout **infléchissement** (*m*) de notre politique africaine semble d'ores et déjà exclu; SEE ALSO **modification**

repatriate (*v*): le gouvernement compte **rapatrier** ce trop-plein d'immigrés (*repatriate*); l'arrivée d'un million de **rapatriés** (*m*) d'Afrique du nord (*repatriated person/settler*); (*Fin*) les bénéfices peuvent **être rapatriés** en France (*be repatriated*)

repatriation (*n*): le **rapatriement** forcé de 59 réfugiés

repay (*v*): cette année, ils ont **restitué** 140 milliards de dollars; SEE ALSO **reimburse**

repayment (*n*): le **remboursement** de dettes contractées au moment du rachat (*repayment*); les **traites** (*f*) mensuelles pour acquérir son logement

repeal

([*loan*] *repayment*); une économie de 62.000F sur les **annuités** (*f*) des prêts (*annual repayment*); SEE ALSO **reimbursement**

repeal (*n*): ⟨Pol/Jur⟩ le Parlement vota l'**abrogation** (*f*) de l'amendement; l'**abrogation** des dispositions de la loi de 1952 (*repeal, abrogation*)

repeal (*v*): ⟨Pol/Jur⟩ **abroger** la loi électorale adoptée pour les législatives de juin; **abroger** l'âge légal de la retraite (*repeal, rescind [esp. a law]*); SEE ALSO **annul**

repeat (*n*): nul ne souhaite une **réédition** de l'affaire Greenpeace (*repeat, repetition*)

repeat (*v*): **rééditer** sa performance de 1990 (*repeat*); empêcher le maire de **réitérer** son exploit de 1992; il a **redit** son hostilité au projet (*repeat, reiterate*)

repeated (*adj*): des grèves **à répétition** (*f*) dans les transports aériens; le pays, secoué par des crises **répétées**

repercussion (*n*): les **contrecoups** (*m*) de la grève se font sentir durement; avoir de lourdes **incidences** (*f*) sur la rentabilité de l'opération; avoir des **répercussions** (*f*) sur le coût du travail; les **retombées** (*f*) sociales de cette politique (*repercussion*); la crise pourrait **se répercuter** sur l'emploi (*have repercussions upon; affect*)

repetition (*n*): SEE **repeat**

report (*n*): le **rapport** établira sans doute la vérité (*report*); le **constat** est sévère (*report, conclusion*); ⟨Admin⟩ le **procès-verbal** de la séance (*report, minutes*)

report (*v*): les médias ont **rendu compte** (*m*) de l'affaire (*report; give an account of*); l'ONU **fait état** (*m*) d'activités militaires dans le sud du pays; ses propos ont été **rapportés** par plusieurs journaux; quelques cas de rage sont parfois **signalés** en Espagne (*report*); l'agent **verbalisait** pour stationnement non-autorisé; il leur a **dressé un procès-verbal** (*report, 'book' for an offence*)

represent (*v*): **se faire l'interprète** (*m*) de l'ensemble des travailleurs (*represent, speak on behalf of*)

representation (*n*): ⟨Pol⟩ le Parlement, en France, assure la **représentation** du peuple

representative (*n*): ⟨Pol⟩ un **responsable** américain a démenti ces affirmations (*representative*); envoyer un **fondé de pouvoirs** pour traiter avec la délégation soviétique (*[authorized] representative*); ⟨Admin⟩ confier ses intérêts à un **mandataire** (*representative, proxy*); **délégué** (*m*) **élu** des parents d'élèves de l'école (*elected representative*); le **délégué syndical** CFDT (*trade-union representative*); SEE ALSO **elected**

repress (*v*): **réprimer** une sédition (*repress, quell*); SEE ALSO **crack down, put down, suppress**

repression (*n*): un tournant dans la **répression** de la Mafia; les dépenses pour la **répression** de la criminalité; SEE ALSO **suppression, crackdown**

185

repressive (*adj*): les régimes **répressifs** (*repressive*); avoir recours à des **mesures** (*f*) **de répression** (*repressive measures*)

reprieve (*v*): ⟨Jur⟩ condamnée à mort, elle fut **graciée** en 1978 (*reprieve*); **surseoir à l'exécution** (*f*) du condamné à mort (*reprieve; grant a stay of execution*)

reprieve (*n*): ⟨Jur⟩ bénéficier d'une **grâce** présidentielle; un **sursis à exécution** (*f*) pour les deux cliniques privées

reprisal (*n*): une décision prise **en représailles** (*fpl*) (*as a/in reprisal*)

reputation (*n*): leur **notoriété** dépasse largement le cadre de leur village (*reputation, fame*); conscients que leur **crédit** (*m*) était en jeu (*reputation, credit*)

request (*n*): le gouvernement a rejeté la **demande** des autorités yougoslaves (*request, demand*); de nombreuses **demandes** de visas ont été déposées (*request, application*)

request (*v*): l'entreprise devait **solliciter** l'aide de l'État (*request, ask for, seek*)

resale (*n*): ⟨Comm⟩ acheter un article **pour la revente** (*for resale*)

reschedule (*v*): ⟨Fin/Comm⟩ Belgrade pourra **rééchelonner** sa dette extérieure

rescheduling (*n*): ⟨Fin/Comm⟩ la Pologne obtient un **rééchelonnement** de sa dette

rescind (*v*): ⟨Ins⟩ **résilier** un contrat d'assurance; ⟨Jur⟩ **annuler** un verdict; ⟨Pol⟩ **révoquer** un arrêt (*rescind, annul*)

rescinding (*n*): le Parlement vota l'**abrogation** (*f*) de l'amendement; SEE ALSO **repeal**

rescue (*n*): Albanie: l'Italie **vient à la rescousse** (*come to the rescue*); ⟨Fin/ Econ⟩ les créanciers ont approuvé le **plan de sauvetage** (*m*) (*rescue plan*)

rescuer (*n*): ⟨Fin⟩ un dépôt de bilan permet au **repreneur** de partir sur des bases financières plus saines (*company rescuer; acquirer of an ailing business*)

resell (*v*): ⟨Comm⟩ acheter et puis **revendre** plus cher

reservation (*n*): les **réticences** (*f*) des Américains (*reservations*); Téhéran **fait des réserves** (*f*) sur l'accord, Bagdad le rejette (*have reservations*)

reserve (*n/adj*): ⟨Econ⟩ les **réserves** (*f*) mondiales du bauxite s'amenuisent (*reserves*); ⟨Fin⟩ les États-Unis, avec une **monnaie mondiale de réserve** (*reserve currency*)

reserved (*adj*): son accueil fut **mitigé** dans les territoires occupés (*reserved, lukewarm*)

reservist (*n*): ⟨Mil⟩ une unité de **supplétifs** (*m*) de l'armée; les harkis, anciens **supplétifs** de l'armée française en Algérie

reshuffle (*n*): ⟨Pol⟩ un **remaniement ministériel** hier à Tunis (*cabinet reshuffle*)

reshuffle (*v*): Phnom Penh **remanie** profondément son gouvernement (*reshuffle, reshape*)

residence (*n*): la **résidence** officielle du Président (*official residence*); **élire domicile** (*m*) à Paris (*take up residence*); **se faire domicilier** à Londres (*give as one's residence/address*); les conditions d'entrée et de **séjour** (*m*) des étrangers en France; SEE ALSO **resident**

residence permit (*n*): ⟨Admin⟩ les titulaires d'un **permis de séjour** (*m*); une **autorisation de séjour** de trois mois; 1916, année de la création de la **carte de séjour**

resident (*n*): entrée interdite sauf aux **riverains** (*m*); indemniser les **riverains** les plus exposés (*[local] resident; people living close by*); un ressortissant turc, **domicilié** à Paris (*legally resident*); SEE ALSO **residence**

residential (*adj*): ⟨Soc⟩ des **maisons** (*f*) **d'accueil** pour personnes âgées (*residential home*)

resign (*v*): **se dessaisir** de ses fonctions de maire; le maire a **démissionné de son mandat**; il était prêt à **quitter ses fonctions** (*f*); **se démettre** de son mandat de député (*resign one's post/office*)

resignation (*n*): les étudiants exigent la **démission** du ministre de l'Intérieur serbe

resite (*v*): SEE **relocate**

resolve (*v*): un plan d'action visant à **résoudre** la crise; la guerre ne va rien **résoudre** (*resolve, solve, settle*)

resort (*n*): pas de **recours** (*m*) à la force (*resort, resorting, recourse*); SEE ALSO **recourse**

resort (*v*): **en venir à** la guerre; en désespoir de cause, **recourir à** la violence (*resort/have recourse to*)

resource (*n*): utilisant tous les **ressorts** (*m*) de la procédure; ceux qui n'ont pas de **ressource** (*f*) (*resources, means*); SEE ALSO **means**

respect (*n*): des relations de **respect** (*m*) mutuel et de bon voisinage

respect (*v*): **respecter** les accords conclus l'an dernier (*respect, observe*); SEE ALSO **observe**

respond (*v*): l'Amérique est prête à **répondre** à toute provocation (*respond, reply; retaliate*)

response (*n*): ⟨Mil⟩ la stratégie de la **riposte graduée** (*graduated response*)

responsibility (*n*): on lui a confié la **charge** de l'enquête (*responsibility*); un transfert de **responsabilités** (*f*) et de charges (*responsibility, duty*); ⟨Jur⟩ la loi reconnaît aux communes les **compétences** (*f*) suivantes (*area of responsibility, competence*); la décision **revient à** eux seuls; le maintien de l'ordre **incombe au** préfet de police (*be the responsibility of; fall to* *s.o.*); **endosser la responsabilité** des dommages causés (*take responsibility*); SEE ALSO **claim**

responsible (*adj*): ⟨Admin/Pol⟩ le Préfet **assure** la direction des services extérieurs de l'État (*be responsible for; carry out*); le ministre **chargé** de la Santé (*responsible for*); les variations de prix ne sont pas seules **en cause** (*f*) (*responsible; to blame*); **auteur** (*m*) de plusieurs assassinats de policiers (*[person] responsible for; perpetrator*)

restart (*n*): **reprise** (*f*) prochaine des exportations irakiennes; **reprise** des discussions sur l'union

restart (*v*): la guerre civile **reprend** (*restart, begin again*); les deux fabricants de pneumatiques **renouent le dialogue** (*restart talks*)

restoration (*n*): le **rétablissement** de leurs relations diplomatiques; ils réclament la **restitution** de leur statut professionnel

restore (*v*): reconstruire le pays et **restaurer** son économie (*restore [to health]*); ⟨Pol⟩ **rétablir la paix** dans la région (*restore peace*); la France **rétablit des relations** (*f*) **diplomatiques** avec les républiques baltes (*restore diplomatic relations*); SEE ALSO **bring back**

restraint (*n*): faire preuve de **retenue** (*f*) face aux provocations terroristes; l'armée a fait preuve d'une **retenue** inaccoutumée

restrict (*v*): c'est le budget global qui **restreint** les dépenses hospitalières (*restrict, curb*); SEE ALSO **keep down**, **limit**

restricted (*adj*): l'influence de la France y est assez **restreinte** (*restricted, limited*); SEE ALSO **limited**

restriction (*n*): les **blocages** (*m*) législatifs et réglementaires (*restriction*); ⟨Econ/Fin⟩ à l'époque, le crédit était **encadré** (*subject to restrictions*); SEE ALSO **ease**

restrictive (*adj*): les lois **contraignantes** sur l'exercice du droit syndical (*restrictive*); ⟨Comm⟩ des **ententes** (*f*) qui faussent la concurrence (*restrictive practice*)

restructure (*v*): ⟨Econ⟩ la société **se restructure**, bilan: 400 personnes sans emploi (*restructure, reshape*)

restructuring (*n*): un **réaménagement** de la fiscalité des carburants (*restructuring*); ⟨Econ/Ind⟩ dans l'industrie informatique en crise, des **restructurations** (*f*) se multiplient (*industrial restructuring*)

result (*n*): l'**issue** (*f*) du scrutin (*result*); faillites en rafales, chômage **à la clé** (*as a result; resulting*)

result (*v*): une négociation qui va peut-être **déboucher sur** des résultats concrets; l'élection **s'est soldée par** le triomphe de la droite (*result in*); cette politique **se traduit par** une augmentation du chômage (*result in; give rise to*)

resume (*v*): le travail va **reprendre** lundi; SEE ALSO **restart**

resumption (*n*): **reprise** (*f*) des négociations syndicats-direction (*resumption*); ⟨Ind⟩ l'usine Renault du Mans a décidé la **reprise du travail** (*resumption of work, return to work*); SEE ALSO **restart**

resurgence (*n*): une **résurgence** du mouvement pro-démocratique de Pékin; 〈Comm〉 le **redémarrage** de l'activité féminine après la guerre

retail (*adj*): 〈Comm〉 les **commerces** (*m*) **de détail** sont moins euphoriques (*retail business*); un réseau de **points** (*m*) **de vente au détail** (*retail outlet*); les **prix** (*m*) **de détail** ont fortement progressé en octobre (*retail prices*); le volume des **ventes** (*f*) **de détail** (*retail sales*); la **valeur marchande au détail** est estimée à 400 millions de dollars (*retail market value*)

retail (*v*): 〈Comm〉 dans le commerce, cet article **se vend** à 100F (*retail, sell*)

retailer (*n*): 〈Comm〉 **revendeur** (*m*) d'articles en cuir; entre marchand en gros et **détaillant** (*m*) le prix a doublé (*retailer, retail dealer*)

retailing (*n*): 〈Comm〉 dans le **commerce de détail** (*m*) l'emploi reste un gros point noir (*retailing, retail business/trade*); les relations établies entre l'industrie et la **grande distribution** (*volume retailing*)

retake (*v*): 〈Mil〉 la troupe a pu **reprendre** la ville sans effusion de sang (*retake, recapture*)

retaliate (*v*): Israël **ripostera** à toute provocation (*retaliate, reply, respond*)

retaliation (*n*): 〈Comm〉 la menace de **rétorsions** (*f*) américaines (*retaliation, retortion*)); la saisie de cargaisons **en rétorsion contre** des impayés sur des livraisons antérieures (*in retaliation for*)

retaliatory (*adj*): en les menaçant de **mesures de rétorsion** (*f*) économique (*retaliatory measures*)

retire (*v*): la société **met à la retraite** 300 personnes (*retire, make redundant*); à 60 ans, on peut **prendre sa retraite**; **partir à la retraite** est l'ambition de beaucoup de gens (*retire, take retirement*)

retirement (*n*): épargner pour préparer mieux sa **retraite**; l'âge de **départ** (*m*) **en retraite** (*retirement*); des militaires **à la retraite** (*in retirement, retired*); prendre sa **retraite anticipée**; le financement des **pré-retraites** (*f*) (*early retirement*); 〈Fin〉 4.000 ex-employés seront privés de leur **pension** (*f*) **de retraite** (*retirement pension*); des **systèmes** (*m*) **de retraite** et de prévoyance (*retirement pension scheme*); les promesses du candidat aux **personnes** (*f*) **du troisième âge** (*person of retirement age; the elderly*)

retiring (*adj*): 〈Pol〉 l'équipe municipale **sortante** se représentera (*retiring, outgoing*)

retract (*v*): 〈Jur〉 finir par **revenir sur ses aveux** (*m*); remis en liberté après **s'être rétracté** (*retract/withdraw a statement*)

retraction (*n*): (*Jur*) son aveu fut suivi d'un **désaveu**; il a fini par signer une **rétractation**

retrain (*v*): 〈Econ〉 **recycler** le personnel mis à pied; **donner une nouvelle formation** au personnel plus âgé (*retrain, train for a new skill*); **se recycler** dans le marketing (*retrain, convert to a new activity*)

retraining (*n*): 〈Econ〉 un **recyclage** constant imposé par le développement technique (*retraining*); en cas de licenciements, les possibilités de

189

reconversion (*f*) sont quasiment nulles (*retraining; redeployment of displaced workers*); le plan social offre à tous 24 mois de **congé-conversion** (*m*) (*period of paid retraining*)

retreat (*n*): une nouvelle **reculade** face aux syndicats; le gouvernement vient d'effectuer une spectaculaire **marche-arrière** (*retreat, climb-down*); les conservateurs sont **en recul** (*m*) (*on the retreat*)

retreat (*v*): ⟨Mil⟩ les troupes **se replient** devant l'avance des alliés

retrial (*n*): ⟨Jur⟩ il y aura un **nouveau procès** (*retrial, fresh trial*)

retry (*v*): ⟨Jur⟩ malgré le verdict d'acquittement, il va être **rejugé**

return (*n*): ⟨Ind⟩ la **rentrée sociale** promet d'être chaude (*return to work*); une **reprise du travail** dans les bassins concernés (*return to work [esp. after strike]*); **renouer avec** le chômage et avec la récession (*see a return to*); ⟨Fin⟩ un **rendement** minimum assuré (*return [esp. on investment]*); **rentabiliser** son investissement (*get a return [esp. on investment]*)

return (*v*): ⟨Fin/Comm⟩ le vendeur doit vous **restituer** le dépôt de garantie (*return, repay*); remplir et **retourner** un questionnaire (*return, send back*); **renouer avec** la prospérité (*return to; re-experience*); ⟨Pol⟩ le gouvernement **sorti des urnes** (*f*) en mars 1986; **être élu** à une majorité écrasante (*be returned/elected*); la gauche pourrait **retourner au pouvoir**; les Travaillistes espèrent **revenir aux affaires** (*fpl*) (*return to power*)

reveal (*v*): le graphique **fait apparaître** les changements intervenus en un an; les chiffres **font ressortir** une baisse du pouvoir d'achat; les résultats **font état** (*m*) d'une croissance globale de 7,5% (*reveal, show*); SEE ALSO **indicate, show, point out**

revenue (*n*): ⟨Econ/Fin⟩ les **recettes** (*f*) pétrolières du Mexique; les dépenses étaient inférieures aux **rentrées** (*f*) (*revenue, income*)

reversal (*n*): un **revirement** de la politique étrangère que rien ne présageait (*reversal, change*); on prédit une lente **inversion de la tendance** de l'économie britannique (*reversal of trend*)

reverse (*n*): SEE **setback**

reverse (*v*): les autorités **ne reviennent pas sur leur décision** (*f*) (*reverse a decision*); ⟨Econ⟩ **inverser une tendance** dans un sens favorable (*reverse a trend*)

review (*n*): devant la presse, il a fait un **tour d'horizon** de la situation

review (*v*): ils ont passé **en revue** (*f*) l'état des négociations en cours (*review, give a review of*); ⟨Pol⟩ son refus de **revoir** la fiscalité; la politique nucléaire a besoin d'être **réexaminée** (*review, re-examine*)

revise (*v*): le gouvernement est obligé de **revoir** son budget (*revise*); l'institut de prévisions **révise à la baisse** ses estimations (*revise downwards*)

revision (*n*): une **révision** des priorités s'impose (*revision*); la **remise à jour** du référendum espagnol de 1976 est maintenant achevée (*revision, bringing up to date*)

190

revival (*n*): il est urgent d'assurer un **renouveau** du syndicalisme (*revival, renewal*); un **regain** d'espoir chez les blancs; la Yougoslavie secouée par le **réveil** des nationalismes (*revival, reawakening*); ⟨Econ⟩ la **relance de l'économie** (*f*) tarde à venir (*economic revival*)

revive (*v*): ⟨Comm⟩ les affaires **reprennent**

revoke (*v*): SEE **rescind, repeal**

revolt (*n*): une **révolte** gronde dans les républiques; la **fronde** des centristes embarrasse le gouvernement; la **jacquerie** des paysans en colère (*revolt, insurrection*)

revolt (*v*): une partie des députés de la majorité **frondent**

revolution (*n*): la **révolution** technologique n'épargne personne

revolving (*adj*): ⟨Pol/Admin⟩ assurer la **présidence tournante** (*revolving presidency/chairmanship*)

rife (*adj*): à un moment où le chômage **sévit** (*be rife/widespread*)

rift (*n*): SEE **split**

right (*n*): la **faculté** d'ouvrir le dimanche (*right, option, freedom*); ⟨Jur⟩ un **droit d'appel** (*m*) des décisions de la Commission (*right of appeal*); disposer d'un **droit de regard** (*m*) sur tout projet d'augmentation des impôts (*right to examine/inspect*); l'Ukraine estime que la flotte lui revient **de plein droit** (*as of right, rightfully*); SEE ALSO **option**

rightness (*n*): nos partenaires comprendront la **justesse** de nos thèses; il est sûr du **bien-fondé** de son action (*rightness; legitimacy*)

ring-road (*n*): une seconde **rocade de contournement** de l'agglomération nancéenne; sur la **périphérique** le trafic était bloqué; SEE ALSO **bypass**

riot (*n*): les **émeutes** (*f*) d'hier ont fait 18 morts (*riot, rioting*)

rioter (*n*): les procès des **émeutiers** (*m*) passionne l'opinion publique; la mairie était la première cible des **manifestants** (*m*)

rise (*n*): une **élévation** du niveau de vie (*rise; raising*); le deuxième **gain** mensuel, après six mois de baisse; une **hausse** du niveau général des prix (*rise, increase*); ⟨Fin⟩ les gains réalisés, grâce à l'**envolée** (*f*) des cours (*sharp rise*); la Bundesbank stoppe la **montée** du dollar (*rise in price/value*); avec la **remontée** du chômage (*renewed rise*); forte **poussée** (*f*) du chômage en février (*rise, upsurge*); SEE ALSO **increase, result**

rise (*v*): le chômage a cessé d'**augmenter** dans l'ex-RDA; les salaires continuent à **progresser** rapidement (*rise*); le chômage **remonte** (*rise again*); les cours du pétrole avaient **monté en flèche** (*rise steeply*); ce chiffre devrait **s'élever à** 70% dans un proche avenir (*rise to, reach*); SEE ALSO **increase**

rising (*adj*): endettement **en hausse** (*f*), bénéfice en baisse (*rising*); ⟨Fin⟩ depuis mars, le marché est **orienté à la hausse** (*rising, on a rising curve*)

risk (*n*): comme tous les placements, il est soumis aux **aléas** (*m*) de la bourse (*risk, hazard*); la RFA **faisait le pari** de l'ancrage à l'Ouest (*take a* *calculated risk; stake all*); ceci avait un temps **hypothéqué** la stratégie d'Israël (*put at risk, jeopardize*); ⟨Soc⟩ des dossiers d'assistance éducative d'**enfants** (*m*) **en danger** (*children at risk*)

risk (*v*): ⟨Jur⟩ les putschistes **encourent** la peine de mort (*risk, be liable to*); SEE ALSO **incur**

risky (*adj*): ⟨Comm⟩ une augmentation de capital est toujours **aléatoire** (*risky, chancy*); la rentabilité de celle-ci devient **aléatoire** (*risky, uncertain*); SEE ALSO **uncertain**

road (*n*): le Département est responsable de la **sécurité routière** (*road safety*); l'entretien du **réseau routier** départemental (*road system*); des plans de **voirie** (*f*) qui ignorent les quartiers traversés (*roads and highways department*)

rota (*n*): ⟨Ind/Econ⟩ cette solution est moins chère qu'un **roulement de personnel** (*rota system; working by rota*); ⟨Ind⟩ le mouvement de **grèves** (*f*) **tournantes** entre dans sa deuxième semaine (*striking by rota*)

round (*n*): ⟨Pol⟩ les deux **tours** (*m*) des élections (*round*); entamer une importante **tournée** diplomatique (*round of visits*); SEE ALSO **tour**

round-table (*adj*): une nouvelle **table ronde** direction-syndicats hier; la **table ronde** chargée d'examiner la question (*round-table discussion; discussion panel*)

row (*n*): la perspective d'une rude **empoignade** entre les deux candidats (*row, set-to*)

rowdy (*adj*): débat **houleux** à l'Assemblée hier (*rowdy, noisy*)

rubbish (*n*): dans de nombreuses villes, les **ordures** (*f*) ne sont plus ramassées (*[household] rubbish*); SEE ALSO **refuse**

ruin (*v*): ⟨Fin⟩ le krach a **ruiné** des milliers d'épargnants

rule (*n*): dans toute entreprise, il y a un **règlement intérieur** (*rules, regulations*); SEE ALSO **regulation**

rule (*v*): ⟨Jur⟩ **statuer** sur un litige; la Cour de cassation **tranchera** fin juin (*rule; give a ruling*); l'arbitrage du GATT **donne raison** (*f*) **à** la France (*rule/find in favour of*)

rule out (*v*): l'ex-premier ministre **exclut** un compromis avec le président; il n'**exclut** pas une modification de la loi (*rule out*); l'hypothèse est définitivement **écartée** par la police (*ruled out*); SEE ALSO **exclude**

ruling (*adj*): une élite fortement intégrée à la **classe dirigeante** (*ruling class*)

ruling (*n*): ⟨Jur⟩ d'après le **jugement** du tribunal, ce contrat est légal (*ruling*); le Conseil d'État va **statuer** en appel (*give a ruling*); SEE ALSO **rule**

rumour (*n*): la **rumeur publique** l'accuse, malgré le démenti de ses amis (*rumour; public opinion*)

rump (*n*): ⟨Pol⟩ un gouvernement **croupion** (*m*) dirigé par le chef des insurgés; une solution consistant à créer un **État-croupion** palestinien

run (*n*): un attentat dont les auteurs **courent** encore (*be 'on the run'*)

run (*v*): ⟨Admin⟩ **diriger** une entreprise; **gérer** une affaire commerciale; ⟨Comm⟩ **exploiter** une petite entreprise de mécanique générale; ⟨Pol⟩ **être candidat** (*m*) à la présidence (*run for office/election*)

run-down (*adj*): la rénovation des quartiers **dégradés**; la capitale, dotée d'un vieux tissu urbain **dégradé**; SEE ALSO **dilapidated**

running (*n*): ⟨Admin⟩ confier la **gestion** à un entrepreneur du privé (*running, management*); ⟨Comm⟩ une autorisation d'**exploitation** (*f*) de salles de jeux (*running, operating*); les **frais** (*m*) **d'utilisation** d'une voiture (*running costs*)

rural (*adj*): dans les cantons **ruraux** (*rural*); la drogue se propage aussi **en zone** (*f*) **rurale** (*in rural areas*); le tourisme **en milieu** (*m*) **rural** (*rural, 'green'*); comment freiner l'**exode** (*m*) **rural**? (*rural depopulation*)

rush (*n*): ⟨Comm⟩ il y a eu une **ruée** sur les actions dès la cotation en bourse

rush (*v*): la France **expédia d'urgence** (*f*) des dragueurs de mines (*rush, dispatch urgently*)

S

sack (*v*): ⟨Pol/Admin⟩ le roi **démit** son ministre de ses fonctions; **limoger** un haut fonctionnaire; **congédier** du personnel; le président peut **révoquer** son Premier ministre (*sack*); le ministre vient d'**être démissionné** par le Président (*be sacked*); les deux hommes **mises à l'écart** (*m*) en 1979 (*sacked, dismissed*); SEE ALSO **dismiss, redundant**

sacking (*n*): ⟨Ind⟩ après son **limogeage** (*m*) de la direction de la société; un droit de regard sur les promotions et les **révocations** (*f*)

safe (*adj*): ⟨Fin⟩ placer son argent dans des valeurs **sûres** (*safe, sound*)

safety (*n*): la **sûreté** nucléaire n'a pas de prix (*safety, security*); une **clause de sauvegarde** (*f*) serait adoptée en cas de récession du marché (*safety clause*); SEE ALSO **security**

salaried (*adj*): ⟨Econ⟩ cadre **salarié** de la société Waterman (*salaried; wage-earning*); le **salarié** est aujourd'hui un privilégié (*salaried person/staff*); d'où un formidable rejet du **salariat** (*salaried status*); SEE ALSO **wage-earner**

salary (*n*): toucher un **salaire** en contrepartie d'un travail fourni; un **traitement** (*m*) indexé sur le coût de la vie; les députés sont imposés sur l'ensemble de leurs **indemnités** (*f*) (*salary, pay*); les revendications **salariales** du personnel (*pertaining to salaries/wages*); la **grille des salaires** de la Banque de France (*salary scale*); les entreprises essayent de réduire les **coûts** (*m*) **salariaux** (*salary/wage costs*); SEE ALSO **wage**

sale (*n*): ⟨Comm⟩ achat et **vente** (*f*) de meubles anciens (*sale, selling*); un **chiffre de ventes** (*f*) qui est encourageant (*sales figures*); ⟨Journ⟩ la **diffusion totale** du mensuel (*total sales*); SEE ALSO **disposal**

salesman (*n*): ⟨Comm⟩ se méfier des **vendeurs** (*m*) peu scrupuleux; la vente à domicile assurée par des **démarcheurs** (*m*) (*door-to-door salesman; canvasser*)

sample (*n*): ⟨Pol⟩ une enquête réalisée auprès d'un **échantillon** de 805 personnes (*sample*); ⟨Comm⟩ remise d'**échantillons gratuits** (*free sample*)

sanction (*n*): ⟨Pol/Econ⟩ la France **prend des sanctions** (*f*) **économiques** contre le régime (*impose economic sanctions*)

sanction (*v*): le vote a **sanctionné** la politique française au Proche-Orient (*sanction; approve*); ⟨Educ⟩ l'obtention d'une qualification **sanctionnée** par un diplôme (*sanction, officially recognize*)

sandwich course (*n*): ⟨Ind/Scol⟩ la **scolarité en alternance** (*f*) entre l'école et l'entreprise; avec la **formation en alternance**, l'entreprise peut contourner le SMIC

satisfaction (*n*): **se féliciter** du large consensus pendant la guerre du Golfe (*express satisfaction/pleasure*)

satisfy (*v*): ces propositions ont peu de chance de **venir à bout** de la grogne des syndicats; le décret du 27 juin vient de leur **donner satisfaction** (*f*) (*satisfy*); 600 emplois sont créés pour **pourvoir aux besoins** (*m*) immédiats (*satisfy needs*)

saver (*n*): ⟨Fin⟩ au détriment des **petits épargnants** (*m*); les **petits déposants** (*m*), affolés par des rumeurs, suite à la faillite de la banque (*small saver, small investor*)

saving (*n*): assurer la **sauvegarde** de 120 emplois (*saving, keeping*); ⟨Econ⟩ l'**économie** (*f*) attendue est de quelque 60.000F (*saving, economy*); la baisse du **taux d'épargne** (*f*) **des ménages** (*domestic saving*); (*npl*) maintenir le niveau d'achat de vos **économies** (*f*) (*savings*); ⟨Fin⟩ virer de l'argent sur un **compte d'épargne** (*savings account*); la popularité des **caisses** (*f*) **d'épargne et de prévoyance** (*f*) (*savings bank*)

scale (*n*): l'**ampleur** (*f*) de ce revers a de quoi inquiéter; nous n'avons aucun organisme d'**envergure** (*f*) nationale (*scale, scope*); organisé **à l'échelle** (*f*) **nationale** (*on a national scale*); peur de l'anarchie **à une échelle gigantesque** (*on a gigantic/huge scale*); SEE ALSO **economy, schedule, magnitude**

scapegoat (*n*): la France ne tient pas à être un **bouc émissaire** (*scapegoat*); le voici soudain **traité en bouc émissaire** (*make a scapegoat of*)

scarce (*adj*): ⟨Fin⟩ les acheteurs solvables **se rarifient** (*become scarcer*); la confiance, une **denrée rare** en ce moment (*scarce commodity*)

scarcity (*n*): l'industrie souffre d'une **pénurie** de main-d'œuvre qualifiée; la **rareté** de tant de produits de première nécessité; SEE ALSO **shortage**

scenario (*n*): trois **scénarios** (*m*) peuvent être envisagés

scene (*n*): le risque d'une balkanisation du **paysage politique** (*political scene*); le **paysage audiovisuel** français (*broadcasting scene; world of broadcasting*); des contacts **en coulisse** (*f*) ont eu lieu (*behind the scenes*)

schedule (*n*): les **grilles** (*f*) **horaires** sont peu modifiées; respecter le **plan de travail** (*work schedule*); l'émission a été supprimée de la **grille des programmes** (*broadcasting schedule*); SEE ALSO **timetable**

scheme (*n*): ⟨Soc⟩ le **régime** général de la Sécurité sociale (*scheme, regime*); ⟨Fin⟩ l'équilibre financier des **régimes de retraite** (*retirement scheme*)

scheming (*n*): les **agissements** (*m*) des fauteurs de trouble; une lutte sur fond de **combinaisons** (*f*) et de petites rivalités (*scheming; intrigue*)

scope (*n*): cela **dépasse la zone de compétence** de l'ONU (*go beyond the scope of*); ceci **est prévu** par le nouveau règlement (*come within the scope of*); **élargir le champ** de leurs activités (*extend the scope*); SEE ALSO **framework**

scuffle (*n*): une **échauffourée** hier au cours d'une manifestation de mineurs (*scuffle, clash, skirmish*)

seal off (*v*): le quartier fut **bouclé** par la police (*seal off; surround*)

search (*n*): la police pratique des **fouilles** (*f*) impromptues (*search [esp. of the person]*); une **perquisition** effectuée à son domicile (*police search*); obtenir un **mandat de perquisition** (*search warrant*); ⟨Mil⟩ une opération de **ratissage** (*m*) de l'armée (*search/combing operation*)

search (*v*): la police **ratisse large** après l'attentat (*search far and wide; comb an area*); **arraisonné** par la police, le bateau est revenu en rade de Brest (*[stop and] search*)

seasonal (*adj*): ⟨Econ⟩ les **emplois** (*m*) **saisonniers** et à temps partiel (*seasonal job/employment*)

seasonally-adjusted (*adj*): ⟨Econ/Fin⟩ des chiffres **corrigés en fonction des variations** (*f*) **saisonnières**

seat (*n*): ⟨Mil⟩ au **siège** du quartier-général des forces armées (*seat, headquarters*); ⟨Pol⟩ conserver son **siège** (*seat [esp. in parliament]*)

secede (*v*): ⟨Pol⟩ le nord du pays **fait sécession** (*f*)

secession (*n*): ⟨Pol⟩ la **sécession** de l'ex-Somaliland britannique (*secession*); une véritable **guerre de sécession** se livre entre les rebelles et les troupes du gouvernement (*war of secession*)

second (*adj*): ⟨Jur⟩ un violeur **récidiviste** (*second-time offender, recidivist*)

second (*v*): ⟨Admin⟩ il a été **détaché** à Athènes après la guerre (*second, send on secondment*)

secondment (*n*): ⟨Admin⟩ le personnel anglais **détaché** à l'étranger (*on secondment, posted*); **chargé** (*m*) **de mission** dans un organisme parapublic (*on secondment, on a mission*))

secret (*adj*): le financement **occulte** des campagnes électorales (*secret, hidden*); ⟨Pol⟩ élire **au bulletin secret** le nouveau comité central (*by secret vote/ballot*)

secretly (*adv*): accusant Moscou de soutenir **en sous-main** l'Arménie

sectarian (*adj*): ⟨Pol/Rel⟩ les élus locaux, empêtrés dans leurs querelles **partisanes**; SEE ALSO **partisan**

sectarianism (*n*): ⟨Pol⟩ sans **sectarisme** (*m*) ni esprit de chapelle

section (*n*): la première **tranche** de l'autoroute (*section*); ⟨Admin⟩ la **direction** des affaires culturelles; le **service** des contentieux d'un grand cabinet parisien (*section, department*); à la **sous-direction** de la politique foncière; le **bureau** de l'urbanisme (*section; divisional office*)

sectional (*adj*): ⟨Pol/Ind⟩ de nombreux mouvements **catégoriels**, des agriculteurs aux chasseurs

sector (*n*): les **secteurs** (*m*) les plus touchés: la Poste, l'enseignement (*sector; branch of activity*)

secular (*adj*): l'éducation **laïque** est sur la défensive (*secular, lay*); la **laïcité** de l'enseignement est toujours son crédo (*secular/lay ethos*)

secularization (*n*): les tenants d'une **laïcisation** totale de l'enseignement

secure (*v*): ⟨Fin⟩ un emprunt **gagé** sur des avoirs à l'étranger; SEE ALSO **guarantee**

security (*n*): la **sécurité** de la détention des grands criminels (*security*); ⟨Pol⟩ une atteinte à la **sûreté intérieure** de l'État (*internal security*); entretenir un état d'esprit **sécuritaire** (*security-conscious; relating to security*); ⟨Pol/Soc⟩ un projet de loi sur la **sécurité** (*[sense of] security*); **sécuriser** les immigrés (*give a feeling of security to*); ⟨Fin⟩ des titres, déposés **en gage** (*m*) auprès des banques (*as security*); investir des économies dans des **valeurs** (*f*) qu'on peut revendre (*securities, stocks and shares*); SEE ALSO **job security**, **stock**, **safety**

seize (*v*): une quantité de résine **saisie** par les douanes (*seize, confiscate*); la maison sera alors vendue ou **saisie** (*seize, repossess*); ⟨Pol⟩ le bloc serbe **s'empare du pouvoir** (*seize power*)

seizure (*n*): la **mainmise** du pouvoir sur la télévision (*seizure, taking control*); ⟨Jur/Admin⟩ une **saisie** de 60 kilos de résine de cannabis lors d'une opération de douanes; ordonner la **saisie** du quotidien incriminé (*seizure [esp. of assets]*)

select (*v*): ⟨Pol⟩ son successeur a été **désigné**; l'erreur de l'avoir **désigné** comme candidat (*select, choose, designate*)

selection (*n*): la **désignation** du nouveau responsable (*selection, choice*); ⟨Educ⟩ partisans de la **sélection à l'entrée** (*admission by selection*)

selective (*adj*): les **mesures** (*f*) **ponctuelles** ne suffisent plus à contenir les dépenses de santé (*selective measures; one-off measures*)

self-determination (*n*): ⟨Pol⟩ le droit des peuples à **disposer d'eux-mêmes**; l'**autodétermination** (*f*) au moyen d'un référendum sur l'indépendance

self-employed (*n*/*adj*): ⟨Pol⟩ le grand parti des **indépendants** (*m*) et des paysans (*self-employed*); ⟨Comm⟩ l'avantage d'**être à son compte** (*be self-employed*)

self-financing (*n*): ⟨Econ⟩ avoir recours à l'**autofinancement** (*m*) ou à l'emprunt; l'**autofinancement** ou le financement des investissements à partir des ressources propres de l'entreprise

self-government (*n*): SEE **autonomy**

self-sufficiency (*n*): ⟨Econ⟩ grâce à l'**autosuffisance** (*f*) procurée par le pétrole de la mer du Nord; ce pays mène une politique d'**autosuffisance**

self-sufficient (*adj*): ⟨Econ⟩ l'incapacité du pays à **subvenir à ses propres besoins** (*be self-sufficient*)

sell (*v*): ⟨Econ/Comm⟩ la France **commercialise** plus de 50% de ses produits à l'étranger (*sell*, *market*); une tonne d'aluminium **se traite** à $23.000 (*be sold/traded*); **écouler** les stocks existants (*sell*, *clear*, *dispose of*); le groupe va **céder** trois de ses filiales (*sell*, *sell off*)

seller (*n*): ⟨Comm/Jur⟩ si le **vendeur** se désiste, il doit rembourser le double des arrhes (*seller*, *vendor*); ⟨Fin⟩ profiter d'un **marché à la hausse** (*seller's market*)

selling off (*n*): ⟨Comm⟩ les socialistes crient au **bradage** du patrimoine national (*selling off*, *selling at cut price*)

sell off (*v*): ⟨Comm⟩ le cuivre **se bradait** à 900 dollars la tonne; il se défend de **solder** le patrimoine économique de son pays

semester (*n*): les très bons résultats du premier **semestre** (*semester*, *six-month period*)

semesterly (*adj*): hausse de 20% du bénéfice **semestriel** (*semesterly*, *half-year*); (*adv*): renouvelable **semestriellement** (*semesterly*, *half-yearly*)

semi-skilled (*adj*): ⟨Ind⟩ des postes vacants pour **ouvriers** (*mpl*) **spécialisés** (*semi-skilled worker*)

senate (*n*/*adj*): ⟨Pol⟩ lors de la première lecture du texte au **Sénat** (*senate*); la majorité **sénatoriale** votait comme un seul homme (*in the senate*; *senatorial*)

send (*v*): la France **achemine** des renforts; **faire parvenir** de l'aide aux plus démunis

send back (*v*): il a été **refoulé** à la frontière suisse (*send back*; *expel*)

sending (*n*): hostile à l'**envoi** (*m*) d'une force militaire (*sending*, *dispatch*); ⟨Jur⟩ en cas de **renvoi** devant la cour d'assises (*sending*, *referral*); 40% des sondés souhaitent le **renvoi** des immigrés (*sending back*)

senior (*n*/*adj*): un parlementaire **chevronné** (*senior*, *experienced*); le **doyen** des juges (*most senior*)

seniority (*n*): la progression automatique, **à l'ancienneté** (*f*) (*by seniority*)

sensitive (*adj*): une commune **sensible** de la banlieue (*sensitive*); éviter la polémique sur une question de cette **sensibilité** (*f*) (*sensitive nature*);

c'est un problème de **sensibilisation** (*f*) des jeunes (*making sensitive to/ aware of sth*)

sentence (*n*): ⟨Jur⟩ le récidiviste doit accomplir les deux tiers de sa **condamnation**; détention sans inculpation ni **jugement** (*m*) (*sentence*); six mois de prison **avec sursis** (*m*) (*suspended sentence*); SEE ALSO **death**, **reduction**

sentence (*v*): ⟨Jur⟩ **être condamné** à dix ans de détention (*be sentenced/ condemned*)

separate (*v*): ⟨Jur⟩ décider d'un commun accord de **se séparer**

separation (*n*): ⟨Jur⟩ en cas de **rupture** (*f*) **de la vie commune** depuis plus de six ans; une requête en divorce ou en **séparation** (*f*) **de corps** (*judicial separation*)

series (*n*): les entreprises annoncent d'importants **trains** (*m*) de licenciements (*series*); Pérou: attentats **en série** (*f*) (*a series of; in series*); SEE ALSO **measure**

serious (*adj*): ⟨Jur⟩ une peine maximale de deux ans pour les délits même **aggravés** (*serious, aggravated*)

serve (*v*): le port de Dunkerque **dessert** tout le nord-ouest du continent; une ville assez bien **desservie** (*serve [esp. by public transport]*); ⟨Jur⟩ **signifier** des actes de procédure (*serve, deliver*)

service (*n*): ⟨Econ⟩ le coût de la **prestation** (*service; provision of a service*); les **services** (*mpl*) en ont été les principaux bénéficiaires; les **activités** (*f*) **de service** ne cessent de s'étendre (*service industries/sector*)

servicing (*n*): assurant la **desserte** de la région Pays de la Loire (*servicing [esp. by transport system]*)

session (*n*): ⟨Pol⟩ hier soir, au cours d'une **séance** extraordinaire; le projet de loi sera présenté à la **session** de printemps

setback (*n*): l'idéologie communiste connaît de sérieuses **déboires** (*f*); un **revers** important pour la résistance (*setback*); le parti a subi un cuisant **revers électoral** (*electoral setback*)

setting (*n*): SEE **fixing**

setting up (*n*): l'objectif reste l'**établissement** (*m*) d'un État palestinien; la **formation** d'écoles pour les immigrés islamiques; la **constitution** d'un fonds de garantie; la **mise sur pied** d'un directoire mondial; la **mise en place** d'un organisme de transition (*setting up*); ⟨Econ⟩ l'aide à la **création d'entreprise** (*setting up a company*); de nouvelles **implantations** (*f*) créeront une centaine d'emplois (*setting up of factory/ manufacturing operation*)

settle (*v*): une réunion pour **régler** les problèmes de la région (*settle*); des manœuvres visant à **liquider** la question palestinienne (*settle/resolve once and for all*); les immigrés n'ont pas automatiquement le droit de **s'y établir**; beaucoup d'immigrés polonais **s'implantèrent** dans le Nord (*settle, settle down*); SEE ALSO **pay**

settlement (*n*): ⟨Pol⟩ le conflit semblait proche d'une **issue**; la **liquidation** d'un litige vieux de onze ans; un **règlement** du conflit (*settlement, solution*); ⟨Fin⟩ dès **règlement** de la facture (*settlement/payment of account*); la **donation-partage** permet de réaliser le partage de ses biens de son vivant (*settlement [esp. of money/estate]*); SEE ALSO **solution, wage**

settling (*n*): le **règlement** des problèmes du Proche-Orient; SEE ALSO **settlement**

set up (*v*): ⟨Pol⟩ **instaurer** en Tunisie une démocratie réelle; **constituer** un gouvernement; **mettre en place** un plan de redressement (*set up*); leur décision de **se constituer** en États indépendants (*set o.s. up; form*); ⟨Econ/Comm⟩ Michelin **implante** une usine dans l'Ouest (*set up a factory*); pour pouvoir **s'implanter** durablement à l'étranger (*set up a commercial/industrial operation*)

sever (*v*): SEE **break off**

severance (*n*): le salarié licencié peut prétendre à une **indemnité de licenciement** (*m*); le plan social comprend des **indemnités de départ** (*m*) (*severance pay*); SEE ALSO **breaking-off, redundancy**

severe (*adj*): ⟨Comm/Econ⟩ en vue de la **rude** concurrence qui les opposera bientôt; une **dure** récession (*severe*); la sélection est **draconienne** (*very severe*)

sewerage (*n*): la Région intervient dans le renforcement du **tout-à-l'égout** (*mains sewerage*); le service d'assainissement comprend aussi l'**évacuation** (*f*) **des eaux usées** (*sewerage, sewage, effluent disposal*); SEE ALSO **drainage**

sexual (*adj*): ⟨Jur⟩ le tribunal n'a pas retenu les accusations de **sévices** (*m*) **sexuels** (*sexual abuse*); le personnel féminin se plaignait de **harcèlement** (*m*) **sexuel** (*sexual harassment*); SEE ALSO **abuse**

shadow (*adj*): ⟨Pol⟩ le ministre de l'Énergie du **cabinet fantôme** (*shadow cabinet*)

shake (*v*): ils ont été fortement **secoués** par la nouvelle; les événements qui ont **secoué** la vieille URSS depuis 1985

share (*n*): la **part** des hydrocarbures dans les exportations (*share*); ⟨Comm⟩ de nouveaux producteurs ont pris de grosses **parts de marché** (*m*) à son détriment (*market share*); ⟨Fin/Econ⟩ les **actions** (*f*) qui constituent des parts de capital d'une entreprise (*shares, stocks*); **intéresser** directement le personnel aux résultats de l'entreprise (*give a share/ interest in profits*); SEE ALSO **stock**

share (*v*): en matière d'élimination des déchets, les deux villes ont décidé de **se répartir** les tâches (*share, share out*)

shareholder (*n*): ⟨Fin⟩ proposer aux **actionnaires** (*m*) un dividende net de 17F; le nombre de **détenteurs** (*m*) **d'actions** a doublé (*shareholder*); 400.000 **petits porteurs** (*m*) sont devenus actionnaires de la chaîne de télévision (*small shareholder/investor*)

shareholdership (*n*): ⟨Fin⟩ pour assurer la stabilité de leur **actionnariat** (*m*) (*body of shareholders, shareholdership*)

share issue (*n*): ⟨Fin⟩ procéder à une **augmentation du capital**; l'**émission** (*f*) **de nouvelles actions** ramène l'endettement du groupe à 35% de ses fonds propres

share ownership (*n*): ⟨Fin⟩ un coup de pouce à l'**actionnariat** (*m*) populaire (*share ownership*); les partisans de l'**actionnariat du personnel** (*employee share ownership; share incentive scheme*)

sharing out (*n*): la nouvelle **répartition** des compétences entre l'État et la région; l'**allocation** (*f*) des pouvoirs au sein du cabinet; SEE ALSO **distribution**

sharp (*adj*): ⟨Comm⟩ les achats d'automobiles ont subi un coup d'arrêt **brutal** (*sharp, sudden*); provoquant une **hausse brutale** des prix (*sharp/ sudden rise*)

sharply (*adv*): sa consommation **chute brutalement** en 1990 (*fall sharply*)

shelve (*v*): le gouvernement semble vouloir **mettre en veilleuse** (*f*) ce projet (*shelve, postpone indefinitely*)

shelving (*n*): la **mise en veilleuse** (*f*) du droit de vote des étrangers (*shelving, postponing indefinitely*)

shift (*n*): ⟨Pol⟩ le **renversement** idéologique le plus remarquable (*shift, reversal; swing*); tout **infléchissement** de cette politique semble exclu (*[small] shift, modification*); ⟨Ind⟩ quatre **équipes** (*f*) de six heures, six jours par semaine (*shift, gang*); la direction en profite pour modifier le **travail posté** (*shift work*); les **travailleurs** (*m*) **postés** qui travaillent l'après-midi (*shift-worker*); SEE ALSO **swing**

ship (*n*): un **bâtiment** battant pavillon libérien; aucun **navire** n'est à l'abri d'une avarie

shipowner (*n*): les **armateurs** (*m*) pourraient préférer Anvers au Havre

shipping (*n*): les droits de pêche accordés aux **armements** (*m*) de la CE

shop (*n*): ⟨Comm⟩ un **magasin** d'alimentation (*shop*); fermer sa **boutique** (*[small] shop*); **s'établir** antiquaire (*set up shop/in business*); ⟨Ind⟩ les **ouvriers** (*m*) ont voté la grève (*shop-floor [workers]*); SEE ALSO **closed**

shopkeeper (*n*): ⟨Comm⟩ la survie des **petits commerçants** (*m*) confrontés à la multiplication des grandes surfaces (*small shopkeeper/trader*)

shoplifting (*n*): son inculpation pour **vol** (*m*) **à l'étalage**

shop steward (*n*): ⟨Ind⟩ le **délégué syndical** a communiqué la décision patronale aux travailleurs

shortage (*n*): la **disette** endémique dans les pays du Sahel; une forte **pénurie** de logements; une **pénurie** de vivres, d'eau et de médicaments; SEE ALSO **food, scarcity**

shortcoming (*n*): à cause des **carences** (*f*) de notre législation; la principale **carence** alors était l'insuffisance d'autoroutes; l'État avoue ses

insuffisances (*f*) passées dans ce domaine; les **défaillances** (*f*) du système scolaire français (*shortcoming, defect*); SEE ALSO **defect**

short-term (*adj*): une solution **à court terme** (*m*) (*short-term*); ⟨Econ⟩ les difficultés sont **conjoncturelles** (*short-term, temporary*); l'extension des **emplois** (*m*) **précaires** (*short-term contract/employment*); ⟨Fin⟩ consentir un **prêt à court terme** (*short-term loan*)

short-time (*adj*): ⟨Ind⟩ Air France va avoir recours au **chômage partiel** (*short-time working*); 14.200 personnes seront **mises en chômage technique** (*put on short-time working*)

show (*v*): les statistiques **affichent** une diminution du chômage (*show; reveal*); cela **témoigne** de l'importance que la France attache à la question (*show, demonstrate*); SEE ALSO **reveal, point out, indicate**

shut (*v*): ⟨Ind/Comm⟩ **chômer** le 1er mai (*shut, close [esp. business]*); SEE ALSO **close**

shuttle (*n*): malgré les multiples **navettes** (*f*) qu'il effectue (*shuttle*); la **navette** aérienne Paris-Bruxelles (*shuttle service*)

shuttle (*v*): ⟨Pol⟩ le texte a **fait la navette** entre Assemblée et Sénat (*shuttle, be sent from one parliamentary chamber to another*)

sickness (*n*): ⟨Soc⟩ toucher des **indemnités** (*f*) **d'arrêt-maladie** (*sickness benefit*)

sign (*v*): ⟨Admin⟩ **signer** en bas de la page (*sign*); syndicats et patronat **paraphent** un accord sur le recours au travail temporaire (*sign; initial*)

signatory (*n/adj*): ⟨Jur⟩ les **signataires** (*m*) d'un contrat; la pétition a recueilli 30.000 **signataires** (*signatory, person who signs*); ⟨Pol⟩ les treize **pays** (*m*) **signataires** (*signatory country*)

significance (*n*): la **portée** historique de ces accords (*significance, import*)

significant (*adj*): dans le bâtiment, on a constaté une amélioration **significative** (*significant, considerable*)

signing (*n*): la **signature** d'un traité de l'union (*signing, signature*)

sign on (*v*): ⟨Ind⟩ renvoyé, il n'a plus qu'à **pointer au chômage** (*sign on the 'dole'*)

single (*adj*): ⟨Pol⟩ le futur candidat **unique** aux présidentielles (*single*); un parlement **monocaméral** (*single-chamber*); on opta pour le **scrutin uninominal majoritaire** (*single-member constituency electoral system*); ⟨Econ⟩ érosion de la **mono-industrie** charbonnière (*reliance on a single industry*); dans le **marché unique** de demain (*single market*)

single mother (*n*): ⟨Soc⟩ le nombre de **mères** (*f*) **isolées** s'accroît parallèlement au développement du divorce; une **mère célibataire** vivant chez ses parents

single parent (*n*): ⟨Soc⟩ l'allocation de soutien familial dont bénéficient beaucoup de **parents** (*m*) **isolés**

single-parent (*adj*): ⟨Soc⟩ les familles **mono-parentales** représentent un cas exceptionnel; le **monoménage** augmente, surtout dans les grandes villes (*single-parent family unit*)

single party (*n*): ⟨Pol⟩ le **mono-partisme** est terminé au Zaïre; ils contestent le **parti unique** (*single-party system/rule*)

single person (*n*): ⟨Soc/Fisc⟩ une pension de 2.300F par mois pour une **personne seule**

sit (*v*): ⟨Pol⟩ le droit de **siéger** à la table des négociations; **siéger** parmi les non-inscrits à l'Assemblée nationale (*sit*); ⟨Educ⟩ pour être admis à **passer une épreuve** (*sit an examination*)

sit-down strike (*n*): ⟨Ind⟩ le personnel a riposté par des **grèves** (*f*) **sur le tas** qui ont arrêté la production

sit-in (*n*): ⟨Ind⟩ une **grève avec occupation** (*f*) **des locaux** à l'usine de Sochaux (*sit-in; sit-down strike*)

situation (*n*): en fonction de la **localisation** géographique (*situation, location*); ⟨Econ⟩ le ralentissement de la **conjoncture** du logement (*general situation [esp. economic]*)

size (*n*): l'**ampleur** (*f*) des fluctuations au mois le mois; malgré l'**importance** (*f*) des aides à l'embauche (*size, scale*); la seule société française de **taille** (*f*) européenne (*size, dimension*)

skill (*n*): une tâche exigeant une **habileté** technique; le **savoir-faire** ancestral des horlogers du Doubs (*skill, expertise*); juriste possédant de solides **compétences** (*f*) en sciences humaines (*skills, qualifications*); ses très grands **talents** (*m*) de négociateur (*skills; talent*)

skirmish (*n*): ⟨Mil⟩ les premières **escarmouches** (*f*) sérieuses éclatèrent en fin de journée; SEE ALSO **clash**

slack (*adj*): ⟨Econ/Comm⟩ la production est **étale** en Allemagne; les mois **creux** de l'année (*slack*); une bonne année, puis le **creux** de 1990 (*slack period/year*); le **marasme** actuel semble appelé à se prolonger (*slack trading conditions*)

slacken (*v*): ⟨Comm⟩ l'activité commerciale a **ralenti** en 1992; SEE ALSO **relax**

slackening (*n*): ⟨Pol⟩ le risque d'un **relâchement** des réformes est bien réel; SEE ALSO **relaxing**

slander (*n*): ⟨Jur⟩ porter plainte pour **diffamation** (*f*); accusation qui constitue une véritable **diffamation**; SEE ALSO **libel, defamation**

slash (*v*): ⟨Comm⟩ la firme japonaise **casse les prix** de la télévision haute définition (*slash prices; undercut a competitor*)

slide (*n*): ⟨Fin⟩ la **glissade** du dollar devient inquiétante; ⟨Comm⟩ le **glissement** des prix était déjà de 0,4%

sliding scale (*n*): ⟨Fin⟩ avec ou sans **barème** (*m*) **dégressif** (*sliding scale [esp. of charges]*); les frais de souscription sont **dégressifs**; l'allocation servie est réduite **de façon** (*f*) **dégressive** (*on a sliding scale*)

slight (*adj*): commerce extérieur: **légère** amélioration en mars (*slight, small*)

slightly (*adv*): le commerce extérieur a **faiblement** augmenté; un niveau de vie **légèrement** supérieur à celui des ouvriers

slim down (*v*): ⟨Econ⟩ la firme va **dégraisser** ses effectifs (*slim down [esp. the workforce]*)

slimming down (*n*): ⟨Econ⟩ le **dégraissage** des effectifs annoncé (*slimming down [esp. of workforce]*)

slow (*adj*): Bagdad **tarde à** livrer sa réponse à Moscou (*be slow to*); la reprise attendue **tarde** (*be slow in coming/to come about*)

slowdown (*n*): ⟨Ind⟩ la grève perlée, un **freinage** volontaire de la production; ⟨Econ⟩ **tassement** (*m*) de la croissance du commerce international en 1991; aéroports: **croissance** (*f*) **ralentie** du trafic; **ralentissement** (*m*) de la croissance allemande en 1991 (*slowdown*); à cause du **ralentissement de l'économie** (*economic slowdown*)

slow down (*v*): les obstacles qui **freinent** l'avancement des femmes (*slow down; put a brake on*); ⟨Comm⟩ les ventes de cognac **se sont ralenties** en 1990 (*slow down, fall back*)

slum (*n*): les **taudis** (*m*), construits au siècle dernier pour les ouvriers (*slum, slum dwelling*); un programme de **démolition de logements** (*mpl*) **insalubres** (*slum clearance*); un enfant d'immigrés, né dans la **zone** (*slum area/belt [esp. of Paris]*)

slump (*n*): ⟨Econ⟩ chacun a ressenti les effets de la **crise**; la **dégringolade** du marché; comment s'expliquer le **marasme** actuel du marché?; peu avant la **dépression** du marché de l'informatique; la **baisse d'activité** (*f*) du travail temporaire (*slump*); Comm⟩ hausse des prix, **crise des logements** (*housing slump*); une période de **mévente** (*f*) en début d'année (*slump in sales*)

slump (*v*): ⟨Comm⟩ les ventes vers les États-Unis **se sont tassées** en 1989 (*slump, fall back*)

slush fund (*n*): ⟨Comm⟩ le parti était financé par les **caisses** (*f*) **noires** du KGB

small (*adj*): la somme **modique** de 200F; une quantité assez **réduite** d'articles (*small; modest*); lorsque le marché du produit est **restreint** (*small, limited*); son audience est encore **confidentielle**; la **faible** majorité au Congrès (*very small*)

small business (*n*): ⟨Comm⟩ l'opposition du **petit commerce** à l'ouverture des magasins le dimanche

smallholder (*n*): ⟨Agric⟩ les **petits cultivateurs** (*m*) dominent dans le Midi

small saver (*n*): ⟨Fin⟩ un krach ne touche pas les **petits déposants** (*m*); les **petits épargnants** (*m*), principales victimes du krach

smoothly (*adv*): les réformes voient le jour, **sans accroc** (*m*) ni retards excessifs; la transition s'est faite **sans heurts** (*mpl*)

soar (*v*): 〈Comm〉 les cours du pétrole avaient **monté en flèche** (*f*); les prix **se sont envolés** hier à Paris; le Franc français **fait un bond** hier sur les marchés de change (*soar, shoot up*)

soaring (*adj*): le chômage à nouveau **en flèche** (*f*); 〈Comm〉 la **flambée des prix** de l'été dernier; 〈Fin〉 les gains réalisés grâce à l'**envolée** (*f*) **des cours** (*soaring prices*)

social (*adj*): 〈Soc〉 un véritable **problème de société** (*f*) (*social problem, problem of society*); mettre tout en œuvre pour favoriser la **vie associative** dans les villes nouvelles (*social activities; clubs and associations*); SEE ALSO **fabric**

social aid (*n*): 〈Soc〉 les **dispositifs** (*m*) **d'aide sociale** tendent à détruire toute motivation (*social aid programme*)

social harmony (*n*): 〈Soc〉 un monde de **convivialité** (*f*) et de solidarité; la **convivialité** ne se décrète pas, elle se construit (*social harmony; good social relations*)

social measures (*npl*): 〈Soc/Econ〉 dans cette zone sinistrée, le gouvernement a prévu un **plan social d'accompagnement** (*m*); alors que le **traitement social** du chômage s'essouffle (*social measures [esp. to alleviate unemployment/plant closures]*)

social mobility (*n*): 〈Soc/Econ〉 le rêve de **mobilité** (*f*) **sociale** s'efface (*[upward] social mobility*)

social security (*n*): 〈Soc〉 les cotisations aux diverses caisses de la **sécurité sociale**; recevoir de l'**aide** (*f*) **sociale** (*be in receipt of social security/state benefit*); SEE ALSO **social welfare, welfare**

social services (*npl*): 〈Soc〉 la santé et l'**action** (*f*) **sociale** relèvent du département comme de la région; des familles à problèmes connues des **services** (*m*) **sociaux**

social welfare (*n*): 〈Soc〉 l'**aide** (*f*) **sociale** place un enfant dans une famille d'accueil (*social welfare department*); les **prestations** (*f*) **sociales** auxquelles ces cotisations ouvrent droit (*social welfare benefit*)

social work (*n*): 〈Soc〉 le **travail social**, généralement mal rémunéré et peu valorisant; un métier dans l'**assistance** (*f*) **sociale** (*social work/welfare*)

social worker (*n*): 〈Soc〉 des **travailleurs** (*m*) **sociaux** et des bénévoles; **assistante** (*f*) **sociale** de son état

society (*n*): se constituer en **association** (*f*) (*society; club*); 〈Soc〉 les créateurs de richesses hautement profitables à la **collectivité** (*society at large*)

soil (*n*): 〈Pol〉 les étrangers expulsés du **sol français** (*French soil*)

sole (*adj*): 〈Comm〉 exportateur **exclusif** pour la France (*sole, exclusive*)

soliciting (*n*): 〈Jur/Soc〉 inculpée de **racolage** (*m*) sur la voie publique

solicitor (*n*): 〈Jur〉 c'est l'**avoué** (*m*) qui représente les plaideurs; tout acquéreur devrait faire appel à un **notaire en droit** (*m*); les fonctions de solicitor s'apparentent à celles de l'avoué et du **notaire**

solution (*n*): chercher une **issue** au conflit saharien; s'acheminer vers la **solution** d'un conflit; SEE ALSO **settlement**

solve (*v*): un problème qu'on n'a pas pu **résoudre**; pour **régler** le problème des sureffectifs (*solve*); ⟨Jur⟩ l'affaire n'est pas près d'être **élucidée** (*solve, elucidate*)

solvency (*n*): ⟨Fin⟩ la **solvabilité** soviétique paraît de plus en plus incertaine

solvent (*adj*): ⟨Fin⟩ **solvable**, c'est-à-dire capable d'assurer à tout moment le paiement de ses dettes; on prête volontiers à un débiteur **solvable**

soon (*adv*): se doter **dans les meilleurs délais** (*m*) d'un missile performant; si une réforme n'est pas mise en œuvre **à brève échéance** (*f*)

source (*n*): ⟨Fisc⟩ un impôt **prélevé à la source** (*pay/deduct at source*)

sovereignty (*n*): ⟨Pol⟩ proclamer la **souveraineté** de la Slovaquie

speak (*v*): il va **prendre la parole** au nom de son parti (*speak, make a speech*); **se faire l'interprète** (*m*) de l'ensemble des travailleurs (*speak for/on behalf of*)

spearhead (*n*): l'Éthiopie, **fer** (*m*) **de lance** des régimes marxistes en Afrique

specialized (*adj*): une politique d'acquisitions dans des domaines **pointus** (*specialized, advanced*); ⟨Comm⟩ lancer un magazine très **ciblé** (*specialized; aimed at a specific market*)

specific (*adj*): dans ce cas **précis**; étudier un cas **particulier**

specification (*n*): ⟨Comm⟩ une brochure avec **fiche** (*f*) **technique** et tarifs; le prix des articles ainsi que leurs **caractéristiques** (*fpl*); imposer un **cahier des charges** (*fpl*) précis (*specifications [esp. in contract]; brief*)

specify (*v*): la nature des charges doit être **précisée** dans le bail (*specify, set out [clearly]*)

spectrum (*n*): des gens d'un large **éventail** socio-économique (*spectrum, range*); de part et d'autre de l'**échiquier** (*m*) **politique** (*political spectrum*)

speech (*n*): une **allocation** d'une heure trente (*speech, address*); lors de son **intervention** (*f*) télévisée en mars (*speech*); ⟨Jur⟩ la **réquisition** du parquet est accablante (*concluding speech for the prosecution*); SEE ALSO **freedom**

speed (*n*): l'ampleur et le **rythme** des réformes sont déconcertants (*speed, rate*)

spend (*v*): **dépenser** sans compter

spending (*n*): ⟨Fin⟩ les **dépenses** (*f*) sont à peine couvertes par les rentrées (*spending, expenditure*); les **dépenses militaires** sont en baisse (*military spending*); les consommateurs, saisis d'une **frénésie d'achats** (*mpl*) (*spending spree*); SEE ALSO **expenditure**

spendthrift (*adj*): SEE **extravagant**

spin-off (*n*): ⟨Econ⟩ les **répercussions** (*f*) **économiques** potentielles de cette percée diplomatique (*economic spin-off*)

spiral (*n*): l'**engrenage** (*m*) **de la violence** (*spiral of violence*); ⟨Econ⟩ l'économie est menacée par cette **spirale inflationniste** (*inflationary spiral*)

splinter group (*n*): ⟨Pol⟩ un petit **groupe dissident**, réfractaire à la ligne officielle

split (*adj*): une opposition elle-même **divisée** (*split, divided*)

split (*n*): éviter une **scission** ouverte au sein du parti; on cherche à sortir du **clivage** juifs-musulmans; **rupture** (*f*) entre sociaux-chrétiens flamands et socialistes francophones (*split, division*)

split (*v*): le parti **s'est scindé** en deux clans irréconciliables; la société avait **éclaté** en deux branches

split up (*v*): le conseil **s'est séparé** sans avoir voté aucun des projets (*split up, break up*)

splitting up (*n*): le mouvement est menacé d'**éclatement** (*m*); après la **décomposition** de l'URSS en 1991 (*splitting up, breaking up*)

spokesman (*n*): il espère leur paraître comme un **interlocuteur** valable; le **porte-parole** de la présidence italienne

sponsor (*n*): ⟨Pol⟩ le **rapporteur** du projet de loi (*sponsor [of parliamentary bill]*); ⟨Comm⟩ les **sponsors** (*m*) veulent adapter l'épreuve aux exigences de la télévision; le **parraineur** sans qui le spectacle n'aurait pas eu lieu (*sponsor*)

sponsor (*v*): ⟨Comm⟩ les producteurs d'alcools ne peuvent plus **parrainer** des manifestations sportives; **patronner** une émission de télévision

sponsorship (*n*): ⟨Comm⟩ le **mécénat** industriel et commercial; se financer par le **parrainage** ou par la publicité (*sponsorship, sponsoring*)

spouse (*n*): ⟨Jur/Soc⟩ un étranger dont le **conjoint** est français; le **conjoint** de l'assuré est également couvert

spread (*n*): l'**extension** (*f*) de l'agitation sociale en Algérie (*spread, spreading*); le blocage de l'**étalement** (*m*) **suburbain** (*suburban spread*); SEE ALSO **distribution**

spread (*v*): le mouvement de mécontentement **se généralise**; l'agitation **s'étend** dans les Balkans (*spread*); l'évacuation va **s'étaler** sur une période de douze ans (*be spread*); prendre des mesures **étalées dans le temps** (*spread over a period of time*); 280 filiales **réparties** dans 35 pays (*be spread/distributed over*)

spreading (*n*): l'**étalement** (*m*) des dépenses sur plusieurs mois (*spreading over a period of time*); des activités ayant en commun la **diffusion** de l'information (*spreading, broadcasting*); ⟨Pol/Mil⟩ même l'Italie est menacée par une **étendue** du conflit (*spreading, spread*)

squander (*v*): fortune qu'il a **dilapidée** au jeu

squandering (*n*): la lutte contre la **dilapidation** des fonds publics

squeeze (*n*): SEE **credit**

squeeze (*v*): ⟨Econ⟩ une stratégie pour **serrer** les coûts de production (*squeeze; reduce*); le quotidien, **laminé** par la concurrence; on a beau **tasser les prix** (*m*) (*squeeze prices*)

stabilize (*v*): ⟨Fin⟩ elle a pour fonction d'**assainir** le budget de l'État

stable (*adj*): à la recherche d'un **emploi permanent** (*stable/permanent job*)

staff (*n*): les besoins en **personnel** (*m*) d'une entreprise; les **effectifs** (*m*) ont été réduits d'un tiers (*staff, personnel*)

staffing (*n*): le plan de restructuration conduira à une **compression du personnel**; la restructuration implique un **dégraissage des effectifs** (*m*) (*staffing cuts*)

stage (*n*): un nouveau **degré** dans l'escalade de la tension; une nouvelle **étape** a été franchie (*stage; step*); la première **tranche** du projet sera achevée, assure le promoteur (*stage, phase*); libération **par étapes** (*fpl*) des prix; le départ **échelonné** du ministère des Finances (*in stages; step by step*); SEE ALSO **introduce**

stagger (*v*): **étaler** une réforme sur plusieurs mois; les heures du travail seront **étalées**; **échelonner** les départs en vacances sur les mois d'été (*stagger; carry out in stages*)

staggering (*n*): l'**étalement** (*m*) des vacances est loin d'être la règle (*staggering of holidays*)

stagnation (*n*): ⟨Econ⟩ la **stagnation** du pouvoir d'achat des familles

stagnate (*v*): les rendements céréaliers risquent de **stagner**; les exportations continuent à **marquer le pas**

stake (*n*): ⟨Fin⟩ céder ses **intérêts** (*m*) dans la firme; certains actionnaires ont déjà accru leurs **participations** (*f*) (*stake, shareholding*); **être actionnaire** (*m*) à hauteur de 25% (*hold a stake*); **détenir 25% du capital** de la société suisse (*hold a 25% stake*); Honda **entre dans le capital** de Rover (*acquire a stake*); aucun intérêt matériel n'est **en jeu** (*m*); c'est tout l'avenir du pays qui est **en cause** (*f*) (*at stake; in danger*); tel est l'**enjeu** (*m*) crucial en cette fin d'année (*question at stake*)

stalemate (*n*): ⟨Pol⟩ même **blocage** (*m*) concernant les négociations du GATT; l'**impasse** (*f*) des négociations avec les pays arabes (*stalemate, deadlock*); le conflit est **au point mort** (*in stalemate, deadlocked*); l'espoir d'un **déblocage** politique en Irlande du nord (*breaking/end of stalemate/deadlock*); SEE ALSO **deadlock**

stamp (*n*): ⟨Fisc⟩ un **droit de timbre** (*m*) est redevable lors de certains transferts de biens (*stamp duty*)

stamp (*v*): faire **viser** le document à la mairie du domicile (*stamp*); des enveloppes **affranchies** avec ces nouveaux timbres (*stamped*); joindre une **enveloppe retour timbrée** 4,20F (*stamped addressed envelope*)

stance (*n*): trouver une **position commune** aux députés de l'opposition (*common stance*)

stand (*n*): sa **prise de position** (*f*) en faveur des déshérités (*stand; taking a stand*); **prendre position** contre la guerre (*take a stand*)

stand (*v*): ⟨Pol⟩ le président **se représentera** aux prochaines élections (*stand for re-election*); le candidat socialiste **s'était désisté** en faveur du communiste (*stand down*)

standard (*n*): une nouvelle dégradation du **niveau de vie** (*f*); une réduction du **train de vie** américain (*standard of living*); SEE ALSO **living**

stand-in (*n*): ⟨Admin/Pol⟩ le vice-président **suppléant**; SEE ALSO **interim**

stand in (*v*): ⟨Admin/Pol⟩ **suppléer aux fonctions** (*f*) du président démissionnaire (*stand in/deputize for*)

stand up to (*v*): Algérie: le FLN **tient tête** (*f*) au pouvoir (*stand up to, confront*)

staple (*adj*): ⟨Econ⟩ les subventions aux **produits** (*m*) **de base** (*staple produce*)

start (*n*): la campagne électorale a connu un **démarrage** hésitant; poste évolutif, **salaire** (*m*) **de départ** motivant (*start/starting salary*)

start (*v*): les deux pays viennent d'**engager** un timide dialogue; **esquisser** un rapprochement avec la Chine (*start, begin, initiate*); le congrès devait **s'ouvrir** dimanche (*start, open*); ⟨Mil⟩ **déclencher une offensive** dès le matin (*start/launch an offensive*)

starting (*adj*): un **salaire à l'embauche** relativement modeste (*starting salary*)

start-up (*n/adj*): ⟨Comm⟩ les défaillances sont plus nombreuses que les **créations** (*f*) **|d'entreprises|** (*start-up [of a business]*); les **frais** (*m*) **initiaux** de qui veut se mettre à son compte (*start-up costs*)

start up (*v*): ⟨Comm⟩ les particuliers prêts à **démarrer** dans l'année qui vient (*start up/set up in a business*)

state (*n*): ⟨Pol⟩ l'**État** (*m*) prélève une partie (*state; government*); les **affaires** (*f*) **de l'État** préoccupent le président (*affairs of state*); SEE ALSO **head**

state (*adj*): ⟨Pol/Econ⟩ un système **étatique** de retraite (*state; state-run*); toujours opposée à l'**interventionnisme** (*m*) **étatique** (*state intervention*); les parents d'élèves face à l'**école** (*f*) **publique** (*state school; state schooling/education*); ⟨Jur⟩ le **ministère publique** a requis une peine de deux ans (*state/public prosecutor*)

state aid (*n*): ⟨Pol/Fin⟩ des **aides** (*f*) **de l'État** sous forme de subventions ou de dotations (*state aid*); les plus défavorisés, habitués à **vivre des deniers** (*m*) **publics** (*live on state aid/on the state*)

state control (*n*): ⟨Pol/Econ⟩ le résultat d'une excessive **étatisation** (*placing under state control*); vingt sociétés **sont passées sous contrôle** (*m*) **de l'État** (*come under state control*)

208

stateless (*adj*): ⟨Pol⟩ des exilés politiques, des **apatrides** (*m*) (*stateless person*)

statement (*n*): dans un **communiqué officiel** (*official statement*); l'**énoncé** (*m*) des principes d'un ordre international nouveau (*statement, exposition*); ⟨Fin⟩ le **relevé de compte** pour les opérations effectuées; un **extrait de compte** est envoyé en fin de mois; un **relevé** trimestriel, envoyé à chaque titulaire de compte (*statement of account; bank statement*); ⟨Jur⟩ tout au long du procès, il a maintenu sa **déposition** (*statement, deposition*); ⟨Ins⟩ faire établir un **constat** (*statement, report [esp. of accident]*); SEE ALSO **deposition**

stationary (*adj*): à partir de 1993, le nombre de cotisants va **stagner** (*remain stationary*)

statistical (*adj*): le principal enseignement de ces **données** (*f*) **statistiques** (*statistical data*)

statistic (*n*): les **statistiques** (*f*) sont éloquentes à cet égard

status (*n*): bénéficier du même **statut** que le travailleur national; pour préserver le **statut** de superpuissance unique

statute (*n*): cette situation n'est pas prévue dans le **texte des lois** (*f*) (*statute book*)

statutory (*adj*): sans transgresser leurs obligations **statutaires**; les dispositions **réglementaires**

step (*n*): un nouveau **degré** a été franchi (*step, stage*); on multiplie les **démarches** (*f*) pour sauvegarder la paix (*step, initiative*); un processus **gradué** et négocié (*step by step*); il est un peu **décalé** par rapport à l'opinion; ceci place le président **en porte-à-faux** avec son cabinet (*out of step/line*)

stimulate (*v*): ⟨Econ⟩ le système des primes **donne un coup de fouet** à la production (*stimulate*); les exportations, **dopées** par la faiblesse de la livre sterling (*stimulate, boost*); **prendre des mesures** (*f*) **incitatives** en faveur de l'épargne (*take measures to stimulate*)

stimulus (*n*): ⟨Econ⟩ les dépenses de consommation sont le principal **moteur** de la croissance; SEE ALSO **driving force**

stock (*n*): 700.000 logements [près de 10% du **parc** (*m*) hexagonal] (*[housing] stock*); le **parc** des hypermarchés s'est accru de 41 unités en 1989 (*stock, total number*); ⟨Comm⟩ en raison d'une **rupture de stock** (*being out of stock*); ⟨Fin⟩ un dealer de **fonds** (*mpl*) **d'État** britanniques (*[government] stock*); 70.000 **titres** (*m*) changèrent de main hier à la Bourse; une hausse record des **valeurs** (*f*) françaises (*stocks and shares*); SEE ALSO **equity, share, supply**

stock (*v*): ⟨Econ⟩ grâce aux armements **entreposés** sur leur territoire; des organismes d'intervention qui **stockent** les marchandises (*stock, store*); **s'approvisionner** soit auprès du producteur, soit auprès de grossistes (*stock up; obtain supplies*); SEE ALSO **supply**

Stock Exchange (*n*): ⟨Fin⟩ la **place** parisienne retrouve son optimisme des derniers jours; 1802, date de l'acte constitutif de la **Bourse des valeurs** (*f*) de Londres (*Stock Exchange*); la **cote** réagit avec mesure à la nouvelle (*Stock Exchange index*); SEE ALSO **stock market**

stockbroker (*n*): ⟨Fin⟩ les **agents** (*m*) **de change** remplacés par des sociétés de bourse

stocking (*n*): ⟨Comm⟩ les conditions de transport, de **stockage** (*m*) et d'emballage

stock market (*n*): ⟨Fin⟩ devenir une véritable **place boursière** internationale (*stockmarket, stock exchange*); SEE ALSO **Stock Exchange**

stocktaking (*n*): ⟨Comm⟩ procéder à l'**inventaire** (*m*) **des stocks**

stop (*n*): ⟨Econ⟩ les **ratés** (*m*) de la croissance (*stop and start*); Tripoli y **met le holà** en fermant provisoirement ses frontières (*put a stop to sth*); SEE ALSO **cessation, stopping**

stop (*v*): ⟨Ind⟩ **débrayer** pendant plus d'une heure (*stop work, come out on strike*); SEE ALSO **search**

stopgap (*n*): ces subventions ne sont qu'un **palliatif** utile pour gagner du temps (*stopgap [measure]*); un chef de cabinet **intérimaire**; SEE ALSO **interim**

stoppage (*n*): ⟨Ind⟩ une journée nationale d'action, avec **arrêts** (*mpl*) **de travail** et débrayage d'une heure hier; les organismes syndicaux appelaient à des **débrayages** (*m*) (*stoppage [of work]*); ⟨Fisc/Soc⟩ les **retenues** (*f*) pour la Sécurité sociale étaient de 6,5% (*stoppage, deduction*)

stopping (*n*): lutter pour l'**arrêt** (*m*) de tous les programmes autoroutiers; tous aspirent à une rapide **cessation** des hostilités (*stopping*); l'**arraisonnement** (*m*) du yacht par la police maritime (*stopping and searching*)

strained (*adj*): ⟨Pol/Ind⟩ la libération d'otages contribua à **décrisper la situation** (*make relations less strained; take the heat out of a situation*)

stream (*n*): ⟨Educ⟩ le système des **classes** (*f*) **de niveau** a beaucoup de détracteurs (*stream*); mettre un élève en **section** (*f*) scientifique ou littéraire (*stream, section*)

stream (*v*): ⟨Educ⟩ en mathématiques, on préfère **répartir les élèves par niveaux** (*mpl*) (*stream, divide class into streams, set*)

streaming (*n*): ⟨Educ⟩ la **répartition des élèves par niveaux** (*mpl*) est inévitable

strength (*n*): les **atouts** (*m*) et les faiblesses de ce secteur (*strength*); loin de s'essouffler, le mouvement paraît **s'affermir** (*gain strength, consolidate*); ⟨Fin⟩ la **bonne tenue** du franc prime sur toute autre considération (*strength, solidity*)

strengthen (*v*): les élections partielles **confortent** le PCF, après une série d'échecs; la France **renforce** son dispositif militaire en Méditerranée;

ils voudraient **muscler** un texte qu'ils estiment un peu flou; ⟨Fin⟩ cette nouvelle a **raffermi** la devise nipponne

strengthening (*n*): Washington s'inquiète du **renforcement** des troupes cubaines en Afrique australe; ⟨Econ⟩ malgré un **raffermissement** de la demande étrangère

stricken (*adj*): ⟨Econ⟩ la reconversion des sites sidérurgiques **sinistrés**; la production laitière, **sinistrée** par l'instauration de quotas (*stricken, badly affected*); SEE ALSO **hit**

strike (*n*): ⟨Ind⟩ une **action** de 24 heures paralyse les transports parisiens; les **mouvements** (*m*) **de grève** se sont limités aux houillères du Nord (*strike action*); installer un **piquet de grève** devant l'entrée de l'usine (*strike picket*); la **consigne de grève** a été largement suivie (*strike call*); lancer un **mot d'ordre de grève** (*f*) **générale** (*strike call; call for a general/all-out strike*); ⟨Mil⟩ les missiles **de première frappe** (*f*) (*first strike*)

strike off (*v*): **radier** les chômeurs qui refusent un emploi (*strike a name off a register*); ⟨Admin⟩ **être radié** de la fonction publique (*be struck off*)

striker (*n*): ⟨Ind⟩ les **grévistes** sont soutenus par l'opinion

striking off (*n*): pratiquer des **radiations** (*f*) des listes de l'ANPE (*striking off [esp. a list/register]*)

strive (*v*): des centaines d'hommes **s'acharnent** à détruire cette forteresse

strong (*adj*): ⟨Fin⟩ le dogme du **franc fort** (*strong Franc*)

stronghold (*n*): ⟨Mil/Pol⟩ la troisième circonscription, **fief** (*m*) traditionnel de la gauche

structural (*adj*): ⟨Econ⟩ ne pas confondre le conjoncturel et le **structurel** (*structural, deep-seated*)

study (*n*): **réaliser une étude** sur la vie et le travail des femmes; des **études** (*f*) **menées** sur l'impact du chômage (*carry out a study*)

study (*v*): **se pencher** longtemps sur une question; un groupe de spécialistes vont **plancher** sur le rapport (*study/examine closely*)

subcontract (*n*): ⟨Econ⟩ les PME locales espèrent décrocher un **contrat de sous-traitance** (*f*)

subcontract (*v*): ⟨Econ⟩ **sous-traiter** certaines activités pour mieux maîtriser les coûts; la plupart **sous-traitent** la restauration à des sociétés privées

subcontracting (*n*): ⟨Econ⟩ de petites unités de **sous-traitance** (*f*); on fait très peu appel à la **sous-traitance**

subcontractor (*n*): ⟨Econ⟩ plusieurs **sous-traitants** (*m*) touchés par la déconfiture du constructeur automobile (*subcontractor*); recourir massivement à une **sous-traitance locale** (*local subcontractors*)

subject (*adj*): la délivrance d'un chéquier est **subordonnée à** l'accord de la banque; **sous réserve d**'un délai de résidence; votre décision n'est pas **soumise à** l'accord de votre employeur (*subject to*)

211

subject (*n*): une mesure qui **fait l'objet** (*m*) d'une vive concertation (*be the subject of*); ⟨Educ⟩ les **filières** (*f*) techniques débouchant sur des emplois (*subject, discipline*)

subject (*v*): en les **soumettant** à un contrôle plus efficace

submission (*n*): après la **remise** du rapport; la date de **dépôt** (*m*) des candidatures (*submission, sending in*); ⟨Jur⟩ la **saisine** du Conseil constitutionnel par le simple citoyen (*submission/referral [esp. of a case to a court]*)

submit (*v*): **remettre** le texte aux organisations syndicales (*submit, hand in*); Bonn refuse de **céder à** la pression des manifestants (*submit/give way to*); **se plier à** la décision du Conseil d'État (*submit/bow to*); SEE ALSO **present**

subscribe (*v*): **prendre un abonnement** de six mois reviendra moins cher (*subscribe, take out a subscription*)

subscriber (*n*): les **abonnés** (*m*) au téléphone reçoivent ce service gratuitement (*subscriber, customer [esp. of a public service]*); ⟨Fin⟩ la liste des **souscripteurs** (*m*) s'allonge (*subscriber [esp. of loan, share-issue]*); SEE ALSO **contribution**, **dues**

subscription (*n*): le prix de l'**abonnement** (*m*) à ce nouveau mensuel est de 240F (*subscription*); Canal Plus, la **chaîne à péage** (*m*) (*subscription TV channel*)

subsequent (*adj*): les versements **ultérieurs** seront de 3.600F

subsidiary (*n*): ⟨Econ⟩ le groupe a une **filiale** en Suisse (*subsidiary*); **filiale à 100%** de l'État (*wholly-owned subsidiary*); SEE ALSO **jointly**

subsidize (*v*): ⟨Econ/Fin⟩ en **subventionnant** aussi les implantations nipponnes; des postes **subventionnés** par l'État, proposés dans les entreprises privées

subsidized (*adj*): ⟨Econ⟩ fournir des produits **à des prix** (*m*) **subventionnés** (*at subsidized prices*); la vente à leurs occupants des **logements** (*m*) **sociaux** gérés par la collectivité locale; l'accès à des **logements** (*m*) **subventionnés** (*subsidized housing; [GB] council housing*)

subsidy (*n*): ⟨Fin⟩ la faiblesse des **dotations** (*f*) de l'Opéra (*subsidy; general grant*); ⟨Econ⟩ les **subventions** (*f*) dont bénéficient les agriculteurs; malgré les importants **subsides** (*m*) communautaires (*subsidy; handout*); des **primes** (*f*) pour la cessation de la production de la viande bovine (*subsidy, premium*)

substantiate (*v*): on veut ainsi **accréditer** la thèse des enquêteurs

subtract (*v*): SEE **deduct**

subtraction (*n*): SEE **deduction**

succeed (*v*): les négociations ont **abouti**, et un accord a été signé (*succeed, be successfully concluded*)

successful (*adj*): si la négociation avec Tokyo **aboutit** (*be successful*); on a bon espoir de **faire aboutir** enfin ce projet ambitieux (*bring to a successful conclusion*); SEE ALSO **succeed**

successfully (*adv*): lutter **avec efficacité** (*f*) contre la concurrence étrangère

sue (*v*): ⟨Jur⟩ s'estimant volé, il décida d'**engager des poursuites** (*f*) (*sue*); il compte les **poursuivre en dommages-intérêts**; la victime décida de **se constituer partie** (*f*) **civile** (*sue for damages*); SEE ALSO **damage, file, libel**

suffer (*v*): ⟨Econ⟩ l'usine de Sochaux **subira** 180 suppressions d'emploi (*suffer; be hit by*); le tourisme **pâtit de** la désaffection des étrangers (*suffer because/on account of*); les actionnaires sont contents, mais les salariés **'trinquent'** (*suffer; pay the price*)

suit (*v*): l'accord **arrange** tout le monde; une solution qui **convient à** tous

suitable (*adj*): les expulsions de locataires se font sans solution de relogement **adapté**; SEE ALSO **appropriate**

sum (*n*): ⟨Fin⟩ pour un **montant** total de 5 MF; la commission est de 2% du **montant** de tout marché

summary (*n*): ⟨Fin⟩ un **relevé** des opérations passées à votre compte en banque; SEE ALSO **sum up**

summary (*adj*): ⟨Jur⟩ la procédure du **référé** vise à obtenir une décision rapide; cité dans le cadre des **comparutions** (*f*) **immédiates** (*summary judgement/proceedings*)

summit (*n*): ⟨Pol⟩ la prochaine **réunion au sommet** (*summit [meeting]*); au **sommet** d'Ottawa (*summit meeting between political leaders*)

summons (*n*): ⟨Jur⟩ une sommation, ou **citation** (*f*) à comparaître en justice; un résident sur trois recevra bientôt une **citation d'huissier** (*bailiff's summons*)

summons (*v*): ⟨Jur⟩ **être cité** à comparaître comme témoin (*be summonsed/ subpoenaed*)

sum up (*v*): le porte-parole du gouvernement **fait le point** sur la situation (*sum up, give a summing-up/summary*)

Sunday (*n*): ⟨Comm⟩ la législation sur l'**ouverture** (*f*) **dominicale** (*Sunday trading*)

superannuation (*n*): ⟨Fin⟩ la société gère sa propre **caisse de retraite** (*f*) (*superannuation fund*)

superior (*n*): ⟨Admin⟩ des fonctionnaires, hautement appréciés par leur **hiérarchie** (*f*) et par leurs collègues; les déclarations faites par ses **supérieurs** (*m*) **hiérarchiques**

supervise (*v*): ⟨Pol⟩ des mesures dont l'application serait **supervisée** par les Préfets; les casques bleus **surveillent** le cessez-le-feu; envoyés pour **veiller au** bon déroulement du scrutin (*supervise*); ⟨Comm⟩ **assurer le suivi** des projets d'aménagement et d'urbanisme (*supervise; follow through*)

supervision (*n*): ⟨Pol⟩ la **surveillance** du cessez-le-feu (*supervision*); sous la **tutelle** du ministère de Finances (*[administrative] supervision*); ⟨Soc⟩ on offre aux anciens détenus un hébergement et un **suivi social** (*social follow-up/supervision; after-care*)

supervisor (*n*): ⟨Ind⟩ les **agents** (*m*) **de maîtrise** et les cadres moyens

supervisory (*adj*): ⟨Pol/Admin⟩ l'administration du fisc, dont il est le **ministre de tutelle** (*f*) (*minister with supervisory powers*); un PDG ou un directoire assisté d'un **conseil de surveillance** (*f*) (*supervisory board, board of supervisors*); ⟨Ind⟩ lettre ouverte des ingénieurs de la **maîtrise** au personnel; des mouvements sociaux des **agents** (*m*) **de conduite** (*supervisory staff*)

supplier (*n*): ⟨Comm⟩ Pékin, le deuxième **pourvoyeur** d'aide après le Japon; l'ex-RFA était notre **fournisseur** (*m*) principal; SEE ALSO **arm, provider**

supply (*n*): ⟨Comm⟩ un contrat pour la **fourniture** de gaz liquéfié (*supply, provision*); la guerre fait peser de sérieuses inquiétudes sur l'**approvisionnement** (*m*) **pétrolier** (*oil supplies*); ⟨Econ⟩ l'**offre** (*f*) reste insuffisante dans beaucoup de secteurs (*supply*); la loi de l'**offre et de la demande** (*supply and demand*); SEE ALSO **availability, stock, water**

supply (*v*): ⟨Econ⟩ **fournir** des armes aux rebelles (*supply, equip*); le barrage **alimente** en eau les deux villes (*supply, feed*); les marchés, toujours bien **approvisionnés** (*supply, stock*); la France **se ravitaille** difficilement en sources énergétiques (*be supplied; obtain supplies*); SEE ALSO **stock**

supplying (*n*): les conditions d'**approvisionnement** (*m*) alimentaire (*supplying, provision*); SEE ALSO **provision**

support (*n*): ⟨Pol⟩ l'idée recueille une très large **adhésion** auprès de la population (*support*); le Chancelier affirme son **appui** (*m*) à Moscou; la France voudrait apporter sa **caution** à un éventuel compromis (*support, backing*); une proposition susceptible de **rallier** la France (*gain the support of*); les États arabes **se rallient au** plan (*give support to; back*); ⟨Econ/Fin⟩ les **aides** (*f*) versées par l'État à la Régie (*financial support, funds*); une réduction des **soutiens** (*m*) **agricoles** (*agricultural support payments*); SEE ALSO **backing**

support (*v*): les pouvoirs publics refusent d'**appuyer** des initiatives privées; la police, accusée de **soutenir** le parti indépendantiste; le ministre, venu **épauler** le candidat (*support, back*); SEE ALSO **back**

supporter (*n*): les **adeptes** (*m*) de la ligne officielle; **fidèle** (*m*) et ami de toujours du président; ses **partisans** (*m*) ont défilé hier dans les rues; en tant que **sympathisant** (*m*) socialiste; les **tenants** (*m*) de la tendance communiste; les **zélateurs** (*m*) de la perestroika; SEE ALSO **advocate**

suppress (*v*): ⟨Mil⟩ l'armée a violemment **réprimé** la manifestation; **étouffer** une révolte; on a tout fait pour **étouffer** le scandale; SEE ALSO **cover up, hush up, put down, repress**

suppression (*n*): ⟨Mil⟩ la **répression** du soulèvement fut brutale; SEE ALSO **banning, repression**

surety (*n*): ⟨Fin⟩ il a laissé des documents comme **caution** (*f*) (*surety*); son tuteur **s'est porté caution** pour lui (*stand surety*)

surplus (*n*): ⟨Econ⟩ un léger **surplus** de l'offre sur la demande; le problème des **excédents** (*m*), notamment laitiers (*surplus*); après trois années de récoltes **excédentaires** (*in surplus*); ⟨Fin⟩ il laisse la Sécurité sociale **en excédent** (*in surplus*)

surplus (*adj*): le problème des 1.500 salariés **en surnombre** (*m*) (*surplus [to requirements], excess*)

surrender (*n*): ⟨Mil⟩ la **reddition** des rebelles (*surrender*); ⟨Pol⟩ les **abandons** (*m*) **de souveraineté** entraînés par les accords de Maastricht (*surrender of sovereignty*); SEE ALSO **abandonment**

surrender (*v*): ⟨Mil⟩ il **s'est constitué prisonnier** (*m*); les rebelles **se rendirent** aux forces régulières (*surrender, give o.s. up*); ⟨Ins⟩ une police d'assurance peut être **résiliée** à tout moment (*surrender, discontinue*)

surrogate (*adj*): ⟨Soc⟩ le débat sur les **mères-porteuses** (*f*) (*surrogate mother*); la loi actuelle sur la **maternité de substitution** (*f*) (*surrogate motherhood*)

survey (*n*): il n'existe pas de tarif fixe pour une **expertise** (*survey, expert's report*); le **rapport d'expertise** confirme les dommages (*survey, report*); lors d'une **enquête d'opinion** effectuée début mars (*survey, opinion poll*)

survey (*v*): **passer en revue** (*f*) l'état des négociations (*survey; review*)

surveyor (*n*): l'**expert-géomètre** (*m*) cumule souvent le rôle d'agent immobilier; le terrain a été évalué par un **expert foncier**; l'**expert immobilier** procéda à l'état des lieux de l'immeuble

survival (*n*): c'est la **survie** d'Israël qui est en cause; les conditions de **survie**: flexibilité et marketing

survive (*v*): sa femme lui **survit**

surviving (*adj*): ⟨Soc/Jur⟩ améliorer les droits du **conjoint survivant** (*surviving spouse/partner*)

suspect (*n*): ⟨Jur⟩ la détention par la police d'un **suspect**; renvoyer le **prévenu** devant la cour d'assises; la confrontation des témoins avec le **prévenu**

suspend (*v*): **surseoir à** la signature du traité (*suspend, postpone*); la moitié des grévistes **mis à pied** par la direction (*suspend; dismiss*); ⟨Admin⟩ **être mis en disponibilité** (*f*) pendant la durée de l'enquête (*be suspended from duty; be granted leave of absence*)

suspended (*adj*): ⟨Jur⟩ condamner à six mois de prison **avec sursis** (*m*); le système anglais de la **condamnation suspendue** avec mise à l'épreuve (*suspended sentence*)

suspension (*n*): un détournement de fonds a entraîné la **mise en congé** (*m*) de deux responsables du parti; ⟨Ind⟩ le patron décida la **mise à pied** immédiate des grévistes; SEE ALSO **lifting**

suspicion (*n*): vaincre la **défiance** de l'Occident; l'opinion a perdu de ses **préventions** (*f*) à l'egard de l'Europe (*suspicion, hostility*); SEE ALSO **hostility**

suspicious (*adj*): décès **suspect** d'un bébé à Dieppe (*suspicious, suspect*)

sustained (*adj*): après sept années de progression **soutenue** (*sustained, continuous*)

swear in (*v*): ⟨Jur⟩ il **fut assermenté** et tenu au secret; le nouveau gouvernement a **prêté serment** (*m*) devant le président (*be sworn in/take an oath*)

swell (*v*): ne voulant pas **grossir** les deux millions de chômeurs; l'arrivée des réfugiés a **gonflé** le nombre de sans-travail (*swell, increase*)

swindle (*n*): une belle histoire d'**arnaque** (*f*) et de magouilles politiciennes (*swindle, swindling*); une peine de prison pour **escroquerie** (*f*) aux chèques volés (*swindle, fraud*)

swindle (*v*): accusé d'avoir voulu **escroquer** ses clients (*swindle, defraud*); le risque de **se faire arnaquer** par le vendeur (*be swindled*)

swing (*n*): ⟨Pol⟩ des **déplacements** (*m*) **de voix** considérables en fin de campagne; le **transfert des voix** (*f*) est de 1,7% au profit du Labour (*[voting] swing*); un **renversement de tendance** (*f*) inespéré entre les deux tours des élections (*swing, shift of opinion*); SEE ALSO **shift**

swingeing (*adj*): **forte** augmentation des loyers à Paris (*swingeing, hefty*)

system (*n*): le nouveau **dispositif**, mis en place cette année (*system, arrangement*); un **système politique** qui a fait ses preuves (*political system*)

T

table (*n*): SEE **round table**

table (*v*): ⟨Pol⟩ une vingtaine d'amendements ont été **déposés**

tabling (*n*): ⟨Pol⟩ lors du **dépôt** (*m*) de la motion de censure

take-off (*n*): ⟨Econ⟩ l'État accepte de financer le **décollage** de l'économie du Sud-Ouest

take off (*v*): ⟨Econ⟩ la production agricole est prête à **décoller** (*take off*); ⟨Jur⟩ un jeune juge, brutalement **dessaisi** de son dossier (*take off/remove [esp. from a case]*)

take out (*v*): ⟨Fisc⟩ l'impôt sur le revenu **ponctionne** moins de 6% de la richesse nationale (*take out, tap*); ⟨Ins⟩ **contracter une assurance** contre le vol (*take out an insurance policy*); SEE ALSO **insurance**, **insure**

take-over (*n*): ⟨Comm⟩ les entreprises peuvent s'unir par **absorption** (*f*) ou par fusion; une fièvre d'**acquisitions** (*f*) a gagné les pays membres de la CE; la **prise de contrôle** (*m*) du sidérurgiste espagnol; le **rachat** de la firme suisse; l'an passé il y a eu environ 60.000 **reprises** (*f*) **[d'entreprises]** (*take-over*); la tentative d'**OPA [offre publique d'achat]** échoua; on assiste à une fièvre d'acquisitions et de **raids** (*m*) (*[hostile] take-over bid*)

216

take over (*v*): ⟨Fin/Comm⟩ en **rachetant** son concurrent, la société devient le numéro un de la grande distribution; Siemens **reprend** l'activité automation de Texas Instruments (*take over, acquire*); une élite capable de **prendre la relève** au moment de l'indépendance (*take over*)

take place (*v*): la rentrée **s'est effectuée** dans le calme (*take place*); les récents massacres **survenus** en Afrique du Sud; des affrontements **se sont déroulés** à Beyrouth (*take place, happen*); ce changement **interviendra** avant trois ans (*take place, come about*); SEE ALSO **occur**

talk (*n*): des **pourparlers** (*mpl*) indirects entre Kaboul et Islamabad (*exploratory/preliminary talks*)

target (*n*): l'**objectif** (*m*) est largement atteint (*target, aim*); les céréaliers sont la **cible** principale visée par la réforme; ⟨Econ⟩ fixer des **objectifs** (*m*) **de production** (*production target*); le Conseil d'État est **dans la ligne de mire** du gouvernement (*be the target; be in the line of fire*)

target (*v*): ⟨Comm⟩ la publicité **ciblait** la tranche d'âge des 16-25 ans; **viser** la catégorie des jeunes célibataires (*target [a specific market]*)

targetting (*n*): ⟨Comm⟩ bon **ciblage** (*m*) vaut mieux que fort tirage (*targetting [of a specific market]*)

tariff (*n*): ⟨Econ⟩ élever des **barrières** (*f*) **douanières** contre les importations japonaises (*tariff barriers*)

tax (*n*): ⟨Fisc⟩ payer une **redevance** pour l'utilisation des brevets (*tax, fee*); leurs produits d'exportation ont été frappés de **droits** (*mpl*) anti-dumping (*tax, duty*)

tax (*v*): ⟨Fisc⟩ la fiscalité qui **frappe** le patrimoine des Français; le nouveau système **impose** chaque adulte d'un montant égal (*tax*); le citoyen français est un des plus **ponctionnés** du monde (*taxed*)

taxable (*adj*): si le revenu **imposable** ne dépasse pas 20.000F

tax adviser (*n*): ⟨Fisc⟩ faire établir sa déclaration d'impôts par un **conseiller fiscal**

tax allowance (*n*): ⟨Fisc⟩ un **abattement** d'une partie des revenus du contribuable; augmenter la **tranche de revenu exonérée d'impôt** (*tax allowance, allowance against tax*)

taxation (*n*): ⟨Fisc⟩ la **fiscalité** est plus lourde en Allemagne; financer par l'**impôt** (*m*); les bénéfices réalisés ne font objet d'aucune **imposition** (*f*); nouvelle augmentation de la **ponction fiscale**; la **taxation** du patrimoine y est bien plus élevée qu'en France

tax avoidance (*n*): ⟨Fisc⟩ l'**évasion** (*f*) **fiscale** est parfaitement licite; l'accroissement des possibilités d'**évasion fiscale**

tax band (*n*): ⟨Fisc⟩ toutes les **tranches** (*f*) **d'imposition** sont relevées

tax-collection (*n*): ⟨Fisc⟩ le rôle du fisc est la **collecte des impôts** (*m*); il s'agit d'améliorer le **recouvrement des taxes** (*f*) (*tax-collection*); les services de la **recette-perception** dans de nouveaux locaux (*tax-collection department*)

tax-collector (*n*): ⟨Fisc⟩ la suppression du poste de **percepteur** (*m*); le percepteur ou un **agent de recouvrement** (*m*) (*tax-collector, collector of taxes*); aller à la **perception** payer ses contributions; travailler aux **Contributions** (*fpl*) (*tax-collector's office*)

tax cut (*n*): ⟨Fisc⟩ des **allégements** (*m*) **d'impôts** pour contenter les électeurs

tax-deductible (*adj*): ⟨Fisc⟩ les intérêts d'emprunts sont **déductibles de l'impôt** (*m*); ces fonds sont alors **déductibles d'impôts**

tax evasion (*n*): ⟨Fisc⟩ la **fraude fiscale** est aussi répandue ici qu'ailleurs (*tax evasion, tax fraud*)

tax-free (*adj*): ⟨Fisc⟩ un compte qui produit des intérêts **exonérés d'impôt**; réaliser un rachat **en franchise** (*f*) **d'impôt**; les achats **hors taxes** dans les zones franches (*tax-free, free of tax*)

tax haven (*n*): ⟨Fisc⟩ on ne saurait assimiler ce pays à un **paradis fiscal**; les enquêteurs se heurtent au système des **paradis fiscaux**

tax increase (*n*): ⟨Fisc⟩ les **hausses** (*f*) **fiscales** décidées par le gouvernement

taxpayer (*n*): ⟨Fisc⟩ le déficit public est supporté par le petit **contribuable** (*taxpayer*); les **assujettis** (*m*) **à l'impôt** nouveau vont se plaindre (*taxpayer; person liable to tax*)

tax rate (*n*): ⟨Fisc⟩ une diminution de 40% du **taux d'imposition** (*f*) des revenus les plus élevés

tax rebate (*n*): ⟨Fisc⟩ le **remboursement d'un trop perçu d'impôt** à la fin de l'année

tax relief (*n*): ⟨Fisc⟩ un **abattement fiscal** de 10%; des **allégements** (*m*) **fiscaux** en faveur des ménages à bas revenus (*tax relief*); certaines catégories sociales bénéficient d'un **dégrèvement fiscal** (*tax relief; tax exemption*)

tax return (*n*): ⟨Fisc⟩ faire une **déclaration d'impôts** (*mpl*); le montant de ses **déclarations** (*f*) **fiscales**

tax revenue (*n*): ⟨Fisc⟩ grâce à de bonnes **rentrées** (*f*) **fiscales**

temporary (*adj*): ⟨Comm⟩ l'**intérim** (*m*) est en pleine déprime (*temporary work/employment sector*); embauché enfin après sept mois de **missions** (*f*) **d'intérim** (*temporary employment; 'temping'*); une dizaine de **vacataires** (*m*) s'occupent des jeunes (*temporary worker*)

tenancy (*n*): choisir entre la **location** et l'accession à la propriété (*tenancy/ renting of a property*); SEE ALSO **renting**

tenant (*n*): 40% des **locataires** (*m*) ont des ressources précaires (*tenant; occupier of rented accommodation*); ⟨Agric⟩ dans le **fermage**, un exploitant loue le fonds au propriétaire (*tenant farming*); SEE ALSO **leaseholder**

tendency (*n*): ⟨Pol⟩ la **tendance** était à une augmentation du chômage (*tendency, trend*); ceux qui sont proches de la **mouvance** islamiste; les sept partis représentent des **sensibilités** (*f*) très différentes (*tendency, movement [esp. political/religious]*); SEE ALSO **movement**

tender (*n*): ⟨Econ/Comm⟩ verser des pots-de-vin lors de l'**adjudication** (*f*) de travaux publics (*putting out to tender; awarding of contracts*); remporter un **appel** (*m*) **d'offres** pour la réfection des locaux (*invitation to tender*); adjudication au **plus bas soumissionnaire**; confier les travaux de réfection aux artisans les **moins-disants** (*lowest tender*); SEE ALSO **bid**

tender (*v*): ⟨Comm⟩ **faire une soumission** pour le contrat du siècle; une déclaration d'intention de **soumissionner** (*tender, bid*); **soumissionner** la construction du tunnel (*tender for a contract*); le gouvernement oblige France-Télécom à **faire des appels d'offres** internationaux (*invite to tender/bid for contract*); SEE ALSO **invite**

tenure (*n*): ⟨Admin/Scol⟩ les enseignants qui n'optent pas pour la **titularisation** (*tenure; holding of a tenured post*)

term (*n*): ⟨Pol⟩ un **mandat** de cinq ans (*term of office*); ⟨Fin/Soc⟩ 150 **trimestres** (*m*) de cotisations (*term; period of three months*); la France voudrait **renouer avec** l'Algérie (*get back on good terms with*); obligé de **composer avec** l'opposition (*come to terms with*); après dix ans de **brouille** (*f*), des relations diplomatiques ont été restaurées (*being on bad terms*)

terminate (*v*): son mandat qui va **venir à terme** (*m*) en juin (*terminate, end, expire*); le contrat peut être **résilié** à tout moment (*terminate, rescind*)

termination (*n*): demander une **résiliation** du contrat de location (*termination; cancellation, rescinding*); SEE ALSO **abortion**

territorial (*adj*): un épineux **contentieux territorial** (*territorial dispute*); SEE ALSO **frontier**, **integrity**

territory (*n*): les habitants du **territoire** de Belfort (*territory*); quatre **territoires d'outre-mer**, dont les îles Wallis et Futuna (*overseas territory*)

tertiary (*adj*): ⟨Econ⟩ l'industrie décline au profit du [secteur] **tertiaire** (*tertiary sector*)

test (*n*): ⟨Educ⟩ une **épreuve** écrite (*test, examination*)

test (*v*): le gouvernement est une nouvelle fois **mis à l'épreuve** (*f*) (*test, put to the test*)

testify (*v*): ⟨Jur⟩ il est prêt à **déposer** devant la commission; elle **dépose** à la barre des témoins (*testify, give evidence*); SEE ALSO **evidence**

testimony (*n*): ⟨Jur⟩ un **témoignage** qui fera pencher la balance en faveur de l'inculpé (*testimony, statement*); maintenir sa **déposition** (*testimony [on oath]*); SEE ALSO **deposition**

thaw (*n*): une volonté de **dégel** (*m*) de part et d'autre (*thaw/improvement in relations*)

theft (*n*): ⟨Jur⟩ le **vol** d'une bicyclette (*theft, thieving*); commettre de **menus larcins** (*m*) (*minor theft*); SEE ALSO **larceny**, **pilfering**

think-tank (*n*): la **commission de réflexion** (*f*) étudiera notamment les problèmes soulevés par l'épargne-logement

third (*adj*): ⟨Pol/Econ⟩ les pays du **tiers-monde** (*third world*); ⟨Ins⟩ l'assurance dite **au tiers** (*third-party*)

thorough (*adj*): le dossier mériterait un examen **approfondi** (*thorough, detailed*)

threat (*n*): une **menace** manifeste à l'ordre public (*threat*); ⟨Ind⟩ les dockers décident une journée d'actions contre la **remise en cause de** leur statut (*threat to, putting in jeopardy of*); ils **passent à l'acte** (*m*), en arrêtant les exportations de pétrole (*carry out a threat*); l'**hypothèque** (*f*) qu'on fait peser sur la stabilité sociale du pays (*threat, danger, menace*)

threaten (*v*): on **menace** Belgrade de sanctions (*threaten*); le second tour ne pourra pas **mettre en cause** (*f*) la majorité obtenue au premier (*threaten, endanger*); agitation qui pourrait **remettre en cause** la croissance de l'économie (*threaten; jeopardize*)

threshold (*n*): ⟨Fin⟩ le **seuil** est périodiquement réactualisé par décret (*threshold*); ⟨Soc/Pol⟩ le **seuil de tolérance** (*f*) a été largement dépassé (*threshold of tolerance*)

throw out (*v*): ⟨Pol⟩ le projet de loi fut **repoussé** (*throw out, defeat*)

tie up (*v*): ⟨Fin⟩ cela évitera d'**immobiliser** un argent rare (*tie up [esp. capital]*)

tier (*n*): ⟨Admin/Pol⟩ un troisième **échelon** de l'administration locale (*tier [esp. of government]*)

tight (*adj*): des règles de procédure plus **contraignantes** (*tight, restrictive*); une négociation **serrée** se joue en coulisse (*tight; closely conducted*); ⟨Econ/Fin⟩ une politique monétaire **restrictive** (*tight, restrictive*)

tighten (*v*): ⟨Pol⟩ **verrouiller** leur emprise sur l'appareil du parti (*tighten*); ⟨Fin⟩ la réserve fédérale a préféré **resserrer** sa politique du crédit (*tighten, tighten up*)

tightening (*n*): un **resserrement** de la politique monétaire; **durcissement** (*m*) des règles de publicité en faveur de l'alcool (*tightening, tightening up*)

time-share (*n*): acheter un **appartement en temps partagé** (*time-share apartment/flat*)

time-sharing (*n*): la **multipropriété**, ou l'achat du droit de jouissance d'un local pour une période donnée de l'année; la croissance de la multipropriété, ou **propriété** (*f*) **en temps partagé**

timetable (*n*): le débat sur le **calendrier** continue; le programme d'investissements se poursuit selon l'**échéancier** (*m*) fixé (*timetable, schedule*)

time-wasting (*n*): les **manœuvres** (*f*) **dilatoires** se poursuivent (*time-wasting tactics*)

timid (*adj*): ⟨Pol⟩ Londres, **frileux**, retarde l'échéance européenne

timidity (*n*): il critique la **frilosité** des entreprises françaises; SEE ALSO **confidence**

title (*n*): le **titre** de comte ou de duc (*title*); ⟨Jur⟩ déposer les **titres de propriété** (*f*) à la banque (*title deeds*)

topical (*adj*): un sujet **d'actualité** (*f*); la question de l'école est à nouveau **d'actualité** (*topical, in the news*)

topicality (*n*): la question retrouve soudain toute son **actualité** (*f*)

topple (*v*): SEE **overthrow**

total (*n*): le **montant** des économies décidées par le gouvernement (*total, sum*); le **montant total** de ses économies (*total sum/amount*); **dresser un bilan** des victimes (*arrive at a total*)

total (*v*): le manque à gagner **se montait à** 2.000F par jour; le parc automobile français **s'élève à** 25 millions de véhicules; le coût de la construction **se chiffre à** plusieurs milliards de francs (*total, amount to*)

totality (*n*): exporter l'**intégralité** (*f*) de son brut via le Golfe (*totality, the whole of*); SEE ALSO **entire, whole**

tough (*adj*): la concurrence était **rude**

tour (*n*): ⟨Pol⟩ au cours d'une **tournée** en province (*tour*); son **périple** dans les pays du Maghreb (*[extended] tour; series of visits*); SEE ALSO **round**

tower (*n*): un ensemble d'HLM comprenant sept **blocs** (*m*); les grands ensembles et leurs **tours** (*f*) lugubres (*tower housing block*)

town (*n*): les deux **municipalités** (*f*) conjuguent leurs efforts dans ce sens (*town; town/city council*); ⟨Pol⟩ ses chances de reconquérir l'**hôtel** (*m*) **de ville** sont minces; les Socialistes tiennent le tiers des **mairies** (*f*) (*town hall; municipality*)

town planning (*n*): un plan d'**urbanisme** et de résorption des bidonvilles (*town planning*); un effort a été fait pour l'**aménagement** (*m*) **du territoire** (*town and country planning*)

trade (*n*): ⟨Comm⟩ apprendre un **métier** (*trade, job, profession*); ⟨Econ⟩ une relance des **échanges** (*mpl*) franco-bulgares; le **négoce** des céréales continue entre les deux pays (*trade, commerce*); SEE ALSO **balance, foreign trade, profession, traffic**

trade (*v*): ⟨Fin⟩ le Franc **s'échangeait** hier à 9,25F; ⟨Comm⟩ **commercer** avec les pays scandinaves (*trade, carry out trade/business*)

trade deficit (*n*): ⟨Econ⟩ le dollar malade du **déficit commercial** américain (*trade deficit*); l'aggravation du **déficit extérieur** inquiète la City (*foreign trade deficit*)

trader (*n*): SEE **dealer**

trade surplus (*n*): ⟨Comm⟩ l'**excédent** (*m*) japonais avec les États-Unis

trade union (*n*): ⟨Ind⟩ peu de Français adhèrent à un **syndicat** (*trade union*); les femmes **se syndiquent** plus volontiers que les hommes (*join a trade union*); SEE ALSO **union**

trade unionist (*n*): ⟨Ind⟩ les **syndiqués** (*m*) étaient encore au nombre de cinq millions en 1978

trading (*n*): ⟨Econ⟩ en cas de cessation d'**activité** (*f*) (*trading, operations*); la firme a été obligée de **mettre la clef sous la porte** (*cease trading*); le **déficit d'exploitation** (*f*) du groupe ne cesse de s'alourdir (*trading deficit/loss*); les comptes de l'**exercice** (*m*) **[fiscal]** ont été approuvés (*trading year*); la **dénomination sociale** de la nouvelle société reste à décider (*trading/trade name*); SEE ALSO **Sunday**

traffic (*n*): ⟨Comm⟩ le **trafic passager** avec la Corse (*passenger traffic*); le **trafic illicite** des stupéfiants (*traffic, illicit trading*); une fortune gagnée par le **trafic de la drogue** (*drug traffic, drug running*); SEE ALSO **racket**

traffic (*v*): ⟨Comm⟩ **faire le trafic** des stupéfiants (*traffic/deal in [esp. illicit goods]*); SEE ALSO **deal**

trafficker (*n*): ⟨Comm⟩ un **trafiquant** de cigarettes volées

train (*v*): un effort pour **former** le personnel (*train*); il faut **se former**, se recycler constamment (*be trained, undergo training*); les ingénieurs **entraînés aux** méthodes modernes (*trained in*)

trainee (*n*): obtenir un poste de **stagiaire** (*m*); jeunes travailleurs, ou **stagiaires** d'une formation professionnelle; SEE ALSO **probationer**

training (*n*): la part de la masse salariale consacrée à la **formation** (*training*); accomplir un **stage professionnel** (*vocational training scheme*): bénéficier d'**actions** (*f*) **de formation** d'une durée de 300 heures (*training programme*); SEE ALSO **on-the-job**

transaction (*n*): ⟨Fin/Comm⟩ le volume des **échanges** (*m*) à la Bourse de Paris a doublé

transfer (*n*): ⟨Ind/Comm⟩ favoriser les **mutations** (*f*) entre différents services (*transfer*); le **déplacement** en province de 3.500 emplois publics (*transfer, removal*); les personnels dont la **délocalisation** n'est pas encore annoncée (*transfer [esp. to new locality]*); ⟨Fin⟩ le transfert de fonds s'est effectué par **virement** (*m*) (*credit transfer*); ⟨Fin/Fisc⟩ un taux de 35% pour les **transmissions** (*f*) entre frères et soeurs (*transfer of property; bequest*); ⟨Pol⟩ un mauvais **report des voix** (*f*) écologistes sur le candidat socialiste (*transfer of votes*)

transfer (*v*): en poste à Paris, il s'est trouvé **muté** en Bourgogne (*transfer [esp. job]*); ⟨Econ⟩ la production **délocalisée** en Malaisie (*transfer, relocate*); ⟨Pol⟩ les électeurs **reportent** leurs suffrages sur le candidat d'union; ⟨Fin⟩ **virer** une somme sur un compte bancaire (*transfer, transfer by banker's draft*)

transformation (*n*): une période de **mutation** (*f*) profonde; en pleine **mutation** économique (*transformation, change*)

transition (*n*): pour gérer la **transition** (*transition, change-over*)

transitional (*adj*): une période **transitoire** de six ans (*transitional*); une fois l'accord signé et la **procédure de transition** (*f*) mise en place (*transitional arrangements*); prévu seulement **à titre** (*m*) **transitoire** (*as a transitional/temporary measure*)

treason (*n*): ⟨Pol⟩ sauf cas de **haute trahison** (*f*) (*high treason*)

treasury (*n*): ⟨Fin⟩ mutisme au **ministère des Finances** (*f*) (*[GB] Treasury; Ministry of Finance*); le **Trésor public** a lancé cette initiative (*[French] Treasury*); les mesures de relance prises par le **Trésor** américain (*[USA] Treasury Department*)

treat (*v*): comment **traiter** le chômage? (*treat; deal with*); **assainir** les eaux du lac (*treat, purify*)

treatment (*n*): le principe de l'égalité de **traitement** (*m*) (*treatment*); ⟨Med⟩ la revalorisation de l'**acte** (*m*) **médical**; les médecins dépassent les tarifs pour certains **soins** (*m*) (*medical treatment/consultation*)

treaty (*n*): ⟨Pol⟩ un **traité** sur la sécurité collective

trend (*n*): la politique d'immigration **s'oriente** vers le laxisme (*show/exhibit a trend*); ⟨Fin/Comm⟩ la **tendance** hier était à la hausse (*trend [esp. in Stock Exchange]*); SEE ALSO **reversal**

trial (*n*): faire l'objet d'une **expérience probatoire** de trois ans; la **période d'essai** (*m*) et le délai de préavis (*trial/probationary period*); admis à **l'essai**, après un stage de deux ans (*for a trial period; on a trial basis*); ⟨Jur⟩ les inculpés vont bientôt **être jugés**; devoir **passer en jugement** (*m*) (*stand trial*); la **mise en accusation** (*f*) ou décision de renvoi devant la cour d'assises (*sending for trial*); SEE ALSO **probationary**

trial of strength (*n*): ⟨Pol⟩ le **bras de fer** se poursuit entre patron et ouvriers; une **épreuve de force** entre gouvernement et opposition (*trial of strength*); SEE ALSO **confrontation**

tribunal (*n*): ⟨Jur⟩ une **juridiction** créée pour statuer sur des affaires d'espionnage (*tribunal, court*); ⟨Ind⟩ traduit devant le **[conseil des] Prud'hommes** (*m*) (*industrial disputes tribunal*)

trigger off (*v*): cette mesure va **déclencher** un véritable tollé

trouble (*n*): déjà **sur la sellette** pour une affaire de pots-de-vin (*in trouble; in the hot seat*); on a pu identifier les **fauteurs** (*m*) **de trouble**; des consignes de fermeté à l'encontre des **perturbateurs** (*m*) et des casseurs (*trouble-maker*)

truce (*n*): ⟨Mil/Pol⟩ une fragile **trêve** s'est instaurée

true (*adj*): si ces prévisions **se vérifient** (*prove to be true*)

trust (*n*): ⟨Econ⟩ les cartels et **trusts** (*m*) faussent la concurrence

trustee (*n*): ⟨Admin⟩ un **fondé de pouvoirs** agissant au nom de la société (*trustee*); lors d'un **conseil de surveillance** (*[meeting of] board of trustees*)

truth (*n*): la **vérité**, et rien que la vérité (*truth*); vérifier la **véracité** de ses déclarations (*truth, veracity*)

try (*v*): la formule sera **expérimentée** dans plusieurs régions (*try out, experiment*); ⟨Jur⟩ **être jugé** pour viol (*be tried/prosecuted*)

turn (*n*): on se félicite de la **tournure** prise par les événements (*turn, direction*)

turn (*v*): ⟨Pol⟩ les mineurs **se sont retournés** contre le pouvoir roumain (*turn/revolt against*); ⟨Comm⟩ tenter de **redresser** une situation dégradée (*turn round, rescue*); un nouveau PDG saura **redresser l'affaire** (*f*) (*turn round a business*)

turning-point (*n*): il s'agit d'un **tournant** capital; les négociations sont arrivées à un **tournant**

turn-out (*n*): ⟨Pol⟩ faible **participation** (*f*) **[électorale]** aux cantonales dans le Vaucluse (*[electoral] turn-out*)

turnover (*n*): ⟨Comm⟩ un bénéfice de 2 MF pour un **chiffre d'affaires** (*f*) de 53 millions (*turnover, sales*); pour compenser une **rotation de stocks** (*mpl*) insuffisante (*turnover of stock*); la **rotation du personnel** prouve que les cadences étaient trop élevées (*turnover of staff*)

turn-round (*n*): ⟨Comm⟩ des entreprises en voie de **retournement** (*m*) (*turn-round, recovery*); le **retournement de conjoncture** (*f*) aux États-Unis (*economic turn-round*); SEE ALSO **recovery, reversal**

two (*adj*): ⟨Pol⟩ les élections scellent la fin du **bi-partisme** (*two-party system*); opter pour le **bicamérisme** (*two-chamber system*)

typical (*adj*): une des opérations-**types** du commerce juridique, la transmission d'une entreprise

U

ulterior (*adj*): une initiative qui n'est sûrement pas sans **arrière-pensée** (*f*); leur soutien pour cette réforme n'est pas exempt d'**arrière-pensées** (*ulterior motive*)

unable (*adj*): un dispositif policier faible et **inadapté** (*unable to cope; inadequate*); SEE ALSO **incapable**

unaffiliated (*adj*): ⟨Ind/Pol⟩ à la CGT, et chez les **autonomes** (*m*) de la RATP (*unaffiliated members*)

unambiguous (*adj*): un soutien **sans ambiguïté** (*f*) au processus de démocratisation (*unambiguous, clear*)

unanimity (*adj*): l'**unanimité** (*f*) syndicale a permis le succès de la grève (*unanimity; solidarity*)

unanimously (*adv*): les socialistes soutiennent **unanimement** sa candidature; élu **à l'unanimité** (*f*) à la présidence (*unanimously*); cette proposition **fait l'unanimité contre elle** (*be unanimously opposed/unpopular*)

unauthorized (*adj*): ⟨Pol/Admin⟩ la lutte contre l'entrée et le séjour **irréguliers** (*unauthorized, illegal*); des immigrés **en situation** (*f*) irrégulière; ceux qui sont **en situation de** travail **irrégulière** (*unauthorized/illegal [esp. immigrant] worker*)

unbeatable (*adj*): ⟨Comm⟩ offerts **à des prix défiant toute concurrence** (*at unbeatable prices*)

unbridled (*adj*): les contraintes d'une immigration **débridée**; SEE ALSO **uncontrolled**

unceasingly (*adv*): la France œuvre **sans relâche** (*f*) pour la paix

uncertain (*adj*): la rentabilité est trop **aléatoire** (*uncertain; risky*); SEE ALSO **risky**

uncertainty (*n*): l'**incertitude** (*f*) règne sur l'avenir des institutions (*uncertainty*); les **aléas** (*m*) de la Bourse (*uncertainty; risk, hazard*)

unchallenged (*adj*): le chef **incontesté** de l'organisation

unchanged (*adj*): une situation **inchangée** (*unchanged, unaltered*); les institutions européennes **restent inchangées** (*remain unchanged*)

uncompetitive (*adj*): ⟨Econ/Comm⟩ subventionner à fonds perdus une industrie **non compétitive**

unconditional (*adj*): le scrutin majoritaire a ses **farouches** partisans (*unconditional, unwavering*)

uncontrolled (*adj*): ⟨Pol/Econ⟩ l'État-Providence cède la place au libéralisme **effréné**; un interventionnisme **débridé**; Paris voit se développer une urbanisation **sauvage** (*uncontrolled, unbridled*); ⟨Econ⟩ l'économie est aux prises avec une **inflation incontrôlée** (*uncontrolled inflation*)

undeniable (*adj*): il paraît **établi** que l'IRA en est responsable (*undeniable*); les effets pervers de l'immigration **ne sont pas niables** (*be undeniable*)

underemployment (*n*): ⟨Comm/Ind⟩ le taux d'**inemploi** (*m*) des dockers, en 1990, a été de 18% (*underemployment, idleness*)

undergo (*v*): l'obligation de **subir** un nouvel examen (*undergo, go through*)

underground (*adj*): ⟨Pol⟩ un mouvement **clandestin** (*underground*); il décide alors d'**entrer dans la clandestinité**; **prendre le maquis** avant l'occupation de son pays (*go underground/into hiding*)

underlie (*v*): les arrière-pensées qui **sous-tendent** cette initiative n'échapperont à personne

underlying (*adj*): on devine sans peine les sentiments **sous-jacents** (*underlying*); ⟨Comm⟩ les causes **structurelles** de l'inflation (*underlying; deep-seated*); ce tableau flatteur cache une **tendance de fond** préoccupante (*underlying tendency/trend*)

underprivileged (*n/adj*): ⟨Econ⟩ une région longtemps **défavorisée** sur le plan économique; un quartier **déshérité** de la ville (*underprivileged; deprived*); ⟨Soc⟩ défenseur du prolétariat et des **exclus** (*m*); les problèmes des **économiquement faibles** (*m*) (*the underprivileged*)

undertake (*v*): le gouvernement va **entreprendre** une révision du code (*undertake*); **s'engager** à réduire les impôts (*undertake, promise*)

undertaking (*n*): SEE **promise**

undesirable (*adj*): les réformes pourraient engendrer des effets **pervers** (*undesirable*); on s'efforce de limiter ces **effets** (*m*) **pervers** par la législation (*undesirable effects*)

undivided (*adj*): dix ans de **règne** (*m*) **sans partage** des communistes (*undivided rule*)

unearned (*adj*): ⟨Fisc⟩ depuis sa retraite, il a pu **vivre de ses rentes** (*f*) (*live on unearned income*)

unemployed (*n*/*adj*): ⟨Econ⟩ un **chômeur** à vie; le nombre des **sans-emploi** (*m*) monte inexorablement; le nombre des **demandeurs** (*m*) **d'emploi** a diminué en avril (*unemployed person*); les chômeurs **inscrits comme demandeurs** (*m*) **d'emploi** (*registered as unemployed*)

unemployment (*n*): ⟨Econ⟩ les travailleurs réduits au **chômage** (*unemployment*); être réduit à l'**inactivité** (*f*) (*unemployment, idleness*)

unemployment benefit (*n*): ⟨Econ⟩ il faut revoir les systèmes d'**indemnisation** (*f*) **du chômage**; les **allocations** (*f*) **de chômage** se montent à 68% du dernier salaire brut (*unemployment benefit*); le chômeur **touche des indemnités** (*f*) à condition de suivre une formation (*receive unemployment benefit*)

unequal (*adj*): la **lutte inégale** des démocraties contre le terrorisme (*unequal fight*); l'**inégalité** (*f*) **des chances** face à l'éducation (*unequal [educational] opportunity*)

unequivocal (*adj*): Israël: le 'non' **sans équivoque** (*f*) des orthodoxes

unequivocally (*adv*): condamner **sans équivoque** (*f*) le coup d'État

unexpected (*adj*): à moins d'un retournement de situation **inopiné** (*unexpected, unforeseen*)

unfair (*adj*): le système se révèle socialement **injuste** pour les petits salariés (*unfair*); ⟨Comm⟩ des pratiques commerciales **déloyales** (*unfair, inequitable*); la **concurrence déloyale** de la firme espagnole (*unfair competition*); ⟨Ind⟩ une protection contre le **licenciement abusif** (*unfair dismissal*)

unfilled (*adj*): plusieurs postes sont restés **non pourvus** (*unfilled, vacant*)

unforeseen (*adj*): **sauf imprévu** (*m*) le sommet se tiendra en octobre (*barring unforeseen circumstances*); SEE ALSO **unexpected**

unfounded (*adj*): une accusation **sans fondement** (*m*) (*unfounded, unjustified*); ⟨Jur⟩ la plainte **n'a aucun fondement juridique** (*be unfounded/groundless*)

unfreeze (*v*): ⟨Fin/Pol⟩ le gouvernement **dégèle** les avoirs libyens en France (*unfreeze; release*)

unfreezing (*n*): ⟨Fin/Pol⟩ le **déblocage des crédits** (*m*) nécessaires ne saurait tarder (*unfreezing/releasing of funds*)

unidentified (*adj*): tomber sous les balles d'un commando **non identifié**

unification (*n*): ⟨Pol⟩ depuis l'**unification** (*f*) des deux républiques allemandes

unify (*v*): **unifier** la police en supprimant la distinction entre police en civil et police en tenue

unilateral (*adj*): ⟨Mil/Pol⟩ proclamer un cessez-le-feu **unilatéral** (*unilateral*); prôner le **désarmement unilatéral** inconditionnel (*unilateral disarmament*)

union (*n*): ⟨Ind⟩ patronat et **section** (*f*) **syndicale [d'entreprise]** sont accusés de complicité (*union branch/local branch of trade union*); SEE ALSO **trade union**

unionization (*n*): ⟨Ind⟩ le faible **taux de syndicalisation** (*f*) des femmes

unionized (*adj*): ⟨Ind⟩ une industrie qui, en France, **est** faiblement **syndicalisée** (*be unionized*)

unique (*adj*): la France est **unique** à cet égard (*unique*); cette gratuité des soins **était une singularité** en Europe en 1990 (*be unique*)

unit (*n*): ⟨Mil⟩ une des premières **unités** à partir au combat (*[military] unit*); ⟨Comm⟩ les ventes prévues sont estimées à 850 **unités** (*f*) (*unit*); la vente s'est effectuée sur la base d'un **prix unitaire** de 290F (*unit price*); ⟨Econ⟩ nos **coûts** (*m*) **unitaires** ont augmenté plus vite que les coûts allemands (*unit costs*)

unite (*v*): alors que la Gauche tente de **se rassembler** (*unite, come together*); les Douze **font bloc** (*m*) pour confronter les États-Unis (*unite; stick together*)

united (*adj*): sur cette question l'opposition semble **unie** (*united*); l'opposition s'est trouvée **soudée** comme jamais auparavant (*solidly united*); la France est totalement **solidaire de** ses alliés (*united with*)

unity (*n*): comment préserver l'**intégrité** du pays menacé d'éclatement? (*unity, wholeness*)

unjust (*adj*): SEE **unfair**

unjustified (*adj*): l'utilisation **abusive** de la procédure (*unjustified*); le ministre du Commerce s'attaque aux rabais **abusifs** (*unjustified, unjustifiable*); des critiques totalement **infondées** (*unjustified, unfounded*)

unjustly (*adv*): ⟨Jur⟩ **injustement** condamné à payer une lourde amende

unlimited (*adj*): la garantie de débouchés **illimités** pour ses produits

unofficial (*adj*): le quotidien **officieux** du parti socialiste

unofficially (*adv*): il parlait **à titre** (*m*) **officieux** pour son chef de file

unpaid (*adj*): ⟨Econ⟩ l'offre et la demande d'**emplois** (*m*) **non rémunérés** (*unpaid work*); se consacrer à un **travail de bénévolat** (*m*) (*unpaid/*

voluntary work); faire appel à des **bénévoles** (*m*) pour ce travail (*unpaid worker*); ⟨Comm⟩ la facture des **impayés** (*m*) s'élevait à quelque 2.000F (*unpaid bill*); SEE ALSO **arrears**

unpopular (*adj*): des mesures **impopulaires** (*unpopular*); assez **mal accueilli** au début, il est maintenant accepté; l'impôt de solidarité sur la fortune est **mal perçu** (*unpopular; unwelcome*); SEE ALSO **popularity**

unprecedented (*adj*): la Lorraine connaît une crise économique **sans précédent** (*m*); cette situation **sans exemple** (*m*) dans l'histoire du régime; une situation complètement **inédite**

unprofitable (*adj*): ⟨Comm⟩ le groupe se débarrasse d'activités **déficitaires**; l'État a renfloué quelques entreprises **non rentables**

unpublished (*adj*): un rapport **non publié** sur la haute fonction publique

unpunished (*adj*): ⟨Jur⟩ le défi lancé par la Mafia ne peut pas **rester impuni** (*go/remain unpunished*)

unqualified (*adj*): ⟨Econ⟩ les emplois créés, pour la plupart **non qualifiés**

unquestioned (*adj*): remporter un succès **sans partage** (*m*)

unreliability (*n*): la **non-fiabilité** des sondages d'opinion

unreliable (*adj*): des chiffres qui sont **sujets à caution** (*f*); une méthode de calcul **peu fiable**

unresolved (*adj*): la question **non résolue** de l'avenir de la fédération; l'existence de nombreuses questions **non résolues** (*unresolved; unanswered*)

unrest (*n*): ⟨Pol/Soc⟩ **agitation** (*f*) islamiste dans les universités tunisiennes (*unrest*); une vague d'**agitation sociale**; des **troubles** (*m*) **sociaux** ne facilitent pas la tâche du gouvernement (*social unrest*)

unrestricted (*adj*): le fonctionnement **sans entrave** (*f*) du marché du travail; **concurrence** (*f*) **sauvage** dans l'industrie automobile (*unrestricted/ unregulated competition*); la **libre circulation** (*f*) des personnes entre les pays membres (*unrestricted/free movement*)

unscathed (*adj*): l'audiovisuel **sort indemne** des coupes budgétaires (*emerge unscathed*)

unskilled (*adj*): ⟨Econ⟩ simple **manœuvre** (*m*), dans un petit atelier du Nord; des **ouvriers** (*m*) **non spécialisés**, sans diplômes ni qualifications (*unskilled labourer*)

unsuitability (*n*): l'**inadaptation** (*f*) des solutions proposées

unsuitable (*adj*): un dispositif policier faible et surtout **inadapté**; des intérimaires ayant une formation **inadaptée** à leur tâche (*unsuitable, unsuited; inappropriate*); SEE ALSO **inappropriate**

untimely (*adj*): les remarques **intempestives** du ministre n'ont pas été appréciées à Bruxelles

unwelcome (*adj*): **mal accueilli** au début, il a fini par se faire accepter; SEE ALSO **unpopular**

update (*v*): on **actualise** les chiffres au 31 décembre; **réactualiser** les statistiques (*update, bring up to date*)

updating (*n*): l'**actualisation** des fichiers; la **mise à jour** d'une publication de 1978 (*updating, bringing up to date*)

up-market (*adj*): ⟨Comm⟩ les marques **haut de gamme**

upper (*adj*): ⟨Pol⟩ rapporteur du projet de loi à la **Haute Assemblée** (*Upper House, [in France] Senate*); SEE ALSO **ceiling**

uprising (*n*): ⟨Mil/Pol⟩ Sri-Lanka, ravagée par des **insurrections** (*f*) depuis 1983; incertitude sur l'état de la **rébellion**; Bagdad annonce la fin du **soulèvement**

upsurge (*n*): la nouvelle **poussée** de la gauche (*upsurge*); une année marquée par une **recrudescence** de la violence (*[fresh] upsurge/outbreak*); SEE ALSO **outbreak, renewed**

up-to-date (*adj*): les dernières précisions **actualisées**; les comptes sont **à jour** (*m*) (*up-to-date; updated*); une étude **très récente** sur le problème (*up-to-date, most recent*)

upturn (*n*): ⟨Econ⟩ un **redressement** de la demande a marqué le premier semestre (*upturn, rise*)

upward (*adj*): ⟨Econ/Fin⟩ une **pression à la hausse** des taux d'intérêt (*upward movement*); une nouvelle **poussée**, après une période d'accalmie (*upward trend*); **réviser à la hausse** ses prévisions (*revise upward*)

urban (*adj*): un canton à la fois rural et **citadin**; le problème de la sécurité **en milieu** (*m*) **urbain** (*urban*); en zone rurale et dans les petites **agglomérations** (*f*) (*urban centre*); ces problèmes d'**aménagement** (*m*) **urbain** (*urban development*); des politiques de **rénovation** (*f*) **urbaine** (*urban renewal*); un exemple réussi de **réaménagement** (*m*) **urbain** (*urban redevelopment*)

urgency (*n*): l'**impératif** (*m*) d'économies budgétaires; être conscient de l'**urgence** (*f*) de réformes dans ce domaine (*urgency, necessity*)

urgent (*adj*): l'aide alimentaire **d'urgence** (*f*) a été suspendue (*urgent*); le nouveau ministre s'est fixé trois **urgences** (*urgent task*)

use (*n*): l'**usage** (*m*) de l'ECU permettra de réaliser des économies; l'éventuel **emploi** (*m*) des forces armées; ⟨Jur⟩ au titre d'indemnité pour privation de **jouissance** (*f*) du terrain (*use, enjoyment, possession*)

use (*v*): le policier a **fait usage** (*m*) **de** son arme; **user de** son droit de véto (*use, make use of*)

user (*n*): les **usagers** (*m*) d'un service public; SEE ALSO **customer**

use up (*v*): ayant **épuisé** ses droits, il est sans ressources (*use up, exhaust*)

usual (*adj*): il est **d'usage** (*m*) de confirmer par écrit; faire les vérifications **d'usage** (*usual, habitual*)

usufruct (*n*): ⟨Jur⟩ au conjoint survivant sont attribués des droits en **usufruit** (*m*) sur la succession; le droit de **jouissance** (*f*) légale des parents sur les biens des enfants (*usufruct, right to hold*); demeurer l'**usufruitier** (*m*) d'un terrain ou d'une propriété (*person enjoying usufruct, usufructuary*); acheter la **nue-propriété** d'un appartement (*ownership without usufruct*)

utility (*n*): ⟨Admin⟩ ces **services** (*m*) **publics** ont bénéficié d'un régime de prix avantageux (*public service, utility*)

U-turn (*n*): le Premier ministre multiplie les **volte-face** (*f*); un **renversement** idéologique imposé par les circonstances (*U-turn, volte-face*)

V

vacancy (*n*): ⟨Comm⟩ un **poste vacant** à la comptabilité; des **postes à pourvoir** dans la fonction publique (*[job] vacancy*)

vacant (*adj*): des postes **vacants**, faute de candidats (*vacant*); un certain nombre de postes sont **à pourvoir** (*vacant, to be filled*)

vacate (*v*): locataire de son appartement, il doit **libérer les lieux** (*mpl*) (*vacate premises*)

vagrancy (*n*): ⟨Soc⟩ les problèmes de santé liés à l'**errance** (*f*); le **vagabondage** relève du service de l'aide sociale

vagrant (*n*): ⟨Soc⟩ un centre qui héberge une cinquantaine de **vagabonds** (*m*)

valid (*adj*): une analyse qui est **valable**, sur le court terme (*valid*); une carte d'identité **en cours de validité** (*f*) (*valid, current*); cela **vaut** pour l'agriculture comme pour l'industrie (*be valid*)

validate (*v*): le Conseil constitutionnel a **validé** le report d'un an des élections cantonales

validity (*n*): la **validité** du contrat liant les parties

value (*n*): ⟨Comm⟩ le **rapport qualité-prix** tourne à l'avantage de l'hôtellerie italienne (*value for money*); ⟨Econ⟩ la **valeur ajoutée** par habitant est sensiblement plus faible (*added value*); ⟨Fin⟩ les cambistes prévoient l'**appréciation** (*f*) de ces titres (*increase in value, appreciation*); les valeurs **s'effritent** hier à la Bourse de Tokyo (*lose/fall in value*); ⟨Fisc⟩ une demande de remboursement de la **taxe sur la valeur ajoutée [TVA]** (*value added tax*); la **revalorisation** de leur métier est leur première revendication (*reassertion of the value/importance of*); il s'engage à **revaloriser** le pouvoir législatif (*reassert the value/importance of*)

value (*v*): faire **estimer** un terrain par un expert; **expertiser** un tableau (*have sth valued*)

valuer (*n*): faire faire une expertise par un **expert en estimations de biens mobiliers** (*valuer, appraiser; assessor*)

verdict (*n*): ⟨Jur⟩ le **jugement** sera rendu (*verdict*); la justice a pu **se prononcer** (*give a verdict*); le juge, après interrogatoire des parties, **rend la décision** (*pronounce/return a verdict*)

veto (*n*): ⟨Pol⟩ il opposa son **véto** à la candidature britannique

veto (*v*): ⟨Pol⟩ Londres pourrait **mettre son véto** au projet d'union politique

viability (*n*): le problème de la **viabilité** d'une armée de professionnels

viable (*adj*): une politique **viable** sur le long terme; un projet **qui a des chances** (*f*) **de réussir**

vice (*n*): ⟨Jur⟩ confier une enquête à la **brigade des mœurs** (*Vice-Squad*)

vice- (*pref*): ⟨Admin⟩ **vice-président** (*m*) de la société depuis 1992 (*vice-chairman*); ⟨Pol⟩ candidat à la **vice-présidence** (*vice-presidency*); ⟨Educ⟩ **directeur-adjoint** (*m*) du collège (*vice-principal*)

victim (*n*): ce système risque d'engendrer des **laissés-pour-compte** (*m*) (*victim of society/the system; social reject*); SEE ALSO **reject**

viewpoint (*n*): dans l'**optique** (*f*) américaine, les choses ne sont pas si claires

vigorous (*adj*): ⟨Pol⟩ une politique **volontariste** pour faire évoluer les conditions de travail (*vigorous*); **prendre des mesures** (*f*) **énergiques** contre la vie chère (*take vigorous measures*); ⟨Pol/Mil⟩ une intervention **musclée** de la police (*vigorous, strong*)

villain (*n*): un petit **truand**, bien connu des services de la police (*villain, crook*)

violate (*v*): des avions ont **violé** l'espace aérien national

violation (*n*): on assiste au **viol** du droit international; la première **violation** sérieuse du cessez-le-feu

violence (*n*): ⟨Jur⟩ inculpé de **voies** (*fpl*) **de fait** (*assault; violence to the person*)

visa (*n*): ⟨Admin⟩ obtenir un **visa** de séjour (*visa*); pouvoir quitter le pays sans devoir obtenir un **visa de sortie** (*f*) (*exit visa*)

vocation (*n*): si le choix de la profession correspond à quelque **vocation** (*f*) (*vocation*); **avoir vocation** de rassembler toutes les voix de gauche (*have a vocation/purpose*)

vocational (*adj*): des stages rémunérés de **formation** (*f*) **professionnelle** (*vocational training*); des filières de formation à **finalité** (*f*) directement **professionnelle** (*vocational, vocationally-orientated*)

voluntarily (*adv*): le salarié peut **volontairement** résilier son contrat de travail (*voluntarily, of one's own free will*)

voluntary (*adj*): un plan social fondé sur le strict **volontariat** (*voluntary agreement/participation*); ⟨Econ⟩ une possibilité de **départ** (*m*) **volontaire** pour les salariés de plus de 50 ans (*voluntary retirement/ redundancy*); SEE ALSO **volunteer**

volunteer (*n*): les **bénévoles** (*m/f*) qui ont démarré cette opération (*volunteer, unpaid [esp. worker]*); ⟨Mil⟩ des jeunes du contingent, **volontaires** (*m*) pour les actions extérieures (*volunteer*); des appelés, recrutés sur la base du **volontariat** pour cette tâche (*volunteer scheme*); SEE ALSO **voluntary**

volunteer (*v*): ⟨Mil⟩ les jeunes qui **s'engagent comme volontaires** (*m*) (*volunteer for service*)

vote (*n*): ⟨Pol⟩ les trois quarts des **suffrages** (*m*) exprimés; le décompte des **votes** (*m*); ils ont remporté les deux tiers des **voix** (*f*) (*vote*); pragmatique, il attend **le verdict des urnes** (*f*) (*result of the vote/poll*)

vote (*v*): ⟨Pol⟩ **se prononcer** sur l'avenir de leur pays (*vote; vote on*); les Espagnols sont appelés à **se rendre aux urnes** (*f*) dimanche (*vote, go to the polls*); les électeurs ont **boudé les urnes** hier (*not go to vote; ignore the poll*); le **droit de vote** des Européens aux municipales (*right to vote, voting rights*); SEE ALSO **pass**

voter (*n*): ⟨Pol⟩ le **votant** n'a pas un grand choix de candidats

voting booth (*n*): ⟨Pol⟩ dans le secret de l'**isoloir** (*m*)

voting intention (*n*): ⟨Pol⟩ un sondage lui donne 38% des **intentions** (*f*) **de vote** (*voting intention; intended vote*)

voting paper (*n*): ⟨Pol⟩ 10% des votants ont **voté nul** (*submit a spoiled voting paper*)

voting rights (*npl*): ⟨Pol⟩ il siège au conseil d'administration avec **voix** (*f*) **délibérative**

W

wage (*n*): ⟨Econ⟩ hostile à toute **réduction** (*f*) **de salaires** ou de compression de personnels (*wage cut; cut in wages*); une politique laxiste, avec **relèvements** (*mpl*) **de salaire** et allégements d'impôts (*wage rise*); **accord** (*m*) **salarial** dans la Fonction publique (*wage settlement*); une mise en garde contre les **dérapages** (*m*) **salariaux** (*excessive wage settlements*); ⟨Pol/Econ⟩ le gouvernement, lié par sa **politique salariale** (*wages policy*)

wage bill (*n*): ⟨Fin/Comm⟩ les 2% de la **masse salariale** affectés à la formation

wage costs (*n*): ⟨Econ⟩ les **coûts** (*m*) **salariaux**, cause principale de la hausse des prix; SEE ALSO **salary**

wage demand (*n*): ⟨Ind⟩ la montée des **revendications** (*f*) **salariales**

wage-earner (*n*): ⟨Econ⟩ les **salariés** (*m*) et les employeurs y sont également hostiles (*wage-earner, salaried personnel*); SEE ALSO **salaried**

wage freeze (*n*): un **blocage des salaires** (*m*) temporaire; le **gel des salaires** prolongé mena à la chute du gouvernement

wage restraint (*n*): ⟨Econ⟩ la direction décida unilatéralement la **limitation des salaires**; la politique de **restrictions** (*fpl*) **salariales** (*[policy of] wage restraint*)

wait-and-see (*adj*): les positions **attentistes** des Britanniques (*wait-and-see, prudent*); entre l'optimisme des industriels et l'**expectative** (*f*) des consommateurs (*wait-and-see policy; prudence*)

waive (*v*): SEE **exception**

waiver (*n*): la possibilité d'une **dérogation** (*waiver*); une **clause dérogatoire** à la loi de 1982 (*waiver clause*); SEE ALSO **exception**

waiving (*n*): une **dérogation** aux règles du Marché commun; SEE ALSO **exception**

walk out (*v*): ⟨Ind⟩ le personnel riposta en **faisant une grève surprise**; tous les ateliers ont **débrayé** (*walk out, stop work*)

walkout (*n*): ⟨Ind⟩ **débrayage** (*m*) hier dans les ateliers de Rennes; la **grève surprise** a eu l'effet escompté (*walkout, stoppage [of work]*)

war (*n*): la **guerre d'usure** (*f*) entre gouvernement et opposition (*war of attrition*); ⟨Mil⟩ payer des **dommages** (*mpl*) **de guerre** (*war damages*)

ward (*n*): ⟨Soc⟩ sont **pupilles** (*m*) **de l'État** les orphelins de père et de mère n'ayant aucun moyen matériel d'existence (*ward of court*); SEE ALSO **electoral**

warmonger (*n*): les Douze désignent les autorités fédérales comme **fauteurs** (*m*) **de guerre**

warn (*v*): Washington **met en garde** Bagdad contre toute provocation

warning (*n*): multiplier les **mises** (*f*) **en garde** (*warning*); ⟨Econ⟩ emploi: le nombre de **clignotants** (*m*) **rouges** augmente (*warning light; alarm signal*)

warrant (*n*): ⟨Jur⟩ un **mandat d'arrêt** (*m*) fut lancé contre les malfaiteurs présumés (*warrant for arrest, arrest warrant*); SEE ALSO **arrest, search**

wastage (*n*): le **gâchis** que représente cet investissement inconsidéré; un **gaspillage** des ressources naturelles (*wastage, waste*); ⟨Econ⟩ réduire le personnel par **départs** (*mpl*) **naturels**; une réduction des effectifs par **non-remplacement** (*m*) **des départs** (*natural wastage; non-replacement of staff*)

waste (*n*): la lutte contre les **gaspillages** (*m*); réduire les **gaspillages** et les pertes (*waste, wastage*)

waste (*v*): **gaspiller** des ressources naturelles

waste land (*n*): ⟨Econ⟩ transformer une région entière en **friche** (*f*) **industrielle** (*industrial waste land*)

water (*n*): un important marché d'**adduction** (*f*) **d'eau** (*water supply, laying on water*); l'**approvisionnement** (*m*) **en eau** est difficile à assurer en été (*water supply*)

233

way out (*n*): la recherche d'une **sortie** honorable (*way out; solution*)

weak (*adj*): ⟨Fin⟩ le franc reste **faible** sur les marchés financiers

weaken (*v*): le parti sort **affaibli** de cette longue crise; un désastre pour le pays, dont il a **fragilisé** la monnaie (*weaken*); la région houillère, **ébranlée** par la crise (*weaken; shake*)

weakness (*n*): ⟨Econ⟩ confirmant la **faiblesse** de l'économie britannique; ⟨Fin⟩ la **faiblesse** du dollar

wealth (*n*): ⟨Fisc⟩ le nouvel **impôt sur la fortune** a été mal accueilli (*wealth tax*)

wealthy (*n/adj*): ce sont **les riches** qui payent, comme d'habitude (*the wealthy*); seules les **classes** (*f*) **possédantes** en profiteront (*wealthy, well-off, the moneyed classes*); les communes les plus **nanties** (*wealthy, prosperous*)

welfare (*n*): ⟨Soc⟩ assurer le **bien-être** et la qualité de vie de tous les citoyens (*welfare*); ⟨Pol/Soc⟩ la Grande-Bretagne avait été la première à instituer l'**État-providence**; grâce à la **sécurité sociale et les divers avantages** (*m*) **sociaux** (*Welfare State*)

well-being (*n*): les Français trouvent que leur **bien-être** (*m*) se dégrade (*material well-being/conditions*)

well-informed (*adj*): *Le Monde*, généralement **bien informé**

west (*n/adj*): les relations de la Chine avec l'**Occident** (*m*) (*the West*)

western (*adj*): les pays riches du **monde occidental** (*the western world; the West*); les services secrets **occidentaux** (*western, of/belonging to the West*)

white-collar (*adj*): ⟨Econ⟩ les artisans, les commerçants et les '**cols** (*m*) **blancs**' (*white-collar worker*); un nouveau concept: le **criminel en col blanc** (*white-collar crime*)

White Paper (*n*): ⟨Pol⟩ un **livre blanc** sera adressé aux parlementaires (*[government] White Paper*)

whitewash (*v*): ⟨Jur⟩ destiné à le **blanchir** au bénéfice du doute

whole (*n*): conserver la **totalité** de ses forces armées; l'**ensemble** (*m*) de l'industrie militaire (*whole, totality*); redresser l'économie **dans son ensemble** (*as a whole*); SEE ALSO **entire**, **totality**

wholesale (*adj*): ⟨Comm⟩ enquête sur l'épicerie **en gros** à Toulouse (*wholesale*); modeste hausse des **prix** (*m*) **de gros** en avril (*wholesale prices*)

wholesaler (*n*): ⟨Comm⟩ le fils d'un **grossiste** en chaussures; un **négociant en gros** établi à Bordeaux

wide (*adj*): ⟨Pol/Admin⟩ l'octroi de très **larges** pouvoirs à l'Écosse (*wide, wide-ranging, extensive*); une Assemblée **aux pouvoirs** (*m*) **plus larges** (*with wider powers*)

widen (*v*): ⟨Pol/Admin⟩ **élargir** les compétences communautaires à des domaines nouveaux (*widen, extend*); les pouvoirs de la Commission sont **augmentés** (*widen, increase*)

widespread (*adj*): un phénomène très **largement répandu**; absentéisme scolaire **généralisé** (*widespread*); la **banalisation** du divorce (*becoming widespread*); SEE ALSO **commonplace**

widow (*n*): ⟨Soc/Fin⟩ des **veuves** (*f*) n'ayant jamais travaillé (*widow*); toucher l'**allocation** (*f*) **de veuvage** (*widow's pension*)

widower (*n*): ⟨Soc⟩ **veuf** (*m*), il n'est pas près de se remarier

widowhood (*n*): ⟨Soc⟩ un récent **veuvage**; être démuni en cas de **veuvage**

wildcat (*adj*): ⟨Ind⟩ une **grève sauvage**, c'est-à-dire déclenchée en dehors d'un mot d'ordre d'un syndicat (*wildcat strike*)

wilful (*adj*): un geste volontaire, **délibéré** et qu'il ne regrette pas (*wilful, deliberate*)

wilfully (*adv*): accomplir un acte **délibérément** et avec préméditation (*wilfully, deliberately*)

will (*n*): l'absence de **volonté** (*f*) **de** démocratisation du pays (*will, wish for*); il n'y a aucune **volonté politique** de traiter à fond le problème (*political will*)

win (*v*): ⟨Pol⟩ **recueillir** bon an mal an 20% des voix; assuré de **remporter** l'élection; ⟨Comm⟩ la France pense pouvoir **s'octroyer** 10% de ce marché

win back (*v*): ⟨Pol⟩ la gauche a pu **récupérer** les sièges perdus en 1986; le maire **récupéra** le fauteuil perdu en 1976

wind up (*v*): ⟨Fin/Econ⟩ la société a été **liquidée**, et ses biens réalisés; **procéder à la liquidation** de la société (*wind up [a business]*)

winding-up (*n*): ⟨Fin/Econ⟩ lorsque aucune autre solution n'est possible, la **liquidation judiciaire** de la société est prononcée; ordonner la **liquidation des biens** (*m*) du patrimoine du commerçant (*winding-up by official receiver; compulsory liquidation*)

winning (*n*): le **gain** de quatre sièges réjouit les Socialistes (*winning, gain*)

win over (*v*): la France souhaite **rallier** les autres pays à son point de vue

withdraw (*v*): ⟨Econ⟩ le gouvernement va **se désengager de** ce secteur (*withdraw from*); ⟨Admin⟩ le pouvoir de **retirer** les visas touristiques; ⟨Jur⟩ si le vendeur **se désiste**, il devra verser le double des arrhes; impossible de **se rétracter**, une fois le contrat signé (*withdraw*); un témoin qui **se rétracte**; finir par **rétracter son aveu** (*m*) (*withdraw/go back on a statement*)

withdrawal (*n*): ⟨Pol⟩ après le **retrait** du projet néerlandais (*withdrawal; withdrawing*); une quatrième défaite électorale a provoqué le **retrait** de leur leader (*withdrawal, departure, resignation*); ⟨Fin⟩ les **retraits** (*m*) **de fonds** peuvent s'effectuer sans préavis (*withdrawal of money*); ⟨Jur⟩

la partie victime du **désistement** de l'autre partie (*withdrawal [esp. from contractual agreement]*)

within (*prep*): les luttes **au sein** de la direction; **dans l'enceinte** (*f*) **de** l'établissement (*within, inside*); **dans un délai de** sept jours (*within, in the space of*)

witness (*n*): ⟨Jur⟩ être **témoin** (*m*) d'un événement (*witness*); la police a **lancé un appel à témoins** (*appeal for witnesses*); des affirmations du **témoin à charge** accablantes pour l'accusé (*witness for the prosecution*); SEE ALSO **testimony**

witness (*v*): on a **assisté** à une forte régression des ventes dans ce secteur (*witness, observe*); **attester l'authenticité** (*f*) des documents (*witness; vouch for*)

word (*n*): en **reniant sa parole** (*break one's word/promise*); la Président a **tenu parole** (*keep to one's word*); SEE ALSO **promise**

wording (*n*): le **choix des termes** (*m*) est très important; une **formulation** maladroite (*wording, choice of words*)); ⟨Admin/Jur⟩ le **libellé** d'un jugement; la **rédaction** d'une loi (*wording, drafting*)

work (*n*): ⟨Econ⟩ se retrouver **au chômage** (*out of work*); la Belgique a misé sur le **partage du travail** pour réduire le chômage (*work-sharing*); après un **stage d'insertion** (*f*) **à la vie professionnelle** de six mois (*period of work experience*); ⟨Pol⟩ le succès des **travaux** (*m*) **d'utilité collective** [TUC] (*government work-creation scheme*); SEE ALSO **job-creation**

work (*v*): les Françaises sont 10 millions à **exercer une activité professionnelle** (*work outside the home*)

worker (*n*): ⟨Econ⟩ un système de **participation** (*f*) **du personnel** aux grandes orientations de l'entreprise (*worker participation*); l'**autogestion** (*f*) de l'entreprise se maintient tant bien que mal (*joint worker-management control*)

work-force (*n*): ⟨Econ⟩ les petites entreprises, celles dont l'**effectif** (*m*) ne dépasse pas dix salariés; une entreprise aux **effectifs** importants; SEE ALSO **labour force**

working (*adj*): ⟨Econ⟩ un **actif** sur trois est sans emploi; les trois-quarts de la **population active** sont au chômage (*working population; wage-earning population*); lors d'un **déjeuner de travail** (*working lunch*); un **groupe de travail** s'est réuni sur le thème des droits des travailleurs (*working group/party*)

working class (*n/adj*): ⟨Soc⟩ issu de la **classe ouvrière**; le départ des immigrés et des **couches** (*f*) **populaires** (*working/labouring classes*)

working day (*n*): ⟨Econ⟩ l'impact du **temps de travail** (*m*) en termes de santé; l'accord sur la **journée** de dix heures, quatre jours par semaine; un allongement de la **durée quotidienne du travail**

work place (*n*): ⟨Ind⟩ le comportement des hommes envers les femmes **sur les lieux** (*m*) **de travail** (*in the work place*)

work rate (*n*): ⟨Ind⟩ certains problèmes, dont les **cadences** (*f*) 'infernales' (*work rate [esp. in industry]*)

works committee (*n*): ⟨Ind⟩ RATP: le **comité d'entreprise** (*f*) va échapper à la CGT; un **comité d'établissement** (*m*) est convoqué ce matin à l'usine d'Angers (*branch works committee*)

work-to-rule (*n*): ⟨Ind⟩ une **grève du zèle** des douaniers pourrait paralyser le pays

worse (*adj*): une situation **en sensible dégradation** (*f*) par rapport à la fin de 1991 (*much worse; worsening, deteriorating*)

worsen (*v*): le taux d'inflation pourrait même **s'aggraver**; la balance commerciale du textile ne cesse de **se dégrader** (*worsen, deteriorate*)

worsening (*n*): la **dégradation** spectaculaire de la balance industrielle; Brésil: **exacerbation** (*f*) des contraintes économiques; SEE ALSO **deterioration**

worth (*n*): s'estimer à sa juste **valeur**; ⟨Fin⟩ à sa **valeur** en francs de 1960 (*worth, value*); le dinar algérien **valait** 1,85F en 1980; ⟨Econ⟩ le groupe **pesait** 34 millions de livres (*be worth*)

worthless (*adj*): ⟨Fin⟩ un émetteur de **chèques** (*mpl*) **en blanc**; la nouvelle loi sur les **chèques sans provision** (*f*) entre en vigueur (*worthless cheque*)

wreck (*v*): ⟨Pol⟩ **faire échouer** les négociations (*wreck*); pour ne pas **faire capoter** la conférence (*wreck, scupper, put paid to*)

writ (*n*): ⟨Jur⟩ menacer de l'**assigner en justice pour diffamation** (*f*) (*issue a writ for libel*)

write (*v*): un rapport **rédigé** par un groupe d'experts (*write; draw up*); **libeller** une demande de congé (*write, write out*); ⟨Fin⟩ **libeller un chèque** au nom d'un parent (*write/make out a cheque*)

write off (*v*): ⟨Econ/Fin⟩ l'investissement est d'ores et déjà **amorti**; quatre millions de dollars de leur dette extérieure ont été **épongés**

writing (*n*): il faut le déclarer **par écrit** (*m*) à l'assureur (*in writing*)

wrongful (*adj*): des dommages-intérêts pour rupture **abusive** de son contrat de travail (*wrongful*); le **renvoi injustifié** du délégué fit grand bruit (*wrongful dismissal*)

wrongfully (*adv*): condamné à rembourser 15.000F de taxes portuaires **indûment** perçues; être licencié **abusivement** (*wrongfully, unjustly*)

wrongly (*adv*): des intérêts d'emprunt déduits **à tort** (*wrongly, in error*); s'estimer **injustement renvoyé** (*wrongly/unfairly dismissed*)

X

X-ray (*n*): une enquête en forme de **radiographie** (*f*); **radioscopie** (*f*) d'une cité sans histoire (*X-ray, radioscopy*)

Y

yard (*n*): ⟨Ind⟩ un maçon travaillant dans un **chantier** [de construction] (*builder's yard; work-site*); les **chantiers** de La Ciotat (*yard [esp. shipyard]*)

year (*n*): ⟨Fin⟩ le chiffre d'affaires pour l'**exercice** (*m*) clos fin octobre (*[trading] year*); des indemnités calculées sur la base de l'**ancienneté** (*f*) (*years of service; seniority*); 1990, un bien mauvais **millésime** dans les annales boursières (*year; vintage*)

yearly (*adv*): à renouveler **annuellement**

yellow (*adj*): dans les **pages** (*f*) **jaunes** de l'annuaire; dans l'**annuaire** (*m*) **des professions** (*yellow pages of telephone directory/phone book*)

yield (*n*): ⟨Econ⟩ dans la notion de rentabilité, le **rendement** n'est pas le seul facteur; SEE ALSO **output**, **capacity**

yield (*v*): ⟨Fin⟩ un placement qui **rapporte** 8% (*yield a return*); un investissement qui fera **fructifier** vos économies (*yield a profit*)

young (*adj*): ⟨Soc⟩ avec trois enfants **en bas âge** (*m*) (*young*); ⟨Jur⟩ le tribunal qui s'occupe des **jeunes délinquants** (*m*) (*young offender*)

youth (*n*): s'adresser au **service d'orientation** (*f*) **professionnelle pour les jeunes** (*Youth Employment Service*); la mise en place de **programmes** (*mpl*) **de formation des jeunes** (*Youth Training Scheme*); le gouvernement a conclu avec les partenaires sociaux un **pacte national pour l'emploi des jeunes** (*Youth Employment Scheme*)

yuppie (*n*): ⟨abbr⟩ ⟨Soc⟩ une certaine jeunesse aisée, le 'yuppie' ou **jeune cadre** (*m*) **urbain**

Z

zealot (*n*): les **zélateurs** (*m*) de la perestroika ont dû déchanter (*zealot, supporter, strong advocate*)

zero (*n*): ⟨Econ⟩ le pays a connu cette année un **taux de croissance zéro** (*zero growth rate*); ⟨Fisc⟩ les livres scolaires et la confection pour enfants sont **exempts de TVA** (*zero-rated [for VAT]*)

zone (*n*): un changement de **fuseau** (*m*) **horaire** (*time zone*)

zone (*v*): ⟨Admin⟩ le secteur a été **divisé en zones** (*f*) (*zone*); un quartier **réservé à l'implantation** (*f*) **industrielle** (*zone/reserve for industry*)

zoning (*n*): un **zonage** du territoire communal; un **certificat d'urbanisme** (*m*) est requis (*zoning/land-use certificate*)

ACRONYMS AND ABBREVIATIONS USED
IN THIS VOLUME

ANPE	Agence nationale pour l'emploi
ASSEDIC	Association pour l'emploi dans l'industrie et le commerce
BTP	Bâtiment, Travaux publics
CAC40	Compagnie des Agents de change [Paris Stock Exchange Index of 40 leading shares]
CE	Communauté européenne
CEE	Communauté économique européenne
CEI	Communauté des États indépendants
CFDT	Confédération française démocratique du travail
CGT	Confédération générale du travail
ENA	École nationale de l'administration
FAO	Food and Agriculture Organization
FLN	Front de libération nationale
FMI	Fonds monétaire international
FN	Front national
FT	*Financial Times*
GATT	General agreement on tariffs and trade
GIE	Groupement d'intérêt économique
HLM	Habitation à loyer modéré
IRA	Irish Republican Army
IVG	Interruption volontaire de la grossesse
OCDE	Organisation de coopération et de développement économique
OLP	Organisation pour la libération de la Palestine
ONU	Organisation des Nations unies
OPA	Offre publique d'achat
OPEP	Organisation des pays exportateurs de pétrole
OTAN	Organisation du traité de l'Atlantique nord
PCF	Parti communiste français
PDG	Président directeur général
PIB	Produit intérieur brut
PME	Petite ou moyenne entreprise
PMI	Petite ou moyenne industrie
PNB	Produit national brut
RATP	Régie autonome des transports parisiens
RDA	République démocratique allemande
RFA	République fédérale allemande

RPR	Rassemblement pour la République
SDF	(Personne) sans domicile fixe
SFIO	Section française de l'internationale ouvrière
SICAV	Société d'investissement à capital variable
SME	Système monétaire européen
SMIC	Salaire minimum interprofessionnel de croissance
SNCF	Société nationale des chemins de fer français
TGI	Tribunal de grande instance
TGV	Train à grande vitesse
TUC	Travail d'utilité collective
TVA	Taxe sur la valeur ajoutée
UDF	Union pour la démocratie française
UEM	Union économique et monétaire
UNEDIC	Union nationale pour l'emploi dans l'industrie et le commerce